THE EMERGENCE OF MODERN JAPAN
An Introductory History since 1853

Janet E. Hunter

Longman
London and New York

Pearson Education Limited,
Edinburgh Gate,
Harlow, Essex CM20 2JE, England
and Associated Companies throughout the world

Published in the United States of America
by Addison Wesley Longman, New York

© Longman Group UK Limited 1989

First published 1989
Eighth impression 1999

British Library Cataloguing in Publication Data
Hunter, Janet
   The emergence of modern Japan: an
   introductory history since 1853.
   1. Japan, 1868–
   I. Title
   952.03

ISBN 0-582-49407-9 CSD
ISBN 0-582-49408-7 PPR

Library of Congress Cataloging-in-Publication Data
Hunter, Janet
   The emergence of modern Japan.

   Bibliography: p.
   Includes index.
   1. Japan—History—1868– I. Title.
DS881.9.H.87   1989   952.03   88–26634
ISBN 0-582-49407-9
ISBN 0-582-49408-7 (pbk.)

Printed and Bound by Antony Rowe Ltd, Eastbourne
Transferred to digital print on demand, 2002

For my mother

Contents

Romanization

Japanese words are romanized according to the modified Hepburn system, as used in Kenkyūsha's *New Japanese English Dictionary* (4th edn., Tokyo, 1974). Long vowels are indicated by the use of macrons (e.g. Saigō, Ryūkyū), but these are omitted in the case of a few well-known place names (e.g. Tokyo, Osaka) and words commonly used in English language texts (e.g. daimyo, shogun).

Chinese words are romanized according to the Pinyin system now in standard use, but for a few place names or individuals, especially those connected with Taiwan or Manchuria, the most widely used form has been adhered to (e.g. Manchukuo, Taiwan, Mukden). Japanese names are given in the Japanese order, i.e. family name preceding given name.

List of Abbreviations

ASEAN	Association of Southeast Asian Nations
DSP	Democratic Socialist Party
EEC	European Economic Community
GATT	General Agreement on Tariffs and Trade
GNP	Gross National Product
ILO	International Labour Organization
IMTFE	International Military Tribunal for the Far East
IRAA	Imperial Rule Assistance Association
JCP	Japan Communist Party
JSP	Japan Socialist Party
LDP	Liberal Democratic Party
MITI	Ministry of International Trade and Industry
NIC	Newly Industrialized Country
NYK	Japan Shipping Company
OPEC	Organization of Petroleum Exporting Countries
PRC	People's Republic of China
SCAP	Supreme Commander Allied Powers
SDF	Self Defence Force

Preface

Writing a general textbook of this kind is a hazardous exercise. It exposes the limitations of the author's expertise and necessitates the voicing of conclusions unsupported by substantive evidence. I would not have been able to complete the work without the support and help of others. The comments of past and present students, as well as colleagues, have been a major stimulus to my thinking on the history of modern Japan. At LSE the Suntory/Toyota Centre and the Economic History Department have together served as a happy and supportive environment. I would like in particular to thank the following, who read parts of the manuscript: Helen Ballhatchet, Raj Brown, Malcolm Falkus, Rachel Hall, Stephen Hickey, Jay Kleinberg and Michio Morishima. I hope they will feel their advice has not been given in vain. I am, of course, responsible for any errors, as well as the views expressed. Etty Curley has been a patient and indefatigable typist, and Longman have been supportive and encouraging, even when the end product might not have been what was anticipated. To them, and to my long-suffering family, my thanks are due.

Janet E. Hunter
London School of Economics
July 1988

Introduction

Japan is of the utmost importance in the contemporary world, yet in Britain the study of Japan is even now regarded as 'exotic', and too often has little or no place in the knowledge of most students. This preserves the notion that Japan is somehow unique, and so different from other countries that it can be safely ignored by students of mainstream history or other social sciences. Many introductory works on its history tend – perhaps inadvertently – to reinforce this attitude. A chronological approach entirely appropriate for conveying the broad panoramic sweep of a country's history and showing the degree to which historical events are governed by a complex convergence of political, social, economic and other forces, is also an 'all or nothing' presentation which can be particularly discouraging for non-specialists.

This book, by contrast, adopts a thematic treatment. It is premised on a belief that such an approach may make it easier for the individual, non-specialist reader to follow through the development of issues in which he or she is particularly interested. To that extent, this book is conceived almost as a collection of essays, but one which, it is hoped, comes together to form a coherent whole. Some duplication between chapters is inevitable, since history cannot be compartmentalized in the neat way such an approach might suggest, but what is important here is for each chapter to be able to stand as an independent entity. The thematic approach is in addition based on a belief that it is only possible to gain a clearer understanding of the development of modern Japan, and its position in the world, by being aware of cultural and institutional continuities, most of which the Japanese themselves take for granted. Such continuities are often obscured in a chronological approach.

Defining 'modern' Japan is not easy. Western historians tend to interpret 'modern' Japan as meaning Japan since the reopening of relations with the West in 1853. Japanese historians tend to refer to the sixteenth-nineteenth centuries as 'recent' (*kinsei*), and the years from the mid-nineteenth century as 'modern' (*kindai*), but contemporary (*gendai*), is also frequently used for the twentieth century. This book focuses on the critical years between the reopening of Japan to the West in the mid-nineteenth century and the regaining of national independence after the Pacific War in 1952. Of course, no single date can ever mark a total break with the past, and it is impossible to comprehend the enormity of the transformation of modern Japan without some knowledge of what it was transformed from. While the emphasis in this text is on the 'modern' and 'contemporary' periods of Japanese history, substantial attention is paid to earlier years when this is essential for an understanding of the modern era. Similarly, to bring the story up to date – at least in outline – each chapter seeks to provide pointers up to the present, and the concluding chapter (Chapter Fourteen) ties the ends up in the context of the 1980s. The 1950s are in historical terms still very recent, and Japan has changed startlingly in the last few decades. Historical legacy and the framework established by the Occupation together laid the foundations on which the developments of recent decades have taken place, and it is with these that this book is concerned. Only in this context can Japan's response to the dramatically different international environment of the postwar years be even partially understood.

The main emphasis of the text is on political, social and economic developments. Intellectual and cultural history have been included only in as far as they have a crucial bearing on the developments which are the core of the book, and the treatment of religion and ideology particularly are clearly not comprehensive. Chapter One outlines the major events and controversies in the period under review with the aim of providing a sense of the broad chronology of modern Japanese history.

The main body of the text can be divided into three sections. Chapters Two and Three are concerned with Japan's interaction with the outside world. More than anything else, the modern period of Japan's history is set off from the past by the degree to which Japan has been compelled to respond to, and seek influence in, other countries. It is the history of a nation in an international environment. The basic parameters of Japan's recent history are diplomatic, military and economic relations between states, and the more nebulous cultural influences and personal attitudes which govern such relations. The dichotomy between Japan's relations with Asia and with the rest of the world is in a sense artificial, since the two are closely interdependent, but the existence of a strong dichotomy in cultural inheritance and social attitudes is beyond doubt.

Chapters Four to Seven are concerned with social and economic change, the patterns of life in the community and the shift from an agricultural to an industrial economy. These spheres of activity are both foundation and backdrop for the development of the Japanese nation-state from the Restoration of 1868 through to the Occupation, and were in turn influenced by it. In recent times women in Japan have played a less obvious and less direct role in the political and diplomatic spheres which have been the object of conventional historiography, and much of Japanese women's history remains to be written. It is therefore particularly important to underline the significance of the role of women in the functioning of economy and society as a whole.

The Japanese nation-state has to a conspicuous degree been a focal point of the modern Japanese experience, and the final group of chapters (Eight to Thirteen) is concerned with the Japanese state, its ideology and structures, the competition to control it, what different people wanted it to be, and the activities of those who secured power or were excluded from it. The subject-matter is not merely politics in the narrow sense. It includes consideration of institutions, ideology and popular sentiment.

An explicit stress on continuity is a dangerous path for historians of Japan. It can lead them to ignore the remarkable similarities between the experience of Japan and those of other countries, perpetuating the very sense of impenetrability they seek to dispel. It is, of course, as misleading to pretend that Japan can only be understood in terms of the continuity of its traditions as to claim that industrialization and capitalist economic development produce identical patterns of development in all nations. The existence of what one author has called 'the myth of Japanese uniqueness' is the result not merely of British insularity, but must also be understood in the context of external pressures facing Japan. The need to operate in an international environment after the 1850s compelled Japan to try to present a specific national identity and image to the outside word. An appearance of national unity and homogeneity was cultivated in the pre-1945 years on a foundation of earlier cultural developments. It has been fostered since then by many Western observers and by the Japanese themselves. So persuasive has the publicity been that most of us have become convinced that the Japanese nation is a monolithic entity untroubled by substantive internal divisions. Westerners sometimes conclude that the Japanese not only look the same, but act and think the same. We fail to recognize in their society divisions such as we have in our own, and assume that divisions do not exist. It is thus also an aim of this book to demonstrate that Japanese society has embraced both divisive and unifying tendencies. Any understanding of how divisions and conflicts are mediated and reconciled with the existence of a broader picture of unity must make our approach to Japan more sensitive.

CHAPTER ONE

Restoration and Occupation

The islands which make up the nation of Japan lie in an
arc off mainland northeast Asia. There are four main islands –
Hokkaido, Honshu, Shikoku and Kyushu – which stretch southwest
to northeast for over 2,000 kilometres from the 31st to the 45th
parallels. Clustered around are a host of smaller archipelagoes
and islands. The northernmost tip of Hokkaido is less than 50
kilometres from the now Russian-owned island of Sakhalin. The
point on mainland Asia closest to Japan is the southern tip of the
Korean peninsula over 200 kilometres from northern Kyushu. The
variation in latitude bestows considerable climatic differences on
different areas of Japan; northern Hokkaido is subarctic, whereas
southern Kyushu and Okinawa are near tropical. For the most
part the climate is temperate, with strong seasonal fluctuations,
harsh winters in the central and northern areas, warm summers
and abundant rainfall. The total land area is less than 0.3 per cent
of the world's total; little more than 50 per cent greater than that
of the United Kingdom. Much of the area is mountainous, with
only around one-fifth permitting of cultivation. The staple crop
has for centuries been rice, and wet-rice agriculture has been of
crucial significance in the evolution of Japanese society. While the
volcanic nature of the country means much of the arable area is
intensely fertile, earthquakes, typhoons and other natural disasters
are frequent. Mineral resources are sparse, and the raw materials
for modern industry particularly so. Natural endowments are not
such as to suggest the astonishing prominence achieved by Japan
in the twentieth century.

The exact origins of the contemporary ethnic Japanese are
unclear, but in prehistoric times the Japanese islands received

1

various waves of immigrants from the mainland, to which they were once joined. Gradually members of these groups coalesced to form a dominant racial group; an elemental Japanese state appeared in the second–third century AD. The Ainu people, a proto-Caucasian racial group driven ever further northwards by the ethnic Japanese, are thought to be the remnants of an earlier wave of immigrants. Only a few hundred still survive on the island of Hokkaido. Through the centuries Japan's proximity to Asia allowed for the absorption of Asian cultural influences, yet the distance proved sufficiently great to assist the emergence and maintenance of indigenous cultural traits and enable Japan to avoid a succession of invasions or new influxes of other peoples. From just over 30 million in 1870, the number of Japanese grew to 44 million in 1900, 64 million in 1930 and 83 million in 1950. By 1986 the population was 121 million. Most of these people are packed into the small area of flat land; the coastal strip – running from the Kantō plain round Tokyo to Nagoya and then through to the Kansai plain, with its cities of Osaka, Kyoto and Kobe – has some of the highest population densities in the world. Population pressure, along with vagaries of climate and terrain, and geographical location, have strongly influenced Japan's relations with the outside world over the last 150 years and have played a crucial part in shaping Japan's evolution for much longer.

Two epochal events have dominated the history of modern Japan. The revolution of 1868, commonly called the Meiji Restoration, and the American-dominated Occupation of 1945–52 both proved major watersheds in Japan's development. Each produced a significant shift in course and within a short space of time wrought a substantial transformation in the direction of national policy and popular attitudes. Such is the importance of these events that none of the radical changes in Japan over the last 150 years can be properly understood without reference to them. Yet modern Japan is also the product of much more than recent upheavals.

Japan has, for the last twelve hundred years and more, been reigned over by an imperial house which claims descent from the Yamato clan, whose control of the central part of Japan long predates written record. The secular and religious authority enjoyed by this clan was recognized over the years in an ever wider area of the country, and during the seventh century the head of the clan used the title of emperor or empress on the Chinese model. The family sought to legitimize its power by fostering a belief in its divine descent, claiming the first emperor, Jinmu, as a descendant of the sun goddess; his reign was dated to 660 BC. Although in the early years control did largely rest with the imperial family, others increasingly came to wield power in its name, and the years after 1185 saw hegemony pass to a succession of military rulers who achieved pre-eminent influence by virtue of superior military strength. These rulers did not seek to usurp the position of emperor, or to abolish the institution. Instead, they manipulated it to legitimize their own rule. They exercised power in the name of the emperor, and the imperial family maintained its nominal supremacy and its role as the nation's highest religious authority. For centuries Japan had a dual system of rule: a reigning emperor based at Kyoto and a military government whose seat was normally outside the capital. Many of these military rulers were granted by the emperor the title of shogun¹, a designation according formal recognition as the emperor's military deputy. This title often passed to successive members of the same family, creating military dynasties. The shogun presided over a military administration known as a Bakufu, but there was considerable diffusion of regional power to local warrior-lords. Bakufu control over the country was never absolute, but rested on the administration's ability to hold in check the ambitions of various provincial lords and play them off against each other. Not until the late sixteenth century, under the warlords Oda Nobunaga and Toyotomi Hideyoshi, was the country unified under a single military hegemony, and this was only achieved by building on a series of successful military alliances.

In the military realignment which followed the death of Hideyoshi in 1598, power fell to Tokugawa Ieyasu, a lord from the Kantō area. The decisive victory won by Ieyasu and lords allied to him at the Battle of Sekigahara in 1600 established his supremacy over rivals throughout the islands of Honshu, Shikoku and Kyushu. He had himself declared shogun in 1603. By 1614 he had eliminated Hideyoshi's heir and overcome the final military opposition to his hegemony. Ieyasu sought to establish a system of rule that would ensure the continued dominance of his heirs. His son, Hidetada, was an equally able administrator and politician, and by the time of his death in 1632 his family's position was unchallenged. For over 250 years after Sekigahara the title of shogun was handed down through the males of the Tokugawa family. The Bakufu administration that went with it was located in Edo (now Tokyo), the traditional seat of the Tokugawa family, and served *de facto* as the government of Japan.

The Tokugawa were essentially no more than *primus inter pares*. Influence rested on the various branches of the family's directly controlling around one quarter of the total land area. The Tokugawa confirmed their hold on power by a complex structure of physical, political and economic controls over the several hundred local lords (daimyo) whose domains *(han)* made up the rest of the country, the samurai (warrior) class who constituted their followers and the populace who resided within their territories. The system of rule is often referred to as the Bakuhan (Bakufu-han) system, and many historians, both Western and Japanese, use the term 'feudalism' to describe it. The use of the term 'feudal' in relation to Japan is, however, a matter of some debate. Defined by early translators as the equivalent of the Japanese term *hōken* used to describe the Tokugawa system, the finer points of distinction between 'feudal system' and *hōken seido* soon became obscured. Further confusion was created by the inclination of many Japanese historians to adopt a Marxist framework. Suffice it to say here that the word 'feudal' is used frequently and loosely in relation to Japan, and this use has been based either on the existence in Japan of certain features associated with European feudalism, such as a military code of honour, or on a specific interpretation of the relations of production in Japanese society before the late nineteenth century.

Under the Bakuhan system daimyo were divided into two major categories: *fudai* (hereditary vassals) and *tozama,* those whose families had submitted to the Tokugawa only after Sekigahara. Disposition of territory and offices, public works, enforced residence in Edo, were only some of the means used to prevent daimyo from becoming too powerful. Notwithstanding the arbitrary demands of the Tokugawa, domains enjoyed a certain amount of autonomy. As long as daimyo did not contravene the rulings of their nominal liege lord, the shogun, they could handle their own territory pretty much as they chose. Mechanisms of political control were backed up by a harsh system of regulation, which attempted to minimize all social, political and economic change among the population at large. A rigid hierarchy of hereditary, occupation-related caste was presided over by the warrior *(bushi)* or samurai élite. An official orthodoxy based on Neo-Confucian doctrines emphasized the preservation of order and maintenance of social hierarchy. Potentially damaging foreign influences were minimized after 1640 by cutting off the country from virtually all contact with the outside world.

While these careful measures succeeded in preserving Tokugawa rule for some two and a half centuries, they could never hope to prevent all social, economic and political change. The Bakufu's position was fatally flawed by its having little economic or political status as a national government: it wielded political power as proxy for the emperor using only the income from its own lands. The dynamic forces within society and in the economy eventually came into conflict with a national polity which sought to avoid change. By the early to mid-nineteenth century, many of the realities of life were totally at odds with the prescribed system of rule. Caste divisions became blurred; occupation, status, wealth and influence were no longer commensurate with each other or in accordance with legal stipulation. Advances in commerce and the use of money were placing great strains on the rice-based economy. The political control of the Bakufu was also weakened. In the face of acute financial difficulties besetting the whole ruling class, the balance of economic power had shifted to powerful *tozama* lords traditionally hostile to the Bakufu. The shoguns themselves lacked the personal charisma of their early predecessors and divisions within the Bakufu hierarchy and Tokugawa followers increased. New intellectual currents began to question aspects of the status quo, demanding reconsideration of the relationship between emperor and shogun. Lower status samurai, increasingly influential in domain or Bakufu bureaucracies, began to demand a greater say in the running of political affairs.

By the 1850s the tensions brought about by social, economic and political change were already beginning to pose a serious threat not merely to the rule of the Tokugawa but to the system itself. The reopening of foreign contacts with the United States and the imperialist powers of Europe rapidly brought matters to crisis point. From the early nineteenth century Japan had been approached on several occasions by Western nations active in Asian waters and anxious to initiate trading and other contacts. Unable to maintain the seclusion policy any longer in the face of strong pressure and superior military strength, Japan concluded her first international agreement in 1854 with the US. Agreements with other nations followed, and the extraterritorial, most-favoured-nation relationships adopted in China and Thailand were extended to Japan.

The development of foreign contacts posed a series of dilemmas for the Bakufu. It showed the Bakufu to be militarily weak and ineffective. It forced many Japanese to recognize the need for reform and a strong national government which might achieve for Japan a

5

better deal in external relations. Yet reform could spell disaster for a regime whose very fundamentals rested on a resistance to change. From 1853, when the crisis over US demands for formal relations led the Bakufu to solicit the opinions of all daimyo, a move quite without precedent, Tokugawa authority went rapidly downhill.

While the Bakufu administration had for several decades been subject to criticisms from within its own ranks, a more serious threat to its supremacy emerged from within domains traditionally hostile to it. During the late 1850s radical samurai from powerful *tozama* domains, especially Satsuma in southern Kyushu, and Chōshū at the western tip of Honshu, began to steer domain policy towards open opposition to the Bakufu. At the same time the Bakufu was held responsible by the powers for attacks on foreigners by anti-foreign elements, over which it had little control. The question of ratification of treaties with Western nations opened up a gulf between the Bakufu and an imperial court whose nominal supremacy Tokugawa enemies were beginning to realize could be fruitfully exploited to the regime's disadvantage. Pressured on one side by nations willing to exert force to achieve satisfactory trading relations, the Bakufu was by its domestic opponents accused of usurping imperial authority by giving in to them. Both the issue of imperial power and the question of foreign contacts became sticks with which to beat the Bakufu. The Tokugawa's enemies took up the rallying cry of 'revere the emperor and expel the barbarian' (*sonnō jōi*), and kept it long after their leaders realized the impossibility of bringing external contacts to an end.

At the same time the Bakufu's weakness was exacerbated by problems over the shogunal succession; the selection of the nearest blood heir, a young boy, to succeed to the title in 1858, highlighted the problems of Bakufu leadership at a time when the institution required all the strength it could muster. The assassination of the Bakufu's foremost leader, Regent Ii Naosuke, in 1860 was a fatal blow to the regime's attempt to re-establish Tokugawa supremacy. The re-emergence of the court onto the political scene and its collusion with many of the Bakufu's other opponents promoted an attempted rapprochement between the Tokugawa and imperial factions in the early 1860s, but this proved short-lived. Divided among themselves over how far to adhere to the traditional policies and how far to adapt to a changing foreign and domestic environment, the Bakufu's members became incapable of decisive action. More and more the sworn enemies of Tokugawa political power openly flouted Bakufu authority. In 1866 an alliance between the Bakufu's two leading opponents, Satsuma and Chōshū, was signed, ending disagreements which had hitherto prevented concerted action, and depriving the Bakufu of Satsuma support for a military expedition mounted to chastise the more radical Chōshū for its insubordination. The Bakufu's inability to demonstrate military superiority over Chōshū late in 1866 made it apparent to all that the Tokugawa no longer possessed the *force majeure* on which their power ultimately depended, and with their opponents allied with each other under the banner of imperial rule the Tokugawa's fate was sealed.

Through late 1866 and 1867 conspiracy against the Bakufu mounted. Many of its own supporters advised Bakufu leaders that concessions were the only way to forestall more radical action. During 1866 Tokugawa (Hitotsubashi) Keiki, whose claims to the office of shogun had been rejected in 1858 on the grounds of precedent, succeeded to the headship of the Tokugawa family and subsequently to the title of shogun. Keiki was an able individual, an astute politician prepared to take heed of the views of both advisers and enemies. He pursued a programme of reform aimed at strengthening the regime and the Tokugawa's position within it, but was unable to stem the hostile tide. Late in 1867, despite calls for resistance from among his more conservative supporters, he formally returned political authority to the emperor, but this move proved inadequate to appease his more extreme opponents, who argued that while the Tokugawa continued to control more than 25 per cent of the country they were bound to play the dominant role in councils of state. Early in January 1868, forces from Satsuma and Chōshū and other Tokugawa opponents siezed the palace in Kyoto, announcing an imperial restoration and the establishment of a new government from which the Tokugawa were excluded. Shogunate lands were to be confiscated and the title abolished. Keiki accepted this *fait accompli* and withdrew towards Osaka, but this acquiescence was not supported by some of his followers, who attempted to occupy Kyoto and clashed with troops mainly from Satsuma and Chōshū fighting as the 'imperial army'. The Battle of Toba-Fushimi was a resounding victory for the imperial troops which, though outnumbered, were better equipped. After this defeat the Bakufu's supporters gradually retreated towards Edo following the shogun's appeals not to offer resistance. The imperial troops marched on the capital in pursuit of them, and the city fell with minimal resistance in May 1868. An alliance of northeastern domains led by Aizu had been forced to capitulate by the end of the year, and much of the country was little affected by the civil war[2]. Only a last remnant of Bakufu supporters held out on Hokkaido through to 1869. The new government stripped the Tokugawa family of most of its land and Keiki was forced to resign its headship; many Bakufu supporters also lost their domains. National power passed to a new group of court nobles and activists from the four leading domains of Satsuma, Chōshū, Tosa and Hizen, who moved quickly to consolidate their power. The dual system of rule which had prevailed for centuries was formally ended and national government brought under the aegis of the reigning sovereign whose authority was recognized throughout the country.

This transfer of power is referred to as the Meiji Restoration, or the Meiji Revolution, after the reign name now adopted by the young emperor who had succeeded to the throne the year before. The years from 1868 until his death in 1912 are known as the Meiji period. During these years Japan's new leaders embarked on a programme of radical reform aimed at transforming Japan into a modern industrialized nation capable of dealing on equal terms with the nations of the West, and throwing off 'unequal' treaties viewed as a national insult. The new regime ruthlessly crushed all semblance of armed opposition which threatened national unity.

By the end of the Meiji period control was focused in a highly centralized state whose functions were carried out through Western style political, administrative and judicial institutions operating in the name of the emperor. Western style armed forces upheld the position of the Japanese state at home and abroad. Western style financial institutions, infrastructure and factory-based industry were promoted to provide the requisite economic foundations for international strength. A highly efficient education system served the aims of the state. Japan had already been victorious in two major wars, against China in 1894–5 and Russia in 1904–5; she was a world power and possessor of colonies.

Such was the speed of the changes in Japan at this time that it is easy to draw a somewhat misleading impression of unilinear progress, a clearly conceived plan of action from the beginning, logically carried out step by step. While motives may have been broadly consistent and widely shared, progress was in fact often erratic and haphazard, disagreements were many and the early Meiji leaders could scarcely have foreseen some of the longer term consequences of their policies. The course of this transformation, which followed on the events of 1868, and the degree to which it was fundamental or superficial, will constitute a major part of the subject-matter of this book.

The interpretation of the events of 1868 has become a major topic of controversy among historians of Japan. Even the term 'restoration' used in English has overtones of a return to the past; the revival of a hallowed Japanese tradition which accorded supreme power to the imperial family. Japan's post-1868 rulers utilized this nationalistic focus and claimed throughout to exercise power in the name of the emperor. Yet the Japanese term normally used for the transfer, *ishin*, is more correctly translated as 'renovation' – a term which implies not retrospection but a sense of renewal and looking forward. This terminological ambiguity symbolizes a basic contradiction embodied in the whole process of change which followed 1868, a running tension between those who looked back and sought to revive what they saw as the best in Japanese tradition in the face of a Western onslaught, and those who looked to the future and were prepared to accommodate the values and techniques of their competitors, if only to compete effectively with them. In fact, of course, many of Japan's new rulers shared both aspirations: modern methods and Western techniques could be embraced as wholeheartedly by those who saw them as the key to a restored 'traditional' Japanese independence based on indigenous social structure and values as by those who desired to embrace not only Western techniques but some version of Western ideology.

Interpretation of the restoration has broader implications for understanding Japanese history as a whole, particularly for the many Japanese historians who have sought to locate it within a Marxist historical framework. Marxist–Leninist ideas became highly influential among the intelligentsia in the 1920s and have remained so ever since. During the late 1920s to early 1930s conflict over the correct strategy for the Japan Communist Party generated an enormous amount of scholarly research aimed at substantiating the views of the main factions. Debate focused on the question of whether the Meiji Restoration was a bourgeois revolution, albeit with remnants of feudalism persisting, in which case activists should work for a proletarian revolution; or whether it was an incomplete bourgeois revolution, necessitating a two-stage revolution in the future. The debate was a major exercise in the application of Marx's framework to a non-European, late developing country, and continues to this day.

Among Western interpreters the Canadian, E. H. Norman, in

Japan's Emergence as a Modern State (1940) was clearly influenced by the Japanese dilemma. Norman saw the Restoration as a revolution carried out by lower level samurai acting against the frustrations of their position. The degree of capitalist development implied the momentum of a bourgeois revolution. Other historians have seen the Restoration as a counter-revolution; a palace *coup d'état* in which power passed from one part of the élite to another; and a transfer of power which was an integral part of the growth of national, and nationalist, awareness among a people faced for the first time in centuries by real threats from the outside world. The Restoration is, perhaps, all of these things, and can only be understood in terms of the background of those who participated, the pressures for economic, social and political change and the context of the Western threat. Clearly it was not a popular revolution in the sense of an uprising by the masses, although popular discontent was widespread, legitimate and frequently manifest: those involved in the transfer of power did not seek to exploit this discontent for their own purposes, either before or for many years after 1868. The revolution was carried out by a small élite, as was the transformation that followed.

The results of the changes in the latter part of the nineteenth century were certainly dramatic. By 1914 Japan had not only achieved revision of the unequal treaties, but also alliance with Britain and the beginnings of an empire. Her modern industrial sector was growing rapidly; she was one of the world's leading exporters of textiles. World War I brought an unprecedented economic boom and recognition of Japan's acquisition of Great Power status – the only Asian country able to compete with the West on its own terms. The flourishing of more liberal trends during the latter part of the war and the early 1920s seemed to mark a shift from autocratic, oligarchic rule to representative party politics, giving the period the title 'Taishō democracy', after the Taishō emperor who came to the throne in 1912. Yet this burgeoning proved short-lived, barely continuing into the early years of the reign of Hirohito, the new Shōwa emperor, who succeeded his father in 1926. Economic problems in the 1920s were compounded by the onset of the Great Depression, although Japan's recovery after 1932 was rapid, and a flourishing export trade helped the country to build up a substantial heavy industrial sector. The ambiguities within the constitution and the sacrosanct elements of patriotism, nationalism and emperorism embodied in the orthodox ideology assisted other élites to wield national power with a considerable degree of freedom and legitimacy. The political role of the army became ever greater as the 1930s progressed, and the problems posed by population expansion, protectionism in international trade and agricultural impoverishment helped to unite much of the population behind an aggressive search for territorial expansion, Asian leadership and economic autarky. The Japanese seizure of Manchuria in 1931 went relatively unchallenged by the Western powers as an intra-Asian affair, but as Japanese ambitions grew they aroused growing concern in nations further afield, notably the European powers with territories in Southeast Asia, and the US with its Pacific interests. War with China from 1937 was followed by war with the US and its European allies, 1941–5. It culminated in the total defeat of Japan and initiated the second major watershed in modern Japanese history, the reforms carried out under the Allied (*de facto* US) Occupation of 1945–52.

Occupation policy had two stated objectives: demilitarization and democratization. A massive programme of institutional reforms was premised on a belief that certain elements in the economy, polity and society of Japan had been conducive to the rise of militarism in the country and the waging of aggressive war. Many outside observers saw the events of the 1930s and early 1940s as the logical outcome not only of the policies adopted after 1868 but also of long-standing socio-economic factors. For others, aberrant leaders and the socio-economic conditions of the interwar years had combined to deny the full fruition of democratic government aspired to by so many Japanese. The Western allies shared a belief in the existence in Japan of a conspiracy to wage aggressive war, for which those responsible must be punished. War criminals were charged and their supporters purged. The militarist state was dismantled by disbanding the armed forces, the forces' ministries and munitions production facilities. Positive reforms to secure 'democratization' included a reorganization of the political system under a new constitution, a transformation of the system and content of education, anti-monopoly and deconcentration measures to extend ownership and control of big business and finance, land reform to widen land ownership and reduce tenancy. The civil code was revised. Sexual equality, freedom of belief, political activity, labour organization and other rights were guaranteed. In effect a total institutional restructuring of Japanese society, economy and politics was imposed within the space of a few years. Japan regained her independence in the spring of 1952, under the San Francisco Peace Treaty. The US–Japan Security Treaty which came into force simultaneously tied Japan firmly to the interests of the United States and its allies.

For much of the population, numbed by defeat, the reforms were initially tangential to efforts to maintain a basic standard of life, but while the reforms themselves were accepted with considerable resignation, none could remain untouched by their effects for long. At one extreme the Occupation changes were an unwelcome imposition of alien Western standards on the evolution of Japan's indigenous culture. At the other they were an opportunity, perhaps the only opportunity, of breaking with institutions and attitudes which had led to disaster; an opportunity which had to be grasped because such radical change could only be imposed from outside. After regaining autonomy some wished to strengthen the changes, others to reject them. The Occupation changes, like the events following the Restoration, aroused in the people of Japan reactions which looked both back to the past and forward to the future, and which highlighted Japan's dependence on, yet difference from, the other cultures of the world.

In the 1980s we are still sufficiently close to the Occupation to make it difficult to assess some of the longer term significances of its reforms. What is clear is that the degree to which the reformers achieved their stated aims was muted first of all by a partial backtracking on policy after 1947 under the pressures of worsening relations between the United States and the Soviet Union, and the burden which an economically prostrate Japan placed on the US taxpayer. This shift in policy is often referred to as the 'reverse course'. Since the end of the Occupation Japanese authorities too, with or without American blessing, have sought to change some provisions of the reform and to circumvent others. The effectiveness of the reforms has also been constrained by the resistance to change of many longstanding attitudes and patterns of operation of political, economic and social activity. Theory frequently does not accord with practice. Nevertheless, the pattern of Japan's postwar history owes much to Occupation policy. Dispute may rage as to the effectiveness of this or that particular reform, but US policy 1945–52 has been a major arbiter of two fundamental axes of postwar development – the integration of Japan, economically and politically, into the Western capitalist camp and the extraordinary growth of the Japanese economy. Historians, economists and other observers of Japan have devoted considerable efforts to locating the Occupation-initiated reforms in the context of Japan's phenomenal advance into the world economy. However, while the policies of the late 1940s were immensely important in providing an altered framework for economic and political activity, what becomes increasingly clear in the course of any serious investigation is the degree to which many factors in Japan's 'success' substantially predate the postwar reforms.

The importance of continuity has in some ways been underlined by the approach adopted in much of the Western, particularly US, scholarship on Japanese development. In the frenzied atmosphere of the Cold War and its aftermath, historical research on Japan was strongly influenced by political imperatives. The Pacific War was viewed less as a failure brought about by long-term institutional factors and class and other divisions within society. Instead Japan's modern development was seen in more positive terms. Japan was a country which had achieved 'modernization', which could offer a model to other industrializing nations; the militarism and aggression of the 1930s was an aberration, explicable largely in political terms, the ability of a small group to turn back the liberal trends of the twenties. English language scholarship at this time failed to reflect the broad range of Japanese language scholarship, in particular the strong Marxist influence on interpretation and conceptualization. To say that it has been the poorer for it is not to denigrate the work that was done. Nevertheless, the broader range of perspectives reflected in recent scholarship has added immeasurably to our understanding of the pre-1950s era and the context it provides to postwar growth.

On the face of it, the postwar transformation of Japan appears even more astonishing than the prewar changes. Japan is a 'phoenix rising from the ashes', whose postwar experience has been a 'miracle'. A single-minded commitment to economic recovery and growth has produced a dramatic rise in material standards of living and the world's second largest capitalist economy. Economic growth has occurred within a framework of close ties with the US and membership of the capitalist camp. At home a constitutional commitment to democracy has resulted in an almost unbroken dominance of conservative political parties. Japan's pivotal role in the world economy has provoked a search for the reasons why Japan's economy has continued to prosper in the face of a lack of natural resources and a high degree of dependence on international trade. Both developed and developing countries have sought to learn from Japan's experience.

Japanese society has changed substantially under the impact of material prosperity and international influences. Yet many Japanese consider their countrymen excessively insular for the contemporary world. Calls for the increased 'internationalization' of the economy, of society and of political attitudes suggest that many of the postwar changes may be less substantive than are often imagined. Such perceptions reinforce the need to view postwar Japan in the context of the country's earlier history.

NOTES

1 Shogun is an abbreviation of *seii-taishōgun*, lit. 'great general who subdues barbarians'.
2 Often referred to as the Boshin War, after the Japanese calendar year.

CHAPTER TWO

Japan and the West

Japan's modern history is the story of a country in an international environment. The active involvement between Japan and the Western world which began in the 1850s has been so important for both that a consideration of Japan's place in the world order is an appropriate starting point for any discussion of her recent history. Yet geographical remoteness had earlier assisted the minimizing of contacts even with neighbouring states, and only 150 years ago Japan was one of tne most isolated countries in the world. The legacy of isolation remains of fundamental importance. Japanese society has evolved singular features, which must be understood in the context of a very particular historical development, in which a profound sense of uniqueness, separateness and isolation has been a major element. The shift away from isolation has been variously interpreted. Was Japan recognizing herself as one country among many, balancing domestic priorities and concerns against the demands of the broader international order, opening up and adjusting her internal arrangements to effect a more cosmopolitan perspective? Or was the change a more superficial one in which a crude, but no longer viable, form of isolation was replaced by a more subtle variant, in which the techniques of the West were adopted to preserve and strengthen an essentially unchanged sense of cultural uniqueness and social order, and ensure survival in an unpredictable and hostile world? This ambiguity – not yet fully dispelled – has been of immense importance both to the international community and to Japan herself.

Japan experienced a brief period of European contact in the late sixteenth and early seventeenth centuries, but in 1639 the government of Japan, the Tokugawa (Edo) Bakufu, effectively severed all contact with the West. Its main motivation was a desire to exclude the potentially subversive influence of Christianity, which had proved impossible to divorce from trading contacts. Foreign contact was seen as a threat to political stability. All that was left of the previous Dutch, English, Spanish and Portuguese contacts was a small Dutch trading station restricted to the island of Deshima in Nagasaki, which remained the only formal Western presence for over 200 years. Japanese nationals were cut off from personal contacts with Europeans and the import of foreign artefacts, books and anything which might convey Western knowledge was banned. Japanese were prohibited from travelling abroad. This 'seclusion' was not always as complete as the authorities might wish. Some knowledge of Western scientific advances seeped in through 'Dutch scholars' based at Nagasaki. In 1720 the ban on the import of foreign books was relaxed, and a series of encounters with foreign representatives from the late eighteenth century portended that seclusion could not permanently be maintained. Nevertheless, despite these breaches in the policy, for a period of over two centuries Japan essentially developed in total isolation. Despite sporadic contacts with China and Holland, when Japan was eventually forced to deal with the international environment she was almost totally ignorant of the intellectual, economic, scientific, technological and cultural advances made by the West during her seclusion period.

Of course Japan herself did not stand still during this time, but the substantial advances that did take place were not influenced by external models or ideas. Herein lie the origins of a fundamental dichotomy that has dominated Japan's recent history; the simultaneous existence of both 'indigenous' and Western modes of thought and behaviour has resulted in acute cultural conflict. Japanese attempts to change Japan in the last 150 years have been both imitative and derivative, but have been accompanied by conscious and unconscious retention of indigenous characteristics and the 'simulation' of traditional Japanese attributes, plus a fair measure of originality. Although accommodation between the two cultural traditions is often achieved, the conflicts provoked have also been intense. Reconciliation sometimes proves impossible, and continuing strains within Japanese society are the result. That discord between indigenous and Western cultures would prove unremitting was suggested by the arguments of domestic political protagonists even before Japan was forced to reopen contacts with the West in the 1850s. At one end of the spectrum of opinion were xenophobic seclusionists who argued that relations with foreigners would be morally as well as politically disastrous. At the other were those with some knowledge of Western technology who saw that Japan, like China, was militarily incapable of resisting Western force, and believed Japan had much to learn from Western culture.

Within Japan economic and social changes during the Tokugawa period imposed severe strains on the political system, but despite growing concerns over the implications for Japan of foreign advances in Asia, seclusion remained for many an article of faith. Sporadic attempts by Western nations to penetrate Japan's isolation from the 1790s were all rebuffed. During the 1840s official approaches increased, but were not pressed forcefully. However, the growth of US interest in East Asia consequent on the opening of the American West and the expansion of US shipping and fishing activities in the Pacific produced more determined action. In July 1853 Commodore Matthew Perry, officially commissioned by the US government to initiate relations with Japan, arrived in Uraga, at the southern end of Tokyo Bay, with a squadron of four ships. He refused to make his approaches at Nagasaki, a customary means of diverting troublesome foreigners, and presented the Japanese with what was effectively an ultimatum, demanding that some agreement be reached to cover the provisioning of US ships, the treatment of shipwrecked American sailors and the development of formal relations. He departed after announcing that he would return for his answer with a larger squadron the following spring. The demands threw the Japanese ruling class into chaos. The Edo Bakufu had dominated political decision-making for 250 years. It now made open confession of its inability to cope alone with the crisis initiated by Perry's arrival. Foreign relations now became a major factor in the final fall of the Tokugawa, whose impotence to resist foreign demands became apparent to all.

In the spring of 1854 Perry returned with an enlarged fleet of nine vessels. He concluded with the Bakufu a convention opening Hakodate (in Hokkaido) and Shimoda as ports of refuge, permitting sailors to be returned and the appointment of consuls at a later date. Consideration of trade was deferred. Before long Britain and Russia had concluded similar treaties. Further pressure was exerted for the establishment of full commercial relations. In 1856 the first US consul, Townsend Harris, arrived in Japan, and it was largely due to his tenacity, and his use of the British as bogeymen, that the July 1858 US–Japan Treaty of Amity and Commerce was concluded. (It took as its model the Chinese treaty port system.) This was the first of several treaties concluded with the Western powers that year, known collectively as the Ansei Treaties, after the era during which they were concluded. They are also frequently referred to as the 'unequal' treaties, since inequality was the essential keynote of their provisions. Diplomatic representatives were to reside in Edo, and trade was to be free of official intervention, with more ports due to be opened in future years. Western traders allowed into Japan were to be restricted to foreign settlements and other prescribed areas, but were to have the benefits of extraterritoriality, i.e. they were not to be subject to the laws of Japan, but any misdemeanour or problem (including those that concerned Japanese) was to be dealt with by a court presided over by the consul of the country of the national concerned. Later agreements fixed tariffs for foreign goods coming into Japan at the low rate of 5 percent *ad valorem;* and a 'most-favoured-nation' clause extended to each country new rights secured by any other. Westerners in Japan were therefore virtually outside any control by the Japanese. The rights Westerners enjoyed were not reciprocated for Japanese abroad. This situation was defended on the grounds of Japan's relative backwardness in economic, social, legal and political terms.

The circumstances of Japan's opening to the West thus seemed calculated to reinforce rather than diminish a sense of separateness and need for security in the face of manifestly unequal treatment. Admittedly the interaction of Western ambitions and Japanese response was such as to prevent Japan's becoming a European colony, or even suffering the impairment of sovereignty which befell China. Nevertheless, an awareness that Japan was acutely vulnerable to threats of superior force, a resentment that Japan was considered inferior because she did not conform to Western standards and models, and a perception that other nations were prepared to act 'unfairly' to maximize the advantages that could be gained from any particular situation, made Japan determined to achieve equal status with the so-called Great Powers, or indeed, to surpass them. Japan was both militarily and economically vulnerable and the lack of outside support for her resistance to great power domination reinforced a sense of national isolation which originated in national myth, grew in the seclusion period and was strengthened by an awareness of the cultural divide between Japan and the West. Removal of this national vulnerability and dependence on other nations became the prime aim, and so compelling an aim was it that it came to be achieved by fair means or foul. Diplomatic activity and international agreements became in a sense tactical, adhered to only when upholding the pursuit of the all-important 'self-sufficiency'.

The first decade after the Ansei Treaties produced a rearguard action against a Western intrusion which Japan was powerless to resist. Early foreign residents were exposed to sporadic physical attacks by extreme anti-foreign elements, and anti-foreignism continued to be exploited by the Bakufu's enemies to compound its political difficulties. Most members of the ruling élite, though, were becoming increasingly aware that Western contacts were inevitable, and should not merely be passively endured but exploited to Japan's advantage. Some knowledge of the West was encouraged and a few individuals travelled abroad. The use of Western skills to strengthen Japan, often summed up in the slogan 'Western technology, Japanese values', was a course of action supported by many. While the impact of renewed foreign contacts on both politics and the economy in these years was considerable, the growing power struggle within the country postponed any substantive attempt to resolve the issue of foreign relations on a long-term basis. With the change of government in 1868, and the new regime's consolidation of its hold on power, attention was again brought to bear on the issue.

The new government's first thought was to attempt a revision of the treaties. Various governments were approached, and in 1871 a top-level delegation was despatched to Europe and America in the hope of substantive negotiation. Led by Prince Iwakura Tomomi, a court noble, the delegation included Ōkubo Toshimichi and Kido Kōin, two of the major architects of the Restoration, and Itō Hirobumi, who dominated the ruling oligarchy for much of the Meiji period. Everywhere they were informed that treaty revision negotiation was premature.

The trip was to have beneficial results despite this. Stunned to realize how very far and in how many aspects the West was ahead of Japan, the members of the mission made extensive observations on various aspects of the civilization of the nations of Europe and America. Their return to Japan in 1873 saw the implementation of a strategy based on a realization that a repeal of the 'unequal' treaties could only be achieved by trying to bring Japan up to Western standards in the things Westerners considered important – legal system, political structure, economic legislation and a general level of 'culture' and 'civilization'. Domestic reform had to precede any thought of international strength. Competition with the West had to take place on the West's own terms.

The result of this realization was a massive programme of change along Western lines. Changes had been partially attempted before the Restoration. The last shogun, Tokugawa Keiki (Yoshinobu), had initiated tentative reforms under the aegis of the French representative Léon Roches. Various domains had done likewise. Prior to the departure of the Iwakura Mission, the Meiji regime too had started a limited programme of industrialization and social change, much of it contingent on the dismantling of the political, social and economic structure that had prevailed under the Tokugawa. The post-1873 programme, however, went far beyond the destruction of the old order. The details of this programme are covered in greater depth elsewhere in this book. It is enough here to note the span of its coverage and the scale of the undertaking. Changes in political institutions culminated in cabinet government from 1885, the promulgation of a constitution in February 1889 and the opening of an elected assembly in 1890. The haphazard bureaucracy of the early Meiji years was reorganized into a formal bureaucratic hierarchy, its entry governed by examination. Radical reform of the legal system brought about the implementation of new civil and criminal codes modelled on European lines and Western-style judicial procedures. A new state education system provided for universal basic education as well as vocational and higher education. Powerful Western-style armed forces were built up. The infrastructure of a modern state – for example, transport, post, banks – was created, and a variety of methods used to promote the building of a modern industrial sector and the exports to help pay for the undertaking. The groundwork of this change was substantially completed by the turn of the century. It was motivated in large part by the desire to rid Japan of the unequal treaties, which remained the arbiter of Japanese diplomatic activity almost to the end of the century.

No single country was taken as the model in implementing change. The degree of eclecticism was considerable, and efforts were made to find the Western model, or the aspects of it, that would be most appropriate to the Japanese situation. In the case of the constitution, for example, it was the German model that was the most influential, while in other spheres it might be the French, British, Dutch or American system that was most closely copied. Nor was there any question of imposing an unadulterated Western model on Japan. Western practices and ideas were modified to fit in with Japanese reality – though there were periods when 'Westernization' was very much the vogue. Much emphasis continued to be laid on the importance of Japanese tradition. Not only did real or supposed elements of Japanese tradition – or simulations of such traditions – serve to focus national feeling and efforts, but a continuing assertion of the importance of 'things Japanese' also served to retain an element of self-respect in the face of foreign cultural pressures and the threat of cultural, economic and political imperialism.

The adoption of the programme for change served to accelerate and deepen contacts with the West. As contacts came to comprise not just diplomatic intercourse, but a whole range of economic, military, social and cultural interests, the scope for both friendship and conflict became greater. The opening of relations had largely been dictated by the powers' own interests in the East Asian region, but now the issues became far more complex; account had to be taken of factors as diverse as Japan's economic imperatives, the growth of Japanese military power and the emergence of national sentiment in response to foreign contact. The unequal treaties did not provide for this growing complexity, but it was clearly reflected in a process of treaty revision negotiation which, despite its ultimate success, did little to reassure Japan regarding the benevolence of Western intentions.

By the mid 1880s the Japanese government felt that it could reopen negotiations concerning revision of the unequal treaties. Some small successes had already been achieved; for example, by 1880 foreigners had agreed to entrust their mail to the Japanese postal system. Between 1885 and 1887 Foreign Minister Inoue Kaoru, an ardent advocate of 'Westernization', negotiated with the Western powers. Inoue reached an agreement on revision which provided for the legal system to be Westernized along approved lines, foreign judges to sit in cases involving non-Japanese nationals, and for tariffs to be raised without the achievement of tariff autonomy. The agreement leaked out and Inoue was forced to resign in July 1887. He was succeeded by Ōkuma Shigenobu, who re-negotiated to restrict the inclusion of foreign judges to the Supreme Court; foreign approval for the new legal code was also waived. This agreement, too, was vigorously opposed, and was a major factor in a bomb attack on Ōkuma in 1889, in which he lost a leg. The degree of hostility to these treaty revision proposals stemmed in large part from feelings that any continuing unsolicited Western involvement in the legal system was an insult to Japan, and that Westernization had in any case gone too far. A few opposed the proposals on the ground that they gave international sanction to an undemocratic regime, but it was the more nationalist elements which were particularly vocal, and there was a broad measure of support for their sentiments. Even Japan's foreign legal advisers opposed any such agreement, so both efforts proved abortive.

As Japan's legal and political system conformed increasingly to Western models it became more and more difficult for foreign governments to refuse to entrust their nationals to Japanese jurisdiction. The delay in conceding what Japanese considered legitimate sovereign rights brought a real danger of unilateral denunciation. Most foreign nationals in Japan continued vociferously to oppose any change in their advantageous position, but their views had less and less weight with government representatives both on the spot and at home. In summer 1893 another foreign minister, Mutsu Munemitsu, initiated a new round of negotiations with Britain which reached a successful conclusion in the Anglo-Japanese Treaty of Commerce and Navigation of July 1894. Under this agreement, British nationals in Japan would, after 1899, be subject to the prevailing Japanese laws. The tariff problem was dealt with separately and a tariff convention was subsequently negotiated, but tariff autonomy was not achieved until 1911. The other powers followed Britain in concluding new treaties.

In theory, at least, Japan was now the equal of the Western powers. Before very long, however, it was to be made abundantly clear to her that legal equality was not enough; the ability to exert force was the key not merely to ascendancy, but also to genuine equality. The nation that was to provide this salutary lesson was Russia, and it was a lesson that was to have a profound effect in Japan.

Japan's contacts with Tsarist Russia, the only Western power with which Japan shared a border, had remained relatively friendly while Japan was sufficiently weak to pose no threat. There had been sporadic contact even before the 1850s treaties, and subsequent relations had been on the same unequal basis as those with the other powers. In May 1875 Japan and Russia had concluded a treaty whereby Japan acknowledged Russian suzerainty over the island of Sakhalin in return for her own possession of the Kurile Isles, the archipelago running northeast from the coast of Hokkaido. By the late 1880s, however, Japan had growing interests in mainland Asia, and there was a danger that Japan's attempts to assert herself in Korea and in Manchuria would bring her into direct confrontation with the expanding Russian empire. Both countries claimed that in these areas of Northeast Asia their political and economic rights and interests were paramount to national security. Both wanted to extend their influence in the same region.

In 1894 war broke out between Japan and China over competing rights and interests in Korea.[1] Japan's newly modernized armed forces achieved a resounding victory, and the terms of the peace treaty exacted from the Chinese not only a massive indemnity, but also the cession to Japan of Formosa (Taiwan), the Pescadores Islands and the Liaodong Peninsula, which lay off the Manchurian coast west of Korea. The war marked Japan's acquisition of her first colonies, and made her a force to be reckoned with in East Asian affairs. A Chinese victory had been widely expected, and many Westerners were shocked by the apparent totality of Japan's triumph. For the first time the possibility of a serious non-white challenge to the nations of Europe or the United States was raised. It was during these years that Emperor Wilhelm II of Germany enunciated his famous 'yellow peril' theory, the idea that the millions of China, led by Japan, would overrun Europe and destroy its civilization. China was far from being in a state to overrun anyone, but the spectre had been evoked, and the West was now forced to note the existence of a non-white imperial power.

Yet Japan's gains in the war did not go uncontested. Russia was vehemently opposed to cession of the Liaodong Peninsula which seemed to offer Japan a valuable foothold from which to extend her influence in Manchuria and northern China. Within a week of the signing of the peace treaty, in April 1895, Russia, Germany and France had joined forces in what was known as the Triple (Tripartite) Intervention. The three powers issued a joint ultimatum to Japan demanding retraction of the Liaodong cession on the grounds that it endangered Beijing and invalidated Korean independence. The ultimatum contained the implied threat of military force. Japan looked around for diplomatic support, but this was not forthcoming from either Britain or the United States. Japan was in no state to risk military confrontation with Russia, backed up by France and Germany. She was forced to concede, accepting in return an additional indemnity of 30 million taels,[2] which China could ill afford to pay.

This tripartite intervention left a legacy of resentment in Japan, a bitterness at being unable to retain concessions fairly won in war except with the sanction of other powers. This long-lasting resentment was far in excess of the significance of the Liaodong Peninsula itself. It served to stimulate further Japan's belief that she was highly vulnerable in military terms and that her only course for survival as a strong and independent state must be the strengthening of her own military capacity. This resentment was strengthened still further in 1898 when as part of the struggle for slices of the Chinese 'melon' Russia herself took out a twenty-five year lease on the southern tip of the Liaodong Peninsula. Japan was powerless to stop her.

The threat of Russo-Japanese confrontation grew around the turn of the century. Japan, bolstered by victory against China, expended considerable efforts and sums of money on the expansion of her armed forces. Russia strove to complete the Siberian Railway and its opening to traffic in 1903 facilitated troop transport to the area. A series of agreements from 1898 onwards tried to channel the tension between the two powers along 'Manchuria for Korea' lines, i.e. Russia was to have the dominant interest in Manchuria, while Japan dominated in Korea. Yet the degree to which Russia tried to control Manchuria, as well as retaining Korean interests, seemed intolerable to many in Japan. Following the eight-nation occupation of Beijing during the Boxer Rebellion of 1900 Russia failed to withdraw completely from Chinese territory, occupying a considerable part of the territory of Manchuria. Representations and ultimata from Japan and other nations were ignored, and it was this Russian occupation of Manchuria that was to serve as the immediate *casus belli* of Russo-Japanese confrontation. The more fundamental causes of conflict lay far deeper – in the basic conflict of two powers anxious to expand their interests and influence in the same region.

Japan had for several years been building up her armed forces in anticipation of conflict with Russia, but many hoped that matters could still be settled amicably. A sizeable body of opinion, led by the veteran statesman Itō Hirobumi, advocated alliance with Russia with a view to reaching a local settlement. Mistrust of Russia was widespread, though, and discussions with Britain concerning a possible alliance were also carried on during 1901. Britain was amenable to these approaches; alliance with Japan was seen as a means of containing Russian expansion in the East, avoiding a Russo-Japanese partition of Northeast Asia and preserving the treaty system in China.

The Anglo-Japanese Alliance was concluded in January 1902. It recognized Japan's dominant interests in Korea. Its main provision was that if either party were engaged in war with one other country in East Asia the other party would remain uninvolved, but should two enemies become involved the other party to the alliance would join forces. This provision was highly significant in terms of any Japanese–Russian conflict. Russia was formally allied to France, and Germany too was keen to encourage Russian activity in Northeast Asia. Any assistance to Russia in a struggle with Japan in East Asia would involve these powers in war with Britain, so the alliance effectively restricted any such conflict to Russia and Japan alone. It thus encouraged the Japanese to adopt a firmer stance in negotiations with Russia. The Japanese also viewed the alliance as a considerable accolade. For several decades Britain's policy had been splendid isolation, and that Europe's most powerful nation should emerge from that isolation by concluding an alliance with Japan was seen in Japan as a triumph.

During 1903 relations between the two powers became increasingly strained as Russia failed to withdraw her troops on schedule from Manchuria. On 6 February 1904 Japan cut off diplomatic relations. Attacks were launched on Russian held territory and on 10 February war was declared. The Japanese advanced rapidly, crossing into Manchuria in May, and moving up the Liaodong Peninsula, but the pace soon slowed. Port Arthur (Lushun), at the tip of the Liaodong Peninsula, held out until early 1905, after eight months of a siege into which the Japanese threw everything they had. A series of hard fought campaigns brought Russian withdrawal, but the Japanese victories were costly and Japan's resources to continue the war were fast being exhausted. The Manchurian winter took its toll on both sides. With ships of the Russian Far Eastern fleet based at Port Arthur badly damaged, or blockaded in port, the Baltic fleet was sent to the scene of battle. Departing in October 1904, it eventually reached the waters between Japan and Korea in May 1905 (after a tortuous journey round the Cape of Good Hope), only to be virtually annihilated by a Japanese fleet under Admiral Tōgō Heihachirō in the Straits of Tsushima.

Moves for peace had begun as early as summer 1904, when it was becoming apparent that the struggle would be long drawn out. As the war progressed the two combatants became increasingly receptive to representations from non-involved powers. While Russia had greater reserves of economic and military strength, revolution threatened at home. Japan had few reserves to continue the struggle, though to have admitted this would have courted political disaster.

In August 1905, President Roosevelt of the US brought the two adversaries together for a conference at Portsmouth, New Hampshire. The Portsmouth Treaty of 5 September recognized

Japan's dominant interests in Korea. Russian troops were to be withdrawn from Manchuria. Japan succeeded to all Russian rights in Manchuria and gained possession of the southern half of the island of Sakhalin. Yet the victory failed to produce gains such as an indemnity[3], which the Japanese public had been led to expect. Announcement of the terms in the late summer of 1905 led to a wave of resentment among a public which had constantly been informed that Russia was on her knees. At an illegal rally opposing the peace terms in Hibiya Park, Tokyo, on 5 September, speakers fired chauvinist sentiments among crowds who then clashed with police. This sparked off two days of rioting, with widespread looting and burning: it was put down only after the declaration of martial law. Hundreds were wounded, including some fatalities, and over 2,000 arrested. The riots demonstrated the ease with which public opinion in Japan was moved to chauvinism and nationalism where foreign policy was concerned, as well as highlighting a gap between reality and what the public was led to believe, which was recurrent up to the postwar period. Although the treaty was ratified, Prime Minister Katsura was forced to resign. Victory in her first war with one of the European powers had the paradoxical effect not of reassuring Japan that she was now a major power able to compete effectively with the others as at least an equal but, instead, of convincing her of her continuing vulnerability and the need to strengthen further her military capability.

The war and the domestic Russian situation together did, however, shelve for a while the problem of confrontation in Northeast Asia. A rapprochement in Russo-Japanese relations was marked by a series of agreements between the two countries in 1907–16 covering the apportionment of rights and interests in the East Asian area. These agreements were renounced after the fall of the Tsarist regime in 1917, and Japan became one of the nations to intervene against the Bolshevik seizure of power. In 1918 Japan announced that 12,000 soldiers would be sent to Siberia to assist anti-revolutionary forces, but the contingent eventually numbered over 70,000, the increase claimed necessary to protect Japanese interests in Manchuria. In May 1920 Soviet partisans killed some 120 Japanese soldiers and civilians at the town of Nikolaevsk and Japan also occupied the northern half of Sakhalin to enforce a demand for compensation. Unable to extricate herself despite the Soviet advance, Japanese troops stayed in Siberia after the remainder of the foreign contingent had been withdrawn, leaving only in 1922. Northern Sakhalin was not evacuated until 1925, when a series of sticky negotiations between Japan and various Soviet authorities eventually culminated in recognition of the USSR and the restoration of diplomatic relations. From then on the course of relations was again downhill; there was an inherent ideological conflict between the two governments, and the common border (with Japanese troops in both Manchuria and Korea) was a constant source of tension. Each country regarded the other as a major military threat.

Thus for a time after 1905 alien influence in Northeast Asia became a less immediate question. The problem which dominated Japan's foreign relations following the war with Russia was the highly sensitive one of Japanese emigration to the US, and the situation of the large immigrant community on the west coast. Racial discrimination was widespread, most Americans showing an unwillingness to treat Japanese in the same way as white immigrants. For Japanese to be discriminated against because of the colour of their skin, despite Japan's success in proving herself the military and political equal of other powers, implied the virtual impossibility of Japan's being accepted as a full equal by the industrialized nations of the West.

Japanese emigrants had been going abroad since the 1880s, the majority of them to Hawaii, then an independent kingdom. From there many went to the mainland US, especially after the US annexation of Hawaii in 1897. By 1899 California had a 35,000-strong Japanese community, economically successful, culturally discrete and less inclined to integrate into the 'melting pot' than most other national groups. The arrival of increasing numbers of Japanese exacerbated the tensions. By 1908 there were over 100,000. Open discrimination against Japanese in California and a threat of total exclusion forced negotiations between the two countries, and the problem was temporarily dealt with by voluntary Japanese restrictions, but the emigration question remained a source of anxiety in Japan. Many believed Japanese territory alone could not sustain the rapidly growing population, and the economic pressures for emigration, mainly to Manchuria, Brazil and the US, were considerable. During the 1920s these pressures became, if anything, even stronger, but in 1924 US legislation effectively placed a ban on Japanese immigration. The exclusion on the grounds of race of a people who laid as much emphasis on their own ethnic origins as did the Japanese, and who implicitly believed in their own superiority, appeared an unpardonable insult. The immigration issue left a long legacy of US–Japanese hostility which surfaced in the injustices suffered by many US citizens of Japanese descent during the war with Japan, 1941–5.

The outbreak of the First World War in August 1914 brought a permanent change in Japan's position *vis-à-vis* the West. Under the terms of the Anglo-Japanese Alliance, Japan was not obliged to enter the war as a belligerent, but Foreign Minister Katō urged the benefits to Japan of joining in, including possible gains in East Asia. Nor was a desire to retaliate for the Triple Intervention of 1895 totally absent. Japan declared war on Germany on 23 August, seized German interests and territory in China, and the German Pacific colonies of the Marshall, Mariana and Caroline Islands. She played little further part as a combatant, stalling later British requests for reinforcements and providing minimal naval assistance in the Mediterranean. She was thus in a position to reap considerable economic benefits from the conflict. Japan supplied export markets formerly dominated by the belligerents, as well as supplying the belligerents themselves. The war years integrated the Japanese economy far more closely into the international economy, and made Japan a major competitor to the capitalist economies of the West. The pressures of war also diverted Great Power attention away from East Asia, leaving Japan a freer hand to extend her interests there and bringing about a permanent weakening in the ability of Western powers to influence affairs in the area.

Formal entry into the war also entitled Japan to a victor's place at the 1919 Versailles Conference, with a vote equal to those of France, Britain and the US. Japan was awarded former German interests in China, although China refused to accede to these concessions. She participated in the founding of the League of Nations and was on the Council, though she failed to get a racial equality clause inserted in the League's charter. The German Pacific Islands continued to be held by Japan under a League of Nations mandate. By 1919 Japan had secured for herself a formal position as one of the world's most powerful nations. As such she became integral to international strategic thinking and power politics in subsequent years. It became apparent that Japan was not to be viewed merely within the context of East Asia. That the implications of her increasing influence were world-wide was demonstrated in the postwar disarmament conferences of the 1920s and 1930s with their emphasis on the naval balance between Britain, the US and Japan. In a world where cooperative security and attempts to reach multilateral, international agreements were replacing formal alliances and balance of power diplomacy, Japan did not seek to exploit unduly her new found recognition. The growth of the economy – and the problems it caused – persuaded Japanese governments during the 1920s that it was in the country's interest to go along with the internationalist trend. The Anglo-Japanese Alliance was allowed to lapse, and Japan became a signatory to two multilateral pacts relating to East Asian affairs. This peaceful strategy eventually failed not so much in the face of Western attempts to restrict Japan's military strength to a lower level than that of Britain or the US, but in the face of rising nationalism and militarism at home and the economic depression and protectionism on which they flourished.

Despite this, Japan's own perception of her relationship with the West remained one of insecurity. This sentiment was based less on perceptions of military inferiority than on an awareness of economic vulnerability, and a sense that, because of history and geographical isolation, Japan's interests differed from those of other industrial nations. Through the 1920s growing pressures were exerted by a rapidly increasing population, a growing industrial sector largely dependent on imported raw materials and fuel – for example, raw cotton, iron ore and oil – and a lack of self-sufficiency in basic foodstuffs such as soya beans and rice. The course of agricultural and industrial development between 1919 and 1935 produced abundant evidence that Japan was closely tied to the fluctuations of the world economy and highly constrained in the resources at her disposal during a period of growing protectionism. The pressure to safeguard by more than diplomatic or economic means external sources of supply, territories for emigration and markets for Japanese goods, coincided with growing nationalism and army influence from the late 1920s, crystallizing in efforts to secure control over large parts of East and Southeast Asia and build an autarkic economic sphere. Within the 1920s cooperative framework Japan had sought to enhance her position in China, but as domestic conditions in China by the late 1920s increasingly undermined the rights of the powers there, Japan's interests in adjoining areas also seemed threatened. In 1931 Japan resorted to force and occupied Manchuria, but the West, absorbed in its own problems, was able to turn a blind eye to such encroachments within the confines of East Asia. The Lytton Commission's report to the League of Nations on the Manchurian incident in effect found Japan guilty of aggression and brought her withdrawal from the League, but the phrasing of the report was highly conciliatory and there was no further action. In 1937 Sino-Japanese friction erupted into full-scale war, but even this failed to rally much more than token support for China in the West. However, as foreign ambitions and the dragging on of the war in China increased the threat of Japanese action in neighbouring territories, the implications for European colonies and nationals, as well as for the broader Asia–Pacific region, forced the industrialized West to take notice.

Apart from encroachments on Western-held territories, the trend in Japanese strategic thinking made it inevitable that the crisis in East Asia, resulting from the China War, would become closely tied up with the course of events in Europe. Many Japanese identified with Germany and Italy in their resentment at the privileges of older established powers. In November 1936 Japan and Germany concluded an Anti-Comintern Pact, in which they were later joined by Italy. Mounting nationalist sentiment in Japan, admiration for the Nazi state and its military successes, concern about possible US involvement in the European and China Wars, and fear of Russian military build-up all concentrated pressure for a full alliance. Delayed by domestic opposition, this was eventually achieved by the conclusion of the Tripartite Pact of September 1940, a time when few doubted the Axis powers would be victorious in Europe. It pledged assistance for any signatory attacked by a country not currently involved in the European or China wars. By this pact Japan ranged herself firmly against the European nations with colonies in East and Southeast Asia.

In autumn 1940 Japan moved into northern French Indo-China in an attempt to restrict supplies to the Chinese, and as a preliminary to creating a Japanese-controlled zone in Southeast Asia. This was done through agreement with Vichy France. In July 1941 she made further advances, which raised real fears for the safety of the oil-rich Dutch East Indies and other Southeast Asian colonies. The US was no longer prepared to stand idly by. Economic sanctions, including an embargo on oil and restrictions on other key exports to Japan, were introduced in the hope of pressurizing Japan into withdrawal. These sanctions, depriving Japan of crucial imports, only served to reinforce Japan's feeling of vulnerability concerning raw materials and fuel supplies. As stockpiles dwindled, the continuing impasse in negotiations rendered military conflict increasingly likely.

The decision to extend Japanese control to areas of Southeast Asia was not taken lightly. A southern advance which risked conflict with, for example, the US, posed strategic difficulties for the defence of Japan's northern front in Korea and Manchuria against the Soviet

Union. Frictions along this border were constant in the late 1930s. Serious confrontations with Soviet forces on the Manchuria and Korean borders at Zhanggufeng and Nomonhan in 1938–9, in both of which the Japanese came off worse, heightened concern at the growing strength of Russian forces. Concentration on one flank rendered the other one vulnerable, and priorities were disputed. The army, which would bear the brunt of any Northeast Asian conflict, and the navy, with its dependence on Southeast Asian oil, were deeply divided. In April 1941 Japan and Russia concluded a non-aggression (neutrality) pact, which appeared to offer both of them short-term security. The German offensive on Russia only two months later shocked Japan, and many Japanese argued for the breaking of the non-aggression pact. Instead, feeling more secure on the empire's northern borders, Japan's government resolved on a southwards advance in the autumn of 1941. A Soviet spy network in Tokyo, led by the German Richard Sorge, revealed this information to Moscow, enabling vast numbers of Siberian troops to be released for the Western front and prevent the fall of Moscow.

Japan's advance into Southeast Asia was a calculated gamble. While French and Dutch colonies might pose little resistance, and while the British were hindered by entanglement in Europe, provocation of conflict with the resource-rich US was potentially disastrous. Strategists decided that Japan's only chance of victory was to deliver a pre-emptive strike against the US and hope for a series of lightning victories which would force the allies to the negotiating table. A forlorn hope that the US might make concessions on its demands for Japanese withdrawal before dwindling stockpiles compelled Japan to engage in war to renew them, prolonged negotiations after the decision for a southward advance was reached in September 1941, but by November few were convinced there was any alternative to attacking the US. On 7 December 1941 the Japanese launched a pre-emptive strike on the Hawaiian base of Pearl Harbor, putting much of the US air and naval force there out of action. The attack on US territory revealed that the US was ill-prepared for conflict, but provoked united resistance to any thought of a negotiated settlement.

In the early stages of the war things went much as the Japanese had planned. They mounted immediate attacks on European colonies by sea and by land from Indo-China and by mid-1942 were in control of much of Southeast Asia, including the Philippines, Malaya, Singapore and the Dutch East Indies. Their empire stretched from

Manchuria in the north to New Guinea in the south. Contrary to Japanese hopes, however, the fall of Britain and China apparently imminent in 1941 failed to materialize. Gradually mobilizing the vast resources of the nation, the full might of US arms, backed up by British and Commonwealth contingents, was directed against Japan. The Japanese advance was halted with the sinking of four Japanese aircraft carriers at the Battle of Midway in June 1942. The final allied victory against Japan came only after a long and costly struggle. Military casualties on both sides were substantial. The hundreds and thousands of civilian casualties included citizens of Southeast Asian countries, interned allied citizens and Japanese caught in the allied advance and the bombing of the Japanese mainland. Not until mid-1944 did a double offensive on the Philippines and the Japanese-occupied Pacific islands begin to bring Japan itself within reach of allied forces. These offensives enabled the bombing of the Japanese mainland and cut Japan off from the empire so crucial to any continuing war effort. By mid-1945 the country was economically, militarily and psychologically on its knees, but unconditional surrender was still resisted. Allied fears that mainland Japan itself would have to be invaded at the suggested cost of millions of fatalities on both sides, as well as a wish to pre-empt Soviet involvement, led to the dropping of atomic bombs on Hiroshima and Nagasaki, respectively, on 6 and 9 August 1945. On 8 August the USSR unilaterally renounced its 1941 non-aggression pact with Japan and invaded Manchuria and Sakhalin. Japan agreed to unconditional surrender on 14 August. There followed the first foreign occupation of Japan in its long history.

The Occupation brought to Japan a succession of radical institutional reforms. It also brought prolonged exposure to the values and beliefs of the world's most powerful and prosperous capitalist nation. In the circumstances of the Occupation, Japan experienced a growing emphasis on material advancement and a wave of foreign influences as great as, if not greater than, anything in the Meiji period.

The stress on material advancement was initially born of necessity. Japan's pre-1945 attempts to achieve national self-sufficiency through being, to quote Peter Duus, 'truculently self-assertive'[4], had been manifestly unsuccessful. The Japanese ended the Pacific War penniless, starving and exhausted; the economy was in ruins. The first priority of these years was the provision of the basic requirements of life. For a while peace, work, food, clothing and shelter were all that most people hankered after, and the basic rebuilding of the economy and their shattered way of life took some two decades. The Tokyo Olympics of 1964 marked the end of this period. For the Japanese they symbolized Japan's re-emergence onto the international scene and the effective rebuilding of Japan's economy and society. Yet material prosperity is in no way guaranteed. The desire for self-sufficiency and material security has remained a key arbiter of foreign relations. In a world of conflict, tensions and national interests Japan can never be assured of the material base for economic prosperity and military strength. The best she can do is to try to secure it by non-military, legal means, and this she has done with a fair measure of success.

Defeat followed by foreign rule paved the way for a new receptivity to foreign influences in general. War between Japan and the nations of the West had been accompanied by a partial rejection of Western cultural influences. The Japanese had always made an effort to preserve and emphasize domestic traditions, and such tendencies strengthened during the more nationalist 1930s. As the nation became increasingly militarized under the pressure of fighting with China, Japan's leaders again turned to Japanese traditions and values as sources of national unity. Despite an admiration among certain circles for National Socialism, for example, many aspects of Western culture met with disfavour, though Western economic, industrial and military practices were widely followed. Japan had reverted to 'Western technology, Japanese values' – or so, at least, many Japanese liked to think. For a while it proved a highly successful combination, but eventually it became apparent that the Japanese spirit could not compensate for inferiority in industrial strength and natural resources in dispelling any sense of national insecurity.

One effect of the nation's defeat was that many of the elements of 'Japanese spirit', as well as the individuals who had most vocally espoused them, were discredited. Something of a spiritual vacuum prevailed following the discrediting of the orthodoxy hitherto imposed, and the values that had been so obviously tied up with the victor's success and the material prosperity of the US seemed to be espoused with enthusiasm. The Occupation years saw a spread of Western values and customs. Along with democracy and equality came chewing gum and Christmas. The influx of Western innovation has continued ever since. The tendency was reinforced by the subsequent efforts of Japanese governments and of the US authorities to incorporate Japan into the framework of the Western

33

camp. Yet acceptance of the Western 'package' was rarely total and frequently superficial, and, as the inevitable reaction against the Occupation changes set in, receptivity to what the West had to offer became far more selective. Moreover, it would be a mistake to identify commitment to a close relationship with the US with a wholehearted acceptance of Western influences in general. The conservatives who have been the most vocal advocates of alliance with the US and opponents of communist totalitarianism, have been at the same time among the most strident supporters of Japanese rearmament and the revival of 'traditional values'. Socialist parties have often rejected such a close connection with the Western alliance, but claimed a commitment to pacifism, neutrality and equality also found among left-wing parties in the West.

Japan regained her independence long before the period of rebuilding was over, but the terms of that independence dictated Japan's international alignment in later years. Even while the Occupation was continuing the pressures of the Cold War and the conflict in Korea pushed US policy in the direction of rebuilding a strong Japan as a capitalist ally in East Asia. When the Occupation formally ended in 1952 following the conclusion of the San Francisco Peace Treaty the previous year, a Mutual Security Treaty between the two countries also came into force. Renewed in 1960, 1970 and 1980 with only slight modifications, it has kept Japan firmly within the US camp. Under the treaty the role of Japanese troops is almost entirely limited to defence of Japanese territory and sea approaches, but the stationing of US troops on Japanese soil could embroil Japan in any conflict in East Asia.

While many Japanese have been in favour of close relations with the US, the opposition parties in the Diet have consistently opposed the Security Treaty. The renewal in 1960 provoked a major political crisis and a storm of protest throughout Japan, not only from those opposed to the treaty *per se,* but from those who feared it might encourage Japanese rearmament and the placing of nuclear weapons on Japanese soil. The treaty was eventually ratified but the crisis brought down the Kishi government and produced the most widespread political protests of the postwar years. While similar agitation has not recurred, the government cannot take for granted universal support of its pro-US stance.

The Security Treaty, with its underlying motive of making Japan a strong ally in the Pacific area, has thus served to reinforce the close ties with the US that were forged during the Occupation period. Japan remains tied to the Western camp partly because the relationship has become integral to her economy and politics over forty years' association, and partly because it appears to offer the best defence against Soviet aggression and encroachment – a long-standing fear – in Northeast Asia, and the best hope of Japan's integrity overall in a world where she has been proved to be economically and militarily vulnerable. The relationship with the US has remained the most important single arbiter of Japan's foreign relations. It has provided the framework for the acceptance of Japan as a leading member of the top Western nations' club, on the basis of an apparent willingness to accept many Western political and cultural values and a devotion to the pursuit of economic activity within the parameters of the US-dominated international economy. Japan seems again to have become an honorary Westerner.

Japan's growing influence as a member of the Western camp has encouraged a greater questioning within Japan of how far to accept what the West has to offer. Japan's incorporation into the American sphere of influence, her military weakness, her lack of diplomatic room for manoeuvre and her concentration on domestic rebuilding for some twenty years after the war meant that major changes or developments in Japan's relations with the West were infrequently the result of positive action on the part of Japan. Growing international influence since then has led to a reappraisal of earlier decisions and trends. The exercise of new found autonomy has been more apparent in the cultural than in the diplomatic sphere. As the country has become economically and militarily stronger, partially concealed ambiguities regarding interaction with the West have resurfaced. While the appetite for knowledge of concrete scientific and technical advancement remains unabated, abstract values have come under closer scrutiny. With the imported institutions and forms of organization acquired during the Occupation increasingly taking on a distinctive 'Japanese' look, a re-emergence of the 'Western technology, Japanese values' syndrome seems on the cards. In a world where communications are instantaneous and Japan is closely integrated into the international economy, an absolute distinction of this kind is clearly not feasible but the pattern highlights an ongoing dilemma. Japan faces a fundamental problem in reaching an accommodation between those values and practices whose origins are primarily indigenous and those that are broadly termed 'Western'. The persistence of this dilemma is made more likely by the tendency of the Japanese to view themselves as unique and separate.

In Western Europe, unlike the US, physical distance, ignorance and the legacy of the war produced a strong reluctance on the part of many to interest themselves in Japan until forced to acknowledge her economic importance. Although some Japanese still harbour a nostalgia for lost European greatness, the 'Western' package which formerly embraced all cultural, intellectual, physical and institutional characteristics with a source in Western Europe or the US has now come to mean almost exclusively the latter. Neither in terms of practical diplomacy, nor as a factor in Japanese cultural or even economic relations, is Europe of remotely comparable importance to the US.

Japan's incorporation into the US sphere of influence brought with it hostility with the Soviet Union. The Soviet Union and its allies refused to sign the San Francisco Peace Treaty in September 1951 on the grounds that it violated an agreement on 'one peace' reached in 1942, and condemned the Security Treaty. Diplomatic relations between the two nations were resumed in 1955, but a peace treaty has yet to be signed, largely due to disagreements over possession of certain of the Kurile Islands taken by the Soviet Union at the end of the war. This dispute is known by the Japanese as the 'Northern Territories problem'. Irredentism remains a powerful issue for many Japanese and can conveniently be used to fuel anti-Russian sentiment when required. For the Soviet Union, the return to any nation of territory occupied during the war would create a dangerous precedent. For the Japanese, the way in which the Russians gained possession of the disputed islands – by breaking the non-aggression pact which operated, and by an opportunistic advance into Japanese-held Northeast Asia when it was evident that the Japanese were already on their last legs – makes Japan doubly unwilling to allow Russia their possession. The ownership of the islands was not clarified by the 1951 Peace Treaty, and this problem has continued to obstruct close relations between the two nations.

With the rest of the non-Asian world, contacts have been less **dis**putatious, comprising mostly cultural interchange, tourism and now business contacts. Japan has become a leader of the Pacific area and to this extent cultivates close contacts not only with Southeast Asia, but also with Australasia, a valuable source of raw materials, where interest in Japan has become substantial. Contacts with the third world nations of Africa and America are relatively sparse. Countries which can neither supply raw materials nor offer substantial markets play relatively little part in Japanese thinking. Aid has been correspondingly low, and although amounts have increased since the mid-1980s, much is still in loans and benefiting Japanese business interests. The main foci of international relations remain the American connection and the pursuit of trade and investment.

The relationship with the West, and since 1945 particularly with the US, has been the factor which sets the last 150 years of Japanese history apart from earlier centuries. Apart from the obvious importance of this relationship on the world stage, it has been a decisive shaping influence on the nature of Japan herself. The period has been marked by dramatic swings: from total isolation to wide-ranging programmes of Western emulation, from alliance with imperial Britain to alignment with Nazi Germany, from all-out war against the US to a seeming acceptance of American dominance in the political, military, economic and cultural spheres.

It is possible to detect underlying continuities in Japan's approach to international relations. While the old policy of seclusion was proved non-viable, the opening to the West has never been total and unambiguous. Some elements of what the Japanese termed 'Western' were accepted with enthusiasm and effectiveness – notably in technological modernization and economic development. Others, for example social norms and cultural values, were little affected. Everywhere there was a persistent tension between Western forms of organization and operation and the real modus operandi they often cloaked. A continuous thread is also apparent in Japan's dealings with other countries. Having accepted isolation as unfeasible, Japan's main concern has been – logically enough – to secure her needs from abroad. These comprise raw materials, fuel and food, and the foreign exchange required to purchase them. Methods have differed enormously, but the objective is clear-cut.

Paradoxically, Japan's relations with Western countries have continued to be profoundly influenced by a sense of isolation. The circumstances of the move – from seclusion and complete vulnerability to the position of one of the world's most powerful nations, both prewar and postwar – failed to dispel a feeling that, in the end, Japan stood alone. Foreign relations and international involvement have never wholly lost their sense of being essentially instrumental in nature.

NOTES

1   The Sino-Japanese War is discussed in Chapter Three.
2   A tael was the silver unit of account used in China at this time.
3   Japan was in no state to press her demands for this and the possession of the whole of Sakhalin.
4   P. Duus, *The Rise of Modern Japan* (Boston, 1976), p. 1.

Japan and Asia

Long before Western contact Japan had contacts with other Asian nations. Geographical proximity meant that these relations have continued to be of crucial importance through into the post-1945 period. Japan's pre-1945 conflicts with the West, too, were largely sparked off by disputes over Japanese ambitions in Asia. The events of the century up to 1945 convey an impression of Japanese domination and aggression in Asia, but in reality the nature of the relationships between Japan and her neighbours has been fluctuating and ambiguous.

Notwithstanding the significance of Japanese ambitions in continental Asia in the modern period, for many centuries Japan managed to maintain a substantial degree of isolation from the mainland. A sea passage of over 200 kilometres from mainland Asia and hostile terrain enabled her to develop more or less free of some of the pressures encouraged by closer geographical proximity – for example, population movements and territorial aggression – and fostered cultural and racial homogeneity. Only once before the twentieth century was Japan threatened with invasion; the Mongol invasions of 1274 and 1281 were repelled with the aid of natural forces, when the original *kamikaze* (divine wind) annihilated much of the invasion fleet. From the sixth century to the late nineteenth century Japan's only military involvement on the Asian mainland was Hideyoshi's short-lived and abortive invasion of Korea in 1592. Diplomatic missions were received and sent from time to time, and during the sixteenth century Japanese traders and pirates dominated the seas of Southeast Asia, but both channels of contact virtually ceased in the seclusion period. A small amount of trade with China, Korea and the Ryūkyū Islands remained. Japan thus remained isolated while yet being part of Asia, and the imposed seclusion after 1639 reinforced this degree of detachment.

Yet Japan was by no means immune from continental influences, and her historical development has been substantially affected by them. Most important were those emanating from China. The civilization of China is among the oldest in the world, and China has throughout Japan's history been the largest and most powerful of her Asian neighbours. The earliest continental influences came to Japan from China, either directly or via Korea, and mutual attitudes between the two countries have been shaped over 1,500 years and more. The Chinese and the Japanese call China 'the middle country', a term denoting a long-standing view that China was the centre of the civilized world. Chinese influence on all aspects of Japanese society and politics was immense, and while this did not preclude friction between the two countries, nor the development of indigenous Japanese cultural traits, many of the institutions, ideas and attitudes important to Japanese history owe a great deal to China. The eighth century saw the wholesale introduction of Chinese political institutions, religious ideas and legal theory, as well as Chinese educational practice. From China, Japan obtained her first writing system, and hence much of her subsequent linguistic development. The introduction of Chinese practices and ideas continued on a lesser scale for the next eight centuries. While the Japanese often modified Chinese customs, and domestic developments frequently rendered Japanese practice far removed from the original Chinese model, Chinese-based cultural practices remained highly significant in Japan. As late as the early nineteenth century, for example, formal education still consisted largely of study of the Chinese Confucian classics, which served also as the vehicle for achieving literacy. Many letters and formal documents were written in Chinese rather than Japanese. At the same time the orthodoxy upon which the political, economic and social status quo was based was a Japanese version of Neo-Confucianism.

A belief in Chinese superiority stemming from a closer approximation to the natural order of the cosmos governed China's relations with neighbouring peoples, which over centuries had been conducted on a tributary basis. Under this system China's many satellites, including Japan, acknowledged the superiority of Chinese culture by making regular tribute payments. Japan's payment of tribute had lapsed long before the modern period, and such payments had ceased to be the normal basis for trading contacts, but the tribute system and the superior–inferior relationship upon which it was premised remained the basic concept behind the conduct of formal relations between countries.

The long heritage of Chinese influence and superiority has remained a crucial factor in relations between the two countries throughout the modern period. Before 1945 Japan was guilty of substantial imperialist ambitions and aggression in China, and China was often too weak to resist her neighbour's demands, but China retained a special position in Japanese sentiment and a certain pre-eminence in Japanese eyes.

The power of the Chinese empire also influenced Japan's relations with other Asian kingdoms. In as far as they existed at all, relations with these countries were conducted as between tributaries of the Chinese empire. Only Korea was close enough to Japan to command a formal relationship of any significance, but this, too, was virtually halted during the Tokugawa period, when the kingdom of Korea, like Japan, adopted a seclusion policy.

By the mid-late nineteenth century these three East Asian kingdoms were weak and divided, and the East Asian cultural area no longer possessed the might of earlier years. China itself was riven with rebellion, and the ruling Qing dynasty was in decline, unable to withstand the depredations of Western traders and governments or to give the leadership it had been able to offer in former times. Korea was small and impoverished, burdened by a highly reactionary ruling class which, unlike that in Japan, proved unable to adapt to a changed international environment.

So, as Japan re-entered the wider world and embarked on a programme of change to deal with it, in dealing with her neighbours Japan faced a mirror image of her relations with the West. Where the West was far stronger than she was, the Asian countries were weaker. To advance Japan had to learn from the West and drop at least some of her former respect for China. Where the political imperative with the West was to avoid being conquered and dominated, the issue with Japan's Asian neighbours was whether Japan should participate in the new imperialist domination.

Following the establishment of treaty relations with the West in the 1850s Chinese merchants and coolies formed a sizeable contingent in the open ports, and many Chinese served as crew on the ships which used them. Only after the revolution of 1868, however, did Japan concern herself with more formal relations with her Asian neighbours. When she did so, disputes soon arose. As Japan's strength grew, so did her ambitions on the Asian mainland

and her ability to advance them. The motivations – both many and complex – behind Japan's desire to exert her influence in Asia have received considerable attention from historians. Among the earliest was a desire to channel domestic discontent away from the regime of the time. From the 1880s many Japanese also saw their strength on the continent as a strategic and military necessity for their defence against other powers. As the economy grew its need for raw materials and markets expanded, and the Asian continent could offer both of these. Ample territory suggested accommodation for Japan's mushrooming population. Ideology, too, played a part. The duty of Japan to lead Asia in resistance to the West was widely advocated. Modernization and the prevailing orthodoxy encouraged the view that Japan was superior to her Asian neighbours and had a duty to promote change in them and fulfil her own destiny. Last, but not always least, came a desire to emulate Western nations for whom the securing of concessions in East Asia and elsewhere was an indicator of Great Power status.

In September 1871 Japan concluded a commercial treaty with China, under which consular jurisdiction was to operate in both countries, tariffs were fixed at a low level and there was no most-favoured-nation clause. Japan was too weak to impose an unequal treaty on China. This treaty was the basis of Sino-Japanese relations until the Sino-Japanese War of 1894–5. The Chinese initially had no envoy or consuls in Japan and this made the resolution of diplomatic problems difficult. Dispute with China soon arose over the Ryūkyū Islands, which lie southwest of Kyushu, and include Okinawa. The Ryūkyūs were an autonomous kingdom, but during the Tokugawa period their king had paid regular tribute to China as well as trading with the lord of Satsuma domain in southern Kyushu, who treated the Ryūkyūan king as a vassal. From 1871 the Japanese government made a series of moves aimed at incorporating the islands into the national administrative framework, but these unilateral steps were strongly contested by the Chinese, who also claimed suzerainty. Not only was ownership of the islands in itself unclear, but the dispute highlighted the disparities between Japan's attempt to reorganize her administration and diplomacy along Western lines and China's adherence to the traditional tributary relationship as a basis of international dealings.

In late 1871 fifty-four Ryūkyūan fishermen shipwrecked on Formosa (Taiwan) were killed by Formosan aborigines. The Japanese government, who claimed them as nationals, demanded that Beijing punish the offenders and pay compensation. The Chinese failure to pay an indemnity resulted in Japan's sending a punitive expedition to the island. Assertion of Japanese ownership of the Ryūkyūs was not the only reason for this expedition. Military action also served as an outlet for widespread samurai discontent. In May 1874 over 3,500 troops under General Saigō Tsugumichi landed on Formosa and suffered serious casualties in occupying the southern tip of the island. It was October before negotiations reached any resolution and the troops were not withdrawn until the end of the year. Japan's receipt of compensation and China's failure to condemn the Japanese action signified in Western international law an acknowledgement that the Ryūkyūans were Japanese citizens. The islands became Okinawa Prefecture in 1879 and sporadic Chinese objections eventually ceased after the early 1880s. The outcome of the Formosan expedition demonstrated the weakness of China in her external dealings, a lesson that was not lost on Japan.

Japan had long-standing territorial ambitions regarding Korea, her nearest neighbour, but these had been held in abeyance during the Tokugawa period. The country remained a semi-independent kingdom within the Chinese orbit. Sporadic trading relations with Japan were maintained through the intermediacy of the Sō daimyo of Tsushima, and a small Japanese community dwelt at the Korean port of Pusan. Infrequent official contact was conducted through the same agency, but for the most part Korea, like Japan, main-tained a policy of seclusion. Following the revolution of 1868 the new regime in Japan was anxious to establish formal diplomatic relations with Korea. The Korean regime, determined to adhere to an exclusionist policy, ignored Japan's demands. The perceived insult to their self-respect angered many Japanese and calls for the subjugation of Korea *(seikanron)* increased; some, concerned about the decline of traditional martial values at home, sought also to divert the samurai into foreign campaigns. During the absence of the Iwakura Mission, 1871–73, remaining government members, led by Saigō Takamori and Itagaki Taisuke, resolved on a military expedition to the peninsula. Saigō himself volunteered to go to Korea as a special envoy, inviting an assassination that would provide justification, if any were needed, for a punitive expedition. The expedition, they argued, would assist a samurai class demoralized by the loss of their status and, in some cases, of their stipends.

The decision to invade Korea was overruled when the members of the Iwakura Mission, now convinced that domestic development had to precede foreign adventures, returned to Japan during 1873, but the disagreement split the government and brought about the resignation of several of its leading members, including Saigō and Itagaki. Relations with Korea were not formalized until the conclusion (under threat of military confrontation) of the Treaty of Kanghwa in February 1876. The imposition on Korea of an unequal treaty was the first stage in a sustained attempt by Japan to secure dominant influence in the peninsula. The argument over formal relations was the first of a succession of Japanese disputes with Korea and with other countries concerning Korea, which have formed a very substantial part of the story of Japan's relations with both Asia and the West.

During the first two decades of the Meiji period the Japanese continued to take a strong interest in Korea. Korea was ruled by a conservative and authoritarian monarchy. Factional disunity, economic stagnation and Chinese dominance were further hindrances to change. Japan, increasingly aware of the international rivalries at work in Asia as a whole and in Korea in particular, began to regard a weak, backward Korea as a liability. Two other powers contested Japanese influence in the peninsula. The expanding Russian empire was showing an increasing interest in Northeast Asia, and China was likely to challenge any attempt by Japan to intervene in the affairs of a country which for centuries had been her foremost tributary. Though the Treaty of Kanghwa had stated Korea to be independent, the concept of a tributary relationship remained significant in thinking in both China and Korea, and during the early decades of the Meiji period China maintained a strong influence in the peninsula, being closely identified with the more conservative element whose dominance was resented by so many Japanese. Factional conflict within Korea was extended to Japan and China. Japanese nationals cooperated with Koreans wishing to change the status quo, and willingly offered them asylum. In July 1882 an anti-Japanese riot in Seoul (the so-called Jingo Incident) forced the Japanese minister in Korea and his staff to flee the country. The 1882 troubles precipitated the sending of troops by both China and Japan and direct Chinese intervention in the internal affairs of Korea. A further crisis after a failed pro-Japanese coup in 1884 highlighted the rivalry for domination of the peninsula. Negotiations aimed at settling the problem resulted in the April 1885 Treaty of Tianjin. Under the terms of this agreement both countries agreed to withdraw their troops and military instructors and in future to provide written notification before sending any troops to Korea. The agreement merely deferred armed conflict. It failed to resolve the question of foreign influence in Korea, which a decade later led to war between China and Japan.

Meanwhile, the Japanese pressed unsuccessfully for international guarantees of Korean independence. Japan believed that the weakness and conservatism of both China and Korea rendered Japan herself more vulnerable. Phrases such as 'Korea is a dagger pointed at the heart of Japan' were commonly used to denote Korea's strategic significance, and of all the varying motivations governing Japanese policy in Asia it was the issue of national defence which was most crucial at this time. By the early 1890s the view was widespread that Japan's own security could not afford a weak, Chinese-dominated Korea, which could offer no barrier to Russian advance. This view received added impetus from the proposal to construct the Trans-Siberian Railway. After victory over China in 1895 made territorial control a reality, the haphazard search for political and economic influence (direct or indirect) of earlier years became a systematic one, in which emulation of Western imperialism was seen as both practicable and desirable.

In 1894 Chinese troops were sent to Korea in response to the Korean king's request for help against domestic rebellion led by the powerful Tonghak religious sect. Acting under the terms of the 1885 agreement Japan too sent troops. Both parties then refused to withdraw. The anticipated rejection of Japanese demands for radical reforms was used by Japan to provoke hostilities, and in late July the Japanese sunk a British ship chartered to carry Chinese reinforcements. The fighting rapidly escalated. Japanese land forces enjoyed numerical superiority and better preparedness, which provided them with an initial advantage. At sea the larger Chinese fleet rapidly yielded dominance to a better trained and up-to-date Japanese counterpart. By the end of 1894 Japanese troops had driven the Chinese from Korean soil and were advancing through Manchuria to threaten Tianjin and Beijing. Korea itself was under effective Japanese control from the early stages of the war. By the beginning of 1895 the Chinese navy had been virtually annihilated, and China's land forces convincingly beaten. Japan, confident in her position as victor, agreed to requests for a peace conference, and representatives of the two belligerents met at Shimonoseki in southwest Honshu in March. Such was the strength of Japan's negotiating position that it was only marginally weakened by an attempt on the life of the elder statesman Li

Hongzhang, leader of the Chinese delegation. The terms of the Treaty of Shimonoseki concluded on 17 April included Japanese possession of Formosa, the Pescadores Islands and the Liaodong Peninsula in Manchuria, the opening by China of four more treaty ports and the payment to Japan of a sizeable indemnity. A formal acknowledgement of the independence of Korea signified the end of Chinese domination there, but did not clarify Japan's position in the country. A separate Treaty of Commerce and Navigation awarded Japan most-favoured-nation treatment in China.

In the early stages of the conflict the nations of the West concerned themselves little with the war. It was widely assumed that China, with her vast size and resources, would be the victor, and that the status quo in East Asia would remain unchanged. The unexpected course of events aroused considerable alarm, and the terms of the peace treaty provoked open opposition with Germany, Russia and France joining together in the so-called Triple Intervention to demand that Japan return the Liaodong Peninsula to China. Bereft of international support, Japan had little choice but to accede. This forcible intervention by the Western powers in relations between East Asian nations highlights the degree to which East Asia and Western power play were related, and the pivotal position of Japan in this interdependence.

Although Japan was for the first time in a dominant position *vis-à-vis* China, the problem of disputed influence in Korea remained. Japan was in effective control of the country during the 1894–5 War, but her efforts to intervene in Korea's domestic affairs were clumsy in the extreme. The proven complicity of Miura, the Japanese envoy, in the brutal murder of the Korean queen in October 1895 drove the Korean king, fearful for his safety, to seek asylum in the Russian legation. His presence there for over a year was a useful lever for Russia, which therefore replaced China as a contender for dominant influence in the peninsula. The inept policy had provoked the very Russian influence of which Japan was so fearful, and made Korea a potential flashpoint for conflict between the two powers.

The military victory did not end Japan's difficulties in dealing with China. Japan now exercised sufficient influence in China to secure similar concessions and privileges there to those offered the powerful nations of the West. Yet there were two main barriers to the exaction and enforcement of such concessions. The first was that such privileges could be secured only with the sanction of the other powers; this had been clearly demonstrated by the Triple

Intervention. The second obstacle was the nature of China itself; the geographical size of the country, the way in which it traditionally operated, and, above all, its disunity. Chinese governments in the nineteenth century faced a succession of major rebellions, and the defeat by Japan in 1895 hastened the demise of the Qing dynasty. Revolution in 1911 was followed by thirty-eight years of civil conflict during which control of the country was fragmented and China lacked any unified, stable national government. The simultaneous emergence of popular nationalist sentiment meant that concessions extracted from one Chinese government could be flouted by the people and revoked by another regime. Attempts at intervention in China's domestic affairs were the inevitable result of this turmoil.

The first instance of this came in the so-called Boxer Rebellion of 1900. The 'Boxers'[1] were members of a violent anti-dynastic, anti-foreign and anti-Christian religious movement which spread through northern China during 1899. Fearful for its own survival, the imperial house skilfully diverted the frenzy and hatred away from itself towards the foreign presence in China and gave the movement tacit encouragement. Outside Beijing dozens of foreigners and thousands of Chinese Christians lost their lives. On 20 June 1900 the German minister was killed and the legations in the capital besieged. Western attempts to meet force with force led to China's declaration of war on the foreign powers the following day. Eight nations with legations in Beijing gathered together an international force and the two-month seige was lifted on 14 August 1900. The victory was not difficult; the rebels were ill-equipped to cope with Western weapons and forces. Violent retribution followed. Much of Beijing was laid waste, with many Chinese raped and killed. Punitive expeditions were sent to many other cities. Only the Japanese – at 8,000 the largest single contingent in the initial force – were reported to have conducted themselves in an **hon**ourable fashion. In settlement a massive indemnity and further punitive concessions were exacted from China. The intervention also won for the powers the right to station soldiers in Beijing's legation quarter to protect their nationals. It brought onto Chinese territory Russian forces whose reluctance to withdraw from the province of Manchuria sparked off the Russo-Japanese War a few years later.

Manchuria had for long been subject to encroachments by Russia. The position of the territory, situated to the northeast of Beijing, bordered to the east by Korea and with a long frontier with Russia, was somewhat ambiguous. Home of the Manchu

Qing dynasty which ruled China from 1644 until its fall in 1911, it had a distinct status shared with no other part of the empire. After 1911 Manchuria fell under the domination of the warlord, Zhang Zuolin, who effectively controlled the territory until 1928. This semi-autonomous status, compounded by the administrative disintegration of China during these years, persuaded Japan that the future of Manchuria could be separated from that of China.

Japan's interest in Manchuria dated from the Meiji period. Japan had a growing economic interest in the area, and considerable quantities of soya beans and minerals began to be imported from there. Manchuria was known to be rich in raw materials, notably coal and iron ore, and capable of supporting a far larger population than dwelt there at the time. After 1895, as shown by the dispute over the Liaodong Peninsula, foreign interests in the area became a bone of contention between Russia and Japan. Above all the territory was regarded as crucial to Japan's strategic line of defence, but in this respect Korea was a nearer and more immediate problem.

After the Sino-Japanese War both Russia and Japan sought to dominate Korea. Conflict was deferred by the attempt to reach agreement along the lines of 'Manchuria for Korea' *(Mankan kōkan)* (i.e. Manchuria for Russia and Korea for Japan), but the two countries eventually came to blows in 1904 over the failure of Russian troops to withdraw on schedule from Manchuria. The war served to consolidate Japanese influence in both Korea and Manchuria. Korea was controlled by Japan almost from the outset. The Japanese built railways to get their troops to the front, requisitioned supplies, and brooked no opposition to what was dictated by the exigencies of the war. A series of agreements with the Korean government aimed at formalizing Japanese control culminated in a 1905 protectorate agreement which went unchallenged by other countries. The protectorate established a Japanese residency in Seoul, deprived Korea of any independent foreign policy, stationed Japanese troops within the country and installed influential Japanese advisers at all levels of government. The installation of the elder statesman Itō Hirobumi as resident 1905–9 marked the significance of the post. Over the next few years Japanese took over much of the administration and established mechanisms for economic pre-eminence.

The resentment within Korea was intense. Koreans who had formerly looked to Japan for help against a conservative, autocratic government and for encouragement to 'modernize' now found themselves subordinated to those self same Japanese, deprived of an independent voice. An attempt to contest Japan's control over Korean foreign policy at the Hague Peace Conference in 1907 fell on deaf ears; whether Korea was, or was not, independent meant little to most of the nations of the West. The same indifference reigned in August 1910, when Japan annexed Korea, transforming her into a fully-fledged colony. Whether annexation was a long-term aim in Japan is debatable; what is clear is that Japanese believed that their nation's security necessitated a hold on power in Korea of a kind which could only be achieved by colonial status.

By 1910, therefore, expansionism had turned into overt and formal colonialism. Japan had assumed control over Korea, Formosa, the Pescadores and the southern half of Sakhalin, which had been obtained at the end of the Russo-Japanese War in 1905. While there was an element of imitation of Western territorial imperialism, Japan essentially regarded control of neighbouring territories and resources as fundamental to her own safety and well-being, either for reasons of economic security, or because their weakness and backwardness rendered Japan militarily vulnerable and politically isolated, since such countries were easy prey to third party aggression. The possession of colonies and interests in Asia was, for the Japanese, integral to Japan's immediate security. Out of this fundamental rationale, and out of the geographical proximity to Japan of colonies or potential colonies, grew a distinct set of colonial policies.

The lack of systematic policy in Formosa in the late 1890s suggests that Japan was initially ill-prepared to cope with colonies. The first stage, of direct military rule, sought merely to suppress opposition to Japanese control – a short-lived republic was declared in 1895 – and wipe out the widespread banditry and disturbances which had long plagued the island under Chinese rule. The Japanese began actively to develop Formosa after the appointment of General Kodama Gentarō (1852–1906) as governor in 1898. A massive programme of reforms had by the 1920s established law and order, infrastructure and a stable economy based on agriculture – notably the production of tea, rice and sugar – and some state sponsored industrial development. Japanese rule did bring Formosa a certain prosperity. The Formosans had for many decades suffered from imperial Chinese indifference and neglect, and a substantial minority of the island's non-Japanese inhabitants benefited from the new economic and educational policies and enjoyed rising living standards.

Nevertheless, although Formosa was in a sense merely exchanging one overlord for another, resentment at Japanese rule was never stilled. While geographical proximity, cultural affinities and the need to justify Japanese rule encouraged the pursuit of a policy aimed at integrating the interests of ruler and ruled, equality between the two was never a possibility. Japanese in Formosa were mostly short-term residents who enjoyed the traditional privileges of a colonizing race and who, backed by Tokyo, implemented a colonial policy whose basic premise was that the colony existed for the benefit and betterment of mainland Japan, economically, politically and militarily. Any benefit to the native inhabitants of the colony was incidental.

The same basic assumption lay behind Japanese policy in Korea, but the Formosan experience was hardly a useful precedent. Korea had for centuries been an independent nation (though within the Chinese orbit). As Japanese influence in Korea grew after 1895, so too did Korean nationalist sentiment. The protectorate agreement came just as the Russo-Japanese War seemed to suggest new hopes of Asian independence, and Japan's claim to champion the cause of Korean modernization and Asian nationalism was rendered particularly insulting by the brutality with which all manifestations of anti-Japanese sentiment were suppressed under the protectorate. The assassination by a Korean of the resident general, Itō Hirobumi, during a visit to Manchuria in 1909, marked the end of all attempts at conciliation and became the excuse for annexation.

For the initial years after 1910 Korea was under a brutal military regime which attempted to crush all anti-Japanese activity and sentiment. Opposition movements were driven into exile. What remained of the armed independence movement was based in Manchuria, where it later came under communist domination and was headed by Kim Il-sung. The leading faction of the political independence movement was led by Syngman Rhee from Hawaii. Pro-independence demonstrations were ruthlessly suppressed, notably that of 1 March 1919, which claimed a million demonstrators. Political activity was banned and Koreans were subordinated to Japanese at all levels of administrative activity. Koreans were frequently evicted from land and property to be replaced by Japanese, and poverty and homelessness increased, despite improvements in public health and some welfare provisions. Many Koreans went voluntarily or forcibly to Japan, mostly to engage in the most menial of jobs. Economic policy aimed at developing the Korean economy to serve the needs of Japan. As a subject people regarded as inferior to Japanese, Koreans possessed none of the democratic rights enjoyed by Japanese. They were increasingly subjected to a programme of enforced cultural 'Japanization'. In the late 1930s Japanese became the official language and attempts were made to wipe out the indigenous Korean culture. Japan's legacy in Korea was one of brutality, exploitation and suppression, traits which became even more marked in the war years.

Korea and Formosa provide the most durable examples of Japanese colonial policy. Other territories were to be added to the Japanese empire but some were insignificant in terms of size, and elsewhere the occupation was short-lived and constrained by the exigencies of war. With control over Korea and Taiwan secure, Japan's eyes turned to the territories of Northeast China and Manchuria, and Japan's search for the acquisition of control over greater portions of Asian territory governed the development of Asian–Japanese relations during the four decades up to 1945.

While Japanese expansion in Asia was still influenced by a preoccupation with defence and strategy, Japan's need for security in terms of raw materials, trading opportunities and an outlet for her expanding population became of increasing importance. The need for stable markets and raw material supplies became increasingly acute with the advance of industrialization, especially after 1918, when Chinese boycotts and world depression exposed Japan's vulnerability. In these circumstances Manchuria was seen as a justifiable target for Japan's ambitions, and control over certain economic, political and military aspects of China was also sought. Like other empire-builders, Japan justified her expansion by a public relations rhetoric aimed at making it appear as altruism. Japan, it was said, sought the benefit of Asia as a whole and had a national mission to lead and coordinate the nations of Asia in resistance to the West. A Japanese-led bloc of Asian nations would be militarily and economically secure, and able to stand up to the threat posed by the nations of Europe and by the United States. Similar arguments were used in the case of Southeast Asia. The concept that Japan's mission was to save Asia for the Asians, to reject the Western colonizers and influences and lead Asia to greatness was used to justify the idea of the Great East Asian Co-Prosperity Sphere, developed out of Prime Minister Konoe's calls in November 1938 for a 'new order in East Asia'. The scope of this mutually cooperative and self-sufficient economic and political sphere under Japanese leadership was initially Japan, Korea, Manchuria and China, but was gradually extended to include the whole of Southeast Asia, and even Australia and New Zealand. However, Japan's colonial and expansionist policies were hardly such as to strengthen the Asian nations. A stable and egalitarian Asian military and economic alliance was bound to founder on Japan's inability to submerge her own interests for the benefit of Asia as a whole. The Co-Prosperity Sphere became an area whose resources were exploited for the benefit of Japan. Blatantly selfish methods and policies and the degree to which Japan became entangled in the extremes of her own rhetoric inevitably resulted in the pursuit of a course devoted to Japanese, rather than Asian, nationalism.

The acquisition of Korea was followed by the 1911 Chinese revolution and the fall of the Qing dynasty. The inconclusive nature of the revolution and the weak and divided government of the Chinese state in the years that followed appeared to make China easy prey to foreign encroachment. The Western powers and Japan, who had long been attempting to secure rights and interests in China, were now faced with a series of regimes too weak to resist some of their demands, or to see that any concessions were adhered to. The nations of Europe, increasingly taken up with their own military and economic problems, responded by increasingly withdrawing from any attempt to exact further concessions. America, which had always held aloof from more active participation in the exploitation, became the strongest advocate of the 1899–1900 'Open Door' policy, which maintained China's right to national integrity and the equal entitlement of all nations to economic opportunity in China. For Japan the Western withdrawal and the disunity of China seemed to present a golden opportunity to advance her own interests.

The Formosan Expedition in the early 1870s, the Treaty of Shimonoseki (1895) and the Boxer Rebellion (1900) had already secured for Japan substantial political and economic concessions in China. The division of China into spheres of influence gave the Japanese a non-alienation agreement concerning Fujian Province, although this claim was never fully exploited. Japanese could engage in industry and manufacturing outside the open ports and, after 1905, possessed railway rights and territorial concessions in Manchuria. The Japanese-controlled South Manchurian Railway acted as the major base for the expansion of Japanese interests in the province. On the outbreak of war in Europe in 1914, Japan, acting under the terms of the Anglo-Japanese Alliance, declared war on Germany. Disregarding Chinese neutrality, Japan forcibly seized all German concessions in the Shandong Peninsula, as well as taking over German-owned islands in the Pacific. In mid-January 1915 China was presented with what became known as the 'Twenty

One Demands', a call for China to make certain economic, political and military concessions. Many of the demands related to Japanese control of substantial areas of Chinese territory; the fifth and final section included demands for the installation of Japanese 'advisers' at all levels of the administration, armed forces and police. The presence of such 'advisers' would have constituted a severe infringement of China's political autonomy. Stalling for time, China appealed to the West for support, but the response was so muted as to be useless. The European nations were far too absorbed in their own conflict to give heed to China's concerns. The demands were leaked to foreign journalists. Beset by mounting criticism at home, and abroad, over the way the issue had been handled, the Japanese government agreed to defer the fifth group of demands and in May 1915 delivered the remainder in the form of an ultimatum. The Chinese gave way. While the concessions were not as damaging to China's integrity as the original list would have been, they did give Japan a far stronger base in China from which to conduct economic activities, confirming her dominance in Shandong, Manchuria and part of Mongolia. The Versailles peace conference acceded to Japan's takeover of the former German concessions, but the Chinese refused to sign any treaty which did not return them to China, and Japan remained in occupation. At the 1921–2 Washington Conference Japan agreed to restore Chinese sovereignty in Shandong, but only in return for Chinese confirmation of Japan's economic privileges there.

In the years after the Twenty-One Demands Japanese governments tended to adopt a more indirect approach in their attempts to exert Japanese influence in China. In 1917–18, for example, a massive sum in politically-motivated loans[2] found its way from Japan to China, nominally for industrial and infrastructural development, but in fact ending up as political and military funding. The loans were criticized in both China and Japan and achieved little, but the consolidation of Japanese interests using diplomatic and economic means rather than force was pursued under Foreign Minister Shidehara Kijūrō in the years 1924–27.

As Japan's interests in China and Manchuria became more embedded, internal strife and growing nationalist sentiment there increasingly threatened to undermine them. The Twenty-One Demands were a particularly potent factor in the build-up of anti-Japanese feeling, and provoked a mass exodus of Chinese students from Japan. The return of the Chinese students helped to spread wider resentment of Japan's actions and attitudes. The

1919 Versailles Conference decision to award Shandong to Japan sparked off the nationalist eruption of the 4 May Movement in Beijing and a boycott of Japanese goods. From being the Mecca of young Chinese who wished to 'awaken' their nation, Japan had, in little more than two decades, become an aggressor to be kept at bay. Hostility towards Japan's economic policies in China and the policies of Japanese firms operating there, as well as a wider opposition to Japanese attitudes towards China as a whole, led to a succession of anti-Japanese demonstrations and boycotts of Japanese products throughout the 1920s. They were widely supported: Shanghai, with its huge foreign settlement, became the centre of anti-Japanese popular protest. These protests provoked not merely concern, but anger and a desire to retaliate, in Japan.

By the mid-1920s the disunity which had plagued China since the 1911 revolution showed some prospect of ending as the Nationalist Party, the Guomindang, consolidated its control over large areas of the country. By the late 1920s the nationalist government had achieved tariff autonomy and an agreement in principle to give up extraterritoriality, yet enclaves of foreign settlers, foreign interests and foreign troops (nominally for protection of the first two) remained. By far the biggest concentration of Japanese troops in mainland China were those in Guandong Province in Manchuria. The Guandong Army's task was to guard the leased Liaodong Peninsula and Japanese interests in Manchuria, including the South Manchurian Railway and lands controlled by the Japanese adjacent to it. The potential for conflict when Chinese and Japanese troops were in such close proximity was enormous, and became greater as China moved towards unity and greater strength.

Fear of Chinese unification and Japanese resentment at anti-Japanese protests in China combined with a division between military and civilian priorities at home to produce a shift in Japan's China policy away from the 'conciliatory'. When General Tanaka Giichi became prime minister and foreign minister in April 1927 the stance became more 'positive'. Tanaka convened a conference of top military and government officials to discuss Japan's continental policy; a conference statement called for greater Japanese intervention in Northeast Asia and strong moves to protect Japanese interests in China. The conference was also the reputed source of the notorious Tanaka Memorial (Memorandum), a blueprint for continental strategy which Tanaka afterwards purportedly submitted to the emperor. Highly aggressive in tone and content, the authenticity of the memorial has yet to be proved, but it was widely circulated in China, where it was believed to be genuine, especially as the policies of the 1930s seemed to be fully in accordance with it.

The more 'positive' Tanaka approach was soon reflected in policy, as the Japanese attempted to acquire a greater say in Manchuria. During the period of Chinese disunity the Japanese had supported the powerful warlord, Zhang Zuolin, who ruled Manchuria as his private province for much of the 1920s, but Zhang's position, like that of the other warlords, began to come under threat from the rise of the Nationalist movement under Chiang Kai-shek (Zhiang Jishe). As the Nationalists consolidated more of the country under their control in a gradual northwards advance, Japan feared that Zhang would either join forces with the Nationalists or would be replaced by them. On more than one occasion, Nationalist troops clashed with Japanese forces in China, as Japan, realizing the threat to Japanese interests of a unified China, sought to sustain Zhang in power and impede the Nationalist advance. During 1927 Japanese troops were sent to Shandong, ostensibly to protect Japanese residents. Fresh troops arriving in the spring of 1928 clashed with the Chinese, and continuing Japanese occupation of the Jinan area aroused international protest. Agreement on withdrawal was not reached until early 1929.

Zhang himself was initially keen to retain his influence and resisted the Nationalist advance, but by 1928 was in danger of defeat in North China. In the hope of forestalling this he was urged by the Japanese to retreat to his stronghold of Manchuria and establish himself as ruler of an autonomous Manchuria under Japanese tutelage. Zhang was not totally opposed to the idea, but some members of the increasingly politicized Guandong Army felt that more radical action to extend Japanese control in Manchuria could be taken if Zhang, known to be somewhat recalcitrant and a far from willing puppet, were out of the way. In June 1928, as Zhang retreated to his capital, Mukden, his train was blown up by members of the Guandong Army. Zhang was killed instantly, although his death was kept secret for a few days. In as far as the plotters hoped to engineer a state of affairs which might enable Japan to occupy substantial parts of Manchuria, the plot failed. The Chinese kept the situation under control, and Zhang Xueliang, who succeeded to his father's position, harboured considerable resentment at those who had caused his father's death. Regarding the Nationalists as the lesser of two evils he joined with them to resist Japanese encroachments.

The railway was also to play a focal part in a second, more successful, plot aimed at generating direct Japanese action in Manchuria. In the three years after the murder of Zhang Zuolin Japanese–Chinese tension in Manchuria reached new heights as radical young officers from the Guandong Army urged Japanese occupation of the area. On the night of 18 September 1931, an explosion occurred on the South Manchurian Railway line just outside Mukden. The explosion was in fact caused by members of the Guandong Army, but the Japanese announced it to be the work of non-uniformed members of the Chinese army. Claiming to act in self-defence, the Guandong Army occupied Mukden almost before the night was out 'to forestall further disturbances'. Reinforced by troops from the sizeable Japanese army in Korea, which crossed into Manchuria without obtaining prior permission from the Japanese government, the Guandong Army had extended its occupation to three of the four provinces of Manchuria by 1932. The Chinese initially offered no opposition, and later resistance was scattered and ineffective. In March 1932 Japan sponsored the establishment in Manchuria of the nominally independent state of Manchukuo. In occupying Manchuria the Guandong Army effectively acted as an autonomous political decision-making body. Attempts to restrict military advance were ignored on the grounds of operational necessity, and the government in Tokyo, incapable of stemming the advance, found itself forced to act as an apologist for the military's *faits accomplis*.

China appealed to the League of Nations for support against the Japanese occupation and in December 1931 a commission was set up under Lord Lytton to investigate the situation. The commission carried out its enquiries during the first half of 1932 and presented its report in October. Hoping to pre-empt censure by the League of Nations, Japan formally recognized Manchukuo in September 1932. The report allotted some blame to both China and Japan, but much of Japan's case was rejected. The formal acceptance of the report by the League early in 1933 brought Japan's withdrawal from it. The commission and the League, however, offered no real material help to the Chinese.

Manchukuo remained a Japanese puppet state. Recognized by few states apart from Japan, Germany and Italy, it was a colony in all but name, with real power exercised by Japanese administrators ultimately responsible to the commander of the Guandong Army. The authority of Chinese administrators and the head of state, Pu Yi[3], was purely nominal. Political activity was prohibited and the treatment meted out to non-Japanese was harsh and arbitrary. As Manchukuo's raw materials were exploited for the benefit of Japan's industrial economy, the area became a centre for heavy industrial development. No concern was shown for the standard of living of the population or the improvement of the primitive agricultural base. Farmers were evacuated so that their land could be made available for Japanese immigrants or industrial concerns; labour conscription was widespread. Anti-Japanese guerilla activity was insufficient to shake the harsh military regime.

The Japanese takeover of Manchuria caused anxiety among major nations outside Asia, but faced with their own economic and political problems none was prepared to engage in military action or to use economic sanctions to assist China. Japan's withdrawal from the League in any case demonstrated a clear willingness to flout world opinion. China could only wait for a more favourable opportunity to recover her rights. While any Japanese involvement in Manchuria remained there was no hope of a rapprochement between China and Japan, and the presence of Japanese interests and troops in China only made matters worse. Tension was continuous, and it was only a matter of time before the two countries slipped into total war.

As Nationalist China became stronger under Chiang Kai-shek in the years after 1931 there were frequent clashes between Japanese and Chinese troops in mainland China; but on each occasion a local settlement was reached and the incidents did not escalate. One reason was the continued disunity within China itself. While the nationalists controlled much of the country they still faced internal challenges. From the early 1920s Chiang devoted much of his attention to suppressing his communist rivals rather than forming a united front with them to resist the Japanese, but they established a strong base in the northwest following the Long March of 1934. Increasing calls from both sides to end domestic feuding and make resistance to Japanese encroachments a priority were resisted by Chiang until 1936, when he was kidnapped and briefly detained by Chinese troops from Manchuria in Xian. The nationalists eventually agreed to join forces with the communists against the enemy without.

On 7 July 1937 Japanese troops on night manoeuvres at the Marco Polo Bridge near Beijing clashed with Chinese troops. Strengthened by the united front, the Chinese responded more vigorously than in any previous incident, moving troops to the area. Reinforcements sent from Japan embarked on hostilities with the

Chinese at Shanghai. This time the fighting escalated into full-scale war. War was in fact never declared; the Japanese continued to refer to the 'China Incident'.

At first Japan appeared to have the upper hand. Japanese troops advanced rapidly to take most of the main cities of China – Beijing, Canton (Guangzhou), Shanghai and, in December 1937, Nanjing. Here a Japanese orgy of murder, looting and other atrocities brought an estimated Chinese death toll of nearly 200,000. Yet the Chinese refused to capitulate. Chiang's Nationalist regime moved west to Chongqing in Sichuan, where it remained beleaguered. It became increasingly difficult for assistance from outside to reach the nationalists, and their united front with the communists was no more than skin deep, but even so the Japanese could not extract a surrender. With the main cities and lines of communication secured by the end of 1938, Japan's success waned. She became bogged down by the very size of the country, the lengthy supply lines, her inability to have her army spread thickly on the ground, the increasingly effective guerilla warfare waged by the Chinese communists, as well as by debilitating rivalries within the Japanese army itself. In March 1940 a puppet regime under the former nationalist Wang Jingwei was established in Nanjing in a belated attempt to increase Chinese support. The regime never gained credence inside or outside China.

The lack of progress in China was a major cause of Japan's advance into Southeast Asia. Japan's attempts to cut off China from the south provoked the US into sanctions which ultimately led to Pearl Harbor in December 1941. Japan's seizure of Burma in early 1942 blocked the Burma Road, the last remaining major supply route for Chongqing, but the Chinese still held on. The outbreak of the Pacific War meant extension of fighting to a whole new area and made resolution of the Chinese impasse that much harder. Japan had reduced the need for troops in Northeast Asia by the conclusion of a non-aggression pact with the Soviet Union in 1941, but still needed troops in Occupied China, Korea, Manchukuo and Taiwan to forestall internal disturbances against Japanese rule, and fighting forces throughout China and Southeast Asia. The sheer scale of military involvement was bound to place a major strain on her resources, and it was unlikely that a Japan that had been unable to achieve a Chinese surrender in four years when her military efforts were largely concentrated on that country would be able to secure a military victory now that many of her resources were diverted elsewhere. The fusion of the Asian and European conflicts was a gamble which could only come off if a successful *blitzkrieg* were to lead to negotiation.

Occupied China was under strict Japanese military rule, despite the existence of the puppet government. It served as a military base for a foreign power still fighting to subdue the remainder of the country. After Pearl Harbor, US, British and other nationals with whose countries Japan was now at war were interned or repatriated. The Chinese population, for many of whom existing poverty was compounded by the effects of war, were treated with the utmost contempt and ruthlessness. Torture and execution were the fate not only of those suspected of conniving with anti-Japanese activity, but of thousands of innocent Chinese. In so-called Free China distress was acute; resistance was a priority, and even away from the war zone few escaped the effects of the spiralling inflation which beset the non-agricultural sector. Unlike Manchuria or Korea, occupied China was not economically exploited, let alone developed, by the Japanese, except in the crudest manner. The essentially transient regime left behind little but resentment and destruction. The war with Japan, while weakening the Nationalist government, left the nation's internal conflicts essentially unresolved. The defeat of Japan in August 1945 unleashed an all-out race for power in China.

In Southeast Asia one consequence of the Japanese invasion was to hasten the destruction of European colonialism in the area. Following her early advances into French Indo-China, Japan occupied with astounding speed the remainder of colonial Southeast Asia, and took control over French Indo-China, Singapore, the Philippines, the Dutch East Indies and Malaya, as well as parts of Burma. (Thailand concluded a treaty with Japan and retained nominal independence under Japanese military occupation.) The nature of Japanese rule in these countries varied. Some were allowed a relative degree of freedom, but others, like the Dutch East Indies, were kept under direct military rule, largely due to the importance of their natural resources. Japanese policy everywhere was governed by one overriding consideration, namely the degree to which a country could be made to provide political and economic support for Japan's war effort. Potentially anti-Japanese independence and nationalist movements were vigorously suppressed. Where necessity demanded, as in French Indo-China, Japan cooperated with the colonial power, which was represented by the Vichy regime. The utilization of established or collaborationist governments, as in Thailand or the Philippines, was little more than a façade for Japanese rule. Everywhere Japanese military control used the exigencies of war to subject the populace to harsh and often brutal treatment in what was clearly Japanese domination rather than Asian cooperation. The rhetoric of the Great East Asia Co-Prosperity Sphere still talked of Japanese altruism, but few took it at face value. A Tokyo conference in November 1943 of leaders from nominally independent Southeast Asian countries was supposed to strengthen solidarity and cooperation, but had little impact either in Japan or in Southeast Asia itself. As the Japanese mainland became increasingly cut off from its far flung empire in the later stages of the Pacific War, Japanese control in Southeast Asia weakened. Moreover, any initial support for the Japanese as ousters of Western imperialism had for the most part been transformed into armed nationalist movements anxious to oust the Japanese in their turn and achieve real independence.

The legacy left by the Japanese was a bitter one. The economies of these countries ended the war in ruins. Countries agitated for reparations that Japan was too poor to pay. The return of territories to European rule after Japan's defeat added dissatisfaction to distress. The years of Japanese control had seen the growth of a whole series of independence movements of varying characters. Some, such as the Provisional Government of Free India, had been promoted by the Japanese. In the years after the war these countries sooner or later, peacefully or with bloodshed, achieved independence from Western colonial rule. The Japanese, despite all pretences, had sought to replace European imperialism with their own, but their rhetoric had introduced the concept that total independence was an imminent possibility.

During the years of the Occupation of Japan relations with the rest of Asia were on ice. Japan had no independent foreign policy capability. Moreover, other territories were taken up with their own internal problems. Until 1949 China was preoccupied with civil war. The Southeast Asian colonies struggled for independence. Even for most of the 1950s contact was minimal, although under the San Francisco Peace Treaty agreements were reached with the countries of Southeast Asia concerning Japanese reparation payments. The last of these payments was made in 1976.

Since the 1950s Japan has worked hard to build up contacts with the region, both economically and politically. Japanese business has made substantial advances and much Japanese manufacturing is carried on there. The area is a major source of raw materials for Japanese industry. Marketing of Japanese products has been highly successful. Japan also supplies substantial cultural, technological and financial assistance. The Japan–Southeast Asia relationship is one of the pivotal ones of the Pacific area, but the balance remains unequal. Although the relationship between Japan and the ASEAN nations is by and large cordial but cautious, considerable fears of a new Japanese imperialism, economic if not territorial, exist in Southeast Asia. An explosion of anti-Japanese riots in the early 1970s meant that Japan and her businessmen have had to step carefully in dealing with the area. Southeast Asia remains highly sensitive to Japan's actions, and this sensitivity is not always reciprocated.

Southeast Asia is not the only area where a legacy of hatred, bitterness and injustice has meant that Japan has had to tread very carefully in her relationships. East Asia suffered from the Japanese presence for somewhat longer. Japan's colony of Korea was occupied partly by Russian troops and partly by the US in 1945. Prior discussion among the allies had agreed to aim at international trusteeship followed by independence, but superpower interests and conflict between Korean independence groups rendered agreement on unification impossible, and the two sides became increasingly polarized. By autumn 1948 the split along the 38th parallel had been formalized. The communist-controlled north under Kim Il-sung proclaimed itself the Democratic People's Republic, the capitalist south under Syngman Rhee became the Republic of Korea. With Japan under US control, Japanese contacts were largely with the south. Japan was not militarily involved in the conflict between the two Koreas and their backers during 1950–3, but reaped considerable economic advantage from US military spending. At the end of the Occupation Japan, now firmly in the capitalist camp, established official ties with South Korea. Thirty-five years later diplomatic relations with North Korea have yet to be established.

. For much of the 1950s relations with South Korea were bedevilled by conflict over the territorial waters of the two countries. The memory of the past, not surprisingly, has died hard, but contacts have gradually increased on the basis of certain shared interests, experiences and problems. Japan's economic development has been followed by rapid growth in South Korea, sufficient to challenge Japan's preeminence in some fields. Economic ties are close. Both are Asian capitalist nations existing in close proximity to very different political and economic systems; the awareness of a shared threat, fostered in particular by South Korea, does as much as anything to bring them together. The two states have with difficulty reached a *modus vivendi*, though hardly friendship.

Koreans remain cautious of the Japanese, and the situation of Koreans in Japan does little to remove this suspicion. Koreans, many of them second or even third generation residents, now constitute the country's largest racial minority, numbering some 700,000. Official and personal discrimination is widespread and many Koreans are forced to take inferior jobs. Even those who are successful are rarely accorded the full credit given to their Japanese counterparts. Few are naturalized and most do not wish to be. As aliens, they have to register with the authorities annually. Anger at the fingerprinting this entails has become increasingly rampant in recent years. In a country like Japan where citizenship and race are virtually synonymous, integration between the two races is particularly difficult. The Korean community within Japan remains bitterly divided in its allegiance to north or south, and the 'two Korea' issue has plagued the issue of repatriation.

Japan's formal postwar relations with the People's Republic of China (PRC) are of more recent origin. With the establishment of the communist People's Republic in 1949 remaining Nationalists under Chiang Kai-shek fled to the former Japanese colony of Taiwan. Throughout the 1950s and 1960s the Japanese government followed US leadership in accepting Taipei as the locus of power of the government of China. Trading and personal contacts with the PRC gradually increased over these years, but not until 1972 did a visit to Beijing by Prime Minister Tanaka Kakuei herald Japanese recognition of the PRC. Formal relations led to the conclusion of a Peace and Friendship Treaty in August 1978, which provoked some Soviet opposition. Japan has worked to strengthen the relationship with Beijing, since close contacts with China offer support against the Soviet Union and chances of economic advance. Nevertheless, Japan does not seek a total commitment that would restrict her and endanger contacts with others. Japan's strong economic ties with Taiwan have largely withstood the shift in allegiance. Japan has provided substantial economic and technological assistance to the PRC, but the Chinese have been wary of accepting all that Japan has offered. In general, both sides have been keen to keep their options open.

Eighty years of Japanese aggression in China have left their mark. A continuing sensitivity is demonstrated by Chinese protests over officially approved Japanese textbooks which appear to play down the iniquities of Japanese actions before 1945. The pre-modern relationship which prevailed for centuries has just as enduring an influence. During the 1970s there was a China boom in Japan which seemed to evoke the old image of China as a source of civilization and ideas. Sino-Japanese contacts of all kinds are still eagerly followed in the press and pursued by individuals, national and local organizations, officially and unofficially. Despite the essential superficiality of much of this contact, the traditional empathy between the nations has assisted the Japanese to be on good terms with a regime whose political ideology is the antithesis of their own.

Despite identification with the 'Western' camp, Japan is cautiously trying to build up her position as an Asian nation and as a member of the Pacific community. To regain the trust wiped out by years of Japanese aggression and exploitation requires sensitivity and caution. It requires Japan to demonstrate a genuine concern for the interests of her Asian neighbours which was conspicuously absent fifty years ago and which is made more difficult by Japan's long-standing sense of separateness and uniqueness.

Japan's strength in Asia and her existence as a powerful member of the Western camp mean that Japan's relations with Asia are no longer the mirror-image of those with the West. Nevertheless, Japan's position as the pre-eminent capitalist nation of Asia still makes her a focal point not only for Asian/Western contacts, but also for the clash of differing, and sometimes irreconcilable, cultural traditions.

NOTES

1   The designation 'Boxer' stemmed from a crude translation of the sect's Chinese title as 'righteous and harmonious fists'.
2   A large part of these loans were known as the Nishihara Loans, after Nishihara Kamezō, the Japanese prime minister's personal envoy to China.
3   Pu Yi was the last Manchu emperor, who had abdicated at the age of seven in 1912.

CHAPTER FOUR
Individual and Community

Individualism was well established as one of the cardinal virtues of Western civilization when Japan reopened her doors in the latter half of the nineteenth century. Yet despite nearly 150 years of Western contact Japanese people are still regarded by non-Japanese as group-oriented, lacking individualism and prone to authoritarianism. This view is shared by many Japanese. Although Westerners have invariably regarded a lack of individualism as a negative feature, an impediment to democracy and equality, Japan's recent history suggests that an overriding emphasis on the group and the community can produce considerable strength and may have considerable virtues. Nor is it necessarily undemocratic. Reconciling the desires of the individual and the cohesiveness of the community has not always been easy. Over the last century or so there have been frequent conflicts between individual and group interests. The failure of such tensions to overturn or revolutionize the social structure has rested in the way in which individuals have been socialized and the fundamental norms according to which the society operates. Moreover, social values and structures have shown a remarkable ability to adapt to a rapidly changing environment.

The rulers of Japan from the early seventeenth century attempted to confirm their dominance by restricting all political, social and economic change in the country to within rigidly defined limits. A natural process of development during the Tokugawa period, and the fluctuating pressures to which the regime was subject, meant that this was effectively impossible. Changes over the course of 250 years meant that realities accorded less and less with formal appearances and official regulations. Nevertheless, a rigid hierarchy of hereditary caste continued to prevail both in theory and, to a large extent, in practice. Society as a whole was subdivided into various strata, whose existence was the result not of any process of economic or social change, but of government decree. The hierarchy was headed by the imperial family and court nobility, but these comprised a numerically small and socially insignificant group, largely detached from the rest of society. The remainder of the population was strictly categorized into four groups. These were, in descending order of status, the *bushi* (warriors) or samurai, who were the ruling class; the peasantry, which owed its second ranking to its fundamental role in the national economy and accounted for some 80 per cent of the population; the artisans; and the merchants and traders.[1] A samurai was publicly marked out from the rest of society by his appearance and his bearing of two swords. He was permitted to exert his authority as a member of the ruling class over his inferiors at any time and in any situation. Merchants were relegated to the bottom of the edifice in line with a long-standing Confucian contempt for money-making and commercial activities. Japanese merchants shared this lowly status with their counterparts in China. Outside and below the four official castes there existed the outcasts or untouchables (*eta* or *hinin*), a sizeable group, who, while racially Japanese, had long since been strictly segregated from the remainder of society. Many engaged in certain unclean occupations, such as slaughtering and leather-curing.

Throughout the Tokugawa period the lifestyles, customs, work practices and privileges of each caste were minutely regulated by a host of detailed sumptuary laws and other provisions. Members of each stratum were not expected to deviate from certain prescribed occupations. Within each caste there existed numerous subdivisions, which allotted members a ranking *vis-à-vis* each other. The hereditary nature of social gradation offered little opportunity for social mobility. While these various groups which went to make up the hierarchy were mutually interdependent, the basic principle on which society was organized was this formal system of ranking. Social stratification was affected but not dictated by economic developments. The rigid structure of Tokugawa society was beginning to break down by the early nineteenth century. While the system of formal ascribed status largely held firm, the divisions between classes showed signs of blurring. Wealth, influence and occupation became decreasingly commensurate with formal status. Wealthy merchants purchased samurai rank and landholdings. Impoverished samurai engaged in farming and other occupations to supplement their inadequate stipends. Peasants abandoned the land and fled illegally to towns, while prosperous artisans engaged in commercial activities. The conventional morality and social operation of the various castes remained to a degree distinct from each other at the end of the Tokugawa period. By the early nineteenth century, however, some social values constituted a significant part of the morality of more than one caste. Racial, linguistic and cultural homogeneity in a nation virtually cut off from outside contacts, and the growth of national economic and political integration, in part counteracted the authorities' attempts to perpetuate rigid status divisions. In the years after 1868 the new regime attempted to manipulate selected facets of Tokugawa society to impose a uniform social structure and morality which could then be trumpeted as 'traditional'.

For the cardinal virtues and family structure the Meiji 'tradition' drew on the ethos of the warrior class. In some other respects it relied on centuries of evolution of peasant society. It is difficult to know about the social morality of the peasantry in the early part of the Tokugawa period, but what is clear is that by the 1850s a relatively homogeneous set of social norms prevailed throughout the peasant class, and that their value system was strongly influenced by the agrarian experience. In most peasant communities agricultural operations are of considerable communal significance, and this is likely to be particularly true of wet-rice agriculture where irrigation is the key to survival. Patriarchy and the family are normally of pivotal importance in the social systems of such communities. Japan remained a predominantly agrarian society up to the late 1930s, and the family and the village community are the keys to any understanding of Japanese society in the prewar years.

The Neo-Confucian influenced *bushi* value system of Tokugawa Japan emphasized the virtues of loyalty, filial piety, obedience to seniors, courage and self-sacrifice. Chinese Confucianism enjoined these same virtues, but priorities differed in the two countries. While it is therefore acceptable to talk of Japan as strongly influenced by Confucianism, the emphases of the Japanese brand of Confucianism are in many respects far removed from the Chinese original. The persistent dominance of military society in Japan was crucial to this change. In Japan the supreme virtues were loyalty to one's ruler, one's lord or one's immediate superior, and filial piety. Within families filial piety was the keystone of morality and it led logically to an absolute obedience to the household head. However, where the two virtues conflicted, loyalty tended to take precedence over filial piety. In China the position was normally the reverse; family and lineage took precedence over duty to the ruler. In China perfect virtue, or benevolence, was of overriding importance; a ruler or master lacking this quality could legitimately be overturned. In Japan, with its rigid status system, benevolence was rarely taken into account.

The imposed status system in conjunction with the emphasis on loyalty and obedience, whether to ruler, master, household head or parent, produced what the anthropologist Nakane Chie[2] has called a 'vertical' society. Hierarchical ranking operated within each social grouping as well as between members of different groups. Within a group each individual had a prescribèd status above or below the other members of the group. This was particularly conspicuous in the basic social unit, the *ie* (roughly pronounced as 'ee–e'). *Ie* is normally translated as 'family', but is a more all-embracing concept than that normally signified by the English term. The *ie* was more than a group of individuals; it was a continuing entity carrying on from generation to generation embracing people, property and reputation. It often consisted both of a main line and of branch families. By late Tokugawa inheritance of the property and headship of the *ie*, and the responsibilities this entailed, was among *bushi* determined by primogeniture. This produced differential status between older and younger sons and between sons and daughters. Males were above females and age took precedence over youth. These practices had spread to many families outside the ruling class.

The persistent importance of hierarchy and status in no way negated the significance of the group in defining the position and behaviour of an individual. Apart from their 'vertical' obligations individuals were tied together by belonging to the same group. Small groups provided the context of day-to-day operation. Ties which might provide a basis for group cohesion included regional origins (reinforced by the domain system), shared caste, family relationships or occupation. For the peasant class, the strongest manifestation of group solidarity outside the family was the village. A village essentially consisted of a group of *ie* sharing not only location of residence but often occupation. In the Tokugawa period it enjoyed some autonomy, and was permitted a certain degree of self-reliance and self-government. A cohesion originating in the needs of agriculture and a desire for group protection in times of uncertainty and danger was reinforced by this relative autonomy. Within families, villages and larger social groupings a sense of solidarity prevailed. Group members would help each other in times of need and adopt a united front *vis-à-vis* the outside world, whatever their internal differences. While a strict hierarchy of individuals and families operated within the village, villages also developed a kind of democracy and spirit of mutual reliance and assistance. Decisions were made by reaching a consensus embracing every level of the hierarchy; this made possible a unanimous agreement among household heads. While the village unit remained small there was less chance of a decision's being imposed by the community's more influential members, and in any case the imposition of status and ranking tended to reduce the passive acceptance of inferiority which might have attended its acquisition through achievement or wealth. Nevertheless, in later Tokugawa the polarization of wealth and interest resulting from economic change and exposure to the market economy more and more broke the appearance of village harmony.

The combination of vertical and group ties was such that individuals tended to be viewed by others not as individuals, but as group members, and a network of reciprocal obligations and feelings between group members was the key to the maintenance of social order. The categorization of individuals by position in the hierarchy and group membership made it impossible for an individual to divorce himself from his social role. To that extent individual fulfilment lay in coping with the demands of society and the dividing line between the private and public domains was blurred. This was a basis upon which later propaganda of community of interest between the individual and the state could usefully be constructed.

Thus in society at large the position and role of each individual was strictly prescribed by his or her position within the group or groups to which he or she belonged, and the position of that group in relation to other groups and society as a whole. For most individuals the *ie* grouping and the village were of prime importance, but these might become overlaid by membership of other groups, for example, as a result of occupation or education. Moral behaviour was behaviour that accorded with what was expected from a particular social role or situation, and could not be defined outside the social context. Role-playing was crucial to preserve what is often called *tatemae*, defined by one author as 'the presentation of an appropriate face for any particular situation'.[3] There were no moral absolutes as the moral order was equated to the actual order. Morality then, as now, was determined largely by contemporary trends. Behaviour was subject to the decrees of custom and this led to a strong emphasis on pragmatism and the averting of any confrontation. This avoidance of conflict became the key to the much-vaunted 'harmony' of the Japanese social system. The contrast with the Western civilization Japan encountered after the 1850s, imbued with the virtues of individualism and *laissez faire,* absolute moral values and the righteousness of an individual's conduct in the eyes of God, seemed unbridgeable.

Japanese reactions to Western contact as a whole were widely varied and highly ambiguous. Among Japan's leaders opinions of Western society ranged from utter condemnation of its values to defiant affirmations of its superiority. While the majority of Japanese remained ignorant of Western social values and customs, and of the background which had given rise to them, the new Meiji government was already moving fast to demolish the formal apparatus of Tokugawa society. Its prime aim was to consolidate its own power, but it also hoped to centralise and unify the nation and attain to Western standards required for a revision of the unequal treaties. By 1872 the old caste system had been abolished. Behaviour and occupation were no longer strictly controlled. The designation warrior family *(shizoku)* was no more than an indication of family origins although it continued to have social prestige. Individual members of society were encouraged to work to the best of their abilities and improve themselves, and a translation of Samuel Smiles' *Self Help* became a bestseller. Some Japanese flourished in this enthusiasm for individual improvement. Others proved unable to cope with the rapidly changing conditions with which they were faced, but there is little evidence of a violent breakdown in social or moral standards. The persistence of traditional patterns and of the conventional morality that had dictated behaviour and social structure in Tokugawa Japan proved a source of stability.

The way in which the majority of Japanese conducted their daily lives was not changed overnight by the upheavals at national level. Nevertheless, the political, social and economic reforms undertaken by Japan's leaders, as well as Japan's new relationship with the outside world, were bound before long to have an impact on the lives of all Japanese. Individual response to the altered conditions was, as might be expected, conditioned by conventional morality. The Japanese historian Irokawa Daikichi[4] has suggested that it was only when the economic plight of the early 1880s failed to respond to this conventional morality that some of the lower classes were forced to break out of their limitations in the violent incidents of the time. In response to this threat, Irokawa argues, the ruling classes moved rapidly to reinforce the conventional norms still adhered to by the vast majority of the people, but in a way which removed any spontaneous content and value. The result was a code of morality and social behaviour demanded by the state and its henchmen, and later backed by a variety of legal means.

What is indisputable is that the Meiji government, having abolished the official status system of the Tokugawa, tried to impose a permutation of the Tokugawa social ethos, and this ideal sought a fusion of social structure and social morality. This national policy was in part a semi-conscious response to an intense awareness of vulnerability, to the threat of cultural imperialism and loss of national identity. Its implementation resulted in the enforcement of a social system which permitted little dissent and which could be, and was, used to aid and support a specific political system. The reassertion and manipulation of 'traditional' values to maintain continuity in a time of rapid change and to preserve national identity and order have frequently been undertaken by countries facing an external (or internal) threat. For Japan to react in this way at this time was not in itself culpable. Government policy emerged after considerable in-fighting among ruling circles, and many of its long-term results were unforeseen.

The 1870s was a period of vigorous debate concerning the need to change Japanese society. Groups such as the Meirokusha (lit. Meiji Six Society), a group of enlightened scholars formed in 1874 to discuss and disseminate new ideas, were in the forefront of this debate. Leading members of the Meirokusha included Fukuzawa Yukichi (1835–1901), Nakamura Masanao (1832–91) and Mori Arinori (1847–89). Discussion of the need to introduce certain Western political, economic and social practices would appear to have taken place at many levels of society. From the 1880s onwards, there was a reaction against what many considered excessive aping of Western practices and values. This led to calls for the reassertion of the values and practices of the Tokugawa period, or rather of those that the ruling élite regarded as according to the needs of post-1868 Japan. In the circumstances such calls were not totally unrealistic. Early Western adoptions were often uncritical and foolish. Many Japanese failed to appreciate the background of Western social customs or realize how ill-suited they were to Japan. Social and intellectual imitation was often less eclectic than Japan's borrowing in the more concrete fields of technology, industry, education and defence. Problems raised by the non-transferable nature of social behaviour and structure were compounded by a distinction between social conventions, which were adopted wholesale, and social morality, which could hardly be transformed overnight. A reversion to older morality and convention seemed a safer course to adopt, and one that was not necessarily incompatible with the pursuit of political, legal and economic activities along Western lines.

The official imposition of conventional social forms and norms was achieved largely through the education and legal systems, but its strength lay in its manipulation of existing social values and a long-standing social system which enabled it to be internalized by the average Japanese. Patriotism was added to the warrior virtues of duty, obedience, loyalty and filial piety to become the attributes of morality. The *ie* became more than ever the pre-eminent entity in society. Calculated manipulation and the need for security in a rapidly changing society led to the family mode of operation being simulated in other institutions, giving rise in the early years of the twentieth century to many quasi-family organizations. Parent–child relationships, and the boss-follower *(oyakata-kogata)*[5] relationship widespread in the economy of earlier times, were fundamental axes of social interaction. Employers made claims about the familial nature of their businesses and their warm relationship with their employees. Such statements, though frequently unjustified, indicate the extent to which rhetoric of this kind had become widely acceptable.

During the Tokugawa period the position of an individual was governed by the various groups of which he or she was a member, and this remained true in the post-Restoration years. Beginning with the family into which an individual was born, he or she contracted a series of group memberships in quasi-familial institutions or groups, such as school, college or company. Within each group each individual had a specific ranking, but now the hierarchy was imposed by convention rather than being formally assigned. The most important and all-embracing of these groups was the 'family state', which figured prominently in the official political ideology. All Japanese belonged to this 'family state' purely by virtue of being Japanese; they were the emperor's 'children'.

The structure and ethos of the village community remained pivotal to the whole system. The enduring ties of many new urban residents with rural areas led to a simulation of village structure in the cities. The village came to be represented as the source of all the traditional virtues, the heart of the Japanese tradition. Notwithstanding the difficulties which many members of the agrarian community faced in the new Japan, the continuing economic significance of agriculture and the numerical importance of the rural population made the maintenance of this reputation easier.

The inculcation of the new 'tradition' was backed up by two documents in particular. The Imperial Rescript on Education was promulgated in October 1890 and thereafter read regularly in the schools of the empire until all children knew it by heart. The rescript was a powerful exhortation to patriotism, loyalty, filial piety, obedience and duty within the political framework established by the Meiji Constitution. A more direct influence on the social system itself was the new Japanese civil code of 1898. An earlier civil code drafted in consultation with the French legal expert Gustave Boissonade had been rejected as too influenced by French natural rights theories. The version implemented in 1898 was influenced more by German legal thinking. It was designed to uphold rather than undermine older aspects of Japanese society. This civil code remained in force up until the end of the Pacific War, and provided the legal framework for the social system for nearly fifty years. Family law was a codification of the patriarchal family system, which rested on the existence of the *ie* as the basic unit of operation. The head of the household had privileged legal status, and the right of individual family members to autonomous activity was strictly limited. Primogeniture was enforced and the majority of women became legal incompetents.

The emphasis on the family and quasi-family situations strengthened the concept of the individual as a group member performing a socially ascribed role. Prominent individuals were often prominent by virtue of the groups of which they were leaders. Disapproval was frequently the lot of individualists and non-conformists. In the 'family state' the assertion of individualism was increasingly regarded as being incompatible with the demands of patriotism. This is not to say that there were no outstanding individuals or charismatic heroes. Japan was not a country of nonentities, in which no one stood out from the crowd. Individual social mobility continued to be actively pursued, and many able individuals made the most of a rapidly changing environment and opportunities to rise above their origins, or, in some cases, to enjoy the luxury of non-conformism. The motivation to achieve was strong. For most Japanese there were no longer formal restrictions on mobility, and, especially in the Meiji period, social ranking was relatively fluid. The restrictions which bound individual Japanese to conformity were less those laid down by law than the more pervasive ones of social ethic and social convention which discouraged a 'selfish' individualist approach.

Government efforts to promote national unity and identity and improved communications contributed to Japanese society's becoming more homogeneous by the early twentieth century than it had been in the Tokugawa period. Foreigners were small in number and for the most part temporary residents, but there were two sizeable minority groups in the country. The ethnically Japanese *burakumin* (lit. 'hamlet people'⁶) were descended from the outcastes of the Tokugawa period. In the mid-Meiji period there were over 400,000, a little over 1 per cent of the population. By the late Taishō period the figure had increased to one million. Although as a group they had been officially emancipated in 1871, *burakumin* became the sporadic scapegoats of popular resentment, and social discrimination persisted on a wide scale in spheres such as education, employment and marriage. The early 1900s produced a movement for improvement through self-help, but the failure of this campaign to achieve any notable advance prompted the rise of a more radical emancipation movement. *Burakumin* were conspicuous in the rice riots which erupted in 1918, and during the 1920s *buraku* leaders were drawn into the general upsurge of left wing activism. Many were convinced that only a proletarian revolution could remove discrimination. Their radical national organization, the Suiheisha (lit. Levelling Society), founded in 1922, scored several notable local successes, but at considerable cost. Large parts of the Suiheisha were subsequently caught up in the government's clampdown on radicalism after the mid-1920s. The government started an assistance programme in the early 1920s, but it was totally inadequate to deal with the fundamental problems facing the *buraku*, which were particularly hard hit by the interwar slump. Indications of tangible progress in the late 1930s were stifled by the constraints of war.

Immigrants from Korea were the other large minority. Koreans flooded in from the new colony in search of work and livelihood. By the early 1930s there were half a million, by 1940 over one million. They were disadvantaged by colonial status, which did not permit them full citizenship or equal rights with ethnic Japanese, who looked down on them. Most Korean immigrants were also unskilled labourers, the majority of them men. They often worked for far lower wages than their Japanese equivalents, and turnover was very high. They dwelt mainly in impoverished ghettoes in urban areas and many of their children went uneducated. Success for the few who achieved it was often bought at the cost of Korean ties and identity. Koreans became, like the *burakumin,* an object of social prejudice. They became scapegoats for crimes committed and were widely bruited as potential subversives. They were considered uncultured, undisciplined and dangerous. Japanese hostility towards its Korean minority reached a peak of violence in the unrest after the Great Kantō Earthquake of 1 September 1923, when rumours of organized Korean subversion, systematic rape, poisoning of wells and arson, led to the declaration of martial law and an officially approved anti-Korean witchhunt in which thousands were brutally massacred.

Substantial though both these minorities were, their presence had little impact on the way the majority of Japanese conducted their lives. There was little social intermingling, and the subordinate position forced upon them enabled the ethnic majority to hold themselves detached and distinct. Affinity of conduct and values among this majority did not always make for unity. The persistent importance of the group, which had led to a strong sense of communal identity since the Tokugawa period, could also produce schism within society. Group membership could promote ties which often transcended other loyalties. Competing groups – for example, companies in the same line of business or different universities – engaged in intense and bitter rivalry in which manifestations of loyalty and dedication to the group sometimes went far beyond the bounds of what was normally acceptable. Larger groups were prone to intense factionalism. Membership of a specific group was often the product of a boss–follower relationship with one of its leading members, and thus very large groups were in danger of becoming no more than a coalition of personal factions. The conservative political parties of the interwar years, with their amorphous ideologies, were a case in point. One major factor acted to contain the divisive tendencies inherent in the prevailing group orientation. This was the institution of the nation as a unifying group to which all ethnic Japanese belonged. The establishment worked hard to ensure that allegiance to the nation transcended allegiance to any other group or individual. The exploitation of this allegiance in the circumstances of the 1930s enabled an effective mobilization of society for common national cause and self-sacrifice.

Whatever the 'social costs' of political and economic development in Japan up to the 1940s, it is difficult to find widespread sustained resistance to, or non-cooperation with, the social value system. Reaction even against the political system with which it was so closely integrated was muted. Many writers have therefore looked to pre-modern social patterns and economic relations in analysing Japan's path to authoritarianism and war. It is all too simplistic to explain political developments in late 1930s Japan purely by reference to an inherent susceptibility to authoritarianism in socio-economic relations in the village. No more is it possible to claim that the strict code of social morality and convention which helped to sustain the political system was held in place from outside against the will of most Japanese people. What must be noted here is that much of the strength of the political ethos propagated in prewar years rested on its incorporation and distortion of concepts and assumptions whose origins were far back in Japanese history, and which were broadly unquestioned by the majority of the population; and that it was firmly integrated with the social system and standard code of morality and behaviour.

After 1931, and especially after the outbreak of full-scale war with China in 1937, social regimentation in Japan became more obtrusive. Control over the behaviour of the individual was more overtly stringent, deviation from the norm far less tolerated. Although external organs such as the police networks were used to enforce control, much of it was exercised through existing social institutions, for example, the family and the company, and through official organizations such as the reservists, youth leagues and women's groups, of which membership, where appropriate, eventually became compulsory. An additional mechanism was provided during the war years by the neighbourhood associations *(tonarigumi)*. In the Tokugawa period 'five family groups' had operated as instruments of social control by holding the household heads within the group mutually responsible for the misdemeanours of a member of any of the five households. The neighbourhood associations were larger – up to twenty families, with associations organized in turn into larger village or block associations. The neighbourhood associations were used for administrative functions, but members were also encouraged to spy and report on fellow members to minimize disloyalty and unpatriotic behaviour, encouraging an atmosphere of mutual suspicion. The multiplicity of groups to which each individual was obliged to belong placed further external restraints on his or her activities, and discouraged the expression of independent thought even among close friends or relatives.

The growing economic and physical hardships of the later stages of the Pacific War, and the inability of the authorities to conceal Japan's deteriorating position from the populace, placed new strains on society. Social control networks began to break down as urban civilians fled to the countryside and heavy human and material losses disrupted the normal organization of life. Nevertheless, there is little evidence while the war continued of a widespread rejection of the prevailing code of morality or of the conventions governing social interaction *per se*. Society never became even remotely ungovernable. Official suppression alone cannot adequately explain this apparent docility. By mid-1945 the majority of the population may well have had little stomach for a fight to the finish on Japanese soil, but the threat of the military's being able to drive the populace into such a last ditch stand was taken seriously both inside and outside Japan by all who realized the strength of customary morality and social organization.

Conclusions regarding the existence of the authoritarian tendencies in Japanese society led the Occupation authorities to see the democratization of society as fundamental to any lasting democratization of the country as a whole. Clauses of the existing civil code and other legislation were quickly suspended or modified, and many of the organizations used to mobilize and control the Japanese people were disbanded. (The neighbourhood associations were retained until 1947 for administrative continuity, despite fears of their 'subversive' potential.) The social dislocation of the immediate postwar years resulted less from the Occupation reforms than from the economic and political problems of the country. The general demoralization and effort of coping with day-to-day existence at such a difficult time left many Japanese with little energy to pay attention to the radical changes in social structure and values which the Occupation authorities were attempting to impose on the country.

The wholesale legal and institutional change implemented by the Occupation authorities attempted to undermine concepts fundamental to the organization of prewar Japanese society, for example, the pre-eminence of the *ie*, the dominance of the household head and the subordinate position of women. A total revision of the civil code to uphold the guarantee of individual rights and equality contained in the May 1947 constitution took effect in January 1948. Modelled on the Western idea of the individual's relationship with society, the new version deprived the *ie* of legal status, provided for free choice of spouse and domicile (i.e. the consent of the household head was no longer required) and the equality of all individuals and both sexes in the eyes of the law. The élitist educational system was reformed with a view to providing equality of opportunity, in the hope that this would back up a new, genuinely democratic social structure permitting a high level of individual social mobility. The strong achievement orientation of Japanese society and the degree to which it has become a genuine educational meritocracy have led many to assume that this aim has been achieved. However, official statistics suggest that mobility has not recently been conspicuously higher in Japan than in other industrialized countries, especially since access to good education has too often depended on wealth and background. Despite the educational and other changes, there remained after 1945 an influential hard core of élite families, many descended from the leading business, political or artistic families of the prewar years. Such families have been well placed to secure the best contacts and the best education, and rising young stars have often married into them, so social prestige and heredity have continued to count for a considerable amount.

Even the most optimistic forecasters, though, never expected the Japanese to change their mode of social operation overnight. Legal reform was a prerequisite for social change, but not automatically the immediate precursor of it. While the constitutional and legal changes laid the foundations for a breakdown of the dominance of the household and for greater individual rights, especially for women, considerable importance still attaches to some of the characteristics noted in the prewar period, albeit with modifications.

Writings on postwar Japanese society suggest a consensus on the persistence of its 'vertical' element. For example, the lack of a rigid division of labour such as is found in Britain reflects and reinforces the strength of vertical ties. The *ie* has ceased to exist as a legal entity, but the family unit has remained highly influential. Many families have continued to attach great importance to the family line, adopting their daughter's husband or another male as heir to the family name where there is no son to succeed. The continuing emphasis on family relationships may well affect the way Japan copes with the rapid ageing of the population which faces her over the next three decades. Within most families the roles of husband and wife have remained distinct, with the male the breadwinner and the female caring for house and children. Inheritable property has still tended to go to the eldest son.

Changes in social attitudes in the postwar period have also, not surprisingly, been gradual. Most Japanese have had no wish blindly to imitate Western social customs and attitudes. Many believe strongly in the need for Japan to be different and to retain what they see as its own traditional *modus operandi;* they are quite satisfied with the roles which society expects them to play. Their major concerns remain their nation, their families, their work and their friendship groups. Within the constraints of these traditional preoccupations the majority of the population adheres happily, or unhappily, to the roles which society expects of them, even though there is no legal compulsion to do so.

The major factors behind the change that has taken place are economic and industrial development. More married women now work in activities incompatible with childcare and domestic duties, forcing some couples to hold a less traditional view of their relationship. Even before the Occupation legislation, the rapid industrialization of the 1930s threatened to undermine the position of the *ie* and the authority of the household head. Family ties have been further weakened by old people living apart from their children, and by the pressure on accommodation in urban areas, which has accelerated the decline in three-generation family units. Yet to the outsider postwar Japanese society still seems to be striking not in its similarities to, but in its differences from, the West.

Japan is no exception to the tendency to sum up widely shared social characteristics and attitudes under the heading of 'national character'. Indeed, this predisposition has been reinforced in the Japanese case by the unusual degree of social uniformity which appears to stem from the homogeneity of the people and their customs. Foreigners have too often seen Japan as a monolithic society where individualism is frowned upon and conformity all important, where the tendency is towards harmony and consensus and a healthy element of conflict decidedly absent, and where the role of the group is all-pervasive. Yet this image, allowing for exaggeration, is not totally removed from the reality of prewar Japanese society, and the persistence of some of the same characteristics in the post-1945 period therefore means that such categorization still contains a measure of truth.

In Japan the relationship of the individual to other individuals and to society at large is still governed largely by his or her membership of various groups. In any context an individual perceives him/herself as a member of a particular group, and this perception reinforces an us–them mentality.[7] These groups are the key to the moulding of an individual's identity. They are not so much status-based as functional, but they have an all-pervasive influence on the individual's life far beyond the narrow functions which are their specific object. Conformity with the group is still a major objective. The dependence of the individual on the group and on certain individuals within it has become a major theme in any analysis of Japanese society. 'Harmony' within and between groups is the ideal of Japanese social interaction. Where a grouping is a sizeable one it becomes divided into smaller subgroups. Potentially damaging conflict between these subgroups is avoided by channelling mutual competition into an avenue where it can benefit the group as a whole.

The other side of the coin has also persisted in the form of factionalism and intergroup conflict. The hierarchical loyalty structure promotes intense schism and conflict within large organizations, as is abundantly clear in the case of political parties. Before 1945 the overall unifying entity was the nation as expressed in the 'family state' to which all belonged. The legal and constitutional foundations of the prewar state have been destroyed; the existence of the emperor as the symbol of the Japanese nation is almost the sole relic of the old structure, albeit an important one. Yet postwar experience has shown that the formal foundations of the state were not the *sine qua non* of nationhood. More significant in providing this national group membership has been the racial homogeneity of the Japanese people themselves, the culture, language and traditions common to them, and the shared history and society upon which the political system was constructed. Now, as then, Japanese form a single social group by virtue of being Japanese. This attribute separates them from the outside world and can be shared by no non-Japanese. It is not a mere matter of citizenship; it is a birthright and a shared inheritance. To this extent the nation still acts as the overriding social group whose existence serves to contain the most damaging effects of the conflict and factionalism which are daily occurrences at lower levels.

In the years since 1945, Japan, unlike many other industrial nations, has received few immigrants whose presence might modify this sense of 'being Japanese'. Even the presence of a substantial Korean minority has done little to weaken a sense of identity whose strength is indicated by the virtual denial of Japanese nationality to those who are not racially Japanese. The largest minority group in Japan is still the *burakumin,* who comprise something over 2 per cent of the population. *Burakumin* are still the object of severe social discrimination in all areas of life, although much of it is indirect or covert. There is a reluctance on the part of any social group to engage in overt discrimination against the members of another.

A clear reluctance on the part of many Japanese even to discuss the problem suggests a reluctance to admit to the existence of the *burakumin* as an outcaste group, on the assumption that a problem that is not talked about is not a problem, or at least is one that will go away if it is ignored. Sporadic attempts to justify discrimination by proving that *burakumin* are not Japanese have little credibility, but serve to emphasize the importance of race.

The Korean minority, now numbering over 600,000, have suffered from this racial prejudice. Despite an increasing amount of intermarriage, few Koreans have wished to take up the option of naturalization, difficult enough to achieve in itself. Most have remained registered as citizens of North or South Korea, aliens in their country of permanent residence. In recent years an increasing number of second- and even third-generation Koreans have shown signs of rebelling against a system which has limited their job options and freedom of movement. Members of the Korean minority have started to question the exclusivity of a Japan which has denied citizenship and certain basic human rights even to those born and brought up in the country. This growing discontent has been symbolized by Koreans refusing to comply with the stipulation that all aliens resident in Japan for any length of time have to be re-registered as aliens and fingerprinted at regular intervals, and carry alien registration cards with them at all times. For Korean residents who have known no home other than Japan these regulations are considered particularly insulting.

The non-Japanese community in Japan remains sufficiently small and discrete to highlight, rather than dilute, indigenous customs and attitudes. The prospect of any substantial increase in immigration in the near future is unlikely. Some observers have suggested that the decline of the village as the main social unit in Japan has produced a greater heterogeneity in the smaller groups which go to make up society as a whole. For other commentators the continuing dominance of smaller group attitudes and the persistence of an 'us' and 'them' mentality towards non-members, is no more than a repeat of the older village attitudes. The increasing heterogeneity of the subgroup, it has been argued, means a greater homogeneity in the nation as a whole.

Some Japanese maintain that the way in which society operates has changed little since the 1930s. Others call for a reassertion of 'traditional' Japanese values, saying that changes provoked by Western contact have gone too far, and that 'traditional' Japanese values should be reasserted. The question of what it is desirable for Japan to be and do deeply divides the Japanese, but few fail to acknowledge that being Japanese sets them apart.

NOTES

1   The four strata were often referred to as *shi-nō-kō-shō*, according to the first character of their respective designations.
2   Nakane Chie, *Japanese Society* (Harmondsworth, 1973).
3   J. Hendry, *Understanding Japanese Society* (Beckenham, 1987), p. 204. A distinction is drawn between *tatemae* and *honne*, or real feelings.
4   Irokawa Daikichi, *The Culture of the Meiji Period* (Princeton, 1985).
5   Significantly, *oyakata-kogata* uses the characters for 'parent' and 'child' when written in Japanese.
6   The term originates from the segregated hamlets *(buraku)* where the *burakumin* resided.
7   Analysts of Japanese society use the terms *uchi* (inside) and *soto* (outside) to describe the dichotomy experienced by a child between elements within the family/home and without. This dichotomy is extended to all wider groups of which the individual is a member.

CHAPTER FIVE
Town and Country

For much of the modern period Japan has been a predominantly agrarian country. In the Tokugawa period agriculture served as the cornerstone both of the economy and of society as a whole. The importance of manufacturing increased steadily from the beginning of the Meiji period but until the late 1920s agriculture accounted for over 25 per cent of net domestic production. As late as 1930 over 50 per cent of the population – more than 30 million people – were still dependent on agriculture for a living, and it was not until two decades later that there was an absolute fall in the number of Japanese working in the agricultural sector. The rapidity of Japan's economic and political transformation and the enduring influence of Tokugawa practices and ideas into this century mean that in Japan, as in other late industrializers such as the USSR, agricultural issues and the impact of the rural sector have been of crucial importance throughout the past 150 years.

Rice was introduced into Japan over 2,000 years ago. It rapidly became a staple, and has remained the major crop throughout the modern period. Wet-rice agriculture stimulates economic and social conditions very different from the dry land agriculture of, for example, Europe. Paddy rice production can support a very high population density. Environmental and climatic conditions have combined with agricultural techniques to produce in Japan exceptionally high yields. Rice production is also very labour intensive, but in Japan the intensity of work is not even throughout the year, freeing the population for other work at certain times. Wet-rice production also has considerable implications for the community engaged in it. The building of irrigation systems and paddy fields is costly in terms of time and effort. Construction and cultivation require cooperation within the family unit and within the community. The implications of the existence of wet-rice agriculture in Japan have an important bearing on the development of the rural sector over the past 150 years.

During the Tokugawa period (1603–1867), notwithstanding advances in the manufacturing and commercial sectors, agriculture remained the basis of the economy. Over 80 per cent of the population consisted of peasants. They lived in small villages scattered over the landscape in varying degrees of density. The peasant caste's second ranking in the official status hierarchy below the ruling samurai caste, was a formal recognition of the degree to which the economy as a whole was dependent on the products of peasant labour. The rice and other crops produced by the peasantry did not merely keep the population as a whole alive; rice was also the cornerstone of the formal political and economic organization of the country, at both national and local levels.

In this period the largest landholder was the ruling Tokugawa family. The remainder of the land was subdivided into several hundred domains (*han*), each ruled by a lord, or daimyo. These warrior rulers had overriding rights over the land under their control. Even when private landownership spread in the latter Tokugawa era it did so under this premise. From the late sixteenth century the size of a domain was expressed in terms of the rice production it could command, and this assessment was made in terms of *koku*.[1] Fief size ranged from Kaga (present-day Fukui Prefecture), with around 1 million *koku*, to others with the bare minimum of 10,000 *koku* required for daimyo ranking. Local lords had originally maintained their followers by allotting to each a specific area of land, rather in the nature of a mediaeval European king assigning fiefs to his followers. Even before Tokugawa rule, however, there had begun a shift away from direct land entitlements towards a system of stipends payable by the lord to his followers. In the 1580s an earlier warrior ruler, Hideyoshi, had sought to implement a formal distinction between warriors and farmers. Farmers were deprived of arms and many of the warrior class were removed from direct contact with the land and brought into the castle towns as an urban ruling class with no independent power base. Thus by the early years of the Edo period many samurai families were maintained by a fixed stipend rather than by the fluctuating harvest of a prescribed area of land. By the mid-Tokugawa period this practice was almost universal.

To support himself and his followers a daimyo took as tax a specified proportion of the harvest in all areas under his control.

The tax obligation of each village was measured in terms of *koku*, as were the values of the stipends distributed by the daimyo to his followers. Daimyo took most of their income in the form of rice, and warrior stipends, too, were normally payable in the same commodity. This remained substantially the case despite an increasing monetization and diversification of the economy. The degree to which an individual possessed rights over the rice crop thus defined his position in the whole socio-economic system, and became the major indicator of wealth and status for most of the population.

Peasant family members had no freedom to leave the land. Their task was to maximize output and hand over the requisite tribute to local officials who acted as the daimyo's intermediaries. Villages were normally assessed as a single unit and the distribution of the burden by the village hierarchy was often highly inequitable. The proportion of output given up varied according to such factors as region, land quality and time, some allowance being made for the abundance of the harvest. A further major arbiter was how long it was since the land had last been assessed for tax purposes (if ever). Estimates suggest that the peasantry as a whole was giving up over one-third of its total rice output for much of the period, but in some areas it may have been much higher.

The removal of warriors from the land and the rapid urbanization that took place from the late sixteenth century indicate the availability of a substantial surplus in peasant production. Owing to reclamation, technological improvements and urbanization, agricultural productivity and the level of production rose during the period. Much of this increase in production went untaxed since cadastral surveys were often hopelessly out of date. How much of the increase went to the peasantry is a matter of dispute. While some members may have experienced a steady rise in their standard of living in the latter half of the period, others were in no position to benefit. That the number of town dwellers grew and that such a large proportion of output could be made over to the ruling class without permanent and chronic nationwide famine or substantial evidence of huge tax arrears suggest that peasants continued to produce well above subsistence level. However, in less prosperous areas the large exactions were, for many, such a burden that they still lived at subsistence level. Members of the ruling class sought to increase agricultural production by land reclamation and other projects, and farmers diversified into alternative crops and non-agricultural by-employment to supplement their incomes, but the ruling class was not keen to allow Japan's farmers to reap the benefits of any increase.

Despite the attempt to impose a rigid status system, the division between farmers and warriors was never as clear cut as intended. Nor could peasant society be kept unchanged over 250 years. While the majority of samurai did live as retainers in castle towns, there were some marginal cases who continued to reside in the countryside, often cultivating the land. This group, which included what are known as rural or quasi-samurai, was particularly numerous in a few important domains, such as Satsuma and Chōshū. They often bridged a social and economic division, and held an ambiguous position *vis-à-vis* the daimyo and the hierarchy as a whole. There also developed considerable disparities in wealth and status within the peasantry itself. Such disparities predated the imposition of a rigid social hierarchy, but became more marked during the course of the Tokugawa period. This was not always apparent due to the degree of autonomy enjoyed by villages within the domain. In practice village elders were usually jointly responsible for the payment of the dues of village members as a whole, and as long as the correct amount was forthcoming, and the village itself reasonably peaceful and law-abiding, the domain authorities tended to concern themselves little with how this was achieved. The inadequacies of individual villagers were frequently concealed by the aggregate. If an individual peasant family was for one reason or another unable to produce its share of tax a peasant might borrow, do additional work as a paid labourer or craftsman or forfeit his land rights to another. The number of landlord-peasants and landless or part-tenant farmers increased rapidly, and the growth of landlordism was accelerated by the ingress of merchants, entrepreneurs and moneylenders who saw in land a profitable and respectable locus for investment. While peasants might in theory be tied to the land, many engaged in non-agricultural by-employment. Others gave up their agricultural occupations and even left the rural areas together, migrating to find work and livelihood in the expanding urban areas. These significant changes failed to be reflected in substantial changes in the system of rule. Rice-producing peasants continued to be the workhorses of the nation and the economic support of the ruling class.

A major contributory factor to the polarization of wealth within villages and between regions was the growth of towns and the commercialization and monetization of the economy which accompanied it. Despite continuing dependence on the agricultural economy, the Tokugawa period was a time of rapid urbanization. Towns in the pre-Tokugawa years had, except for Kyoto the imperial capital, been fairly small scale. Patterns of late sixteenth-century warfare encouraged the building of huge castles as daimyo bases. The move of *bushi* away from the land into the 'castle town' of each domain meant substantial concentrations of population. The growth of service and artisan sectors to serve the needs of the élite expanded the urban population still further. By the early nineteenth century there were dozens of towns with a population of over 10,000, many of which had originated as castle towns. By far the biggest of these was Edo, the seat of the ruling Tokugawa Bakufu. Edo mushroomed from the late sixteenth century and had an estimated population of around one million by the mid-eighteenth century, probably making it the largest city in the world at the time. Apart from its strategic position as the seat of Tokugawa government, Edo achieved added importance from the system of alternate attendance (*sankin kōtai*). This was one of the methods used by the Tokugawa to keep potential rivals in check. Under it daimyo had to reside for one year out of every two in the capital, and leave their wives and families in permanent residence there. The disproportionate population of samurai attracted vast numbers of retailers, craftsmen and servants to service the large and wealthy consumer market.

A further category of urban development was the growth of trading and financial centres. Sometimes this function was performed by castle towns, but some centres of the commodity economy were separate from domain administration. Osaka was by far the most important in this category. Its existence as a commercial centre predated the start of the Edo period, but it grew rapidly from the early years of the seventeenth century and by the 1730s had an estimated population of over 300,000. Osaka was a city not of samurai, but of merchants (*chōnin*, lit. 'townspeople'). It owed its rapid expansion to its role as the chief supply centre for the growing metropolis of Edo, above all as the locus of sale and distribution of the rice income of the daimyo and their retainers. Even in the early seventeenth century commercial transactions had advanced far beyond the simple barter level, and with an increasing proportion of the population not directly engaged in agricultural production, non-producers had to be supplied with the cash to purchase the necessities of life, as well as its luxuries. By far the largest part of daimyo tax income, most of it in the form of rice, was shipped to Osaka. There merchants would undertake its storage, marketing, sale and distribution, providing the daimyo and their retainers in return with credit, goods or cash to finance their way of life. Commodity broking functions led to the growth of financial and exchange business as well. Osaka merchants became increasingly specialized in function and their number expanded rapidly. Powerful guilds were established. As their wealth increased they, and the permanently resident warrior retainers with whom they dealt, attracted further tradesmen and craftsmen to the city. The monopoly of Osaka merchants over the rice market, and Osaka's role as a supply source for the demands of Edo and elsewhere, brought substantial prosperity. Osaka became the heart of the merchant culture which was a lasting heritage of seventeenth- and eighteenth-century Japan.

Other commercial centres on a smaller scale were promoted by the increasing transport of goods up and down the country which accompanied the emergence of a national market. Edo itself also acted as a major centre of commercial activity. The growth of coastal shipping to compensate for the inadequacies of land transport encouraged the further development of ports such as Sakai, near Osaka.

Government policy and commercial development thus came together to make the Tokugawa period an era of rapid urbanization; estimates suggest that in the early 1800s around 15 per cent of the population could be considered as dwelling in urban areas. This figure is high compared with most pre-industrial economies. In Russia, for example, as late as 1914 the urban population was only 18 per cent of the total. Japan did not, moreover, have a primate city that accounted for most of the urban population. Large towns and cities existed throughout the country.

Along with the growth of towns went the rise of the merchant class. Although still ranking lowest in the official hierarchy, merchants' expanding wealth and influence, and the degree to which the samurai ruling class was dependent on them, constituted a major anomaly within the system. This anomaly became even more striking as the increase in merchant prosperity was accompanied by deterioration in the economic position of the ruling class. Bakufu and daimyo administrations found themselves in increasing economic difficulties as their income failed to keep pace with rising expectations of consumer expenditure and other demands on their budget. Successive coinage debasements promoted rampant inflation and daimyo borrowed extensively from rich merchants. The price of rice, which was in any case subject to considerable fluctuations, failed to keep pace with the increase in the prices of many other commodities purchased by samurai. Instead of raising samurai stipends, daimyo, who were in straits themselves, shifted the burden to their followers by, in part, withholding the stipends. Samurai retainers, too, borrowed heavily. Warrior indebtedness to the merchant class became endemic until, by the late Tokugawa period, the ruling stratum was in thrall to those it purported most to despise.

The samurai response to the potential threat posed by the merchants was a reassertion of their lowly political and social position. Moreover, the dependence of their prosperity on the status quo discouraged merchants from attempting to end their exclusion from overt political power and social pre-eminence. Merchants sought outlets for their wealth and desire for influence within the system. They found ways of evading the restrictive sumptuary laws. They fostered the development of a new, urban, cultural tradition. They evolved their own codes of conduct and social morality, in part modelled on those of the warrior class. So while merchant prosperity was the reverse side of warrior impoverishment, the vested interests of merchants in the Bakufu-*han* structure meant that they had more to fear from change than from continuation of the system.

The rapid urbanization of the seventeenth and eighteenth centuries was closely integrated with the agricultural economy, and dependent on the manner in which the fruits of agricultural production were distributed. The growth of towns was in large measure the result of an influx of migrants from the villages. The flow was not purely one way. Wealthy merchants often invested in land and rural industries. By contrast, after the 1720s a levelling off of population growth and the increasing economic problems of the ruling élite led to an absolute decline in the population of many towns and cities.[2] A shift in emphasis back to the rural areas was manifested by what might be termed an urbanization of the countryside. The expansion in the number and size of towns had already brought increasing numbers of villages within the urban orbit, stimulating them into commercial production for urban needs. Villages began to engage in increasing specialization within the general sphere of market gardening, with those nearest the towns producing the most perishable or bulky goods. Others engaged in the domestic production of handicrafts. Many village economies became more and more market orientated, but much of this increasingly commercialized production went untaxed, or was only lightly taxed. Here, if anywhere, was the source of peasant prosperity.

As agricultural specialization increased and farmers became less self-sufficient they, too, had consumer needs to be catered for. The division of labour in the towns spread outward to the rural areas. It was a trend that rules and regulations were powerless to halt. Landlords with money to spare and other entrepreneurs took advantage of such factors as space and improved communications to expand productive facilities to rural areas. A new breed of rural merchants flourished. Throughout the Edo period, though, the economies of town and countryside were closely interdependent. The growth of rural manufacturing and commercial dealings served to reinforce the integration of both into a single national economy.

Such integration did not, however, mean identity of interest. Mutual dependence also contained the seeds of conflict. The economic base of Japan as a whole remained overwhelmingly agrarian. Rural areas supplied not only agricultural products but also a considerable proportion of manufacturing output. Yet a tradition of urban centres of political power had been clearly established, and the members of the ruling class who were to determine the course of revolution and change came largely from urban backgrounds. The shift in the relative balance of economic and political power in later Tokugawa away from the Bakufu domains in the more urbanized centre of the country to its rivals on the peripheries, especially those in southwestern Honshu, Kyushu and Shikoku, did little to mitigate this urban emphasis among the national leadership. The limited dispersal of authority that accompanied the decline of Bakufu control in the closing years of Tokugawa rule was ruthlessly reversed by the centralizing policies of the Meiji regime after 1868. The interdependence of the rural and urban sectors remained as strong as ever, but under the impetus of new policies and the drive for industrialization a gulf between town and country, and in particular between Tokyo and the provinces, became increasingly marked.

For the new regime to achieve the economic and political status of a national government – unlike the Bakufu – meant the acquisition of undisputed political control over all parts of the country and the unquestioned right to tap its economic resources. This necessitated the abolition of the whole Bakufu-*han* system and the economic structure on which it rested. In 1871 the domains were abolished and all areas came under the control of administrators responsible to Tokyo. The new government also set about confirming the land ownership rights of individual members of the population, in order to establish the responsibility for tax payment. Land ownership rights were investigated and recognized by title deeds. Most land fell to the peasants who had tilled it for decades and the landlords or rentiers who held large amounts of land, renting it out or tilling it by hired labour. Prohibitions on transactions involving land were removed in 1873, and between 1873 and 1881 a large-scale reform of the land tax assessed all land for tax purposes. The aim of the reform was to provide the government with a stable source of revenue, as agriculture still had to provide the major part of government income. Whereas the old system had taken a percentage of the harvest, the new one levied tax on registered landowners as a percentage of the assessed monetary value of the land, 3 per cent in the first instance, plus a local government levy. This new system took into account the widespread variations in land quality and fertility, and hence output, but failed to allow for scanty harvests as a result of climatic or other factors. The land tax accounted for the lion's share of total government revenue throughout the 1870s and 1880s, and it was only towards the end of the century that it accounted for less than 50 per cent of tax income.

The land tax was thus the major source of funding for government activities during this period. Much of this capital found its way directly into the non-agricultural sphere, funding administration, the provision of armed forces, the building of a national infrastructure and production capacity. Some went indirectly to private industrial development by means such as subsidies. Capital was not the rural areas' only contribution to the development of the industrial economy. The agricultural sector managed to provide for the food needs of Japan's growing population. Very little food was imported up to World War I, and even after 1918 imports of foodstuffs accounted for a much smaller proportion of total imports than in some other industrial nations, particularly Britain. For much of the pre-1939 period agriculture was also a major source of exports, securing foreign exchange, which enabled Japan to purchase capital goods and raw materials from abroad. Silk was most important in this regard. From agriculture, too, came the labour force for Japan's expanding industries. In many countries in the early stages of industrialization agriculture has been a major source of foodstuffs, exports and labour, but the degree to which agriculture in Japan contributed capital over a sustained period is unusual.

Tokugawa agriculture was highly productive, and the amount levied in tax suggests that production was well above subsistence level. There is no reason to suppose that this changed after 1868. The rate of growth of agricultural output in the Meiji period is subject to considerable dispute,[3] but it is probable that a rate of around 1.8 per cent annual growth in output was maintained through to the early 1900s at least, far outstripping the rate of population growth in the same period. Growth was not achieved by any wholesale revolution in agricultural techniques. Central and local government worked hard to improve methods and disseminate new techniques. Active landlords promoted improvements in their villages. Fertilizers were more widely used. The granting of individual landownership rights improved incentives, and facilities for credit and investment improved. Most significant was an increase in working capital and an increase in labour inputs consequent on the technological changes introduced. The expanding non-agricultural sector itself provided farmers with new opportunities and incentives. Rice remained the main crop, but many farmers diversified.

Much of the benefit of this expansion accrued not to smaller farmers, but to central government or to large landowners and landlords. The government made little effort to conceal a belief that the rural sector had to pay for the development of the urban/industrial one. Violent peasant resistance led the government to reduce the tax rate in 1877 from 3 per cent to 2.5 per cent, but the rate of land tax remained high, accounting still for one-quarter to one-third of total production. Large numbers were forced into tenancy or became agricultural labourers. Others went off for extended periods as migrant (*dekasegi*[4]) workers or severed their ties with the land altogether. For many of those who did remain life was very hard; family members frequently had to seek outside employment on a part-time or short-term basis. The bleak accounts of life in the farming villages suggest that the majority of middle and lower peasants were little better off than hitherto. Many lived in squalor and poverty, went short of food when times were hard and were kept from starvation only by the meagre income they gained from non-farming pursuits, whether sidework or the labour of family members working further afield on a temporary or permanent basis. For many the income from agriculture alone could not support them. Farming families worked hard and long for scanty remuneration, and it is difficult indeed to see them as beneficiaries of the government's development policy.

In the depressed conditions of the interwar period and the aftermath of the disaster of the Pacific War, many commentators took the view that the economic, political and social costs to the rural sector of Japan's rapid industrialization were excessively high. The influence of Marxism on Japanese historiography strengthened the feeling that Japanese agriculture had been mercilessly exploited for the sake of industry. Yet we must be cautious in viewing the Japanese farmer as being on the losing end every time. There is evidence of a rise in rural demand and in traditional consumption. The obvious reluctance of many in the rural sector to seek work in the industrial sector, even on a temporary basis, points to an inclination to stay put far beyond what might be expected from a natural conservatism and apprehension of the unknown. The rapid rise in tenancy in the mid-Meiji period and its maintenance at a high level thereafter may not necessarily mean a wholesale polarization of rural wealth, but a keenness on the part of those who were able to work more land to rent extra plots to take advantage of improved market opportunities. Farmers actively responded to changing imperatives. Recent work on the interwar period has disputed that the plight of the peasantry even at this difficult time was as disastrous as has been claimed.[5] These revisions do not ask us to view the prewar Japanese peasant as a prosperous and independent cultivator, but they suggest that at least part of the rural sector was benefiting from the course of development. More significant for any assumptions concerning the long-term effects of rural suffering is the undoubted existence of a widely-held perception that the interests of the rural community were being sacrificed to those of the urban, industrial sector.

The economic hardship facing farmers worsened in the years after 1914. Farmers now suffered from inflation caused by the industrial boom of the war years. An increasing dependency on the market forced them to sell their crop cheaply immediately after the harvest and buy back later when speculation and other factors had increased its price. Nationwide rioting in 1918 over the price of rice started in rural areas and threatened to reduce the country to chaos. The government responded by promoting the expansion of cheap rice imports from the colonies of Formosa and Korea. These imports reached on average over 10 million *koku* a year in the late 1920s, equivalent to over 15 per cent of annual domestic production. They had a generally depressive effect on domestic rice prices, and threatened to undermine the prosperity of the majority of domestic farmers for whom rice was still a staple crop.

They became one of the factors that contributed to a degree of rural depression that persisted throughout the interwar years and was exacerbated by the deflationary policies pursued by successive governments. Another was population expansion. Between 1920 and 1930 the population of Japan jumped by 15 per cent to over 64 million; industrial sector growth was inadequate to absorb the increase. In agricultural production, too, the limits of the changes in working capital and labour input which had brought improvements earlier on were being reached.

From the late 1920s, depression rapidly became crisis. The interwar period was a difficult one for the world economy as a whole, characterized by widespread dislocation of, and fluctuations in, international trade. Japanese farmers were closely tied to the vagaries of the world markets. Many had long engaged in the production of cocoons for the silk industry, and as silk production rose dramatically in the interwar years more and more farmers engaged in this by-employment. Although silk prices fell after 1925 the additional cash income still cushioned farmers against the effects of a simultaneous fall in rice prices. Bumper rice crops in the late 1920s, however, combined with rice imports to produce a catastrophic fall in rice prices in 1930–1. At the same time the collapse of the American silk market in 1929–30 following the onset of the Great Depression brought a fall in silk prices of cataclysmic proportions. Many landlords found themselves in economic difficulties, and there was widespread impoverishment of tenants and small farmers. In the northeast in particular, poor harvests in the early 1930s led to famine conditions in some districts and an atmosphere of growing desperation. Conditions improved after 1933, but a measure of agricultural depression persisted through much of the 1930s. Official moves to alleviate the worst conditions were little more than palliatives. Rural depression was significant in two main ways. It served to prevent the industrial and military expansion pursued during those years from becoming excessively inflationary. It was also skilfully manipulated for political purposes.

Throughout the post-1868 years the rural–urban balance was shifting away from the countryside in the wake of rapid population increase and industrialization, although up to the Pacific War at least half the population continued to reside in small towns and villages, and there was little absolute fall in the rural population until the late 1930s. The rate of urbanization increased after 1868, and by 1920 nearly one-third of Japan's population lived in towns of over 10,000 people. By 1940 the figure was one-half. In the same year 20 per cent of the population was concentrated in a few metropolitan areas each with a population of over half a million. Many of the biggest cities dated back to the Tokugawa period. They included Tokyo (Edo), Osaka, Kyoto and many old castle towns. Other old foundations which were for locational or other reasons less well suited to the changing situation, stagnated or declined. Some expanding cities were the creations of the new era; Yokohama had been a mere fishing village in 1853, and Kobe, too, owed its expansion to foreign trade. Osaka maintained its importance as a financial, commercial and industrial centre, but despite a population of over 1.5 million in 1920 was still dwarfed by Tokyo, which was not only the locus of a highly centralized national administration but attracted financial, commercial, industrial, educational and cultural activities as well. At the time the city was devastated by a huge earthquake in 1923, the population of Tokyo was in excess of 3.5 million.

In a period when the social, political and economic priorities of the rural community would seem to have been largely disregarded, the attention paid to the urban sector did not lead to huge improvements in the social, political and economic environment of the inhabitants of the towns and cities. Many were little better off and little more contented than their rural counterparts, even during the years between the two world wars. Cities and towns were, of course, sometimes able to offer material benefits not available to the residents of the countryside. Drainage, street lighting, gas, public transport and a variety of shops created an aura of improved living standards attainable even by the poor. The better off could avail themselves of banking and credit facilities, shops selling luxury goods, culture in the form of theatres and other entertainment facilities. Educational opportunities might well be better than in the country, not to mention employment prospects outside the home. Yet the disparities of wealth and poverty were, if anything, even greater than in the countryside. While the rich could flaunt their wealth the numerous urban poor lived in a state of penury. Moreover, they were largely deprived of the stability and continuity of traditional rural life. While some city dwellers came from families long settled in urban areas, the vast majority of the swelling populations was the result of an influx from the countryside (temporary or permanent). Efforts to reproduce village patterns of organization and values in urban areas, or the emergence of new ones, could not prevent dislocation in social structure and family life.

The appalling conditions in which some urban and industrial workers lived and worked were first brought to public notice during the 1890s. Intellectuals, journalists and activists in the labour and farmers' movement attempted to gain the attention of the public and force the government to take action on urban and rural poverty, but achieved little substantial change. Despite the implementation of a Factory Act in 1916 and growing agitation in the early 1920s, many urban workers continued to work long hours for meagre wages in unhealthy and dangerous environments, and live on inadequate nourishment in slum conditions. Some who failed to find work remained unemployed and dependent on family or charity; others resorted to domestic contract outwork, where the conditions were just as bad as anything in nineteenth-century Europe. Yet villagers continued to flock in searching for work, lured by often misplaced hopes, discontented with their inability to secure a decent standard of living in the rural areas, or driven out by the impossibility of securing any living at all. There was no famine and for most urban residents conditions of life improved during the 1920s–1930s, but cities were by no means the havens of wealth and prosperity that hostile or covetous agricultural ideologues made them out to be. The vast benefits many farmers saw as accruing to cities as a result of rural exploitation were no more than illusory.

The perceived polarity of the urban and rural sectors was equally false. Industry was not a purely urban phenomenon. While the industrial sector remained small in real terms, much industrial production continued to be located in rural areas. Some employers took advantage of local workforces or environmental conditions. Others built on traditional industries. The all-important production of silk, for example, remained located outside the big urban centres throughout the prewar years. Moreover, much of the growing industrial labour force was not of urban origin. As the industrial sector grew, especially with the rapid post-1918 development of heavy industry, the concentration of industry in urban areas meant that members of the rural population could no longer maintain even a pretence of living off the land, and were more and more drawn away to the expanding cities. There was an accelerated flow of labour from one sector to the other. Some residents of the countryside, particularly younger sons, moved to urban areas on a permanent basis, but many were employed as *dekasegi* workers, away for anything up to three years or more. These workers regarded themselves as temporarily relieving their parents of the burden of supporting them and perhaps contributing something to the overall family budget. This is especially true of the female workers who constituted the bulk of the textile labour force throughout the prewar period, at a time when textiles were the key to exports and industrial growth. Yet other workers were employed in industry on a purely seasonal basis.

Even where workers moved away from their villages for good, most maintained contact with their places of origin and visited at regular intervals. The identification with the 'home town' (*furusato*) was carried on into the next, urban-born generation. When unemployment was bad those without alternative income returned to their native villages, where they might rely for support on family or communal networks. Like most economies in the early stages of industrialization, Japan's industrial workforce could not be immediately divided from its links with the countryside.

The hardships in the countryside in the 1930s were given an added bitterness by official rhetoric on the virtues of rural life. Since the Meiji period the farming community had been trumpeted as the guardian of the so-called 'traditional' Japanese virtues, the embodiment of all that was best in the Japanese family system. At the same time the rural interest had for the most part been neglected by the political powers-that-be. Industrialization had been seen as the key to international strength, and industrial development had been pushed forward regardless of rural and urban poverty, environmental damage and social and economic dislocation.

Calls for the promotion of agricultural development and welfare also dated from the Meiji government's emphasis on industrial and commercial growth. In the 1890s a prominent establishment figure, General Tani Kanjō, had called for greater attention to be given to the interests of the farming population. The mixture of agrarianist views put forward in subsequent years have tended to be lumped together under the heading of *nōhonshugi*, the concept of agriculture as the socio-economic base of society. *Nōhonshugi* was a combination of physiocratic theories, support for the traditional values of village society and structure, and a belief in the spiritual values of rural life. Agrarian thinkers shared a hatred of capitalism and urbanization, and sought to re-establish an owner-farmer based agriculture as the foundation of the national economy. With the continuing preponderance of the agricultural population this aspiration was not then as unrealistic as it might seem today.

Innately more conservative than its urban counterpart, the rural community had not for the most part engaged in widespread and overt political protest in response to the strains that were placed upon it. Radical agrarianism had little support. Even after universal manhood suffrage was introduced in 1925, the 'proletarian' parties gained most of their limited support from urban areas, and not, for all the poverty and discontent, the rural constituencies. Spates of tenant disputes in the early 1920s and 1930s were largely provoked by local issues. Tenants' unions were quashed as part of the suppression of left-wing movements. Yet the size of the rural community gave it a potent voice in political affairs.

The diverging fortunes of the agricultural and industrial sectors during the 1930s gave added substance to agrarian ideologues' claims of rural exploitation. The pro-agrarian rhetoric reached new heights and popular support for radical agrarianism increased. Militant agrarianist leaders such as Gondō Seikyō wielded a growing influence in depressed areas. More significantly, agrarianist sentiment became increasingly associated with extreme nationalist views. Many right-wing thinkers since the late nineteenth century had seen the sufferings and sacrifices of the rural community as just one aspect of Japan's development along an undesirable path. Advocacy of the agrarian community as the manifestation of the traditional Japanese spirit led agrarianist views to become more and more part of a broader nationalist ideology. The aspirations of those who wished to improve the lot of the rural sector became tied to wider political issues, and extremist agrarianists were prominent in some of the violent incidents of the early 1930s.

Evidence of popular agrarian-nationalism is one reason why the rural community was later identified as being a major support of ultranationalism and aggression. A second major factor in this identification was the link between the army and the rural community. The army had strong ties with the agricultural population through the system of conscription. Over the years a physical and emotional connection had been reinforced by the institution of army-sponsored organizations such as the reservists, through which the army established considerable control over village life. As the army's innately conservative values became increasingly influenced by ultranationalist thought, the villages from which many soldiers came continued to be seen as fertile areas of support. As the economic conditions in many areas became more desperate and the existing ruling élites seemed less and less able or willing to take corrective measures, radical domestic reform, external aggression and colonial possessions were seen by some of the rural poor as the only positively proposed solution to their ills. The army put itself forward as the vehicle for such policies, and in taking radical domestic and international action the army could count on a measure of support from the rural community.

Although the unanimity of rural enthusiasm for army policies is open to question, it is clear that the rural community did not really turn to the left in its search for a solution to its problems. There were active liberal or socialist-influenced tenants' and farmers' movements in the interwar period which sought to improve the farmers' lot. Like other elements of the left-wing movement, however, activists in this sphere were subjected to extensive government oppression, which prevented almost all activity until 1918 and hampered it severely from the late 1920s. The socialist movement as a whole was more preoccupied with the urban/industrial population. The rural community in Japan, like those in many other countries, was disinclined to abandon the old ways. Conservative values had been reinforced by the education system, by government policy, and by army activity. Ultranationalist thinking on the rural sector seemed in many ways only a more radical version of official views. All Japanese people were taught that the aggressive foreign policies pursued in the 1930s–1940s were Japan's destiny. For the rural population these policies could also be seen as the direct answer to its immediate problems.

The right wing in Japan was wholly correct in its perception that the industrialization process imposed considerable new strains on society as a whole. Nor did it remove the old ones. Poverty was widespread in town and country, living standards remained low, and even the pollution commonly identified as a postwar phenomenon can be found causing a major uproar in the 1890s.[6] Yet the experience of other countries suggests that the agricultural sector often bears a disproportionate share of the burdens imposed by rapid industrialization. Japan was not unique in the problems faced by her rural population, but her attempts to search for an external outlet for domestic discontent were unusually vigorous. To that extent rural distress, the fate of the agricultural sector at the hands of the industrialization policy and the countryside's position in the official ideology were in a very real sense major contributory factors to the disastrous warfare of 1937–45.

Despite hopes to the contrary, the war gradually worsened rather than alleviated the problems of the rural population. The human suffering resulting from war they shared with other Japanese. The conscription of manpower into the armed forces and war-related industries deprived agriculture of the strongest and most able element of its workforce at a time when the production process was still relatively unmechanized. Supplies of agricultural machinery dwindled, and with the chemical industries geared increasingly towards war production the supply of fertilizers also decreased. With the country more and more forced into self-sufficiency, land was exhaustively cultivated, and by the closing stages of the war, when supplies from abroad had completely dried up, domestic production had fallen far below the 1941 level. The influx of children evacuated from the cities after 1943 meant extra unproductive mouths to feed, and by the time they were followed by adult evacuees in any number the dislocation of the agricultural sector was beyond rapid repair. On top of this came the sundry depradations of military and civilian authorities desperate to feed the armed forces and urban population in the face of totally inadequate harvests.

In as far as they were less likely to be increasingly forced to resort to bribery to obtain scant food supplies at a time when the official ration was totally inadequate, farmers were better off than their urban counterparts. A few farmers even managed to do very well out of the exorbitant prices charged to urban residents for a few mouthfuls of grain. However, the government's implementation of strict price controls and a rigid quota system hindered farmers from benefiting from the shortage or from the black market sales. Some were barely able to support themselves, let alone provide for the urban sector. War failed to be the hoped-for panacea for the afflictions of Japan's farmers. Paradoxically the Occupation came much closer to being that.

In their efforts to pinpoint the causes of Japanese aggression and warmongering, the allies' experts on Japan had long before 1945 reached the conclusion that the structure of land ownership was a fundamental evil. They believed that the conversion of Japan into a nation of prosperous owner-farmers was crucial if a democratic, peace-loving state was to become a reality. A drastic reform of the land tenure system was thus a primary objective of the Occupation authorities and was implemented in late 1946. Under the reform individual private landholding was restricted to an area of 3 *chō*[7] for most of the country; of this area no more than a third could be rented out. Any land in excess of this maximum was subject to compulsory purchase by the government. Absentee landownership was prohibited. The excess land was mostly sold to existing tenants. The purchase and sale of the land was carried out at fixed 1945 prices at a time of rampant inflation, which meant that landlords were virtually expropriated and farmers were able to pay off the purchase price and own their land outright in a year or two. The failure of the reformers to incorporate the all-important forest land into the settlement and the neglect of the landholdings of the imperial family were criticized, but the effects of the land reform were far-reaching. It succeeded at a stroke in reducing tenanted land from over 45 per cent of the cultivated area to under 10 per cent. Remaining tenants were more secure than hitherto. Absentee landlords and large concentrations of landholdings were virtually eliminated. Most farmers were now independent owner-farmers with small holdings. The transformation went far beyond the narrowly economic; it wrought a fundamental change in the structure and behaviour of village society and reduced rural discontent to a genuinely low level.

No reform could of itself guarantee immediate and lasting prosperity for individual farmers, nor would the pattern of landholding established by the reform necessarily last. There was a growth in the concentration of landholdings from the late 1940s, but the limits remained restrictive, and agitation for their relaxation has increased. Overall the patterns established by the 1946 land reform have been remarkably enduring. Little over 15 per cent of farmers are now tenants, and fewer than 2 per cent own no land of their own, most tenanted land being rented to supplement existing holdings. The agricultural sector has continued to be both the supporter and beneficiary of urban and industrial development, and the rural population has enjoyed a very considerable prosperity in the years since 1947. The changes that have affected rural population and landholding patterns are due less to the profitability or otherwise of agriculture itself than to developments pertaining to the economy as a whole.

The conversion into owner-farmers of those who had hitherto been tenants or agricultural labourers provided many for the first time with genuine prospects of making a decent living, unburdened by debts, high rents or heavy taxes. This proved an undoubted incentive for increased productivity and output. Furthermore, despite the neglected state of agriculture at the end of the war, Japan's farmers were in a relatively advantageous position. In the face of appalling shortages and rampant inflation after Japan's surrender, food supplies were at a premium and those fortunate enough to control any of the scarce agricultural output were able to charge high prices. On the rampant black market prices were particularly exorbitant. Farmers had purchased land at quite unrealistic prices at the time of the reform and were not burdened with long-term borrowing. These benefits, which accrued from inflation, far outweighed its disadvantages, such as increased prices for equipment and other working capital. One factor of production that remained cheap in the early years after 1945 was labour. The critical situation in the towns and cities in the closing stages of the war meant that much of the urban population had fled to the countryside. The long-standing links between urban workers and their *furusato* in the countryside were exploited to the full as refugees from urban areas sought help from their country relatives. With the repatriation of around six million Japanese military and civilian personnel from overseas in the years 1945–7, the rural population swelled to even greater proportions. This labour supply was exploited to the full by farmers, though far from all the urban refugees could find agricultural employment. Between 1940 and 1950 the proportion of the working population engaged in agriculture actually rose from 44 to 48 per cent.

Prewar production levels were not regained until the early 1950s, and not until even later were 1930s agricultural productivity levels exceeded. From then on there was a sustained increase in output and productivity, which has continued through to the 1980s. While earlier growth was more dependent on manpower and the recovery factor, increases in working capital and improved techniques played a major role subsequently. The use of better fertilizers and seed strains became widespread. The near universality of agricultural cooperatives for purchasing, marketing and savings activities made for more efficient organization and greater security for farmers. Mechanization had always been difficult due to the dominance of wet-rice production and the small scale of cultivation, but from the early 1960s new forms of mechanization adapted to the conditions of Japanese agriculture were developed. The increasingly urban nature of Japan as a whole after 1950 stimulated diversification of production. By the early 1970s rice accounted for less than a third of production by value, with the biggest increase showing in market gardening and animal-based products. Governmental support for the farming community through the medium of rice support prices has kept rice production well above the level required for domestic consumption and slowed the move away from rice production. The maintenance of rural support is crucial to the continuation of the Liberal Democratic Party in power.

The growth and prosperity of the agricultural sector in the postwar years have stemmed not merely from the new institutional framework and advances in technology. Agriculture has also been the beneficiary of rapid industrial growth and urban development, which have created expanding market opportunities. In return, agriculture's contribution to the industrial and urban sectors, though quantitatively less substantial than in the prewar years, has remained important. Japanese agriculture is no longer a major source of capital and exports, but it has reduced Japan's dependence on foreign foodstuffs. Certain leading commodities, such as soya beans and wheat, have long been imported, but other staple items of the diet are still domestically produced. Imports of foodstuffs as a whole have grown rapidly in recent years. Eating habits have changed under external influences, and it is not always easy for farming to adapt to such changes.

Agriculture has also provided the expanding industrial and tertiary sectors with their labour force. Although much of Japan's population flocked to the countryside after 1943, as urban prospects improved many returned to the cities. The rural sector had been dependent on external aid to support these people, and was in any case unable to employ all of them. The post-1950 returnees were joined by some who had never before left the villages. Right through the postwar decades there has been a steady flow of labour from the rural to urban areas, from agricultural to non-agricultural occupations. By 1985 less than 9 per cent of the employed population was in the primary sector. The flow of labour was sustained by the greater efficiency in farming. The rapid rate of mechanization from the 1960s was particularly important in releasing male labour, and only a small proportion of farmers' sons now expect to follow their fathers on the land. In 1985 only 2.4 per cent of farmers' sons finding employment were engaged in farming.

Even where a household is categorized as a farming household there is a high probability that family members will be employed outside the farming sector and much of the household's income will also be drawn from outside it. There is a long tradition of by-employment, much of it non-agricultural in nature, in Japanese farming families, and the extension of this practice since 1945 – accentuated by the sharp decline of the previously all-important silkworm cultivation – has made part-time farming a dominant feature of the rural sector. Farming, though still relatively profitable, employs few families on a full-time basis. Of a total of 3.75 million farm households in 1985 over 83 per cent were part-time farmers. With much of the labour flow into industry permanent, rather than of the temporary migrant pattern common in the prewar years, the population structure of many rural areas is distorted, with most agricultural work carried out by the elderly, women and children. Rural depopulation is a matter of serious concern.

The mutual interdependence between rural and urban areas which characterized the prewar period is by no means completely gone, but it is waning fast. Agriculture has fewer and fewer workers to give up to industry or the tertiary sector, and short-term migrant or daily labour has steadily declined from a peak in the 1960s. Seasonal work is also on the decline. Many of those who call themselves farmers because they still own land derive the major part of their incomes from non-agricultural occupations. Some urban families do still look back to their rural roots; while they may never have lived in the areas from which their ancestors originally came, they may make regular visits to the *furusato* and bring up their children to do likewise. This practice, however, is becoming increasingly difficult to sustain. As the base of the Japanese economy becomes more and more industrial and commercial, less and less dependent on the support of the rural sector, and as the shrinking agricultural sector in its turn has less to offer to the rest of the economy, this mutual interdependence between the two sectors will diminish still further. Moreover, following the discrediting of the official ideology after Japan's defeat, the concept of the farming family as the haven of traditional virtue and morality lost much of its influence. The rapid decline in the number of such families has further undermined belief in this ideal. The rural idyll remains strongly evocative in most industrialized societies, but the emotional hold it formerly possessed over the minds of most Japanese has been substantially weakened. Calls for a revival of traditional values are not infrequent, but with so many Japanese now detached from the rural sector the farming community could no longer act as the main standard bearer of such a revival. Its role could at best be a backward-looking one, symbolic and historical.

For many Japanese the rural areas are now more important for the welcome respite they offer to those seeking temporarily to escape the pressures of city life, for inevitably the mushrooming of industry and commerce has led to a massive increase in the rate of urbanization. Population growth has slowed considerably, but by the early 1980s around 65 per cent of the Japanese population lived in towns of over 50,000 people, and half the population in what were categorized as 'densely inhabited districts'. In as far as there is an average Japanese, he or she is very much a town dweller. The mountainous terrain predisposes the country to industrial and residential concentration, and a considerable proportion of the population is located in a narrow urban belt running from the Kantō plain round Tokyo down to Kobe. With a population of 121 million by 1987 and limited habitable areas the population density of many Japanese cities was among the highest in the world, and is still increasing.

During the 1950s–1960s the growth of cities followed the growth of industry, but subsequently intense concern over overcrowding, pollution and transport congestion stimulated revived interest in locating industry away from residential areas, in particular establishing strategic industrial and processing centres on the coast where shipping facilities are convenient. Prime Minister Tanaka's *Plan for Remodelling the Japanese Archipelago* published in 1972 symbolized a hope that a fundamental restructuring could be achieved to improve the quality of life in Japan. For the most part, though, these aspirations regarding a new industrialization of the countryside remain unachieved.

The overwhelming dominance of the urban areas – in particular, the metropolitan regions around Tokyo, Osaka and Nagoya – in most areas of national life is having a far more devastating effect on village life than might stem just from better employment opportunities. The cities boast facilities for consumption, recreation and entertainment, with which rural areas cannot even hope to compete. Although urban dwellers troop out to the countryside at the first available opportunity and nature plays a significant part in Japanese sentiment, the cultural and other attractions of the cities have a magnetizing effect in an era which has produced a strong emphasis on material rather than spiritual wealth. The lure of urban life is especially powerful for the rural young, who may not be short of money, but who often have fewer outlets for spending it. Authorities concerned over rural depopulation have attempted to provide for the consumer and cultural needs of rural dwellers, but the drift has persisted. The political influence of the countryside remains disproportionately strong, but in other respects it is now the urban centres which dominate the economic, social and cultural life of Japan.

The perceived difference in interest and the rural hostility towards the urban sector that wielded such a powerful influence in the interwar years have not completely disappeared. The depopulation and lack of facilities in rural areas indicates to a few that industrial expansion is detrimental to country life. The concept of the rural sector being exploited by the urban one retains some potency in such a centralized nation as Japan, and rural resentment at some of the decisions of Japan's urban-oriented rulers is widespread. The fight against the construction of Tokyo's new airport at Narita, although led by environmentalist and anti-establishment groups, tapped this resentment.

As long as the country continues to enjoy prosperity sufficient to accommodate both agricultural and industrial sectors large-scale open conflict is unlikely. Moreover, as the urban/industrial complex becomes ever more predominant agricultural resentment will become less vocal and the rural sector's capacity to oppose weaker. The post-1945 years have produced a fundamental restructuring of the pattern of economic activity on a scale never achieved by the prewar industrialization. Its political influence notwithstanding, the agricultural sector in Japan is no longer of substantial economic importance. In 1984 it produced only 3.1 per cent of GNP. Even a disastrous industrial slump would not now bring a major return to the countryside or substantial growth in the relative importance of agriculture. Sooner or later the political balance, too, must be redressed to the disadvantage of the countryside. Such a change would set the final seal on what is perhaps the most radical transformation Japan has gone through in the last few decades: the disappearance of the farming community as a fundamental axis of politics, the economy and society and the emergence of Japan as a fully-fledged urban, industrial society.

NOTES

1   1 *koku* = 4.96 bushels. (This measurement invariably referred to rice, although it could be used for other commodities.)
2   The levelling off of population growth in the latter Tokugawa era is the subject of much debate among historians and is closely tied to discussion of the standard of living at this time.
3   A good account of this debate can be found in P. Francks, *Technology and Agricultural Development in Pre-War Japan* (New Haven and London, 1984), ch.2.
4   *Dekasegi* literally means 'working away from home'; it embraced all who left their homes to work either on a seasonal basis or for a period of years.
5   See, for example, R.J. Smethurst, *Agricultural Development and Tenancy Disputes in Japan 1870–1940* (Princeton, 1986).
6   The pollution caused by the Ashio Copper Mine in Tochigi from the 1880s was a major and long-running political scandal.
7   Around 7 acres. In Hokkaido 12 *chō* was the permitted maximum, to allow for the sparser population and the less intensive character of farming.

CHAPTER SIX
The Pattern of Industrial Development

One of the most remarkable features of Japan's modern history is the speed, scale and apparent success of the growth of industry. There is evidence of industrial and commercial development long before the modern period, but the past century has transformed Japan from a predominantly rural country into a highly industrialized one. The current debate over how far other countries can learn from Japan's experience makes it particularly important to see Japan's postwar industrial expansion in the context of the country's longer term industrial development.

Agriculture remained the socio-economic base of the country in the Tokugawa period, but there were nevertheless considerable advances in industrial and, in particular, commercial activity. Commerce centred on the merchants of the castle towns and Osaka. Large-scale urban development in turn fuelled increased commercialization and monetization of the economy. Many Tokugawa merchants became highly specialized and engaged in a variety of sophisticated commercial practices, ranging from the issue of credit notes (which served as the most widely trusted form of national paper currency) to speculation in rice and other futures. Elsewhere, ever more of the population – peasants, artisans and samurai – were brought within the sphere of commercialization and the money economy. Even in the 1690s a rare foreign observer, Engelbert Kaempfer,[1] commented on the scale of the retail trade in Japan, and by the mid-nineteenth century commercial activity was something with which almost all Japanese were to some extent acquainted.

Within the parameters of small-scale, traditional modes of operation industrial activity also grew. Manufacturing activity had originally been the exclusive province of the artisan caste, whose status had been defined by their work as craftsmen. At the beginning of the Tokugawa period artisans mostly acted as independent operators maintaining their own workshops for the manufacture and sale of their products. Many continued to operate on this basis. However, as the period progressed the importance of hired labour increased. Members of the merchant class advanced capital to artisans, supplied them with raw materials and tools or sold their products for them. Commercial interests were extended to industrial ones in what often became a putting-out system, although it is difficult to tell how widespread this practice was by the end of the Tokugawa period. Other attempts to control the operations of artisans, especially those in castle towns, came from domain authorities, who, eager to supplement their inadequate incomes, attempted to institute *han* monopolies on the production and sale of certain commodities.

The peasantry also produced many craft items. Such activity had originally been an integral part of subsistence agriculture, and while the production of some commodities was increasingly taken over by specialist artisans, the majority of peasants continued to produce many of their own needs, including food, clothing and tools. With the increasing commercialization of the economy many peasants both bought more for cash and engaged in production for the market. While the bulk of this production was agricultural commodities, including industrial raw materials such as raw silk, it also included handicraft goods. Agricultural work was in any case seasonal, freeing peasants for other activities. Poorer peasants in particular, for whom handicraft income was often essential, found themselves, like the urban artisans, depending on wealthier members of society for loans, raw materials and marketing.

As urban growth tailed off after the early eighteenth century there was an upsurge in industrial activity in the countryside. Operation was often on a semi-capitalist basis, and the labour force was mostly of peasant origin. Prominent in this activity were provincial and rural merchants traditionally involved in operations such as sake (rice wine) brewing and moneylending. Many extended their range of interests and became involved in the production of a whole range of commodities. Textiles, notably silk and cotton, were particularly important. *Han* authorities also became involved with manufacturing production by the peasantry, as they sought to extend *han* monopolies to agricultural products such as indigo, and noted local craft goods. Bakufu and *han* recruited impoverished peasants to work in mines.

There was nothing approaching the modern factory. Levels of mechanization and use of motive power were very low and most production was carried on by individual peasant families in their own homes. Nevertheless by the 1850s there did exist a small number of manufactories where a range of processes were carried on under the same roof. There were also peasant workers operating on a putting-out system, receiving raw materials and even tools from putting-out masters and providing labour in return. For many families such work as this provided a substantial part of the total family income, often exceeding the income received from agriculture. The move towards an emergence of wage labour and the division of labour was apparent in both town and countryside.[2]

The opening of the country after 1853 exposed the economy to goods from the factories of Western Europe and the United States. The treaties Japan concluded with the West deprived indigenous Japanese industries of substantial tariff protection. A flood of foreign products was released into the economy, dislocating both the monetary system and domestic industry. Worst hit were textiles. Indigenous cotton production suffered from the import of cheap machine-spun yarn of a quality with which domestic producers could not compete. Cotton piece goods posed a further threat. The impact on silk was quite different. Silkworm disease in Europe at this time fortuitously meant a massive foreign demand for silkworm eggs, cocoons and raw silk. Exports boomed, but at the cost of forcing up prices to a level where domestic silk weavers could no longer afford to purchase their raw material. Within a few years the silk-weaving industry was in disarray.

The few Japanese able to travel abroad were stunned by the technological gap between the West and Japan, but bridging it was no easy matter. The Bakufu, despite a tradition of official intervention in the economy, was still unsure whether its attitude to the West should be emulation or rejection. Preoccupied by the worsening political position at home, it was too weak to engineer the wholesale adoption of Western industrial practices even had it wished to do so. The devolution of so much decision-making to the various *han* would in any case have limited the influence of any industrialization programme outside its own territories. In the event, official moves in the direction of an industrial transformation were piecemeal and small-scale. Plans formulated under French guidance during the last two years of Bakufu rule to introduce Western-style production methods on a modest scale were thwarted by the Tokugawa fall from power. The Bakufu's only lasting achievements in the introduction of Western technology were in dockyard construction and armaments production. Some Japanese were trained to operate warships and merchant vessels imported from the West.

A few powerful domains pursued similar policies. In the forefront was Satsuma, whose daimyo constructed a water-powered manufacturing complex and later Japan's first steam-powered cotton spinning mills. For the most part, though, domains were no more able and willing than individual entrepreneurs to experiment with new techniques.

With the revolution of 1868 Japan had for the first time a central government with sufficient power to try to implement an ambitious plan of industrialization along Western lines. The programme of change involved the government in industrialization to an almost unprecedented degree. Only imperial Germany pursued a similar interventionist role, at a time when in Britian *laissez-faire* doctrines were still widely upheld. The motivation behind Western-style industrialization seems in retrospect only too obvious. Japan had in the course of less than two decades been made abundantly aware of her own inadequacies in the face of Western pressure. She saw other nations in Asia being subjected to political subjugation, colonization and economic exploitation. The civilization of China was under threat. The only way of protecting economic and political independence appeared to be to build Japan into a strong and united state with Western-style institutions capable of competing with the West on the West's own terms. The adoption of an industrialization policy was an integral part of this strategy, since industrial power seemed to be a foundation of Western strength. The new regime's commitment to radical change became apparent as early as April 1868, when the Charter Oath stated that knowledge would be sought throughout the world and evil customs of the past abolished.

A coherent industrialization policy required activity in a variety of related fields, and government involvement was wide-ranging, if not always systematic. Government activity ranged from the provision of financial, commercial and physical infrastructure, and of industrial and other education and training, through industrial exhibitions and the encouragement of private entrepreneurs by legislative and financial means to direct engagement in industrial production. The fundamental principle was the selective and closely controlled use of Western know-how and personnel in a way which would enable Japan as soon as possible to stand on her own feet. Both government and private business hired large numbers of foreign experts during the 1870s to act as advisers, engineers and administrators. These individuals – referred to as *oyatoi*, 'hired' foreigners – were paid huge salaries and enjoyed a privileged life; in return their experience and expertise were tapped for all they were worth. The danger of excessive foreign influence was minimized by such experts remaining subordinate to Japanese on all but technical matters. By the mid-1880s most had left Japan, in some cases before their Japanese successors were really capable of independent operation. Foreign know-how was also secured by sending Japanese abroad, either for training or to survey the various techniques available in a specific field with a view to selecting those that most accorded to Japan's needs.

The import of foreign technology and capital goods had to be paid for, either by taking out substantial loans or by establishing a successful export trade. Fearing that extensive foreign borrowing might weaken Japan's international position, the Japanese government took out only a very few foreign loans before 1900. They also sought to avoid a deficit on commodity trade. Japan was fortunate in being able to build on the export trade established during the 1860s. The two most important commodities were tea and silk. Tea was already widely produced and Japanese tea quickly proved itself capable of competing with and complementing tea exports from China. The real money-spinner was silk. Most Japanese silk was hand reeled, and much of it was too uneven in texture to be used by the mechanized factories of the West. Well aware that the effects of the silkworm disease in Europe which had initially boosted the silk trade would not last for ever, the government sought to improve both quantity and quality of Japanese raw silk. Systems of inspection and standardization of products destined for export were improved. In 1872 a government-run Western-style reeling mill started operation in Tomioka (Gunma Prefecture). Supervised by French personnel, the aim of this model factory was not so much to produce high-quality goods for export, but to disseminate new techniques to private silk producers. Engineers, technicians and reelers were trained at Tomioka, and then sent to teach in newly established mills elsewhere. As such it was a major focus of training in skills vital to the silk industry.[3] In other respects Tomioka enjoyed mixed success. Few individual entrepreneurs had at their disposal the vast sums poured into Tomioka by the government. Production methods at many privately owned mills were cobbled together from traditional and Western practices and bore little resemblance to those at the model mill. Moreover, Tomioka was never profitable under government ownership. After initial problems of transition in the 1870s, the initiative in the silk industry rapidly passed from the government. Private entrepreneurs spearheaded a vast expansion in silk production, mostly in non-urban areas. Right through to 1914 the industry provided around one-third of Japan's exports by value.

The government was also directly involved in production in the war-related industries, in particular munitions and dockyard work. The Meiji government capitalized upon the enterprises in this field which it had inherited from the Bakufu. By the 1890s Japan was self-sufficient in many items of military equipment and able to repair, though not construct, its own warships. While it can be argued that the vast sums devoted to military expenditure – on average *c*.25 per cent of the government budget per annum 1879–1912 – might have been used more productively, the munitions factories acted as centres for the absorbtion and dissemination of modern techniques and skills, and fuelled the economy as a whole, providing demand and contributing to capital formation. Defence expenditure also made a vital contribution to Japan's retention of sovereignty and independence.

The government also set up other model plants during the 1870s to introduce new techniques in unfamiliar industries which demanded considerable capital expenditure and were associated with considerable risk for the private entrepreneur. They included factories producing cement, glass and bricks.

The growth of production, however, was dependent on the availability of facilities for transport and communication and an internationally recognized machinery for trade and financial operation. Only the government could attempt to provide the necessary infrastructure as a matter of urgency. Roads were inadequate, railways non-existent, shipping largely coastal and sail-powered, and communications in general unreliable and slow. There were no banks, stock exchanges or currency regulation. Provision of many of these facilities entailed capital investment of a scale no private entrepreneur could command and implementation required a nationwide authority which only the government possessed. Thus the government here took over much of the entrepreneurial function. By the early 1880s young bureaucrats located in the Finance, Home and Industry ministries had spearheaded efforts to build an efficient nationwide telegraph and postal network, a coordinated system of road transport on much improved roads and Japan's first railway. Under the guidance of Finance Minister Matsukata Masayoshi[4] Japan had moved towards the establishment of a stable financial and commercial system within which industry and trade could operate with a degree of security.

In some areas, the government had no choice but to move slowly. The undertaking of the building of even a short length of railway track was a costly operation in an unknown field. The first short line, between Tokyo and Yokohama, was built with a British loan and completed in September 1872, but the Japanese government was unwilling to borrow further for railway building, which in so many other countries has been a major focus for foreign investment. Instead it turned to assisting legislation. Not until after the first private railway boom of the late 1880s, however, did railways begin to have a widespread impact upon the country. By the time the government nationalized much of the system in 1906 there were nearly 8,000 kilometres of track.

In the all-important field of commercial shipping the Japanese success was particularly conspicuous. Here the government early on refrained from direct involvement through a state-owned company, instead promoting the business through the considered sponsorship of a leading entrepreneur. Other examples of government patronage of private business exist, but the official assistance given to the Mitsubishi company is the most significant example of this form of industrial promotion. The government had inherited ships from the Bakufu, and in 1872 established its own Postal Steamship Company as the intended nucleus of Japan's merchant shipping fleet. Its main competitor was the Mitsubishi company. Iwasaki Yatarō, founder of Mitsubishi, was a native of Tosa *han* who after the Restoration had taken over his former domain's shipping interests and used them to build up his own flourishing company. So inefficient was the Postal Steamship Company that the authorities did not feel able to award it the contract for carriage of men and supplies on the Formosan Expedition of 1874. This went instead to Mitsubishi. In the light of this failure, officials moved for the government company to be disbanded and its ships handed over to Mitsubishi, and for Mitsubishi to receive government patronage to enable it to form the nucleus of a powerful merchant shipping fleet. The adoption of this policy took Mitsubishi from strength to strength. After 1875 it entered international routes. In 1885 it merged with its main competitor and, under the title NYK, became one of the world's major shipping lines. Responsible for carrying a large amount of Japan's trade, it was a powerful competitor to older European companies in the Pacific area. NYK became independent of other Mitsubishi concerns after 1886, but for the Iwasaki family (Yatarō himself died in 1885), shipping interests served as a foundation upon which to construct a huge commercial and industrial empire.

Numerous other entrepreneurs, many originating from the same domains as the leading members of the government, were the recipients of considerable government favours. Some were referred to as 'political merchants' (*seishō*). Mitsui, for example, handled much of the government's financial business. Others were the beneficiaries of substantial orders for items such as armaments. A conspicuous source of advantage was the sale of government enterprises in the early 1880s. Most of the government's model undertakings, though significant as models of technology and operation, had operated at a considerable loss. As part of its deflationary policy after 1880 the government pursued a withdrawal from direct involvement in industrial development and sold off its enterprises at ridiculously low prices. Their purchasers received, for very little, enterprises which had got through their worst teething troubles. Before long most were operating at a profit. Government-owned mines were also sold off at this time. Government favouritism of this kind helped many of these men to secure monopolistic, or oligopolistic, positions in specific industrial or commercial fields. These served as bases from which they could extend their business interests, enabling the eventual appearance of the huge economic concerns known as *zaibatsu*.[5]

The relationship between government and private entrepreneurs indicates that important as the government role may have been, its significance lay largely in enabling the private sector to innovate and prosper. Japan's development from the Meiji period was dependent on a unique partnership between public and private entrepreneurship. This public–private cooperation stemmed in no small part from the fact that the members of each sector had shared long-term aims and agreed ways of going about things. The gulf between the state and the private sector did widen significantly later on, but in the early Meiji period it scarcely existed. In the 1870s government officials themselves acted as entrepreneurs, and the government's withdrawal from entrepreneurial activity and the increasing professionalization of the bureaucracy after 1880 were accompanied by a marked shift of government personnel into the private sector. Private entrepreneurs were often of the same background as many of the government's leaders; personal contacts were frequently close. The leaders of the public and private sectors comprised a relatively unified entrepreneurial élite, and a community of interest and origins was throughout the Meiji period the foundation of government-business unity. Even afterwards an enduring tradition of government involvement and guidance facilitated the direction of private enterprise along desired channels in ways which appeared not to constrain business decision-making.

Much has been written about the supposed uniqueness of these nineteenth-century Japanese businessmen. The quality of Japanese entrepreneurship has often been cited as a crucial ingredient in Japan's success where other countries have failed. Even before the end of the Edo period entrepreneurship had spread well beyond the confines of the merchant class, and after the Restoration entrepreneurs came from the ranks of samurai, merchants, peasants and artisans. The origins of many remain unclear. A reluctance to engage in new and unknown activities was widespread. Many Tokugawa merchants were too bound up with the old status quo to make a successful transition to the new age. By contrast the Tokugawa merchant house of Mitsui acted as one of the government's bankers in its early years and went on to build up the largest financial and commercial empire in Japan. The survival of Mitsui and other merchant houses was, however, dependent on radical changes in management and attitudes.

Samurai would seem to have comprised the largest single status group among leading entrepreneurs. Such men had a relatively high degree of education, and tended to advance into new and unknown activities for reasons of both curiosity and financial need. Some possessed substantial amounts of capital (mostly through stipend commutation) which could be invested in new enterprises. Their contacts with government were particularly close. Disputes concerning the numerical dominance of samurai or quasi-samurai among rising entrepreneurs cannot detract from the crucial role of samurai entrepreneurs in forging close contacts between political and business leaders or from their willingness to set the pace for the entrepreneurial class as a whole.

Under the Tokugawa regime commercial and industrial activity was considered demeaning and unfitted to a member of the ruling class. More than a relic of this attitude endured the shock of the Restoration. Many Japanese, especially samurai, continued to regard commercial activity in this way and to look down on anyone involved in it. Realization that such views could render abortive any hope of industrialization stimulated the cultivation of a new business ethic. In an effort to dissociate themselves from the despised traditional merchant and achieve substantial status in Meiji society, many Meiji entrepreneurs went out of their way to assert their strong patriotic feelings and proclaim their desire to do what was good for the nation rather than that which most benefited their own pockets. The most articulate voice in this campaign was that of Shibusawa Eiichi, a prodigiously successful businessman who turned his hand to a multiplicity of new enterprises and industries and was one of the major innovators of the time. The government provided powerful support. The evocation of the nationalist businessman, the industrial samurai embarking on new and untried ventures for the good of the nation, proved so persuasive that within little more than two decades the stigma formerly attached to industrial and commercial activity was insignificant. The ethic that Japanese entrepreneurs were not merely profit-seeking capitalists but 'community centred' and patriotic was so well propagated that not only many contemporaries, but many historians as well, have been persuaded of the truth of its claims. In the 'nationalist' approach lies the much-vaunted 'uniqueness' of Japanese entrepreneurs.

Certainly many Meiji businessmen did indeed undertake risky and innovative ventures which were hardly justified on the grounds of profit alone. More than a few took such risks repeatedly, trying their hands at a variety of undertakings, sometimes succeeding in the end, sometimes not. The willingness of these men to risk their capital and reputation (as well as those of others) is not in doubt. That the ultimate rationale for such risk-taking was the good of the nation, however, has been widely accepted, and doubts more recently expressed concerning this *raison d'être* are long overdue. In the first place the Meiji background was such that any undertaking whatsoever was justified on the grounds that it was in the best interests of the nation. This became particularly true after the reaction against unadulterated Western influence in the late 1880s. Against such a background it would have been inconceivable for businessmen to have justified their activities on any other grounds. The attention they have received is perhaps more due to the business class's greater need to make such claims and the effectiveness with which it succeeded in putting its case across, as well as the desire of historians to pinpoint the factors behind Japan's rapid industrialization. It is, moreover, unthinkable to believe that any entrepreneur who time after time makes losses will for long retain the confidence of others. Risks were taken because the period was conducive to risk-taking, because financial support could be mobilized and because, on the occasions when such risk-taking paid off, profits were considerable. The most outstanding businessmen were ultimately those who made the biggest profits and proved themselves as entrepreneurs, not those who could boast only patriotic motivation and a string of failures. Meiji entrepreneurs were certainly nationalistic, but it is hard to believe that as a group they were any more patriotic than the rest of the population. To say that they were convinced by their own rhetoric is not to accuse them of hypocrisy.

The pattern of industrial expansion pursued by public and private sectors at this time had a lasting impact on the structure of Japanese industry. The most significant of these enduring characteristics is perhaps the coexistence within sectors of the economy and individual industries of very large and very small firms, and of the parallel existence of firms making Western-style goods and those catering in traditional needs. This phenomenon, often referred to as 'dualism', is still conspicuous in the postwar Japanese economy.

It is not surprising that the encounter between Japan's highly developed indigenous culture and the industrialized economies of the West should lead to the emergence of both 'traditional' and Western industries. Japan could not transform its way of life overnight along Western lines, and in fact chose to lay a particularly strong emphasis upon the 'indigenous tradition'. Some industries catering to traditional needs in, for example, food production, housing, clothing and artefacts, were capable of adaptation to factory production and mechanization, but for most of the Meiji period even these still tended to produce on a relatively small scale for a local market, in marked contrast to the large-scale factory production dominant in the production of Western-type goods. Production of other traditional items was less amenable to large-scale operation, and this led to the persistence of many operations along traditional craft lines. Over subsequent years traditional tastes and modes of living were, of course, modified by Western contact, and technological advance enabled the mechanized production of a wider range of goods; nevertheless a polarity between 'Japanese' and 'Western' products continued to exist. This polarity has been a major factor in producing the juxtaposition of large and small enterprises which has become so much a feature of Japan's industrial structure.

The trend towards very large-scale production on the one hand and very small on the other was often accentuated by the industrial policy of the Meiji government. Official promotion of Western-style factories and methods did not necessarily lead to the rise of large companies. The model Tomioka mill, for example, operated on a scale which private entrepreneurs found difficult to emulate. The silk industry remained characterized by the relatively small scale of its factory operation and the large number of individual entrepreneurs engaged in production. As time passed factories did become larger in scale and many came under the control of great financial combines, but in the Meiji period at least mechanized silk production retained many of the features of localized, small-scale production that had characterized the family craftsmanship from which the industry had emerged.

The government's sponsorship of specific private entrepreneurs did far more to promote the development of large enterprises, by enabling many entrepreneurs to build up large businesses with semi-monopolistic positions in certain fields. The latter half of the Meiji period saw the rise of huge financial combines known as *zaibatsu*, which dominated many of the new manufacturing and commercial activities. These huge concerns were characterized by certain features. They were essentially united by finance rather than technology. Most had their own bank, which served as the major channel both for funding existing *zaibatsu* enterprises and for bringing new enterprises under the *zaibatsu* aegis. While some *zaibatsu* concentrated on certain fields of industry or commerce, many others, among them the largest, embraced a huge range of activities from textiles, mining and machinery to insurance, trading and transport. The diversification and expansion of these empires was so rapid that by the early twentieth century their control and coordination was fast becoming a problem. The result was a series of reorganizations in the late Meiji and Taishō periods which imposed upon all the biggest *zaibatsu* similar pyramidal patterns of organization. At the apex of the pyramid was a holding company, in which all the shares were owned by the *zaibatsu* family. (These concerns remained for the most part family-owned, although ownership became increasingly separated from management.) This holding company controlled majority shareholdings in all the *zaibatsu* enterprises, including the all-important bank. These enterprises might in turn have wholly or partly owned subsidiaries. One *zaibatsu* enterprise frequently acted as supplier of raw material or parts to another, while a third marketed or exported the product, often using *zaibatsu*-owned means of transport. Such arrangements rendered the whole process of *zaibatsu* production free of dependence on any external enterprise. Control and contact between individual enterprises was further strengthened by interlocking shareholdings and directorates and the 'feudal' method of strategic marriages. These huge conglomerates, led by the four giants Mitsui, Mitsubishi, Sumitomo and Yasuda, came to dominate Japanese commerce and industry, particularly in the interwar period.

In Japan, like in Britain, the textile industries dominated in early industrialization. Silk and cotton were the leading sectors in Japanese industry in the years up to 1914, and remained of crucial importance thereafter. The silk industry, promoted for its export significance, became increasingly mechanized and factory production expanded from the 1870s. Japan's silk workers – mostly women – accounted for a substantial proportion of Japan's total factory labour force. Until the 1930s silk employed more workers than any other industry, the number peaking at over half a million in the mid-1920s. In the early decades silk exports were crucial in enabling the import of foreign capital goods without foreign borrowing, and for most of the prewar period silk remained the biggest single export by value.

By the mid-1980s the cotton industry was also becoming highly significant, not only in terms of domestic consumption but also for its export contribution. Cotton goods production had flourished during the Tokugawa period, but domestic cotton goods production was devastated by an influx of high-quality imported yarn and piece goods during the 1860s, and cotton growing collapsed. Unprotected by any high tariff barrier, the Japanese cotton industry faced total extinction unless it could improve the quality and quantity of its production. Neither the few mechanized cotton spinning mills established during the 1860s–1870s, nor the government's attempt to sponsor the introduction of new machinery by private entrepreneurs, enjoyed much success. In 1883 Shibusawa Eiichi set up the Osaka Cotton Spinning Company, operating by steam power on a scale far larger than anything hitherto attempted. The mill's rapid expansion suggested that modernized cotton spinning could be profitable in Japan. Between 1890 and 1900 the number of spinning mills increased from thirty to eighty as other enterprising businessmen followed Shibusawa. The industry began to compete with foreign products in both the domestic and export markets. The weaving industry also expanded, and by 1914 Japan was self-sufficient in cloth and exported half her own yarn production, around one-quarter of the world's cotton yarn exports. The organization of the industry was very different from that of silk; cotton was produced in much larger scale units, mostly in urban areas. It was more involved with *zaibatsu*, and was more dependent on unskilled labour. Weaving and spinning were increasingly brought under the same roof, creating integrated production units.

The prominence of textile production tended to overshadow the development of new or 'traditional' industries during this period. Wool, cement, bricks, glass, for example, were central to the government's programme for the introduction of new industries. The indigenous industry of sake brewing proved amenable to factory operation and expanded rapidly. A limited expansion in mining, shipbuilding and munitions took place with government help, but the period up to 1914 was very much one of light industrial expansion. The crucial heavy industries – iron and steel, heavy machinery and engineering – failed to experience substantial growth, given the greater technological problems, capital needs and lack of protection against foreign competition. When shipbuilding, for example, began to expand it depended on imported iron and steel.

The process of consolidating the financial and commercial framework within which industry had to operate took several decades. In addition to encouraging the growth of a merchant shipping fleet, the government carried out substantial improvements in road transport and other forms of communication. Railway booms in the late 1880s and late 1890s vastly increased the railway network, and nationalization in 1906 provided a more integrated system. A further rapid expansion in private railway building after 1910 produced a total of over 24,000 kilometres of track by 1930.

The government also made itself responsible for the provision of a stable financial framework. Although the American model of national banks with right of currency issue early on proved attractive, under Matsukata Masayoshi in 1882 the Bank of Japan was established as a central bank along British lines. All other banks became commercial banks with no right of note issue. These commercial banks, in conjunction with specialized government banks, played a crucial role in financing productive industry. Even when a stock market was established its operations were largely speculative, and the joint stock company form of organization failed to spread ownership, investment or shareholder control to the extent of

119

its British counterpart. Strict deflationary policies undertaken by Matsukata in the early 1880s stabilized the currency, and Japan's international financial credibility was assured when the indemnity secured from China after the Sino-Japanese War was used to put Japan on the gold standard in 1897. (Hitherto a bimetallic system, with silver the dominant medium of exchange, had operated.) Not until 1900, with a secure financial base and the unequal treaties a thing of the past, did the Japanese authorities start to borrow widely from abroad, a policy avoided hitherto for fear of foreign control, intervention and dependence. Foreign loans became particularly substantial at the time of the Russo-Japanese War, and by the end of the Meiji period Japan's foreign debts and serious balance of payments position threatened to plunge her into a state of crisis. The outbreak of World War I rescued the country from acute economic depression.

At the outbreak of war in Europe the Japanese invoked the terms of the Anglo-Japanese Alliance to declare war on Germany. Despite rapidly occupying German concessions in China and German colonies in the Pacific, Japan was far enough removed from the main theatre of war to restrict further military activities to a minimum. Japan's position essentially as a non-belligerent enabled the country to reap many benefits from the war situation while bearing few of the costs. Japan was able to supply her belligerent allies not only with munitions, but with other goods which the diversion of their own industries to war needs rendered in short supply. She was able to profit from other nations' preoccupation with war to gain a foothold in their export markets; for example, Japan made inroads into many of the Asian cotton markets formerly dominated by the British, especially in China. With much European shipping damaged or converted to war use, Japan secured a proportion of the world's carrying trade which went far beyond the shipment of her own imports and exports. Japan's merchant marine more than doubled during the years of the war, and related services such as insurance also grew. The halting of supplies to Japan of certain crucial imports forced the development of production in Japan itself. This was particularly true of the chemical industry; Germany had before the war been the world's major supplier and the source of most of Japan's chemical imports.

The economic consequences of the war in Japan were thus a tremendous upsurge in industrial activity and a vast increase in exports. Within a very short space of time Japan went from a debtor nation to one enjoying an immense balance of payments surplus.

Some of these profits could not find their way to Japan due to suspension of the international gold standard and embargoes on gold exports. Japan accumulated considerable balances in certain foreign centres, but this seemed no cause for worry as long as the boom lasted. Industry prospered and huge profits were made. The *nouveaux riches* (*narikin*) of the war years became legendary. Not all Japanese benefited from the war boom. The accelerating inflation which accompanied it hit the agricultural sector particularly hard, and many industrial workers, too, failed to benefit. Rioting erupted over the high price of rice in 1918. Nevertheless, through to 1919 the industrial sector as a whole prospered, and the boost given to many industries during these years provided a sound basis for subsequent development.

In the financial sphere Japan failed to capitalize on her wartime gains. The vast balances accumulated overseas were not used, when available, to pay off Japan's prewar debts. Instead they were largely dissipated in the postwar depression. The domestic economy was further constrained by the deflationary policy pursued by successive Japanese governments through the 1920s with the aim of returning Japan to the gold standard at the prewar parity, when inflation and then depression had left the yen vastly overvalued.

Although Japan's exports continued to be dominated by light manufactures and textiles in the interwar period, these years were characterized by a conspicuous development in heavy industry and the start of a transformation of the whole pattern of industrial management and operation. Government financial policy and the international economic climate were crucial factors in these developments. The early 1920s was a period of world slump and overcapacity in many industries. There was a consequent growth in export dumping, tariff barriers and protectionism. The need for industries to become more competitive to have any hope of success in this new situation was reinforced in Japan by the deflationary trend of policy. Government attempts to impose industrial rationalization were not particularly successful at this time, but a situation where those who did not become more efficient went to the wall reduced the number of inefficient enterprises, concentrated ownership and made remaining enterprises much more competitive and of a size to take advantage of economies of scale. The productivity of Japanese enterprises, in terms of both labour and capital, increased rapidly during these years for the whole range of industries.

One aspect of this drive for increased productivity was the rationalization of labour, and management policies in this period played an important part in the growth of the 'paternalistic' Japanese firm so often branded as our exemplar today. Before World War I most Japanese firms had had an explicit policy of hiring cheap labour wherever possible. Exceptions had to be made, especially where skilled labour was required, but for the most part expenditure on wages, working conditons and welfare was minimized. Whether such a policy was as cost-efficient as it appeared is dubious; recruitment costs and turnover were high, skill levels and productivity low by international comparison. Nevertheless, in the crucial textile industries in particular, this approach was widely adhered to without an apparently adverse effect on the overall labour supply. The few more enlightened employers who later in the Meiji period gave thought to better treatment for their employees were exceptions. The economic and political situation of the post World War I years provoked changes. These were spearheaded in heavy industry, where the dominance of male labour and the need for higher skill levels had always produced somewhat better conditions. They spread to large firms in other spheres of industry.

The idea of the paternalist employer in Japan had been widely proclaimed well back in the Meiji period. The view that the bond between employer and employee was far more than a narrowly commercial one had an even longer tradition. Despite the appalling labour conditions widespread in late nineteenth-century Japan no less that in other countries, many employers of girls and young women in particular claimed to operate *in loco parentis* and have their employees' best interests at heart. Such claims would appear to have been largely propaganda; there is little evidence that most employees, or even their families, considered employers to be fulfilling a parental role. Nevertheless, after the early Taishō period employers utilized this theoretical paternalist tradition in modifying their labour management practices. So skilfully was this done that the development of the paternalist firm appeared to be not the result of the need to cope with increasing labour activism and labour market pressures transformed by the changes in the international economy, but the natural outgrowth of more altruistic company and familial practices dating back to the Tokugawa period.

There is no doubt that employment conditions for some workers in large enterprises did improve in the 1920s. As part of the rationalization process, large firms concentrated on improving productivity by reducing hours, improving the work environment and training workers in skills. Higher wages and bonuses sought to reduce turnover and absenteeism. Welfare facilities increased. Some enterprises permitted unionization, often in company unions. These benefits affected relatively few. Most employees still lacked security of employment, and in the drive for rationalization and more capital-intensive production to compete in declining markets many workers were reduced to the status of temporary workers or made redundant. Few employers were motivated by anything approaching altruism. 'Paternalism' was a route to profitability and survival, a means of combating a potentially dangerous labour movement and general social unrest.

The prevailing economic conditions and policies also reinforced the dualism inherent in the structure of industry, the gulf which existed between large and small firms, between *zaibatsu* enterprises and the rest. Firms already operating on a large scale were able to summon the reserves of capital needed to invest in improvements in labour conditions and capital equipment conducive to increased efficiency. Small operations survived by dependency on larger firms (e.g. by amalgamation or subcontracting) or by concentrating on products where competition from larger firms at home or abroad was minimal. Small enterprises continued to pay very low wages, remained less mechanized[6] and were unable to exploit economies of scale. The small enterprise sector increasingly became the indispensable reverse side of the efficiency of the large, 'paternalistic' enterprises.

This increasing polarization within industry was also in part both the cause and effect of the growth of heavy industry. Prior to World War I shipbuilding and engineering had grown only slowly, and even by 1914 domestic ship production barely equalled imports. The challenge posed by the iron and steel industry proved too demanding for any private entrepreneur. Even after production started at the government's Yawata Iron Works in 1901 development remained very slow. In all these industries vast capital requirements, technological difficulties and a high degree of dependence on imported raw materials severely hindered growth. The war was an important stimulus to shipbuilding, with capacity increasing more than nine times during the war years, but Yawata was still by the early 1920s producing almost all of Japan's iron and steel output, far short of domestic requirements.

This situation was transformed in the interwar years. Among the main beneficiaries of the war boom were *zaibatsu* enterprises, and these concerns benefited further from the 1920s environment, in which they were better able than most to endure depressed conditions and afford the cost of enterprise rationalization. The *zaibatsu* had tended from the start to concentrate on Western-type industries, and were now almost alone in being able to command the capital and expertise and bear the risk involved in heavy industrial undertakings. As the heavy industrial sector grew in the post-1918 years, the dominance of the *zaibatsu* in the economy as a whole increased accordingly. During the 1920s the base for expansion was laid. A change in government financial policy was a crucial factor in the dramatic acceleration of heavy industrial growth which took place in the 1930s.

For most of the 1920s Japanese governments maintained a deflationary policy in the hope of being able to return to gold at the prewar parity. The pursuit of this policy of financial orthodoxy, even after the great depression struck in 1929, exacerbated the effects of the slump upon Japan. Early in 1930 the gold embargo was triumphantly lifted, but the yen remained greatly overvalued and the effects were disastrous. There was a flight of gold, exports slumped and the embargo was eventually reimposed by Finance Minister Takahashi Korekiyo in December 1931. This marked a radical change in economic policy. The yen was allowed to find its own level, depreciating over the next year by around one-half. The watchword became reflation instead of retrenchment. The sudden fall in the yen promoted an export revival, mostly in the traditional light industries. Takahashi led a programme of deficit spending to assist recovery from depression, preceding other industrialized nations in stumbling upon Keynesian policies. The reflationary policy was continued throughout the 1930s, early on under Takahashi, and after 1936 under the aegis of the armed forces, for whose continuing expansion it was crucial.

Deficit spending and the creation of demand, much of it in the field of armaments, assisted individual enterprises and boosted the economy as a whole. Firms which had perforce become more efficient in the 1920s now capitalized upon expanding export and domestic markets. The reflationary policy heralded a massive industrial expansion in which the profits of light industrial exports, an expanding domestic market and government deficit spending together fuelled large-scale development of the heavy industrial sector, undertaken mainly by enterprises with *zaibatsu* associations. During the period 1920–40 the volume of iron and steel production increased eleven times, machinery and chemical production six times. Even textile output was nearly three times as great in 1935 as it had been in 1920, though the volume of textile production then fell sharply with the advent of the quasi-war economy of the late 1930s.

The industrial expansion of the 1930s reinforced the dualism of the Japanese economy, strengthening the division between the production of traditional and Western-style goods, and between large and small enterprises and firms. Many housing, clothing and food consumption needs, for example, continued to be catered for by small, often unmechanized firms or craftsmen. The big export industries and the heavy industrial sector were dominated by large plants and firms, many of them with *zaibatsu* ties. By 1937 the four largest *zaibatsu* (Mitsui, Mitsubishi, Sumitomo and Yasuda) together controlled over 21 per cent of all paid-up capital in banking, 26 per cent in mining, 35 per cent in shipbuilding, 38 per cent in commercial shipping and as high as 61 per cent and 68 per cent in insurance and paper production respectively. A single conglomerate, Mitsui, held 7.7 per cent of total capital in commerce and industry, closely followed by Mitsubishi with 5.5 per cent. Both controlled well over a hundred enterprises.

During the 1920s the *zaibatsu* capitalized on close personal contacts with members of the conservative political parties to much advantage. *Zaibatsu* success was based on a widespread ability to operate in the domestic and international economies without extensive government controls. The emergence of a more protectionist and aggressive environment during the 1930s was therefore not necessarily in their best interest. The strongly anti-capitalist strain found among the radical right wing, as well as on the left, found growing support. In 1932 the managing director of Mitsui, Dan Takuma, was assassinated by right-wing extremists following accusations of speculative currency dealings. Mitsui was accused of being 'a kingdom within a kingdom', whose members put the interests of Mitsui above those of the country. Vulnerable in the face of rising nationalist sentiment and faced by growing protectionism in the world economy to which they were so closely tied, the major *zaibatsu* deemed it prudent to tailor their activities to the changing situation. They did so with considerable success, but their relationship with Japan's military leaders of the late 1930s–early 1940s was never an easy one. Their powerful position within the economy made some degree of government–*zaibatsu* cooperation indispensable, but an absence of trust between the two sides led the authorities to rely where possible on alternative means of promoting the commercial and industrial expansion that would support their growing military ambitions. A major example of this was the so-called 'new *zaibatsu*'.

Between the wars the world's industrial economies were transformed by advances in technology and the emergence of many new products. In Japan the development of these products and the desire to make the domestic economy more self-sufficient in an era of greater trade barriers was capitalized on by a new generation of entrepreneurs, anxious to establish a foothold in the face of *zaibatsu* domination of markets for a whole range of products and services. While the *zaibatsu* themselves did innovate, there was a growing conservatism in many of their investment decisions which resulted in much of the new development's being left to their younger rivals. From the late 1920s there emerged several new conglomerates – the 'new *zaibatsu*' – which benefited considerably from the post-1931 deficit spending boom and build-up in military production. The spheres on which they concentrated – heavy industry, chemicals, mining, vehicles, colonial development – were strategic to the economic and military policies of the 1930s and early 1940s. Most famous was Nissan, which by 1938 was smaller only than Mitsui and Mitsubishi. These groups were less secure financially than the old *zaibatsu*; they had no banks of their own and their dependence on the open market for most of their capital, and the rapid rate at which they expanded and diversified, made them highly vulnerable to sudden fluctuations. This very vulnerability to external pressures led governments in the 1930s to turn to these groups and the adventurous entrepreneurs who headed them as agents in the execution of policy. A conspicuous example of this is the state's cooperation with Nissan in 1937 to found the Manchurian Heavy Industries Development Corporation, the major tool for the industrial development of the puppet state of Manchukuo. Like their predecessors, the new *zaibatsu* were the beneficiaries of government patronage. In the short run, at least, the tie-up brought them phenomenal success.

The rise of heavy industry highlighted the long-standing problem of industrial raw materials supply. Japan's sparse land area and numerous population meant that many agricultural goods had to be imported, and the second largest export industry, cotton yarn and goods, was totally dependent on imported raw materials. Mineral resources were scarce; major metal mines had been all but exhausted during the Meiji period, and much of Japan's coal was unsuitable for shipping and industrial purposes. Almost all iron ore supplies had to come from outside Japan. Japan had no oil; neither the armed forces, nor much of industry, could operate without supplies from Southeast Asia. As heavy industry expanded the need for minerals and fuel became even greater. In the protectionist atmosphere of the interwar years the Japanese felt acutely that such a dependence on others made Japan vulnerable to outside pressure and threatened to undermine any political or economic strength the country might build up for itself. In the face of growing population pressure the absence of secure control – and this eventually came to mean physical control – over raw materials sources and markets contributed substantially to the aggressive and expansionist nature of Japanese policy during the 1930s. Manchuria in particular was a semi-virgin territory, rich in natural resources, which seemed to offer not only an outlet for Japan's expanding population, but a solution to many of her raw material supply problems.

Europeans, in the 1930s, tended to regard Japanese expansion and aggression in East Asia as a localized problem. For most the Japanese economy was destined to be a permanent exporter of light industrial goods manufactured with cheap labour; Japan was always likely to lack the heavy industrial capacity and raw materials that might enable her to pose a serious military or economic challenge to the European empires, let alone the United States. A few writers pointed out, with every accuracy, that Japan now had a sophisticated heavy industrial base even though exports in that field might remain small, and that control of the physical resources and markets of mainland Asia, not to mention Southeast Asia, would render her well nigh unchallengeable in the Asian area.[7] For the most part, though, Western criticism consisted of a mixture of social contempt, accusations of dumping and unfair practices, and exposures of cheap, exploited labour. Sentiments in Lancashire aroused by the success of the Japanese cotton industry epitomized a widely felt sense of pique towards the new upstart who dared to be more successful.

Nevertheless, from early in the 1930s the Japanese economy was geared up for war. A basis for government control was laid in official measures to enforce industrial rationalization and cartelization in the hope of rendering industry more capable of coping with the problems of the international economy. The period 1936–7 is known as the quasi-wartime economy.[8] Full-scale war against China broke out in 1937. Strategic industries were nationalized and in 1938 legislation was introduced permitting the state almost total control of industrial capacity and manpower in the interest of the war. A degree of consensus on the inevitability of a wider conflict existed. The Japanese advance into French Indo-China as part of its China War strategy provoked foreign sanctions and strengthened Japan's desire to gain control of the crucial mineral reserves of the area, especially oil. By the time of Pearl Harbor in December 1941, the Japanese economy, despite already being at war for four years, was as well prepared as it could be for what was to follow. The US, by contrast, took time to mobilize its huge resources.

The advantages conferred by preparedness were limited by the constraints of the economy itself. It was widely realized in Japan that the country's industry could not sustain a lengthy conflict. The extensive raw materials which Japan controlled by mid-1942 were located not in a closely defined, easily defended area, but in a far-flung empire stretching from Korea and Manchuria down to Indonesia. The heavy industrial base in Japan, Korea and Manchukuo could not operate without raw materials, which had to be transported by sea, rendering supplies highly vulnerable to attack en route. As the war dragged on, it became clear that doubts over Japan's ability to support a prolonged conflict were only too well-founded. After mid-1942 Japanese control in Southeast Asia was gradually eroded. The number of ships available for transport dwindled and increasingly effective attacks on shipping convoys depleted the supply of raw materials from the empire to Japan proper. Unrest and other internal problems caused supplies to fall sharply even from territories as near as Manchuria and Korea.

By 1943 lack of raw materials was far from being the only problem faced by Japanese industry. With production geared to war needs, non-essential products, in particular consumer goods, had become in increasingly short supply. Productive capacity had wherever possible been transferred to war-related industries. Such minerals as Japan possessed, especially coal, were being mined exhaustively and wastefully. The drafting of reluctant manpower from the colonies to compensate for a shortage of Japanese labour reduced productivity further. Management had to contend not only with shortages of raw materials but also with inadequate fuel supplies, unrepaired machinery and often reluctant, unskilled and undernourished workforces. The attempt to coordinate industrial production by bringing all capacity under the control of a new, army-dominated Ministry of Munitions in November 1943, had no impact on these fundamental impediments. In the later stages of the war much of the industrial capacity not rendered inoperative by shortages was destroyed by the extensive bombing of the Japanese mainland. Well before August 1945, Japan's industrial production had been reduced far below the level needed to sustain modern, mechanized warfare. By the time of defeat, Japanese industry had been almost totally destroyed. The incoming Occupation authorities were faced with an exhausted people and a society where war and defeat had wrought havoc with all facets of economic life. For the Japanese to sustain a reasonable and peaceful existence in the future the economic foundations of national life had to be at least in part reconstructed.

Such productive capacity as remained intact in 1945 was mostly for war-related purposes. In line with the Occupation policy of demilitarization, factories were dismantled. Equipment was to be sent abroad as reparations payments. Reconversion of plant to civilian use was often difficult, and the rebuilding of capacity which might again be used for the purpose of war – for example iron and steel, shipbuilding – was a sensitive matter. Small firms did slowly re-emerge to cater for immediate civilian needs, but they hardly marked a revival of the modern industry of which Japan had been so proud and which had brought her such export success. It was several years before the pressure of deteriorating relations with the Soviet Union and the continuing financial burden of aid and loans to support the Japanese economy forced the Occupation authorities to give positive support to a rebuilding of Japanese industry.

Concerned also to achieve a more democratic industrial structure, policy-makers took a particular interest in the role of the *zaibatsu*. *Zaibatsu* of all kinds had long since been identified with the rise of militarism, and the evidence suggests that most *zaibatsu* made considerable profits out of Japan's expansionist policy. With the anti-trust movement of the 1930s still fresh in their minds the authorities viewed the *zaibatsu* as excessive concentrations of economic power whose dissolution was essential if a more democratic and competitive industrial structure was to be achieved. Little account was taken of the distinction between old and new *zaibatsu*, or of the competition between *zaibatsu* themselves.

There were two major lines of reform affecting *zaibatsu*. The first of these was the disbanding of the existing *zaibatsu*; the second, a broader anti-monopoly law along the lines of the US Anti-Trust Act to promote competition and prevent cartelization and monopoly. In 1946 a Holding Company Liquidation Commission was established to terminate family ownership of the *zaibatsu* and dissolve the holding companies which held the combines together. Under the Deconcentration Law of 1947 no fewer than 325 businesses were designated excessive concentrations of economic power. The extent of the list, drawn up in secret, raised an outcry in Japan when it was made public. Many saw it as proof that the Occupation authorities (and hence the US) wished to so weaken the Japanese economy that the rebuilding of competitive enterprises would be delayed for decades. Even in the United States the scale of the proposed measures was widely regarded as establishing a dangerous precedent for similar action at home. The pressure of protest against the background of a growing desire to help rebuild the Japanese economy led to the deconcentration programme's being halted in December 1949. Out of the 325 firms and organizations, only the nineteen largest (including all the major *zaibatsu*) had been reorganized. This effective climbdown on deconcentration inevitably meant that Occupation policy was less far-reaching in its effects than originally anticipated. Where they were implemented, deconcentration measures were effective in as far as they terminated family ownership and dissolved most of the formal ties which held the constituent parts of the combines together – in particular, the holding companies.

The Anti-Monopoly Law passed in April 1947 was intended to limit any revival of comparable groupings or monopolistic tendencies. The law prohibited holding companies, cartels, private monopoly and other manifestations and mechanisms of unfair competition. It was to be less effective than anticipated. The effective exemption of banks and financial institutions from the reforms marked a disregard for the significance of banks as central financiers for a conglomerate. Moreover, the deconcentration measures did not – and perhaps could not – dissolve the informal ties that tied enterprises to each other.

For the early years of the Occupation the economy remained in a state of inflationary confusion, and there were few positive steps towards economic revival. Industrial recovery was small and piecemeal; in 1948 the level of industrial production was still little more than one-third of what it had been ten years earlier, and the recovery of trade lagged far behind this. In 1949, however, demands from the US and its allies for a stronger Japan initiated moves to stabilize the economy and curb inflation as a prerequisite for the rebuilding of industry and revival of foreign trade. Under the guidance of the American banker, Joseph Dodge, a nine-point economic stabilization programme was adopted in the budget that year. The new policy established a sound and secure financial basis upon which industry could reasonably be expected to recover. By 1951 the value of foreign trade was well on the way towards recovering prewar levels. The demand stimulated in its turn the recovery of manufacturing.

The boost in international receipts was largely the product of the Korean War, which began in 1950. Japan was ideally located to act as a base for US military and naval activity and her proximity made her useful as a source of war materiel. Personnel far in excess of the number stationed there for Occupation purposes spent their leave in Japan. During the course of the fighting – and for several years after – billions of dollars were spent in Japan on what became known as 'special procurements'. This sudden increase in demand for a whole range of products and services caused a surge of expansion in industrial activity and in the economy as a whole. The sudden influx of foreign currency meant, for the first time since before the Pacific War, a significant ability to purchase from abroad. Some of this currency went toward much-needed capital good replacement. The initial beneficiaries of this demand were industries producing items such as textiles and light engineering products, but soon the production boom spread to cover all areas of heavy industry. Japan was not permitted to engage in the production of armaments, but trucks, tyres, iron and steel for military use were not covered by the ban. Demand was initially supplied by smaller, less capital-intensive enterprises, which had managed to survive during the earlier Occupation years, when large-scale industry had yet to recover. As demand accelerated the multiplier effects of this activity extended beyond the small/medium enterprise sector, and large enterprises again became dominant. The inflow of foreign currency enabled further purchases of raw materials and capital equipment.

The Korean War marked the start of the phenomenal industrial growth Japan has experienced since the war. While it was not until the second half of the 1950s that Japanese industry exceeded pre-1945 levels of production, and later still that the living standards of the Japanese people began to rise markedly, the real rate of growth of the economy was over 10 per cent for most years of the 1960s. With a rapid decline in the contribution of the rural sector Japan has become predominantly an industrial country, and it is industrial expansion and change that have been the key to Japan's immense influence in the international economy. From collapse in 1945, Japan possessed by the early 1980s the third largest GNP in the world. The astonishment which this rapid economic growth has aroused is suggested by reference to it as an 'economic miracle'. Inappropriate though the word 'miracle' may be in its suggestion that no rational explanation can be found for the phenomenon, there is no doubt that many varying factors have been cited as contributing to Japan's rapid industrial growth, ranging from patriotism and the education level of the workforce on the one hand to the complexities of Japanese accounting techniques on the other. These factors cannot be listed exhaustively here, nor is any assessment of the balance between them possible in the present context. It is important to note that Japan's rapid rate of economic growth has taken place within the context of, and benefited from, a favourable international situation. 'Special procurements' proved an enduring boost for much of the 1950s, and the Vietnam War generated further American spending. In the 1950s and 1960s the world economy as a whole was expanding; technology imports, raw materials and energy were relatively cheap and Japan made maximum use of these advantages. Constitutional restrictions on defence spending liberated resources for alternative uses, at the cost of accusations that Japan was having a free ride on the US.[9]

The oil crisis of 1973 initiated a period of far slower growth rates, but the Japanese economy has shown itself remarkably resilient in the face of decreasingly favourable international conditions. This suggests that it is the Japanese response to international conditions which is the key to Japan's rapid economic growth. In the context of Japan's modern history, it is the institutional features in the domestic economy conditioning this response that are of particular relevance. Part of Japan's strength has lain in her responsiveness to a changing economic environment and the adaptability of her industrial structure. No single industry or group of industries has played the leading role throughout the postwar years; at different times iron and steel, shipbuilding, electronics, information technology, for example, have been the major growth sectors. An ability to switch resources from one sector to another with relative ease has been helped by two major features: the nature and effectiveness of government policy and the nature of Japanese firms.

The tradition of government involvement in the Japanese economy is a long one, and Japanese governments in prewar days pursued an active role in setting an overall industrial policy. Postwar government intervention, though frequently exercised through 'administrative guidance' and other informal means rather than through official rules and regulations, has remained pervasive. To this extent it would not be an exaggeration to say that the

Japanese economy, for all its emphasis on the importance of the free market, has been subject to extensive official controls, with central planning playing a not inconsiderable part. The Finance Ministry has been quick to take action when rapid industrial expansion has threatened excessive inflationary pressures. Industrial strategy has been exercised mostly through the Ministry of International Trade and Industry (MITI). Since its establishment in 1949, MITI has been a driving force behind the evolving industrial structure and the development of production and trade. Its strategy has been implemented by formal and informal methods, including selective export credit, a radical scrap-and-build policy, subsidies and sponsorship of selected companies. Close contacts with big business and its political mouthpiece, the ruling Liberal Democratic Party, have played a major role in both formulation and achievement of MITI's aims.

Economic success has also been widely attributed to the nature of Japanese firms; students of Japanese management methods engage in intense debate over how far the industrial nations of the West can and should imitate Japanese practices. The archetypal Japanese firm sets itself up as a paternalistic entity, caring for its employees in a way which breeds intense loyalty and hard work. Employees receive the benefits of so-called lifetime employment, wages rising in accordance with seniority, multiple welfare facilities, and have the opportunity of rising up the hierarchy of the organization. The ideal company lacks a clear-cut division between management and worker of the British type, and unions are mostly organized on a company rather than a trade or industry basis. With membership embracing all members of the enterprise, the union is not dominated by any sectional interest; union officials are part of the management hierarchy. Emphasis on the enterprise rather than on a specific skill makes for greater job flexibility, with restrictive practices virtually unknown. Decision-making in the company is achieved on a basis of consultation, without, it is argued, restricting the right of managers to manage. The company operates as an entity within which all members share the same interest, and unite to achieve maximum results in the face of competition from outside, whether from other companies or other countries.

There is a considerable measure of truth in this image of large Japanese companies, although not all large companies may be as caring as they have been depicted. However, this characterization is only valid, or even partially valid, for Japan's largest enterprises. The system does not extend to the medium/small enterprise sector, without which big business could not operate nearly so effectively. The dualism of products, scale of operation, employee welfare and wages found in prewar Japan has survived through the postwar years. Large firms have continued to hire large numbers of part-time or non-permanent employees who can easily be made redundant and who enjoy few of the benefits accruing to their more permanent counterparts. More importantly, large enterprises have been serviced by a cluster of small ones. In the early 1980s Japan's medium and small enterprises still accounted for a very large proportion of all workers in manufacturing, and an even larger proportion of all firms. In 1939 it was estimated that 46 per cent of the manufacturing labour force was in workplaces with under thirty workers. In 1981 the figure was still over 40 per cent. The same year 80 per cent of the manufacturing workforce was in establishments of under 500 employees. The dominance of very small units was particularly great in the retail and service sectors, due to the prevalence of family-operated units, but even in manufacturing 51 per cent of all enterprises employed less than five people. This substantial majority of the industrial workforce has had little security of employment; these workers receive lower wages and few of the 'paternalist' welfare benefits, such as housing, recreational and medical facilities. By acting as subcontractors for large enterprises, many smaller firms have essentially cushioned large enterprises against recession. When demand has fallen it is the temporary workers and the smaller subcontractors who have been hardest hit; this flexibility has enabled large enterprises to maintain the lifetime employment/no redundancy policy for their permanent 'core' staff. Smaller and medium-sized firms have, of course, also derived certain benefits from their relationship with their larger neighbours, and on occasions may even have graduated to join them, but their existence as a *sine qua non* for the highly efficient operation of the big enterprises has too often been overlooked.

The Occupation reforms aimed at preventing large firms from securing any quasi-monopolistic position or from becoming part of a larger group of economic interests. Nevertheless, some sectors of the Japanese economy have become dominated by very large enterprises, many of them associated with huge conglomerates. The emergence of these large groupings and enterprises has not been prevented by the existence of the Anti-Monopoly Law, nor have they encountered official disapproval. The resulting oligopolistic situation in many industries clearly seems to contravene the basic tenets of the deconcentration measures. Paradoxically, this oligopoly and the existence of other cartel-like measures have rarely restricted competition, since the various groups have continued to vie with each other over the whole range of product markets.

The term applied to these postwar industrial and financial groupings is *keiretsu*.[10] A *keiretsu* has been defined by one authority as 'a closely knit, vertical hierarchy of undertakings centred on a large concern which organizes and in part finances a population of associated firms and their subcontractors'.[11] Some of these groupings are based on old *zaibatsu*, more informally reconstituted. The power of the new *zaibatsu* was largely broken by the Occupation reforms, but solidarity between enterprises in the established *zaibatsu* was more firmly based. The reborn *zaibatsu* have had to compete with new groupings centred on core concerns which have enjoyed phenomenal expansion in the years since 1950. Examples of these new groups are Toyota and Toshiba. *Keiretsu* enterprises usually work in cooperation with each other, and often rely on funding from the banks, although they are not internally funded to the extent of the old *zaibatsu*. They turn to each other where possible for a particular service, a process which perpetually reinforces mutual interdependence. Links between enterprises are frequently informal, although such mechanisms as interlocking directorships are found. The scale of operation of these huge conglomerates not only makes them immensely powerful in the domestic economy, but also enables them to operate efficiently and exert tremendous leverage in the international economy. They are one of the factors that have brought Japan export success. The resources at the group's disposal in terms of such attributes as information gathering, finance and productive capacity are enormous and enable it to carry out extensive undertakings which in many countries could only be undertaken by government.

While success in the international economy has, not surprisingly, provoked a desire to learn from Japan's experience, it has also become apparent in recent years that Japanese industry has to learn how to cope with the friction and resentment which its very success has provoked. While foreign attitudes in the internecine trade disputes the US and the EEC have had with Japan and the accusations of Japanese protectionism in its own financial and commodity markets may be redolent of the prewar indignation at being beaten at one's own game, the friction nevertheless jeopardizes the existence of the whole international system from which Japan has prospered. The degree to which Japan can accommodate her policies accordingly will fully test the responsiveness of the domestic economy.

NOTES

1   Kaempfer was a German doctor attached to the Dutch trading post in Nagasaki. His *History of Japan* was first published in English in 1727, then reissued in London in 1852.

2   The debate on Japanese capitalism mentioned in Chapter One has generated an enormous amount of research on the nature and implications of pre-Meiji industrial development, but a consensus has yet to be reached.

3   Some historians have argued that Tomioka failed to discharge even this role successfully.

4   Matsukata was Finance Minister for fifteen years of the period 1881–1900, and is credited with being the architect of Japan's modern banking and financial system.

5   Lit. 'financial clique'. The term *zaibatsu* is normally retained in Western literature.

6   The introduction of electric motors did, however, transform many small enterprises.

7   For example, see F. Utley, *Japan's Feet of Clay* (London, 1936).

8   Some historians use the term quasi-war economy (*junsenji keizai*) more loosely to refer to much of the 1930s.

9   This is in strong contrast to Japan's massive defence spending in the prewar period, which some historians have regarded as a stimulus to industrial development.

10   *Keiretsu* = lit. 'order', 'system'. Some writers still use the term *zaibatsu* to refer to those groups which had *zaibatsu* status prewar.

11   G.C. Allen, *The Japanese Economy* (London, 1981), p.126.

CHAPTER SEVEN

Men and Women

The disparity between the roles, activities and histories of men and women in Japan is as great as, if not greater than, that in any other society. Traditional historiography has concentrated on the activities of men, in Japan as elsewhere.[1] To redress the balance even partially it is necessary to acknowledge the part played by Japanese women in activities which are not the object of conventional historical record, to emphasize the fundamental role of women as the cornerstone of domestic life and to outline the changing status and role of women in modern Japan. Over the last century Japanese women have fulfilled an essential role both in the domestic sphere and in the economy, but a growing involvement in all aspects of national life has not always been reflected in a marked advance towards sexual equality as it is perceived in the West.

The image of Japanese women as exquisite but subservient adornments – an image still current in the West – was promoted by Westerners' experiences in the late nineteenth century. In as far as this stereotype was valid at all, it applied only to women from the middle and upper classes, or to entertainers; these were the only women encountered by Westerners on a social level. Women had not always been subordinate in Japan; some women enjoyed considerable power in ancient times, and the imperial line did not then exclude women. As late as the Kamakura period (twelfth to fourteenth centuries) women of the ruling class exercised a powerful political influence and enjoyed considerable legal and property rights. Much of Japan's great literature of the Heian period (784–1185) was written by women. However, the growing emphasis on military values helped to erode women's freedoms. In Japan, as elsewhere, the military role was considered unsuited to women, and from the Kamakura period the political, legal and economic power of women gradually declined in relation to that of men. By the mid-Tokugawa period the difference in role which formed the basis for subservience in the middle and upper classes had been rigidly defined within the Neo-Confucian-based official orthodoxy. During the course of the Edo period social values stressed by the ruling class filtered downwards through the other castes of society, and even among the peasantry the crucial importance of women's contribution to agricultural labour could not totally prevent the imposition of inferior status in a rigid family and community hierarchy. By the late Tokugawa period Japan was confirmed as a patriarchal society in which the stated functions of women were twofold: the perpetuation of the family line and the care and entertainment of men. Though mitigated by economic imperatives at the lower levels of the social structure, these two precepts were at least in part the ideal at all levels of society.

The position of samurai women in Edo Japan was based on a principle of respect for men and contempt for women (*danson johi*). At its root was a strict division between the functional roles of men and women, with the woman's place and role being exclusively within the household as wife and mother. Even within the domestic sphere, a woman was still subordinate to the dictates of men. A woman's supreme virtue was submissiveness, and her life was governed by what were known as the 'three obediences'. In childhood she obeyed her father or elder brother, after marriage her husband, and in widowhood her son. She received no legal protection against any abuses to which the male members of her family might subject her. Almost all women were expected to marry, and young brides were at the mercy of a strange household and the whims of an often domineering mother-in-law pleased to be replaced at the bottom of the hierarchy. Wives could be divorced without any substantive grounds and at any time by the husband and his family. No reciprocal right existed. Childbirth was a woman's main function, and any wife who failed to produce male heirs was likely to be returned to her own family; those children she did bear were part of her husband's family, and she had no claim to children or property in that family, remaining essentially an outsider. Only when a wife became a mother-in-law could she in her turn enjoy a brief heyday of influence. Women's education consisted of instruction in how to behave according to their low status, how best to fulfil their roles of childbirth and attendance to the needs of men, and, where the family's economic status allowed sufficient leisure, in gentle arts such as flower arrangement, poetry and the tea ceremony.

While the Western stereotype of the Japanese woman owed much to the ideal aspired to by the ruling élite, a further factor in its formation was the attributes expected of a different group of women – geisha, prostitutes and other women of entertainment. In Tokugawa society concubinage and prostitution were the norm and the number of women involved in male entertainment of some form was considerable. Those at the top of the entertainment hierarchy, for example, the geisha (lit. 'performer', 'artist'), were expected to possess a high degree of personal attractiveness, sophistication and cultural attainment which could be devoted to the diversion of the opposite sex. Necessary skills included musical performance (singing, dancing and playing of instruments), conversation, and often the art of sex. Such women as these existed solely for the diversion of men. Their growing contacts with Westerners arriving in the late nineteenth century enhanced the impression that Japan's women were fragile dolls supremely versed in the gentle arts. The greater degree of freedom and economic activity enjoyed by women in the non-samurai classes failed to shake this impression.

The ideal Western woman of the late nineteenth century, too, was *par excellence* mother and housewife, but even in propaganda the model was more complex. Women became missionaries, for example. They concerned themselves with moral issues and charitable purposes. The new exposure to Western civilization raised questions over the role and status of Japanese women. The years after the 1850s produced no immediate or dramatic change, but some women became active in spheres denied to them during the Tokugawa period and Western cultural influences began to stimulate a greater awareness of the position of women among the more educated. The first perceptible changes were essentially superficial. The initial craze for Western cultural habits was pursued by many female members of the ruling élite. Like men they adopted Western clothes and hairstyles; they were encouraged to participate in Western-style social gatherings to indicate to foreigners how Westernized Japan had become. The traditionally conceived role and position of women were seriously discussed by leading male intellectuals, and Mori Arinori, later Education Minister, went so far in 1875 as to engage in a contractual marriage, followed eleven years later by a contractual divorce. These discussions, however, rarely questioned the need for women to remain the repositories of the traditional attributes of obedience, chastity and gentleness.

Their role was still to support their menfolk. Even the most progressive intellectuals desired an improvement in the status of and opportunities for women for the advancement that might ensue in the upbringing and development of Japan's ruling men, and hence in the welfare of the nation as a whole. There is little evidence of a desire to improve the status of women for its own sake or to encourage women to compete with men in areas traditionally reserved for men. Male and female roles remained strictly divided.

Yet any changes in the education of women and the opportunities open to them made more likely further efforts to step beyond women's allotted role. Women from the better off sectors of society were the main beneficiaries of the first attempts to provide an alternative education for women spearheaded by Western missionaries such as Rev. J. C. Hepburn.[2] Tokugawa female education had been limited to moral training and the arts becoming to women. Women from the commercial classes had received some practical training, and instruction in reading and writing was spreading, but the literacy rate remained far lower than that of the male population, especially among lower social groups. The new Christian-influenced schools talked of equality and the dignity of the individual. Instruction began to include subjects such as languages, history, and even science and mathematics. The Meiji government increasingly subscribed to 'modern' education for women, although on the basis of the old Confucian perception of women's role. Among the first Japanese sent abroad to study by the Meiji government in 1871 were five girls. The most famous of these, Tsuda Umeko, studied for many years in the US and after returning to Japan became a pioneer in higher education for women and English language teaching. The government encouraged women to attend state elementary schools, which under the post-1880s system were coeducational. Normal schools trained female teachers, who in turn provided other girls with instruction. Private and state institutions for girls' education sprang up. Above the elementary level schools were strictly segregated and opportunities for women highly restricted, but by the turn of the century a small female élite was receiving higher education, and the vast majority of girls were attending elementary school, although the instruction they received there was often rudimentary and limited. The influence on women's attitudes of this change was most conspicuous among the highly educated élite, but there were some from outside this minority who sought a reappraisal of the status and role of women in the context of the radical social changes taking place. The Meiji period saw the emergence of an embryonic women's movement.

Some of the earliest female activists were those who were influenced by Christianity to campaign against concubinage and the existence of licensed prostitution in Japan. The Women's Temperance Association prominent in this activity was the Japanese counterpart of Western organizations such as the Women's Christian Temperance Union. The campaign was unsuccessful; both licensed and unlicensed prostitution continued to be legal under national law until after World War II. Nevertheless it signified a limited advance towards a concept of women's rights, albeit within the confines of home and motherhood.

More radical women campaigned as part of the popular rights movement during the 1880s. Two of the best known of these were Kishida Toshiko (1864–1901) and Fukuda Hideko (1865–1927). Kishida, a former lady-in-waiting at court, was a source of inspiration to many women through her fiery speeches in support of women's being equal partners in the building of a new Japan. The outspokenness of her criticism of existing mores made her the subject of intimidation and harassment. Among those enthused by her oratory was Kageyama (later Fukuda) Hideko. Fukuda's association with the radical wing of the popular rights movement led to her imprisonment in 1885–9, but she remained a stalwart and vocal supporter of women's rights in the face of government suppression of the nascent socialist movement and acute poverty. She was dedicated to improving education opportunities and the chance of self-sufficiency for poorer women normally unable to afford them. Many of her later efforts were devoted to raising women's consciousness, particularly through journalistic activity. Though remaining doyenne of the women's movement until her death, Fukuda was an isolated figure. The decline of the popular rights movement put a severe damper on the women's rights' activity it had begun to stimulate. Kishida's activities became less public after her marriage in 1885, and with Fukuda in prison others, too, fell silent.

Notwithstanding the ferment of 1882–5, the mass of women remained relatively untouched by the campaigns of Christians and popular rights activists. Far more significant for them were the changes wrought by the economic transformation taking place in the country, which forced more and more women to adopt a lifestyle at odds with the role and status traditionally ascribed to them. As the number of women employed outside the home grew rapidly from the early Meiji period, the role and occupations of women in the labour force changed dramatically. Women from the artisan and commercial classes had long engaged in business; their numbers now increased, although some existing handicraft industries and commercial undertakings were displaced by newer rivals. Millions of women continued to engage in the arduous, exhausting manual labour of farmwork. The nature of agricultural work altered little at this time; substantial increases in output and productivity were secured by more, rather than less, labour. Many peasant women had traditionally carried on occupations such as weaving and spinning within the home, but the growth of factory-based industry also drove an increasing number to work as wage labour outside the home for extended periods. The textile industries, the cornerstone of early industrialization, had a largely female workforce; around 250,000 women worked in factories by the turn of the century. Most were under twenty; temporary migrants (*dekasegi*) from farming villages, they remitted much of their wages to their families and worked at the most for a few years before returning to their communities to marry. Other women became secretaries, telephonists, teachers, nurses, clerks – a few at first, but from the 1890s in rapidly growing numbers. As women were increasingly able to choose whether to sell their labour to the agricultural or industrial sectors, the prospects and expectations of those employed in the new growth areas had a growing effect on those working outside them.

Economic as well as social change was thus driving women away from the roles which they had traditionally occupied. Yet the essential nature of women's work did not lead to improvements in status or rights. From the 1890s the establishment increasingly sought to reimpose traditional virtues and status on women. Given the difficulty of doing so in the face of dramatic economic and political changes, its success was substantial and long-lasting. Thirty to forty years after the Restoration the majority of Japanese, both men and women, still adhered closely to the Tokugawa ideal of a woman's role, and the new orthodoxy tried to build on and reinforce conservative attitudes of this kind.

The keystone of the political system, the Meiji Constitution of 1889, excluded women from any direct political participation, and other legislation prevented them from campaigning for change.[3] Women began to agitate for the vote in the years after World War I, but legal hindrances rendered their activity constantly vulnerable to official intervention. A more pervasive restriction was embodied in the 1898 civil code, which became the legal foundation of the patriarchal family (*ie*) system in the pre-1945 period, and placed a woman firmly within the locus of the family. Every clause of the civil code relating to women reinforced their subordinate, subservient position in Japanese society. A woman had no independent legal status, but was treated as a minor; all legal agreements on her behalf were concluded by the male to whom she was subordinate – father, husband or son.[4] She had no free choice of spouse or domicile. While women could, in theory, protest against this subordinate position in a non-political manner, to do so directly posed a challenge to the whole social orthodoxy on which the prewar Japanese state was founded. Women thus protested at their peril. Those who demonstrated their dissatisfaction by adopting non-conformist lifestyles or extra-marital sexual relationships could lay themselves open not merely to social opprobrium but to legal action.

Such women's organizations as existed in the late nineteenth century confined themselves to activities which met with official approval. The Christian Temperance movement concerned itself with temperance, prostitution and poverty. The Patriotic Women's Association of 1901 sought to provide physical and material comfort to soldiers and bereaved families in time of war. Upper class women were conspicuous in both these organizations, and although the Patriotic Women's Association, which had one million members by the end of World War I, could claim mass membership, activity at local level was minimal. Organizations such as the Patriotic Women's Association were essentially the creatures of the establishment.

Significantly, literature remained a vehicle for dissent for both sexes, and in the case of women served as the genesis of a renewed political movement for women's rights. Literary expressions of defiance from women unable to develop their creative abilities or express themselves to the full grew into a broader resentment against the subordinate status of women and their lowly position in the 'family state'. This new direction was marked by the formation of the famous Bluestocking Society (*Seitōsha*) of 1911 by a small number of women graduates led by Hiratsuka Raichō (1886–1971). Strongly influenced by the romantic literary movement and the pacifist poet Yosano Akiko and other women writers, the group determined to secure for itself personal liberation through expression in its own journal. *Bluestocking* (*Seitō*) was the first Japanese journal to be edited and written by women. Hiratsuka's declaration in the first issue was a harbinger of later developments. Entitled 'Originally woman was the sun', the statement called on women to regain their 'hidden sun' and reject their position of dependence, in which they could

143

only shine in the reflected light of their men. The implied criticism of the whole family system and existing pattern of male–female relationships alienated many critics from the start.

In successive issues *Bluestocking* found itself moving away from an exclusive concern with individual liberation to the problems of women in society as a whole. Persecution of the group increased. Hiratsuka herself was propelled by her search for personal liberation toward more anti-establishment views, and the struggle to keep the journal going in the face of growing censorship gradually eroded support. The editorship was handed over to the politically radical Itō Noe early in 1915, but her advocacy of anarchism weakened support for the journal still further. It ceased publication in 1916. The membership of the group was never great, nor the circulation of the journal ever more than a few thousand, but its influence was out of all proportion to its size. Hiratsuka herself remained a leader of the women's movement until her death. Many other leaders of the interwar and post-1945 women's movement were readers of the journal or members of the group, and many more were caught up in the renewed concern for the position of women in Japanese society which the Bluestockings had initiated. They included Ichikawa Fusae (1893–1981), one of the founders of the New Women's Association (*Shinfujin kyōkai*) of 1919, which campaigned for greater legal rights for women, and better education and welfare facilities for them. This organization and its successor, the Women's Suffrage League of 1925, pressed for an end to the legal prohibition of political activity by women and female suffrage. In 1922 a partial amendment of the 1900 Peace Police Law allowed women to attend and hold political meetings, but the right to join parties and to vote was withheld until after 1945.

The Bluestockings and other intellectual groups searching for personal freedom were only one facet of women's rights activity after the Meiji period. Just as the 1880s popular rights movement had stimulated feminist ideas, so, too, did the emerging labour and socialist movements attract women who, despite their exclusion from political activity, sought to reassess the position of women in the light of socialist ideology and the growth of capitalist industry in Japan. The female industrial labour force grew rapidly after 1900, but although strikes by female workers in the 1880s had proved relatively successful, employers proved increasingly able to stifle sporadic communal expressions of protest. The majority of female workers endured appalling conditions or got out. The establishment of a women's section by the main labour organization, the Yūaikai, in 1916 acknowledged that women workers were a substantial element in the labour force, but for the most part little effort was made to organize female workers. The perspective that female workers were short term, uncommitted members of the workforce with little to gain from organization, in conjunction with the view that their sex rendered organization effectively impossible, made for a very low unionization rate.

The socialist political movement was no more successful in absorbing women into its ranks, although the legal ban on political activity did not prevent women from being informally involved with left-wing organizations. The Heiminsha of 1903–5 claimed an interest in women's rights, and socialist women's organizations, often with proletarian party associations, existed during the 1920s. A series of women played a prominent part in the movement – Fukuda Hideko, Kanno Suga (executed with anarchist Kōtoku Shūsui in 1911), Itō Noe, Yamakawa Kikue – but the disinterest of male socialist and labour leaders often drove them to sacrifice feminist concerns to what were considered the broader interests of the whole movement. As in other countries, male unionists feared women's advancement in the workplace; women encountered immense hostility to concepts such as equal work opportunities, equal wages and abolition of the patriarchal family system which threatened men's established hegemony. Socialist leaders continued to rely on the automatic liberation of women which they believed would accompany the advent of a socialist society. The activities of the few socialist women interested in women's rights and improving the lot of women workers were doomed to meet apathy, if not outright opposition, from male colleagues. Moreover, the socialist and non-socialist wings of the women's movement rarely came together in a united front.

Dynamic though many of these individuals were, the numbers interested in women's rights, labour and socialist activity paled into insignificance by comparison with the strength of the mass women's organizations, the first of which was the Patriotic Women's Association. These expanded rapidly in the 1920s and 1930s. The Patriotic Women's Association claimed three million members by the late 1930s, the army-sponsored National Defence Women's Association, formed in 1932, around eight million. Both had numerous local branches. These organizations were concerned not with women's rights, but with women's duties. Their task was the reinforcement of the patriarchal 'family state', and both became vehicles for the mobilization of the female population by the state for the purposes of war. They had a major impact on the lives of the majority, while agitation by the few non-establishment organizations and individuals seemed no more than peripheral to the concerns of most women.

Notwithstanding innate conservatism and the official reassertion of the traditional status of women, changing economic and labour market forces continued to exert a substantial influence on women's lives. Apart from their significance as wives, mothers and teachers, women continued to make up a large proportion of the workforce in the agricultural, industrial and commercial sectors. The agricultural smallholdings and tenancies which still sustained over 40 per cent of the population in the late 1930s became increasingly dependent on the labour contribution of the women of the family, both in the work of cultivation and in by-employment inside or outside the home. This process was accelerated by the absorbtion of men into the rapidly expanding industrial sector in the late 1930s, and into the armed forces. By 1940 women comprised over half the agricultural labour force (around seven million workers). This marked a reversal of the pattern earlier in the interwar years, when agricultural depression, climatic fluctuations and increasing population pressure on the land meant that poverty became increasingly severe in some villages. A woman's labour contribution was often considered less valuable to the farm, and the income she brought in had always been viewed as supplementary to the family budget. Thus in times of difficulty young women regarded as little more than extra mouths to feed tended to be among the first to be shed by the farm economy. More and more women and girls were forced to search for alternative sources of income at a time when industrial depression meant that employment opportunities outside the agricultural sector were declining. Male control over the female labour market weakened women's position still further. Since girls had no independent legal status, they had from the Meiji period been despatched to work in factories on the basis of contracts signed by their fathers or elder brothers, with or without the consent of the girl concerned. Although women became increasingly independent of their families in matters of employment in the 1920s and 1930s, they were still largely subject to legal and economic control by the males of the household. In the early 1930s girls from the depressed areas of the northeast were not infrequently sent into prostitution by their parents because no other employment was available. Brothel-keepers, like mill owners, paid a lump sum advance on wages to the head of the family – crucial to tide it over current difficulties – but the woman was in return committed to many years of service, if not life-long bondage. The effective 'sale' of female labour exacerbated by the depression demonstrated that under the law women were little higher than slaves and little more than chattels.

Their weak position at the bottom of the hierarchy made women particularly vulnerable to the impact of economic difficulties, but far from increasing the agitation for change by women, these harsh realities served to reinforce a broader sense of frustration and despair. While women's interests might have come to the fore in a time of prosperity they were now overtaken by the broader discontent among the working classes. Women's rights agitation was a luxury that could not be afforded; repression was certain and there were more immediate economic imperatives. In any case, for the mass of women local conservatism combined with efficient indoctrination and organization by the authorities to pre-empt any thought of feminist protest.

For some women the interwar years brought new opportunities. The number engaged in clerical and non-manual occupations grew apace. While the number of women employed in industry grew only marginally, those working in the tertiary sector expanded by over 70 per cent to nearly 3.4 million between 1920 and 1940. Around half of these were in the service industries. Women advanced further in the professions. The barriers to women's entering such careers as medicine and the law were slowly removed. Women teachers became increasingly responsible for the early education of children. Though poorly represented at higher educational levels, even in girls' schools, they accounted for nearly half of all elementary school teachers by the 1930s.

One of the most conspicuous areas of women's employment remained the entertainments industry. Licensed prostitution remained in operation throughout the prewar period and private prostitution also existed on a large scale. Girls driven into prostitution by destitution invariably found themselves at the bottom of the hierarchy, but the entertainments industry still embraced a range of occupations. All, from the highly sophisticated geisha with their long years of training, through bar girls, hostesses and nightclub entertainers, to a range of classes of prostitute, were dedicated to the entertainment of the male population. The size of this industry was the natural consequence of the position imposed upon the Japanese woman within the family, and a civil code which made adultery a crime for women and a permitted recreation for men. It is estimated that by the 1930s the number of girls involved ran to several hundred thousand.

In the interwar years a relative decline in the significance of female industrial labour was thus counterbalanced by a rise in other employments for women. By 1940 women constituted nearly 40 per cent of the economically active population of 32 million. In all sectors women were on lower grades or engaged in lower status work than their male colleagues, and received lower wages. The continuing predominance of unmarried women as employees and the tendency to leave on marriage produced a high turnover rate, reinforcing the allocation of females to lower status tasks. Married women worked in large numbers, but predominantly in agriculture or retailing. Women's economic activity continued to be regarded as subsidiary to their real role in the home as wife and mother.

The advance of women into the workforce was accelerated during the war years. The conscription of a large number of men into the armed forces meant the mobilization of the remainder of the population into essential occupations. While motherhood granted a privileged status, the unmarried female population was drafted on a vast scale into war-related production and other back-up services for the armed forces. In the face of growing labour shortages as the war progressed educational provision deteriorated and girls not yet in their teens were pressed into productive work.

While women were increasingly forced into the physical occupations and responsibilities formerly monopolized by men, they continued to carry out tasks assigned to them by the official mass organizations. A large proportion of women had already joined these by the late 1930s; in 1942 all were merged into a single body, the Greater Japan Women's Association. Membership for all women over twenty was compulsory; younger women joined youth organizations. Even before the start of the China War in 1937 these groups had coordinated women in specific back-up functions, such as savings campaigns, civil defence and care for the wounded and bereaved. Such functions were extended under the exigencies of war and the new political structure.

These official women's organizations were also a major element in the 'spiritual' mobilization of the female population, and under the influence of the miscellany of ideas they propagated the ideal of Japanese womanhood was built up into the 'mother of the nation'. A subordinate position in society had never concealed women's very real importance as wives and mothers, as the organizers of domestic affairs and the foundation of family life. That these functions were essentially women's major role had long been assumed, but the highly charged militarist atmosphere of the 1930s overlaid this assumption with an idealized concept of the spiritual and emotional role of women in the Japanese state which, though building on this traditional role, yet remained distinct from it.

Military priorities meant that women were important as the bearers of sons who would fight Japan's wars. The sanctity of motherhood was enshrined in official statements and regulations as long as the war situation permitted the luxury of such favourable treatment. All women were depicted as mother-figures and consolers of men fighting overseas or serving on the home front. The ritual of girls seeing off men to the front was a highly charged emotional experience. Soldiers wore a belt or headband with a thousand stitches, each put in by a different woman; these *senninbari* were held to have talismanic qualities. Girls mobilized for overseas duties to cater to the sexual needs of the armed forces were euphemistically known as 'comfort girls' and said to be doing their part for the nation. Women found themselves bearing the burden of emotional support for the war effort which was such an important element in the spiritual mobilization programme.

The treatment to which women were subject was no more consistent with the idealized image than it had been in earlier years. Japanese employers, for example, had never resolved the contradictions over whether to treat their female employees as women or as a factor of production to be exploited to the full. Within the family, men glorified female attributes but expected women to fulfil the role of servants. This inconsistency of theory and reality was at its greatest during the early war years, when the physical and emotional burden on women became ever greater and the image they were expected to live up to increasingly lofty. As the pressures for survival at home increased, they fell to a growing extent on the shoulders of women. At the same time the ability of the official organizations to mobilize women in practical functions or spiritual campaigns was progressively impaired. The hothouse flower of the ideal Japanese woman of the war years was wilting long before the Occupation reforms attempted to kill it off completely. Economic imperatives, war weariness and the need for survival were key factors in its demise. The earlier ideal woman of which it had been an elaboration proved more hardy.

A change in the status and role of women was integral to the Occupation's 'democratization' programme. Even before the new constitution of 1947 guaranteed sexual equality, women were granted new legal and political rights. In the general election of spring 1946, women were allowed to campaign, stand as candidates and vote. Against all expectations 67 per cent of women voted and 39 women – a figure never since exceeded – were elected to the lower house. Local politics also became open to them. Women became a significant force in the burgeoning labour movement; union membership peaked at 51 per cent of employed women in 1949, falling to 30 per cent by the following year. The revised civil code of 1948 removed women's subordination to the family head and the male. The abolition of the *ie* (family) and the end of primogeniture provided women with legal competence, equal rights regarding marriage, domicile, divorce and inheritance. The number of divorces initiated by women dramatically increased. However, the economic and social straits of the immediate post-defeat years were a limiting factor on women's availing themselves of their new rights. The immediate concern of most women was their own and their children's welfare, and 'freedom' was no substitute for income. The imposition of the reforms met with little outright opposition, but it was not to be expected that the old concepts of women's role and status could be abolished by the stroke of a pen. Even forty years on, social practice is far removed from legal possibilities and indirect discrimination is widespread. Although in the household sphere the woman's influence normally exceeds that of the man, in most other aspects of life traditionally the male preserve, for example employment, politics, even education, women remain acutely disadvantaged.

To be a 'good wife and wise mother' has continued to be what is expected of the majority of Japanese girls. If a woman is content to have her aspirations and ambitions lie within this traditional sphere society will delegate to her considerable power. In most Japanese households the woman has a large measure of autonomy over the family finances; the male breadwinner often hands over his income to his wife, who allots him a small amount for his personal expenses. The wife's disposition of the family budget can even extend to such major items as housing. The upbringing and education of children are also largely the responsibility of the wife. She not only cares for their physical wellbeing, but sees them through the competitive education system; postwar Japan has produced the notorious 'education mother' (*kyōiku mama*), who drives her children to study, and, she hopes, to succeed. Though home and children remain the wife's domain more families are consulting on these issues. For some this is a welcome step towards equal partnership. For other women – and there are many who are well-satisfied with the status quo – the increasing intervention by the husband in domestic affairs and the greater time he may spend at home as a result of changed working conditions and new attitudes among the younger generation is an unwelcome intrusion. In a society where social role is of such importance as it is in Japan, involvement by the male in domestic issues threatens the only social role which many women have. Moreover, women exercise this influence in the home merely because most men are content to let them do so.

Yet economic and social pressures and changes in their education and life cycle mean that more women than ever before find it impossible – and undesirable – to remain strictly within the domestic context for the greater part of their lives. Once a woman begins to harbour ambitions outside the household sphere she meets with social prejudice, economic disadvantage and, despite the constitution, legal obstacles.

The granting of voting rights to women after 1945 meant that politically they became a force to be reckoned with, but the momentum of the early years has not been sustained. Female membership of both houses of the Diet together has not exceeded thirty since 1947, and the appointment of a woman, Doi Takako, to leadership of the Japan Socialist Party in September 1986 was more an image-building exercise than a commitment to equal rights. Few women politicians have achieved the stature of Ichikawa Fusae, who was a member of the upper house almost continuously from 1953 to 1981. In the ruling Liberal Democratic Party, where connections are of continuing significance, women are particularly few, and female cabinet ministers since 1945 can be counted on the fingers of one hand. Women constitute a high political risk for all parties, and this limits necessary funding and encourages the appearance of well-known 'talent' candidates not chosen for their political ability. Conservatism at the local level has failed to allow women to build the local base often crucial in securing influence at national level, and it will be a long time before the national bureaucracy provides them with the stepping stone to national politics it grants to their male colleagues. Women have been unable to engineer dramatic changes in their position in society through direct political influence, and such laws as have been passed are weak. What appears a substantial advance, the Equal Employment Opportunity legislation of April 1986, is significantly weakened by lack of any legal penalty for contravention, and the signs are that some employers are managing to circumvent it by indirect means of discrimination.

Lack of achievement in politics is paralleled by lack of success in other careers, for to attain the top a woman has to be of outstanding ability and determination. Parents and husbands are often unwilling or unable to provide the backing upon which most women are dependent if they are to have a successful career. Yet discrimination by men is far from being the only problem. Just as significant are the attitudes of women themselves. A recent survey suggested that no more than 15 per cent of all women wished to work on any long-term, let alone life-long, basis, and the basic assumption by the vast majority of women that careers are not for them reduces openings and saps the confidence of those who do have ambitions in this sector.

Women are also educationally less well qualified than men. Opportunities are fewer, and the persistence of the old hierarchy of higher educational institutions acts to exclude women. Lack of ambition on the part of girls and their families has inhibited active pressure for improvement. More girls than boys continue to high school after completing compulsory education (in 1984, 95 per cent of girls and 92.8 per cent of boys). Almost as many go on to some form of higher education (32.7 per cent of women, compared to 38.3 per cent of men), but there is a substantial difference in the quality and type of higher education received by the sexes. The prestige national universities are dominated by men. The high-ranking private and prefectural/municipal colleges have many more men than women on four-year courses. A large proportion of female students in higher education take two-year courses at junior colleges at the bottom of the institutional hierarchy, and many take such subjects as home economics, which are regarded as suitable preparation for marriage rather than a career. The proportion of well-qualified women is far lower than their representation in higher education would suggest, and the even greater scarcity of women in science and engineering subjects disqualifies them from many jobs in industry and technology.

The continuing assumption that women's main task is marriage and home is reflected both in marriage levels and in employment patterns. In 1985 nearly 93 per cent of women over twenty-five were married or had been married, and this reality dictates the structure of female employment. In 1985 women constituted around 40 per cent of the labour force and nearly a half of all women were in paid employment. The workforce participation rate for women peaks in the early twenties and among those aged thirty-five to fifty-five. Women are represented in all sectors of the economy, but are dominant in trade and retailing, and in the service industries, where they outnumber men. Light industry still employs many women, and as agricultural production becomes less labour intensive and employment opportunities for men elsewhere more attractive, it is the women who increasingly become the core of the productive unit in agriculture. Women are advancing into the professions, where barriers to equality are less conspicuous, but they remain most numerous in the occupations traditionally conceived of as female, for example nursing and teaching.

The pattern of female employment in all sectors shows certain characteristics which largely result from a continuing reluctance to acknowledge the legitimacy of a woman's role outside the home. In the first place, the average duration of service for women is much shorter than that for men. Women work between finishing their formal education and the birth of their first child, and begin to re-enter the workforce after their youngest child starts school. This pattern excludes many women from the famed benefits of seniority wages and lifetime employment. Secondly, women are overwhelmingly concentrated in the lower grades of employment. Businesses such as banking and insurance have large numbers of female clerical and secretarial staff, many designated 'office lady', a term denoting an individual whose job is often little more than to make tea for her male colleagues and enhance the general ambiance of the office. In government employment, regarded as relatively egalitarian, around 20 per cent of all employees are female, but women constitute only a minute percentage of management grade staff. Surveys show that in both national and local government, and in the judiciary, women lack the confidence and desire to fill higher positions and advance slower up the hierarchy. In teaching women predominate in elementary education, but are heavily outnumbered by men in high schools and further education, and almost all heads and administrators are male. Everywhere disproportionately few women reach the higher echelons and an almost exclusively male management structure persists. Thirdly, women's wages are lower than those of men. In 1985 average monthly earnings for women were little more than 50 per cent of those for men. The disparity was particularly great in manufacturing (42 per cent), trade (43 per cent) and finance and insurance (45 per cent). While starting salaries for entrants at all levels are relatively even, men soon move

153

ahead. By the age of thirty, after equal years of service, men are already earning 20–30 per cent more than women.

An important factor in disparities is the recent expansion in the number of female part-time workers. Most women leave work either on marriage or when expecting a child. Where the aspirations of most lie within the domestic sphere the exercise of statutory maternity and other rights and a return to work while children are small can lead to accusations of neglecting family and domestic responsibilities. Childcare facilities are in any case totally inadequate. However, though a women may remain the focus of home and family, these concerns are no longer the full-time, life-long concerns they used to be. Small families of closely spaced children mean that most women are freed of daily care for their youngest child by their mid-thirties. Fewer have parents-in-law for whom to care, husbands are usually out, and housework is much less time-consuming. While some women occupy this new-found leisure with education, social activities or voluntary work, many others seek to return to paid employment, even where the economic returns may be small. These women provide a pool of low-paid, part-time workers. They do not enjoy the benefits of a regular career structure and can be hired and fired almost at will. The number of female part-timers increased by more than four times between 1970 and 1984; a large proportion were in the late thirties to early forties age group, and they were concentrated in small operations where earnings are already lower than average. The growing prevalence of such workers perpetuates the assumption that a woman's income is supplementary to family needs normally provided for by the main, male breadwinner, and hence that conditions and continuity of employment are of less significance than for men. The reluctance of women to register as unemployed even where they may be entitled to benefit suggests that they share this conservative view of their labour. The marginal nature of the jobs that women can secure reinforces their reluctance to compromise in any way their role in the household sphere.

Such restricted opportunities might be expected to provide fruitful soil for a women's movement in Japan. However, the postwar years have produced few campaigns capable of capturing the imagination and interest of a significant number of women. The Occupation reforms, by providing everything the prewar women's movement had striven for, took the wind out of the sails of women's leaders. In the halcyon days after 1945 true legal equality and free participation in politics seemed to offer all that could be wished. To build on this basis, numerous women's groups did spring up. Many sought to raise political consciousness and achieve liberation from old social attitudes, and a vocal campaign for the abolition of licensed prostitution culminated in the passing of new legislation in 1956.

For the most part, though, women's organizations proved unable to work together. The gap between working women and housewives was rarely successfully bridged. The strong influence of the left made the movement vulnerable to the all too frequent application of political dogma and the adverse effects of official hostility. A long-standing role of women as mere adjuncts of reform and revolutionary movements, peripheral beings whose role was to give emotional and physical support to male leaders, seemed in danger of being perpetuated. For much of the fifties and sixties the movement was weak and divided. In the early 1970s the apparent impasse of the reform movements and the legacy of disunity stimulated the growth of a women's liberation movement. Strongly influenced by similar movements in other countries, members advocated individual liberation, sexual liberation and resistance to male rule. Apart from consciousness-raising, the movement conducted a vigorous opposition to proposed restrictions on the freedom of abortion.[5] Small though the number of feminists is, it has helped to stimulate a substantial interest in women's studies and feminist ideology, and some have hailed women's liberation as part of a rising tide of concern for sexual equality. In fact, much of its impact is restricted to intellectual women who might well have succeeded anyway in escaping the restrictions of the domestic sphere.

The failure of elements of the women's movement to appeal to large numbers of women has led many to divert their energies into other fields. Women are not unorganized. Millions of women belong to groups with nationwide affiliations, and these national organizations have proved powerful factors in national policy. Women's political and legal rights do not figure large among their concerns. Given the legal reforms of the Occupation and the persistent emphasis on women's domestic role it is not surprising that the most important manifestations of women's solidarity in the postwar years have been over problems of more immediate and obvious concern to the lives of the majority of women. Parent–teacher associations are run largely by women. Women are a crucial element in campaigns relating to civic concerns – for example, environmental issues. The prominent part played by women in the peace and anti-nuclear movements dates back to the

Occupation years. The massive support given to the Japan Mother's Convention, which started in 1955, demonstrates clearly Japanese women's perceptions of their own role. Most significant, though, has been women's role in the consumer movement, since women are the major purchasers of consumer goods. Involvement in consumer issues dates back to immediate postwar economic dislocation and the founding in 1948 of the Housewives Federation (*Shufuren*), which is still a leading campaigner in this field. Consumer concerns have had a growing appeal as the Japanese economy has prospered, despite male politicians' initial distaste at having to consider such everyday problems.

In the final analysis the women's movement has been confined by having to rebel against social custom and attitudes rather than legal discrimination. A change in the law is just a single stage towards a real shift in the position of women. In the case of milestones such as the Anti-Prostitution Law and the Equal Employment Opportunities legislation it has proved only too easy to find legal methods of circumvention. The gulf between the *de jure* and *de facto* positions of Japanese women is immense; few women wish, or dare, to claim the equality that is their constitutional right since indirect discrimination is difficult to prove and social conservatism exists at every level of society. In a society where women enjoy a certain status as long as they do not try to step outside their traditionally prescribed roles, the attitude of many women is that rapid change is not only impossible but even undesirable. A very large number of women, even some who are highly educated, have little desire to seek a place in what has traditionally been a man's world and are content to find their metier as wife and mother. Japanese men essentially hold just as conservative a view of a woman's place as do women themselves. Most argue that the sexes are equal but different, and that in fact Japanese women are immensely powerful. On the left many advocates of true sexual equality concede that an improvement or change in the position of women is desirable, but tend to argue that women will benefit more by broader reforms of society than through agitation by a specifically feminist lobby. The private lives even of these advocates all too often demonstrate an equally deep-rooted conservatism.

International and economic pressures make some modification in attitudes to women inevitable, but, without a major lead from the ruling élite of society, change will be slow and painful. Such a lead is unlikely. Few attempts have been made to encourage women to enter politics for example, or become business leaders, and the Women's and Minor's Bureau of the Ministry of Labour established in 1947 has hardly proved the hoped for spearhead of change. Anything resembling positive discrimination has been roundly denounced. Laudable bureaucratic intentions have had to contend with a weight of social conservatism and inertia. Consumer and environmental issues demonstrate that Japanese women acting together over common causes of dissatisfaction can be a powerful force, but while they continue satisfied with their role as good wives and wise mothers that potential will not be brought to bear on sexual inequalities and the gulf in status, role and influence between men and women will remain considerable.

NOTES

1   Women's history is an even more recent development in Japan than in this country.
2   Hepburn worked in Japan for over thirty years to 1892, and produced the first English–Japanese, Japanese–English dictionaries.
3   The Peace Police Law of 1900, which prohibited political activity by women, was the major restriction.
4   There were some exceptions – for example, female household heads – but they were small in number.
5   Abortion was a major method of family planning since the pill was largely unavailable.

CHAPTER EIGHT

Emperor and Nation

During the Tokugawa period Japan was divided into several hundred feudal domains, each possessing a high degree of autonomy and a distinctive, regional outlook. Some of these domains harboured a bitter hostility to the central government. The emperor seemed a political nonentity living in virtual seclusion. By the time of World War II the Japanese were, to their enemies, the embodiment of fanatical nationalism. They appeared to be able to make any sacrifice for their emperor and their nation. The last 150 years have seen Japan transformed into a highly centralized nation state.

Under Tokugawa rule Japan was subject to strong regional variations in terms of geographical situation, economic conditions, degree of prosperity, cultural attainments and political involvement. Commercially sophisticated Osaka hardly had the same interests as rural Kyushu, which differed in turn from the wild frontier territory of Hokkaido (Ezo), still only partially under Japanese control. In some ways the country seeemed little more than an amalgam of scattered entities, held together by coercion rather than any genuine sense of unity.

Yet by the Edo era Japan already enjoyed a substantial degree of racial and cultural homogeneity. This was fostered by the small size of the country. The geographical position of the Japanese islands had helped to deter foreign aggression. While successive waves of cultural influences had reached Japan, no foreign military power had ever successfully invaded the country. Even the Mongols of Genghis Khan had been defeated with the aid of the weather in the thirteenth century. Lack of rule by another power had helped Japan to maintain a distinct identity.

Racially the Japanese were virtually unadulterated either by waves of foreign immigration or by other races living in the immediate proximity. The only significant minorities were the *burakumin*, an outcaste class of Japanese racial origin, and the Ainu, original native inhabitants of Japan, who had gradually been driven out by the ethnic Japanese and were by the Edo era found in substantial numbers only in the northernmost island of Hokkaido, on the very periphery of the country. Racial homogeneity was accompanied by cultural and linguistic homogeneity. While regional variations were certainly considerable, as might be expected in a land where communications were deficient and travel uncommon, people in all parts of the country essentially shared the same culture and spoke and wrote a version of the same language. Two centuries of isolation of the Tokugawa period served to isolate the Japanese further as a discrete group.

Part of the cultural tradition shared by Japanese was the position allotted to the imperial family. From the beginning of recorded history the imperial family, and its progenitors, had functioned as chief priests in what had originally been a form of animism. The family claimed to be direct descendants of the Sun Goddess Amaterasu, whom it believed to be the most important of the various Shinto deities. In the Nara period in the eighth century imperial rulers took steps to emphasize the panoply of Shinto mythology and the divine origins of the imperial family in an effort to bolster up their secular power. The Japanese word 'tennō', translated into English as 'emperor', contains the character for 'heaven'. The islands of Japan were said to be born of other gods, allowing their inhabitants as a whole to lay claim to an aura of divinity. By the Tokugawa period the concepts of the emperor as a living god and the divine origin of the Japanese people had received little more than ceremonial attention for many centuries, but the spiritual authority of the imperial house had never been threatened.

The imperial family wielded little influence over the running of the country from the twelfth century; instead, a succession of warrior families exercised power. The majority had the title of shogun bestowed upon them by the emperor, formally appointing them as his military deputy. The administration of the country passed to them, leaving the imperial house with little but a ceremonial function. With no real military power of its own the court had little choice but to sanction the rule of the most powerful lord or family of the time. By doing so it certainly helped to preserve its own existence. Its relation with the Tokugawa house was no exception to this practice. In 1603 Tokugawa Ieyasu, the founder of the regime, sought and was granted the title of shogun, which continued to be borne by his successors until the last one abdicated the office in 1867. With military strength and a total mandate to exercise secular power the Tokugawa family and its followers were in a formidable position, but the nature of this *ex post facto* legitimization was ultimately to prove a factor in their fall.

The securing of the imperial mandate was the major means by which Tokugawa Ieyasu sought to legitimize his position of supremacy, achieved merely by virtue of being the most powerful of many local barons. The early Tokugawa shoguns also sought to provide a political structure that would perpetuate the family's hold on power. This was a combination of highly autonomous elements and a strong measure of centralization; the system has been referred to by some historians as 'centralized feudalism'.[1] The basics of the structure continued almost unmodified until the mid-nineteenth century.

The main problem for the Tokugawa was to maintain their ascendancy over other powerful lords who were potential competitors. Many had only reluctantly accepted Tokugawa hegemony, and the loyalty of this group in particular was suspect. Using their allegiance at the Battle of Sekigahara in 1600 as the yardstick, the lords were divided into two groups: the *fudai*, who had given their allegiance to the Tokugawa in the earlier struggles for power, and the *tozama*, on whom it had been imposed. Land was apportioned to these lords by the Tokugawa, and many daimyo were confirmed in all or part of their earlier holdings at the start of the period. While a daimyo could, in theory, be transferred from his domain, and such transfers were not uncommon in the seventeenth century, they happened less and less as time went on. The pattern of daimyo landholdings overall was thus fairly consistent. The strategic landholding pattern adopted by Japan's rulers concentrated the landholdings of the Tokugawa family and its collateral branches along with those of *fudai* daimyo in the central areas of the country. The lands of the *tozama* daimyo, many of whose individual holdings were of considerable size, were mostly located in areas further from the Japanese heartland, notably the southwest and Kyushu, southern Shikoku and northern Honshu.

A further distinction marked *fudai* off from *tozama*: this was participation in government. Posts in the Tokugawa-run central administration were open only to *fudai* daimyo. Some were even restricted to specific families. The Tokugawa's erstwhile enemies were excluded from all national political or economic decision-making. This exclusion was maintained until the 1850s. It was naturally supported by many *fudai* daimyo.

The Bakufu sought to deprive all daimyo, but especially the *tozama*, of a political and economic base from which to mount successful opposition. Both *tozama* and *fudai* were subjected to a series of checks and balances aimed at keeping them in a position of subjection, designed to prevent collusion in opposition to the Bakufu, or the creation of independent power bases. Apart from the Bakufu's power to transfer a daimyo to a new fief or deprive him of one completely, the most conspicuous of these measures was imposition of the system known as alternate attendance (*sankin kōtai*). Alternate attendance meant that all daimyo, whether *fudai* or *tozama*, had to spend half their time in Edo, the capital, rather than in their own domains, and their wives and children had to be in permanent residence there. It was, in effect, a hostage system, which did deter flagrant opposition to the government.

The Bakufu also sought to deprive the domain lords of economic strength. It possessed itself a powerful economic base, being the largest land owner (the main Tokugawa house and its collaterals controlled some 25 per cent of the total land area) and the owner of major ports, cities and mines. However, while it controlled the disposition of lands to daimyo it could not levy tax revenue on them for the purposes of national administration. Instead, it imposed exactions in the form of compulsory public works programmes and enforced loans. Rigid stipulations regarding lifestyle and conduct served also to encourage conspicuous consumption.

Despite this apparent concentration of power in the hands of the Bakufu, all daimyo enjoyed considerable autonomy in the governing of their own domains. Each daimyo had a greater or smaller number of samurai retainers who owed their allegiance to him, and not to the Bakufu. This élite group served as the administrative and fighting force of the domain, which it controlled in the daimyo's name. The domain was essentially an independent entity, and the size of some domains meant their approximation to small kingdoms. The prerogative of autonomous control of a domain was fiercely guarded, and one on which the Bakufu was reluctant to encroach, except where its own dictates had been blatantly flouted. Each and every daimyo was likely to prove reluctant to sacrifice even the smallest portion of autonomous power, and the dangers attendant on compulsion were considerable.

Throughout the years of Tokugawa rule the various domains thus remained militarily independent units. Superior military force remained the Bakufu's ultimate sanction. This superiority in conjunction with the autonomy enjoyed by domains, deterred the daimyo from attempting to opt out of Bakufu control completely. Moreover, no military challenge was mounted to Tokugawa power until the closing years of the era. One reason for this was clearly the strict system of controls implemented by the regime. Another was disunity and particularism among the daimyo and the domains themselves, which acted further to prevent the formation of an anti-Tokugawa front. The socio-economic changes of the seventeenth and eighteenth centuries went a considerable way towards dispelling many disparities between *fudai* and *tozama*, but a political gulf between them persisted. The overriding importance of loyalty to the domain obscured the possibility of a broader entity that could claim the allegiance of all. Yet if such a basis for a united front could be found, the Tokugawa hegemony could be disputed.

In the long term the regime was also vulnerable on one other count. The regime had sought to exercise control over those who were a threat to it, rather than make any genuine attempt to bring the competing parties together. Political divisions and rivalries were, if anything, perpetuated and reinforced by a political structure founded on suspicion rather than trust. Many *fudai* were unhappy with the checks placed upon them. *Tozama* antagonism, nourished by political impotence, threatened to support any cause likely to have a chance of overthrowing the Tokugawa. The catalyst for dramatic change was the reopening of Western contacts from the first half of the nineteenth century. Significantly, the words 'emperor' and 'imperial' became of growing importance in the language of political debate.

A more questioning view of the relationship between shogun and emperor dates back to the middle of the Tokugawa period. Early in the eighteenth century scholars from the northeast domain of Mito, home of one of the senior branches of the Tokugawa house, produced a work on early Japanese history entitled *History of Great Japan (Dainihonshi)*. This marked the beginning in Mito of a tradition of investigative scholarship continuing to the mid-nineteenth century. While never questioning the necessity of Tokugawa rule, Mito scholarship implied that on occasions members of the Bakufu were overstepping and abusing their mandate. In the early–mid-nineteenth century Mito scholars showed an increasing interest in political and economic affairs and their 'criticisms' of the Bakufu became increasingly tied to specific matters. Another heterodoxy became more explicitly subversive. This was nativism, or national learning (*kokugaku*). Breaking with the Chinese-dominated bent of learning, nativist scholars of the eighteenth century studied the traditional Japanese classics and mythology in an attempt to discover and reassert a pure, indigenous Japanese spirit. Under Hirata Atsutane (1776–1843) the movement demanded a reassertion of the divine imperial and national tradition and delivered a full-blown attack on Confucianism, Buddhism and all other non-Japanese elements.

While the impact of these intellectual debates was largely limited to the ruling class, they offered a justification for opposition to the Bakufu and suggested the existence of an imperial institution which could serve to unite the Bakufu's opponents. It assumed an underlying unity between members of various domains based on a common race and cultural tradition, and built effectively upon it. The justification of acting in the name of the emperor and helping him to regain his true position developed into a crude ideological statement which served to unite the anti-Bakufu movement. The utilization of the imperial institution by the Bakufu's opponents was the logical corollary of the Tokugawa's own use of imperial legitimacy to consolidate their own power. Any ruler or would-be ruler had to claim such legitimacy and any critic had to argue that the imperial mandate was being abused.

The advent of the West in the 1850s demonstrated Japan's acute vulnerability to foreign pressure, and exposed the inability of the Bakufu to deal with it on the nation's behalf. By the late 1850s many opponents of the Bakufu were beginning to call for *sonnō* (respect for the emperor) and *jōi* (expulsion of foreigners), and these slogans became the anti-Bakufu warcry. While the more realistic members of the movement soon realized that the expulsion of foreigners was unlikely to be achieved, most continued to give lip service to the idea, since it was a convenient stick with which to beat the Bakufu, who had first admitted them. The court became a haven for the Bakufu's more radical opponents and the conservative emperor Kōmei (1846–67) and his advisers re-emerged as forces in national political decision-making. Growing court authority could not be tackled by military power, and in the crisis of foreign relations the Bakufu was pushed into seeking court approval for difficult policy decisions to quell opposition to them.[2] Its signing of the Treaty of Amity and Commerce with the US in 1858 without imperial sanction gave rise to accusations of treachery and provoked a major political crisis. The court became a focus of anti-Bakufu intrigue and attracted dissidents from all parts of the country. By 1866 open rebellion against the Bakufu by Chōshū fief highlighted the fact that the Bakufu no longer possessed the military authority to impose its will on a single powerful domain. Late in 1867 the last shogun resigned. A new regime, dominated by men from the *tozama* domains of Satsuma and Chōshū, took power early in 1868. A brief armed struggle ensued. In this struggle the forces arrayed against the Bakufu for the first time abandoned their particularist domain affiliations and called themselves the 'imperial' troops. This, significantly, marked the demise of the domains as militarily independent units and the move towards the creation of a single national army capable of holding the country together under a central administration.

History has too often tended to view the leaders of the new regime as a single-minded body of men, united in their commitment to political, economic and social change and the creation of an internationally strong Japan. In fact, the participants in the revolution were far from united – many had little more in common than a desire to end the dominance of the Tokugawa and to secure some of its power for themselves. Right through to the beginning of 1868 the anti-Bakufu forces were riven by disagreements, and disputes within the ruling élite over the nature and role of the state continued for the next two and a half decades. In the crisis of the late 1860s the adoption of certain tenets of faith managed to produce sufficient unity to enable common action in the various disparate groups that had opposed the Bakufu.

The new ruling group following the *coup d'état* had siezed power in the name of the emperor. The coup was termed a restoration of imperial rule (*ōsei fukkō*). The same credo continued to be utilized not merely to minimize friction within the ruling ranks, but also to strengthen the government's control and achieve some semblance of unity between the disparate interests within the country. The tradition of imperial authority became well established in the early days after the 1868 revolution. Edicts, rescripts and proclamations were issued in the name of the emperor, giving the impression that he was the fountainhead of policies, directing the development of the nation in the best interests of his people. The most famous of the early proclamations is probably the Charter Oath, a commitment issued in April 1868 to unite and involve all groups of the nation in a search for justice, welfare and prosperity, and to educate and reform Japan 'in order to strengthen the foundations of imperial rule'. From the start the government's policy-makers and leaders were in official rhetoric no more than advisers to the emperor. The new regime perpetuated the use of imperial legitimacy and left the way open for critics to suggest the imperial mandate was being abused.

The acts of political centralization carried out after 1868 were aimed at building a united nation capable of withstanding the Western threat. For that purpose it was imperative that the fragmentation and divisions of the Bakufu era be replaced by a substantive unity, at least in the face presented to the outside world. National awareness can only be developed in response to contact with other nations. Before 1853 Japan had been isolated from almost all such contact for over 200 years. The domain particularism emphasized during the Tokugawa period threatened to make any transition to national unity more difficult. In such circumstances the development within the space of less than fifty years of a secure, unified political system, backed up by a shared national ideology, would appear a remarkable achievement, whatever its subsequent perils. The new government's success was helped by the preconditions of ethnic and cultural homogeneity. The size of the country made it easily controlled. Acknowledgement of a shared external threat after 1853 forcibly engendered a collective sentiment which can be called 'nationalism'. The political measures taken by the government were skilfully implemented. They carefully exploited traditional concepts in the achievement of new goals.

The measures of political centralization were not always wholeheartedly supported within the ruling group, and produced temporary and permanent splits in it. They were the product of a gradual trial-and-error progression from one step to another, not of any far-sighted plan conceived before the takeover of power. In their totality they achieved a nation-state with a highly centralized political structure in which government was carried out in the name of the emperor. This system came to be known as the emperor system (*tennōsei*).[3]

The regime's initial priority was to tackle three major problems: the gulf which divided former supporters of the Bakufu from those now in power; the strong indentification with the interest of the domain rather than Japan as a whole; the formal division between the samurai ruling class and the remainder of the population deprived of access to political power. The nation had to be brought under central military control and independent forces disbanded.

The problem of pro-Tokugawa affiliation proved less intractable than might have been expected; a large number of former Bakufu supporters accepted and even supported the change of regime. After the initial eighteen months the new government sought to absorb many former Bakufu supporters into its ranks and avail itself of their much-needed expertise. This proved sufficient to head off serious friction from this quarter. To cope with the problems raised by the domains and their retainers, however, required carefully thought out political measures.

Following the Restoration many of the former Tokugawa lands came directly under 'imperial' rule, but most of the remaining daimyo domains remained intact. Some daimyo held nominally important posts in the central government, but domain interests frequently took precedence over national considerations. It was widely realized among the real holders of power in the government that while this pattern persisted the new regime was no more a 'national' government than its predecessor. Since no daimyo was likely voluntarily to concede power, and the government could ill afford to alienate them, the process had to be gradual. Despite its victory in the civil war, the Meiji regime as yet had no large military force independent of the domains. In 1869 members of the new government from Satsuma, Chōshū, Tosa and Hizen (the main *han* behind the anti-Bakufu movement), persuaded their respective daimyo to particpate in what became known as the return of lands and government to the emperor (*hanseki hōkan*). Each daimyo formally acknowledged imperial suzerainty over his domain. In return he was appointed imperial governor of his former domain, thus retaining control over the territory. The daimyo of many other domains followed suit. In 1871 the centralization was taken a step further; all former domains were reorganized into a prefectural system, which had already been adopted for the administration of former Bakufu territory. Prefectural governorships ceased to be the prerogative of former daimyo, and appointments were made on the basis of factors such as ability and support for the government. In return daimyo were guaranteed nobility status, a stipend and the takeover of domain debts by the state. This system marked the beginning of development towards a fully fledged local government bureaucracy.

While abolition of the domains was likely to make little immediate difference to the average Japanese peasant, artisan or merchant, it constituted a fundamental blow to the formal status of the warriors (*bushi*) as a ruling class. The daimyo and their samurai followers were being deprived of automatic political prerogatives. Since as a group they depended for their livelihood on the tax levied on the peasantry by the domain they were also being deprived of their main source of income. To minimize difficulties, the government initially took over from the daimyo the burden of paying samurai stipends, but in August 1876 the commutation of stipends became compulsory for all samurai who had not already taken up this option. This meant they were effectively paid off with a lump sum, usually in government bonds. The rigid four-caste hierarchy that had prevailed throughout the Tokugawa period was dismantled by steps; from 1872 samurai families were distinguished from the remainder of the populace only by their designation as *shizoku*, a term which came to imply former samurai status. Their prerogatives were further undermined by the abolition of sword-bearing (the traditional mark of the *bushi*) and the introduction of conscription.[4]

Shizoku and their families amounted to over 8 per cent of the population in 1873. They were by far the best educated, most articulate and politically active element in society. Their alienation was potentially highly dangerous. The new government had to try to minimize the possibility of armed opposition to radical change. Various political measures were taken to find an outlet for samurai discontent, but it was also necessary to establish a military authority over the whole country strong enough to quell coordinated opposition. Conscription was seen as the best way of creating a truly national armed force, although some samurai did take up posts as officers. Where samurai discontent did attain serious proportions, notably in the Satsuma Rebellion of 1877, the new army showed itself more than competent to deal with it. Within a decade of 1868 the new central state had not only achieved military superiority, but controlled the only fighting force in the country.

The new regime's leaders needed to create an efficient national apparatus to administer the centralizing Japanese state and implement the radical changes which most of them considered to be necessary. The initial structure of government in 1868–71 gave the sacred authorities theoretical superiority over the secular, but as a factor within government the non-secular side rapidly diminished in significance. For much of the 1870s the greatest power rested with the select group of state councillors (*sangi*) who presided over the work of the various ministries. The structure of government underwent various changes during this time in response to external circumstances and internal divisions, but the fiction of supreme imperial authority was maintained throughout.

This ideology, which had served to provide unity before the fall of the Tokugawa and legitimacy for the new regime afterwards, was formalized during the 1880s in a structure of national government that was to last, largely unchanged, up to 1945. From 1885 major government decisions were taken by a cabinet consisting of the heads of various ministries presided over by a prime minister. He had an imperial mandate to form a government. The cabinet posts were at this point occupied by members of the existing ruling group. In April 1888 a Privy Council was set up, with a remit to advise the emperor on important matters of state. Then in February 1889 the Imperial Japanese Constitution, often known as the Meiji Constitution, provided for an elected diet and laid down the framework for government activity. The constitution took effect from November 1890.

Pressure for constitutional government in Japan dated back to the early 1870s. Popular rights agitation was a major factor in the government's promising constitutional government in 1881. Both for those in power and their opponents constitutional government seemed desirable; for the former it was important to secure Western respect, for the latter it offered a chance of democracy, and a break in the existing monopoly of power. The 1889 constitution was the result of several years of meticulous study and drafting by a team led by Itō Hirobumi, at that time probably the most powerful figure in the Meiji ruling élite. Itō observed firsthand the operation of European constitutions; he had taken careful note of the views of his colleagues and of European constitutional scholars. The team worked against a background of growing pressure for democracy, to which the regime responded with force. The end product was an amalgam of the provisions considered desirable by Itō and his colleagues. Those who might have been expected to express serious differences of opinion had already left, or had been expelled from, the ruling group. A basic aim was the retention of power in the hands of the existing small ruling élite with minimal interference from or responsibility to the majority of the population. The constitution's architects hoped that the provisions for democratic government it contained would be counterbalanced by other safeguarding provisions. The Meiji Constitution was essentially a cautious, conservative document which served to reinforce the influence of the more tradition-minded elements in Japan's ruling class. While distinctively Japanese, it compared most closely with the German model of the monarchy.

By 1889 the official rhetoric of imperial authority was widely accepted. A formalization of the imperial role was adopted by the drafters of the constitution in part as an insurance policy against rapid change. The starting point of the constitution was thus the person of the emperor, who had seen fit, it was said, to bestow a constitution on the Japanese people.[5] The first clause spoke of Japan being reigned over in perpetuity by a line of emperors. The third referred to the emperor as 'sacred and inviolable'. Under the constitution the emperor was the repository of absolute and inviolable sovereignty. He was also the head of government, possessing on paper a sweeping range of executive, legislative, administrative and military powers. Yet the political position of the emperor was ambiguous. He presided over several different bodies, each of which had different, often competing, powers under the constitution, and each of which could have recourse to imperial influence for the pursuit of its own political interests. Pre-1945 Japanese politics has been referred to as a struggle for the body of the emperor, and the degree to which any of the three emperors who reigned under the Meiji Constitution were able, or willing, to exert the political influence that they appeared to have on paper remains a matter of dispute.

The élites given powers under the emperor included a two-chamber diet with elected and appointed members, the Privy Council, the cabinet, the armed forces and the imperial bureaucracy. These bodies operated to a considerable extent independently of each other. The powers allotted to each were secured by certain safeguards, and constitutional government did not mean the existence of parliamentary democracy, cabinets responsible to the diet or a titular head of state. The cabinet and the armed forces were responsible to the emperor and to him alone. Cabinets were 'transcendental' and non-party, appointed by the emperor not necessarily from the majority party in the diet. Important government decisions had in turn to be ratified by the non-elective Privy Council. The leaders of the armed forces had direct access to the emperor and complete autonomy from the cabinet regarding defence matters.

The potential for conflict between these various élites was likely to present little problem as long as their leaderships were relatively homogeneous in background and views, which was the case until the end of the first decade of the twentieth century. When their interests and desires grew apart, however, the constitution could not prevent damaging conflicts. The political structure centred on the person of the emperor was not by itself sufficient to unite the Japanese nation-state. What strength it had came from its reliance on a basic ideological consensus relating the person of the emperor, and the formalization of the weapon of imperial legitimacy. It did not make for long-term political stability any more than it perpetuated control in the hands of the protégés of the Meiji oligarchy.

Itō and the rest of the ruling oligarchy chose to base the 1889 constitution on certain familiar political assumptions and commonly desired moral attributes in the hope that this would perpetuate a strong state structure, prolong their own hold on power and enable constitutional government to operate in practice in a country where its introduction was not the result of many years of evolution. In the years after 1889 the philosophy underlying the constitution was debated and re-debated. Participants in the debate ranged from those who saw the constitutional Japanese state as a purely functional entity, to those who saw it as something mystical, moral and religious. In effect, the more extreme views that were seen to dominate by the 1930s marked a victory of the latter group, but it is fair to say that there was little in what they said that was not a repetition of statements made decades previously. The Meiji Constitution rested on certain assumptions; the definition and elaboration of those assumptions took place subsequently. The core of the philosophy that emerged was referred to as the 'national polity' (*kokutai*) of Japan, the unique fundamental character of the state. The most important elements in this frequently nebulous concept were the existence of the emperor as the wielder of supreme authority; the nature of his relationship with his people: and the claim that Japan was the repository of certain unique virtues.

The reassertion of old customs and beliefs to strengthen an emergent nation-state is not unique in Japan; foreign threats or colonialism have tended to encourage such tendencies. What is striking in the case of Japan, however, is the degree of completeness with which the nation appeared to unite behind the official ideology, and the maintenance of that support over a relatively long period. *Force majeure*, though much in evidence, could not alone have sustained such support. The secret of this unity, it has been suggested, lies in part in the nature of Japanese society, the susceptibility of the Japanese people to central controls and to authoritarianism. Cultural, linguistic and ethnic homogeneity clearly played a part. Indoctrination was efficient. Mass support for the tenets of the 'emperor system' was also inherent in the very nature of the ideology. By vesting the emperor with absolute sovereignty, making the imperial line the ultimate repository of spiritual and secular authority, and not allowing for the existence of any external moral or religious authority capable of sanctioning alternative thoughts and actions, the ruling élite claiming to act in the name of the emperor achieved a monopoly of the symbols of power and effectively made opposition into treachery. Herein lay the potential for a unity that could fall in behind any policy espoused by that sector of society most able to convince the remainder that it was carrying out the imperial will.

This does not mean that the elements of the 'national polity' of Japan went unchallenged. Disagreements within the intelligentsia were not infrequent, but open dissent was discouraged and advocacy of fundamental change harshly suppressed. The majority of the population went along passively with what they were told, even though in private they may not have agreed with all of it. In the light of official suppression and lack of popular support, any political challenge to the ruling élite had to be couched in the political vocabulary permitted by the state. Opposition was therefore pushed away from radical change towards more extreme versions or manipulation of the official rhetoric.

Emotional ties between the emperor and his subjects were exploited to reinforce the emperor-headed ruling structure. As early as October 1890, the Imperial Rescript on Education, often seen as a basic tool in inculcating the orthodox philosophy of the state, showed the strong influence of the Confucian view that the state was essentially a moral order. Propaganda and education taught Japanese children that loyalty and patriotism were the supreme virtues and that the relationship between the emperor and his people was analogous to that of a father and his children. Japan was a 'family state' (*kazoku kokka*), to be ruled in a patriarchal manner by a family head who loved his children and knew what was best for them. They in return owed him total obedience, loyalty and love. The ancient Japanese mythology began increasingly to be approached as history. This mythology stated that Jinmu, the first emperor, was an earthly descendant of the Sun Goddess, Amaterasu. The unbroken lineage of the Japanese imperial family meant unadulterated divine descent; all Japanese emperors were living gods. This qualification offered the ultimate mandate in the exercise of spiritual and secular power. The simulated familial relationship between emperor and people reinforced the aura of divinity attaching to the Japanese people as a whole.

The concept of the Japanese nation as a family, its relationship with the divine, and its possession of unique moral virtues, meant that being Japanese was not merely all-embracing, but absolutely exclusive. The symbols and slogans of the Japanese state could not be shared with any non-Japanese, nor could the unique emotional relationship between the state and the people. It is not difficult to see how the exclusive nature of these ideas, combined with the very real sense of Japan's insecurity in the international environment of the 1930s, contributed to the aggressive sense of national mission whose ambitions led to disaster in 1945. The orthodoxy of the period 1930–45 was a logical extension of the ideas propounded by the leaders of the late nineteenth century in a new context of international and domestic pressures.

The use of the word 'nationalism' in discussing Japan in the pre-World War II period can be highly misleading. Very few Japanese of this period were not nationalists in so far as they felt a certain common identity within the political and cultural unit to which they belonged, wished their country to possess strength and prosperity that would enable it to withstand external pressures, and wanted to 'catch up' with the West. They were also nationalist in their awareness of nation, their pride in their own traditions and practices. These sentiments were officially encouraged and openly asserted from the Meiji period onwards. The word 'ultranationalist', by contrast, has come to be used to refer to those who espoused a rather more aggressive and extreme form of such sentiments and were prepared to use more forceful means in asserting or imposing what they saw as Japan's best interests. All were categorized as right wing; some were clearly revolutionary. The influential, though numerically small, ultranationalist groups conspicuous in the 1930s could trace their heritage back to the Meiji period. The fundamental concepts they had in common were not so different from the official orthodoxy. The difference lay in methods, and degree, and in the more peripheral aspects of their ideologies. It is misleading to designate Japan as a whole in the 1930s as 'ultranationalist', but what did happen at this time was that the activities of ultranationalist groups became more obvious, their contacts with discontented elements in the army grew, and their leverage on the government increased.

The early ultranationalist groups were civilian 'patriotic societies' born out of opposition to the government after the 1877 Satsuma Rebellion. Several were particularly vocal over foreign policy in the 1880s; Japan's posture was seen as weak-kneed, especially in relation to other Asian countries. Such views found considerable support; foreign policy was a sensitive issue at this time, and many Japanese politicians stressed the need for Japan to achieve a measure of influence over Asian countries in order to strengthen her position *vis-à-vis* the industrialized countries of the West. Purported champions of democracy, like Ōkuma Shigenobu,[6] were given to extreme expressions of national chauvinism where foreign policy was concerned. The advocates of an aggressive foreign policy had some success in pushing government decisions in the same direction. From the argument over the invasion of Korea in 1873 onwards, chauvinistic opposition forced a government more intent upon internal reform – at least for the time being – to make concessions to the views of its opponents on foreign policy issues to cling on to its own power. By the time of the Russo-Japanese War (1904–5) an aggressive international approach was widespread among the people. By World War I (when the most immediate aims of internal reform had been achieved) it was being consistently articulated and implemented by Japan's leaders.

This chauvinism was most explicitly expressed in relation to Asia. Japan's victory in the Sino-Japanese War (1894–5) gave substance to the view that Japan was politically, economically and militarily superior to her Asian neighbours. Many Japanese argued that Japan should take the lead in bringing the countries of Asia together to fight Western imperialism. It was thus in Asia's interest, suggested the more extreme, for Japan to gain direct influence over various Asian countries and bring about changes that they were unable to achieve for themselves. The Japanese 'polity' and the imperial vision made Japan best suited for such a guiding role. Such sentiments as these, sometimes referred to by historians as Pan-Asianism, were increasingly common outside the patriotic societies. However, the ideological justification for Japan's leading role contained exclusive elements which made it impossible for the peoples of other Asian countries to receive equal benefits from this 'co-operation under Japanese guidance'. The exclusivity of the doctrine of the 'national polity' and the sense of Japan's mission led inexorably to a belief in a hierarchy of nations which left no doubt that Japanese interests must take precedence. The concept of a hierarchy of nations was not new; inequality had also been a fundamental element in the Chinese Confucian view of the world, in which China was the focus of civilization, and other lands tributary states or out and out barbarians.

While aggressive nationalist views were first expressed in relation to foreign policy, discussion was extended to the ability

173

of the Japanese state to implement the desired foreign policy. For more extreme nationalists the advent of the more liberal atmosphere and domestic policies of the war years and the 1920s was in some respects a retrograde step. The encouragement which 'Taishō democracy' seemed to provide to 'subversive' doctrines and movements – socialism, universal suffrage, parliamentarianism, communism, feminism, to name but a few – seemed evidence that the existing political structure of the Japanese state was inadequate for Japan to carry out her ordained mission. From the latter 1920s some ultranationalist groups engaged in violent attacks on leading political and economic figures.

The more extreme nationalist elements of interwar Japan were not a homogeneous and united group. They were riven with personal and ideological disagreements and their ideas covered a wide span of religious, political, economic and social views. They represented different interests; some, for example, were identified with agrarianism, while others had close contacts with the army. What most had in common was a sense of Japanese mission and a belief in Japanese leadership of Asia to resist the West. All were fervent advocates of the importance of the *kokutai*. They were united in the belief that the essence of the Japanese state was the position of the emperor as the fountainhead of spiritual and secular authority. With this went emphasis on supposedly unique traditional Japanese virtues and the familistic nature of Japanese society. Since these values were shared by those in power, and built into the Meiji Constitution, opposition to the government had to operate outside the constitutional framework which claimed to be the emperor's will. Demands for reform were predictably made on the grounds that the emperor was being misled and ill-served by his advisers, that his true will was not being carried out. To restore the true relationship between the emperor and his people there must be a 'Shōwa Restoration'.[7] For the 'patriots' of the 1930s, no less than for those of the 1860s, direct action against those abusing the imperial mandate was a legitimate, indeed a necessary, alternative.

One of the most influential thinkers of the ultranationalist movement was Kita Ikki (1883–1937), a former socialist who had spent a considerable period in China. Kita believed that Japan could assist China to advance her revolution and expel the West only if Japan herself was subjected to reform. In his *An Outline Plan for the Reconstruction of Japan*, published in 1919, Kita called for a military *coup d'état* followed by a period of martial law, during which the country could be reorganized along the lines of what was, in effect, a national socialist economic system. The other leading theorist of the ultranationalist movement was Ōkawa Shūmei (1886–1957), an ardent advocate of Japan's mission to liberate Asia. Other, less articulate, thinkers drew on conservative values, socio-economic discontent and popular radicalism in calling for domestic reform to enable Japan to fulfil her 'true' role in Asia.

Mostly through informal means, some descendants of the founders of the original nationalist societies of the 1880s–1890s and their followers influenced and infiltrated decision-making at the highest political levels, exercising a power out of all proportion to their small numbers. Party politicians were driven in the direction of their views, for fear of physical attack, or, at the very least, of seeming unpatriotic. This tendency was reinforced by developments in the army, where factional struggles took on an ideological colour, and discontent erupted between radical field-grade officers and their more élite counterparts. Young officers, keen on radical reform at home and a more aggressive foreign policy, combined with civilian groups in the years 1931–6 in a series of attempted *coups d'état* and assassinations. After the suppression of the most famous of these in February 1936 army leaders reasserted a strict control over these radical elements of the military, and the more extreme members of the civilian right wing were rendered less vocal. Nevertheless, the radical right's attempts at direct action in these years were sufficient to pressurize the authorities into suppressing anything redolent of heterodoxy and reinforce the influence in national affairs of the army, which under the Meiji Constitution possessed considerable political autonomy.

In the interwar years the spiritual and political role assigned to the emperor went largely unquestioned in public through fear of being thought guilty of both treachery and sacrilege. Even in the relatively liberal early 1920s the communists were almost alone in maintaining that the emperor had no place in their ideal society; communism was illegal. Most other groups, even on the left wing, incorporated the existence of the emperor into their beliefs. The glorified imperial role made even academic analysis problematic. The most conspicuous case of this was that of Minobe Tatsukichi, professor of constitutional law at Tokyo Imperial University, who had propounded what is known as the 'organ' theory of the emperor's constitutional position. Minobe maintained that sovereignty rested with the state, and that the emperor exercised sovereign power as the supreme organ of the state according to the constitution. When Minobe's theory was first expounded before World War I it aroused the hostility of more conservative and traditionalist legal circles, who asserted that the emperor had a special position of sovereignty above the constitution, rather than being an organ of it, but it provoked little wider interest. In 1935, however, against the background of a strengthening right-wing/ultranationalist movement, cudgels were again taken up in a revival of the attacks on Minobe's ideas. Branded by opposition politicians and the army as incompatible with the *kokutai*, Minobe's views became a national issue. His books were banned, he was stripped of all honours and public office. There was even an attempt on his life.

This controversy became the starting point of a movement for 'clarification of the national polity', whose outcome was a document released by the Ministry of Education in 1937 under the title *Cardinal Principles of the National Polity* (*Kokutai no Hongi*). This was the formal statement of the fundamental concepts behind the nature of the Japanese state.

Like the other basic statement of the nature of the state, the Imperial Rescript on Education of 1890, the *Cardinal Principles* was far from specific. It spoke in broad terms of the unique position of the emperor, his relationship with his people and the existence of a Japanese mission. The text was backed up by extracts from the ancient Japanese classics. This document, which was widely seen as the definitive statement of the official ideology and used as a school ethical textbook, marked the underlying character of the state as aggressively nationalist, imperialist, authoritarian, non-individualistic. For non-Japanese it seemed to epitomize all that was evil and threatening. For Japanese, however, the statements contained in it were an elaboration of ideas propounded over the preceding seventy years, sharpened by a changing international environment. The *Cardinal Principles* said nothing that was unfamiliar to the majority of Japanese.

This concept of the fundamental principles of the state was crucial to the political position of the emperor, but had little direct effect on the formal structure of government below him. A change in the 'emperor-given' constitution was virtually inconceivable, so the constitutional framework laid down by the Meiji Constitution remained unaltered through to 1945. Some changes did occur in the mechanics of government administration, in the make-up of political organization and in representation, but these matters lay outside the confines of the constitution. A 'new political structure' created in autumn 1940 brought the dissolution of remaining political parties, but this, too, was not a constitutional matter. Nor were such things as ministerial jurisdiction. This is not to say that the realities of power did not change; rather that such changes were shifts in balance within the framework of the Meiji Constitution and not fundamental changes in the framework itself.

Much of the strength of the Meiji Constitution lay in its vagueness but this ambiguity was also inherently dangerous. The lack of commitment to popular sovereignty, and its provision for the existence of several different authorities, whose mutual relationships were ill-defined and each of whom was responsible only to the emperor, failed to provide for a clear locus of authority. Inviolable sovereignty remained vested in the person of the emperor, and politics became a battle for control over his person. Despite claims to the contrary, emperors reigned rather than ruled. The Taishō emperor (1912–26) was physically and mentally sick. The Shōwa emperor (Hirohito) who succeeded to the throne in 1926 was reluctant to try and exercise the political power he in theory possessed, preferring to be seen as a constitutional monarch.[8]

The war years 1937–45 produced a heightened emphasis on the need to unite behind the national polity and preserve the virtues of loyalty, filial piety and patriotism. The unity of the nation behind its leaders held till the last days of the war, but as the situation deteriorated the rhetoric became increasingly hollow in the face of economic and social deprivation and demands to sacrifice all other considerations to the successful prosecution of the war. What purported to be the imperial mission was bound in itself to be morally right and could not be openly criticized, but such an assertion had appeared to guarantee success, and this was no longer forthcoming. The failure of the ideology to live up to its promises called its future into question long before outside intervention produced more radical reforms in its manifestations in the machinery of the state.

For the Occupation authorities the dismantling of the 1889 constitution was imperative for the creation of a democratic, peace-loving state, since it had provided the framework within which militaristic governments had operated and enshrined the principles upon which the aggressive nationalistic state was founded. Some provisions of the constitution were immediately suspended in 1945. The emperor had already broken with tradition by broadcasting to the people after the acceptance of surrender. He now broke more new ground by visiting General MacArthur, the head of the Occupation forces (SCAP – Supreme Commander Allied Powers), and having his photograph taken with him. In his New Year's message in 1946 he publicly renounced his divinity, abandoning any claim to rule as a living god. The declaration could not undermine all the authority he might wield as the descendant of gods – the origins of this authority lay in the realm of legend and could not be altered by statute – but it served notice that the concept of the emperor as the ultimate repository of sovereignty, to whom all elements of government were responsible, was being called into question. Other measures, such as the suspension of certain provisions of the civil code, at the same time undermined the traditional social system which had provided the back-up for the whole concept of the 'family state' headed by a paternalistic, yet deified, emperor.

The survival of the imperial institution itself was a matter of fierce debate at the end of the war. Anti-Japanese propaganda had portrayed the emperor as the arch-leader of aggressive Japanese nationalism, and many among the allies subscribed to the view that he had played a leading role in a conspiracy to wage aggressive war. There were many calls for his trial and execution as a war criminal. Only the belief that the emperor's demise would lead to internal chaos, increasing Japanese hostility to the Occupation and rendering future change more difficult, saved both the emperor himself and the imperial institution. Some SCAP advisers, well acquainted with Japan and its people, felt very strongly that since the imperial institution was integral to the sensibilities of the people the emperor's execution would cause more harm than good. Their argument that the emperor could be used as a vehicle for the implementation of reform won the day, although historians since have continued to debate the emperor's political role pre-1945. On the Japanese side, the securing of a guarantee from the allies of the security of the emperor had been a major stumbling block to peace negotiations. This guarantee had not been given, but the Japanese authorities fought hard to save the emperor himself and preserve the institution intact. The price for keeping it at all was a radically different constitutional position.

In seeking to change the constitutional framework, the Occupation authorities initially hoped that the Japanese would spontaneously propose the necessary constitutional revision, but as successive Japanese committees failed to come up with what the authorities considered to be sufficiently radical drafts, Occupation officials drafted their own version. The 1947 Constitution of Japan was a barely modified version of this draft, and has provided the framework for the government of Japan since that time. It formally excised the apparatus of myth and legend that had upheld the old political order, and sought to remedy some of the 'weaknesses' of the old constitution. Under the new constitution the emperor became the symbol of the state and of the unity of the people. Sovereignty was vested not in him but in the Japanese people. Highest authority was vested in the two-chamber diet elected by universal suffrage. The cabinet under the prime minister was to be chosen from the majority party in the diet and was responsible to the diet. The competing élites of the old constitution were abolished or subordinated to the cabinet. The chain of responsibility laid down excluded the emperor. The constitution also provided for the existence of an independent judiciary and contained a guarantee of human rights and equality.

The nature of the radical changes affecting the structure of government and the character of state and emperor swept away much of the all-embracing official orthodoxy towards which most Japanese had seemed to possess genuinely and fervently held sentiments. How far these sentiments were genuine and how far Japanese merely paid lip service to them is a moot point, but successive Japanese governments certainly made every effort to instil their theory of the nature of the Japanese state, and the social values associated with it, into the minds of both children and adults alike. The indoctrination programme was highly effective. Suppression of opposition, brutal though it was, cannot alone account for the degree of fanaticism with which many Japanese in the 1930s and 1940s appeared to approach their supposed duty to the emperor. The removal of authoritarian controls failed to produce a ferment of alternative ideologies. Prevailing conditions explain in part the absence of such a ferment: the shock inflicted by military defeat and invasion; the acute nature of social and economic problems; the presence of the Occupation and the later moves by SCAP to suppress views regarded as too radical; the fundamental enormity of the disaster that had overtaken Japan. However, it also suggests the degree to which the majority of the populace knew no alternative to the orthodoxy.

For these reasons the discrediting of the existing orthodoxy of the state – a discrediting based on its failure to deliver the goods – was followed by something of an ideological vacuum. Vigorous discussions revolved around specific political issues, suggestions for improvements in the way the country was administered, and by whom, as well as around desired changes in the society and economy. These questions were clearly of great significance, but little thought was given to an all-embracing concept of the nature of the state which could replace the previously dominant one. State and nation lacked a fundamental rationale to tell them where they were going and how they could get there. Broader concepts such as democracy seemed unable to reproduce the emotional commitment which made the old ideas so strong; internationalist doctrines such as communism lacked the 'nationalist' emphasis that was of continuing importance to a vast majority of the Japanese people. Even after the Occupation, when Japanese started looking forward to a new international role, a tendency to look within Japan, and hence to the past, for a more fundamental *raison d'être*, persisted.

With its leading exponents dead or imprisoned, and a widespread purge carried out at all levels of Japan's political and economic leadership, few were at first prepared to speak up in support of the old orthodoxy. Survival and peace were more immediate considerations. After the Occupation was over, and especially from the 1960s when the attention given to the economy was beginning to pay off, it became more respectable to call for a return to the old values. The more extreme voices remained small in number; a few patriotic societies in the prewar mould engaged in small-scale covert activities, but they had the support of few of the population, especially where violence was involved. Talk of going back to traditional values and mores is common to conservatives everywhere, but when such talk has been associated with calls for Japan to reassert her international strength and engage in more substantial rearmament it has caused worry to some.

Despite the radical Occupation reform of the structure of government, aspects of the mores and concepts associated with the 'emperor system' have remained very deep rooted as an integral part of the Japanese cultural tradition. The impact of linguistic, racial and cultural homogeneity on national awareness has remained strong – all the stronger perhaps in a world where internationalism has in theory been the order of the day and external pressures of vital importance. Through the postwar period most Japanese have closely identified themselves with the nation and its success. Some have claimed a unique 'superiority' *vis-à-vis* the outside world. There is no question of restoring the emperor either as a living god or as a *de facto* ruler, but he has retained a certain aura due to past history and the efforts of his entourage to detach him from the people, and has remained a potent symbol of national unity and nationhood to most Japanese. How this will change with the death of the Shōwa emperor in January 1989 remains to be seen. Few can recall the times before Hirohito's accession, and his long reign is associated in the minds of all Japanese with a huge range of historical experiences, good and bad. The end of his life marks the end of an era, and is bound to initiate a period of reassessment. However, the strength of the prewar orthodoxy did not lie in legends. It was powerful because of social and political conditioning, and because in a less articulated form its fundamental elements were integral to a tradition shared by the Japanese people as a whole. Like other communities facing an external threat, or perceived threat, Japanese banded together on the basis of the values and customs that they had in common. Both the reality of the threat and the prominence it attained in public statements affected the drive for national solidarity. The enhanced rhetoric of the 1930s drew support because it appeared to offer positive support to a people whose attempts to be accepted as an equal had been rebuffed and who felt themselves threatened from all sides – militarily, diplomatically and economically.

Through the traumas of the last 150 years Japanese national awareness founded on a unique cultural tradition has provided a sure basis on which to present a united front to the outside world. The formal manifestations of the old philosophy of the state have been dismantled, but many of the elements which gave it its strength have continued to operate. While it is right to approach the term 'national character' with caution, the Japanese themselves frequently call attention to certain attributes which unite them as Japanese. A strong concern for the success and prosperity of the nation is almost universal. The national interest, however perceived, has been able to take precedence over the interests of the smaller sub-groups, organizations and individuals who go to make up the nation. The greatest strength of the Japanese state in the years up to 1945 was its success in making patriotism and concern for the national interest the monopoly of the establishment. This enabled it to reject any mass challenge on the grounds of class, or other sectional interest. The persistence of old attitudes after 1945 has meant that the undermining of this monopoly has been a slow process.

NOTES

1   The question of the applicability of the term 'feudalism' in relation to Japan is mentioned in Chapter One.
2   During the early 1860s the Bakufu pursued a policy of rapprochement with the court, referred to as *kōbu gattai* (unity of court and Bakufu), but this attempt to shore up the system using the influence of the court proved unsuccessful.
3   The word *tennōsei* is widely used in Japanese literature, as is the translation in English-language writings. While some historians define it more narrowly, for most it implies the prewar political system of supreme imperial authority, and the social and legal structures that supported it. It is in this looser sense that it is used here.
4   The military aspect of these changes is discussed in Chapter Twelve.
5   The constitution was referred to as 'emperor-given'.
6   Ōkuma Shigenobu was a member of the Meiji oligarchy who left the government in 1881.
7   Shōwa was the reign name taken by the new emperor in 1926, and the word 'restoration' was used to evoke the Meiji Restoration of 1868.
8   The role of the Shōwa emperor in the policies of the 1930s and 1940s has been much debated. After the war the emperor was often seen abroad as a Japanese Machiavelli, but more recent attempts to prove his complicity in policy-making are hardly substantiated.

CHAPTER NINE

Heterodoxy, Orthodoxy and Religious Practice

In Japan, as elsewhere, the ruling class has long viewed both religion and education as vehicles for furthering the purposes of the state. Throughout much of the modern period, too, religious practice and formal instruction have been manipulated by those in power to enhance their own influence and that of their administration. The purpose of education has been primarily to produce the skills required by the state and inculcate the values the state deems desirable. Religious practice has been closely tied to the whole system of formal education and fostered by the state in accordance with its perceived needs. Heterodoxy has been so overshadowed by orthodoxy that its very existence has been doubted. This manipulation has been approached with varying degrees of subtlety and has met with differing degrees of success. This has been a two-way process, with the state compelled to compromise in the face of religious and educational pressures. In the case of religion in particular, state orthodoxy was counterbalanced by heterodox doctrines and by popular sentiment and religious practice.

The Japanese call themselves an areligious people. Religion is for them not a matter of doctrine or metaphysical truth as it is in the West. Religious practice consists of participation in certain rituals rather than adherence to a specific set of beliefs. Religion is primarily interpreted in a pragmatic, utilitarian way, and the benefits accruing from religion are very much of this world. In consequence the Japanese have adopted an eclectic approach to religious beliefs, selecting practices in response to specific material requirements or the need to compensate for specific lacunae in their spiritual life. Over the centuries a variety of rituals and concepts have come together to form what might be called 'the religion of

Japan'. There are three main sources of Japanese religious practice: Shinto, Buddhism and Confucianism.

Indigenous spiritual beliefs, nowadays associated primarily with the categorization 'Shinto',[1] date back to the animism, shamanism and nature worship of the prehistoric period. Shinto is a loose collection of beliefs and practices associated with the worship of *kami*, a term normally translated as 'deity' or 'spirit'. *Kami* could be associated with a particular location or a particular community, and a belief in the existence of myriads of *kami* denoted the sacredness of the cosmos as a whole. The spirits of the dead were also believed to become *kami*. At an élite level these beliefs became increasingly systematized from the eighth century, when they were used to support the claims of the imperial family to the throne, as the Yamato clan sought to impose its religious tradition on other clans. The emperor, as high priest of his clan, was represented as a living *kami* by virtue of his descent from the sun goddess. While this religious tradition was significant in maintaining the position of the imperial family, it had little relevance to the popular religious practices and beliefs observed by individual families or to the spiritual life of the community.

Buddhism had formally entered Japan by the sixth century as part of an influx of Chinese scholarship. Japanese versions of Buddhism multiplied, ranging from the esoteric sects of the ninth century to the rampant nationalism of the thirteenth-century priest, Nichiren, who popularized Buddhist beliefs. Sect leaders frequently took a political stance, and this politicism was, on occasions, reflected in open opposition to the secular authorities. Violent confrontation between Buddhist sects and the dictator Oda Nobunaga in the six-teenth century removed organized Buddhism as a militant political and moral force opposed to Japan's military rulers, but official patronage and manipulation of Buddhist institutions continued. For most Japanese Buddhism provided rituals and practices for specific aspects of life or death, and throughout the Tokugawa period these remained deeply ingrained in the life of the people.

Yet the nature of Buddhism and the diffuseness of Shinto practice outside the formal ritual of the imperial court rendered both inadequate as vehicles for the reinforcement of Bakufu control. It was to Confucianism that the Tokugawa turned for the cornerstone of their official orthodoxy. Confucian doctrines had also been introduced into Japan long before as a focal element in Chinese learning and civilization, and had remained influential. The rise to power of the military élite after the twelfth century had brought about a decline of emphasis on some aspects of Confucianism and had wrought substantial modifications and 'Japanization' in others. The Tokugawa now turned to Neo-Confucianism, a heterodox version expounded by the Chinese philosopher Zhu Xi and introduced into Japan in the Kamakura period (1185–1333). Here, too, a considerable eclecticism was observed. The elements of Neo-Confucianism stressed in Tokugawa Japan emphasized the virtues of loyalty and filial piety which upheld the existence of a rigid social order and accorded well with the static hierarchy which the Bakufu sought to perpetuate as the foundation of Tokugawa family power. The official Japanese version of Neo-Confucianism as manifested in the Tokugawa era was an ethical system and a moral code; it concerned itself with conduct in this world and not with man's existence in relation to the cosmos.

Elements from these three sets of beliefs served different aspects of an individual's life and complemented rather than conflicted with each other. While retaining their own distinct identity, each religion developed its own particular place within the totality of Japanese religious practice. Broadly speaking, Confucianism provided the moral code, Shinto embraced the practices associated with the agricultural cycle, and hence the rituals of daily life, while Buddhism filled the need for the more transcendental, eschatological aspects. Over the centuries Shinto, Buddhism and Confucianism were continually influenced by each other, and the complex inter-relationships between them were constantly evolving, even where the state had no vested interest in promoting one at the expense of the other.

In fact the establishment was always attempting to do just this. During the Tokugawa period official patronage of Neo-Confucianism and Buddhism as instruments of social control resulted in the formal institutions of organized Shinto, for example shrines, being deprived of funding or placed under the control of Buddhist priests. Nevertheless Shinto rituals continued to be observed by the community. The connections of these rituals with the Shinto ceremonial of the imperial court were at best tenuous. A revival of interest in Shinto among intellectuals from the late eighteenth century strengthened its position, and changes in popular sentiment led more and more Japanese to make pilgrimages to Ise, Japan's most sacred Shinto shrine, but its institutional basis remained weak. Conventional historiography maintained that during the Tokugawa period state policies and isolation worked together to produce a relatively unified and homogeneous ethos which became the core of what is now regarded as 'Japanese tradition'. More recent work has suggested that this 'tradition' was largely a creation of the Meiji period,[2] but its creators owed much of their success to the skill with which they manipulated elements of the Tokugawa orthodoxy.

Despite the keen attempts of the authorities to retain strict control over intellectual and spiritual life, non-conformist ideas often surfaced. The intellectual history of the Tokugawa period abounds in writers and thinkers who, both by deviating from the official line and by working within it, achieved the establishment of new, influential schools of thought, some with considerable mass followings. Mito, the Tokugawa domain which was a centre of Confucian scholarship, produced a restatement of the traditional relation between shogun and emperor which was ironically to prove subversive. Confucian scholarship was marked by the emergence of 'ancient learning' (*kogaku*), which looked to the study of ancient China, as well as by further variants of Neo-Confucianism. Nativism, or national learning (*kokugaku*), by emphasizing Japan's indigenous traditions, became an inspiration behind the 1868 revolution and the development of the modern Japanese state. On a more populist level Shingaku doctrines, an eclectic system of practical morality which sought to accord with the everyday lives of the mass of the people, found widespread adherence among the populace of the towns. Although new ideas could ultimately have a major influence on political activity, they rarely challenged the fundamental ethical principles which governed the operation of Japanese society, and for the most part had little relevance to the lives of the majority.

The mainstream of orthodox thought also set the tone for most of the educational practices and precepts of the Tokugawa period, although in Japan, as elsewhere, education could, and did, become a significant means of dissent. Edo society was in both form and practice rigidly hierarchical. It was to be expected, therefore, that any education available should conform to and reinforce the assigned expectations and lifestyle of the stratum of the population which received it. In this respect it was markedly different from China, where education was the key to social mobility. Broadly speaking there were three major types of education: that received by the ruling warrior class; vocational education for townspeople (*chōnin*) engaged in commercial activity; and temple schools (*terakoya*), which provided basic learning for the remainder of the population.

Samurai education was dispensed by schools run by the domain and by individual scholars, whose reputations often became great enough to attract students from outside the immediate locality. Both types grew in significance as the period progressed, and in the later part of the era most warrior sons attended domain schools. With residence concentrated in castle towns, most samurai families had easy access to these institutions. The shared education reinforced a sense of solidarity among the domain ruling class. All domains saw education as having a moral content, as well as giving instruction in skills required for peace and war. Students were instructed in reading through the medium of the Chinese classics, and studied calligraphy, etiquette and military skills. Some added studies in sciences such as mathematics and medicine. Those who wished to pursue their studies further could become followers of individual scholars who had set up private 'schools' either within the domain or elsewhere. These intellectuals became increasingly numerous during the latter part of the period as mobility grew, Bakufu control loosened and heterodox doctrines, especially Dutch learning, aroused growing interest. Many of the political and intellectual leaders of the Meiji period studied under non-establishment scholars who attracted followers from the length and breadth of the country. The instruction provided at these private schools often had significant political implications.

Most domains did not actively seek to spread education among non-samurai. Education for commoners was provided by a heterogeneous bunch of institutions which tend to be called *terakoya*, or temple schools, so-called because temples were frequently the venue. These schools, run on a mixture of charity and contributions from attenders, sought to impart practical information and basic vocational skills, including literacy and numeracy. Moral injunctions also played a part. Instruction of this kind expanded rapidly from the second half of the eighteenth century. Much of the populace continued to receive no schooling at all, but the number receiving some elementary instruction, albeit sporadically and for short periods, was large by comparison with most pre-industrial countries. While members of the merchant class also attended temple schools, some also received instruction geared to practical commercial and economic purposes, concentrating on subjects such as accounting, business practice and marketing. By and large this training was informally structured, with most knowledge being picked up through the medium of apprenticeship and on-the-spot learning. Merchants essentially learnt by doing, and the training they received was highly empirical. During the course of the Tokugawa period some members of the merchant class turned to a classical education in an attempt to achieve social respectability, and more practical learning gained limited currency among their rulers.

As heterodox schools of thought emerged, so, too, did innovations appear in the field of learning. One of the most important was the introduction of a form of Japanese studies from the late eighteenth century. Stimulated both by official Confucian sources and by the activities of the non-establishment nativist movement, the study of Japan had become part of the curriculum in most domain schools by the early nineteenth century. The other conspicuous development was in Dutch learning (*rangaku*), which experienced a boom in the first half of the nineteenth century. Dutch learning rapidly became Western learning, and the core of these studies was science (especially medicine) and military matters. Western learning was propagated by private schools such as that in Osaka of Ogata Kōan, credited with being the founder of Western medicine in Japan. It too, found its way into the domain schools. Other so-called 'schools' existed purely to promote a specific political viewpoint, for example that of the 1850s radical nationalist, Yoshida Shōin.[3] All these innovations posed a potential threat to the traditional orthodoxy, but educational methods and much of the content of education remained intact, and the numbers involved in these innovative educational changes were few. Most intellectuals, like those involved in peasant unrest, sought improvements within the existing social order, and the implications of dissent were rarely spelt out.

Notwithstanding these limitations, the spread of education and literacy in late Tokugawa Japan was substantial. Estimates suggest that over 40 per cent of the male population had been in receipt of some formal education by the end of the Tokugawa period, and there were few Japanese who did not have access to a person with a degree of literacy, someone who could assist, for example, in deciphering official communications or letters. Such education was of practical use to the individual and facilitated the exercise of administrative and propaganda functions by the authorities. It meant being accustomed to the concept of being trained and to the notion that education was a desirable thing which led to the improvement of the individual, at least in moral terms. Many writers cite the degree of access to education as one of the factors which enabled Japan to transform her economy and polity in the late nineteenth century. Yet reservations as to its value are also called for. On a practical level there was a tremendous gulf between the spoken vernacular and the written language, normally classical Chinese or a literary form of Japanese. Learning to read and write at an acceptable level meant acquiring not only a knowledge of thousands of Chinese characters, but a whole new set of grammatical rules as well. Many commoners would not have received sufficient formal education to achieve functional literacy. They may have been able to write their names, but have no hope of reading an official notice. For these reasons the level of literacy may have been exaggerated.

Most education in the Edo period was designed to achieve a submissive populace unquestioning of the morality given it by its teachers. Formal instruction and orthodox religion were instruments of social control and vehicles for the inculcation of 'acceptable' political and social views. The Meiji regime sought to retain a high degree of integration between learning, spiritual life and the political system to further these same purposes.

The early Meiji political framework suggested the building of a theocracy. The significance of the emperor to restoration ideology and to the stability of the early Meiji government, and the proclaimed desire to revive a former golden age, initially produced a governmental structure in which the religious arm took formal precedence over the secular. This predominance was removed in 1871, but Shinto continued to enjoy the status of a national religion. This privileged position was reconciled with the freedom of religion provided for by the Meiji Constitution through the fiction of 'State Shinto' as a national moral and patriotic cult which did not preclude adherence to a variety of religious beliefs. The rise and continuing importance of State Shinto as the under-pinning of the Meiji political system did not challenge the pivotal role of Confucianism as an ethical and moral code. Elements of Tokugawa Neo-Confucianism were powerfully incorporated into the official value system. By contrast, institutional Buddhism was severely weakened by an attempt to re-establish a firm line between it and Shinto. The disestablishment that followed the Restoration deprived Buddhism of official financial support and undermined its formal institutions to such an extent that for decades it lacked the national influence normally accruing to a major institutionalized religion. Only since 1945 has any element of organized Buddhism assumed an influence that cannot be ignored at national level.

These official attempts to change the religious balance of people's lives were less than wholly effective. They betrayed an insensitivity regarding the functioning of religion at a popular level. The state's attempts to tamper with the coexistence between

Shinto and Buddhism, for example, did little to impair the balance of ritual in people's daily lives, while the programme of shrine mergers in the later Meiji period suggested a total disregard for the relationship between *kami* and community. The formal division of Shinto practice into different categories was highly artificial.

, The opening up of Japan to the West not only introduced new ideas and approaches, but established a dramatically changed overall environment. Most Japanese shared an ambiguous attitude towards the West – an acute awareness of vulnerability combined with pride in the country's success in responding to it. This ambiguity goes some way towards explaining the coexistence of orthodoxy and heterodoxy in modern Japan and the existence of apparently contradictory attitudes even within the same individual.

Some of the first foreigners to arrive in Japan in the mid-nineteenth century were missionaries. Christianity was banned for most of the Tokugawa period, although a small number of 'hidden' Christians, against all odds, covertly kept a form of Christian belief alive for more than 200 years. Restrictions on Christianity were relaxed under Western pressure in the early Meiji period, but while Christianity remained illegal for Japanese, or at least officially discouraged, there was little prospect of large-scale conversion. Instead, missionaries worked to exert influence through medical care and educational activities. They set up hospitals, treatment centres and hostels for the disabled. Christian schools run by foreigners became educational leaders from the 1860s, and Christianity established itself as a major vehicle for education in Japan, especially for women. Writers, journalists, social commentators and religious activists could not remain uninfluenced by it. Some Japanese responded to the first flush of pro-Western enthusiasm by accepting Christianity as the basis of the Western package. Prominent Japanese Christians included the educationalist Niijima Jō, the social movement activist Kagawa Toyohiko and Christian socialists like Katayama Sen and Abe Isoo. However, Christian education and welfare was rarely the key to religious conversion that its proponents hoped. The Japanese approach to religion precluded acceptance of a body of doctrine which seemed to shut out other religious observances. The vast majority of the population had little knowledge of the Christian religion and equally little desire to acquire it. Christianity was an alien creed closely identified with Western civilization and tainted by prohibition in the past. The authorities viewed it as potentially subversive, and as time went on Japanese were more and more encouraged to assert their own 'indigenous' traditions. Christianity was identified with 'non-Japaneseness'. The accusations of *lèse-majesté* levied in 1891 at the leading Christian Uchimura Kanzō for lowering his head rather than bowing to the Imperial Rescript on Education[4] were a clear indication of the perceived incompatibility of Christian belief with loyalty to the Japanese state. So while Christianity remained significant as an educational medium it had less religious impact. The separation of Western culture and institutions from the religious foundations that had produced them became almost total.

In a country where religious life was so strongly identified with the community, the state's attempts to manipulate that relationship were likely to be not merely ineffective, but counterproductive. Moreover, the rapid growth of new communities presented strains which the authorities were ill-equipped to handle. The beneficiaries of this dislocation included a series of new sects. Spontaneous religious sentiments combined with factionalism within both Shinto and Buddhism to produce vigorous new offshoots of these religions or new foundations eventually categorized as quasi-religions. Many of these sects embraced a strong element of mysticism and revelation. Some grew out of the mystical experiences of a charismatic leader, often a woman. Some of the most famous of a succession of cults in the post-1868 years had Shinto connections – Kurozumikyō, Tenrikyō and Ōmotokyō. Followers of these new religions were numerous and vocal enough to disturb the authorities, who sought to keep a tight rein on any potentially subversive influence, particularly in the political arena. Only as long as they offered a quiet vent for popular religious feeling and complemented rather than contravened the official orthodoxy could they be tolerated. The control of the authorities was in most cases made easier by the fact that few of these sects stipulated social value systems radically different from the Neo-Confucian-based ethos of most Japanese. Some were uniquely 'Japanese' religions whose view of the nation precluded any conflict between religion and state. Tight control over these and other sects incorporated their adherents into the orthodoxy of a state termed by one writer as 'immanental theocracy'.[5] In the years after 1868 the state attempted to fuse the ethnocentric amalgam it called State Shinto with the traditional rituals of life and death to provide the basis of 'religiosity' for all Japanese.

Christianity had by the 1870s become a major educational medium, but it was soon overhauled by the rise of an increasingly monolithic state education system. While the literacy rate was relatively high by the late Tokugawa period, the new government was well aware that the level of education was totally inadequate for its purposes. The spread of literacy, a wider knowledge of sciences and humanities, and the training of specialists, were all imperative if Japan was ever to compete with the West on its own terms. The 1868 Charter Oath from the Meiji emperor declared: 'Knowledge shall be sought throughout the world so as to strengthen the foundations of imperial rule.' A wave of enthusiasm resulted in many new educational institutions, but early ambitions for a national system proved well in excess of the government's capacity to implement them. The first educational ordinance (*Gakusei*) of 1872 announced a grandiose plan for the introduction of a comprehensive system of education. This entailed the division of the country into eight educational districts, each served by one university, thirty-two middle schools and 6,720 primary schools (a total of 256 middle and 53,760 primary schools). Old temple schools were often converted into new style primary schools, but in the short term implementation of the plan proved impossible, not only because of lack of financial resources and expertise on the part of the authorities, but also because educational charges and popular resistance meant that the four years of 'compulsory' education which were the rationale of the system could exist in no more than name.

One economic constraint on implementing the comprehensive system was the large proportion of the educational budget that went on higher (Western-style) and practical (vocational) education. During the 1870s and 1880s substantial advances in these fields were made under both private and state aegises, but they had to turn to foreign specialists whose services could only be bought at considerable cost. Foreign teachers were imported in particularly large numbers to teach in scientific subjects such as engineering and the various branches of physics and chemistry at new institutes of higher education, research or apprenticeship centres. At the state-run College of Engineering, which in 1886 became part of Tokyo Imperial University, for example, the first teachers were exclusively non-Japanese. Other foreigners were attached to government departments, where they were not only assigned to practical projects but also spread new skills and techniques relevant to industrial and mercantile development. In an attempt to bridge the huge technological gulf which separated Japan from the industrial nations of the West, training in the applied sciences and practical techniques was given clear priority over pure scientific research. Western influences in the introduction of a national elementary education system were more indirect, but also important. An American, David Murray, was superintendent of education 1873–8, and especially in this decade educational administration, methods and curricula owed much to the systems of other countries, but educational policy in the seventies remained bedevilled by financial constraints and policy disagreements.

The basis of the prewar education system was eventually laid by Mori Arinori, Minister of Education 1885–9. Mori had been educated in the United States, but by the time of his appointment as education minister the wave of pro-Westernism of the 1870s had receded in the face of denunciations from conservatives and calls for a return to the old Confucian educational values. Mori needed to find an accommodation between these two competing schools of thought, and his compromise, which took account of and rejected the extremes of both liberal and Confucian education, was an education system which operated largely unchanged for the next fifty years. In a sense Mori was himself a symbol of this dilemma. In youth he was accused of excessive pro-Westernism and in later life of extreme chauvinism, yet he was assassinated in 1889 by a nationalist who thought he lacked respect for the emperor. The post-1880s education system owed as much to the environment of mid-Meiji Japan as to Mori the individual. The prime objective of the structure was the needs of the state; its main goals were the provision of skills and patriotic morality among the many to produce a literate and pliable workforce, and the production of a skilled élite with a highly sophisticated training. It possessed from the start a capability of systematic political indoctrination, which was exercised more and more explicitly as the years passed.

Under the new system all the nation's children went through four years of elementary education; this was raised in 1907 to six years. Many then left to find employment. Those aiming for higher education went on to five-year middle schools, while others attended a variety of institutions of technical and vocational training. Only a minute proportion of middle school graduates advanced to the few élite higher schools and then to university, the others being compelled to settle for less prestigious training. Elementary schools were coeducational, but single-sex schools were the norm at higher levels, and the separate system established for girls provided them with limited educational opportunities, counterbalanced only in part by the Christian contribution to women's education.

In the early years, elementary education, though in theory

compulsory, was not free. Elementary schools had to be supported by students' fees and contributions from local authorities. Since many families could not afford to have their children dependent for so long, let alone pay for their schooling, the attendance rate was still under 50 per cent in 1890. Concessions over the timing and spread of the years of schooling in an individual's childhood were of some help, but not until after 1900, when elementary schooling became free, did attendance rise to the desired level; by 1907 over 98 per cent of children were receiving six years of education. It was the 1920s before this schooling had worked its way through the population to achieve near 100 per cent literacy.

While the formal instruction they received rarely culminated in academic achievement, all children were susceptible to the moral and political inculcation of which the education system was a principal agent. Textbooks, teaching methods and topics of study were all strictly controlled by the state, which continued in the time-honoured tradition to view education as its servant, and not as a means of individual development. Children were instructed in ethics and from the 1890s listened to regular recitations of the Imperial Rescript on Education. Discipline and regimentation were strict, and in the 1920s military drill was introduced.

At the apex of this broad-based pyramidal structure of educational institutions were the prestigious national universities. Tokyo University became the Imperial University in 1886. A second imperial university was set up at Kyoto in 1897, and by the mid-1930s there were six in all. These national universities, like other educational institutions, were dedicated to the provision of instruction and pursuit of learning in the interests of the state. They were closely supervised by the bureaucracy, and trained most of the nation's leaders, but this close relationship with the state by no means precluded a capacity for independent activity. By contrast with lower levels of the educational system a critical approach was encouraged and rebellious voices were frequently heard within the state system. In the enthusiasm for socialist views which followed the 1914–18 War, the imperial universities were not immune to the attractions of Marxism, for all that it was anathema to their bureaucratic masters. A radical student group called the Shinjinkai founded at Tokyo Imperial University in 1918 had strong connections with the left-wing and labour movements, and set up settlements in slum areas. Many other students showed an interest in non-establishment views. The Shinjinkai-dominated student movement of the early 1920s was an active and vocal opposition to the official line; its growing radicalism and associations with communism so alarmed the government that its suppression after 1925 was as vigorous as that of the radical elements of the trade union and socialist political movements. Student leaders were arrested or expelled from their universities, and overt student anti-government activity had effectively ceased by 1930, although the intermittent protests of faculty members were never stilled completely.

In this particular agitation private colleges, with a few exceptions, played a subordinate role, although some had a long tradition of independent, anti-establishment thinking. Parallel with national and local government's provision of education, private schools were established at all levels. Some of the independent schools dated back to the late Tokugawa period. Most famous of these was the Keiō school, founded by the leading intellectual Fukuzawa Yukichi. Fukuzawa aimed to provide a practical education distinct from the needs of the establishment. Keiō produced many leaders of the business world but even in later years very few bureaucrats. Another leading private institution was Waseda, founded in 1882 by the politician Ōkuma Shigenobu who had recently been ousted from the government. Its avowed aim of 'independence of learning' led Waseda to be viewed in its early years with deep suspicion by the authorities. Its students, too, tended to pursue non-governmental careers such as journalism. These were but two of a number of private institutions of higher education which emerged in the early decades after the Restoration, some secular and some with denominational associations. The educational standard of many was high, but not until 1919 did private institutions enjoy the full university status granted the public ones. During the interwar years private education expanded rapidly, but it continued to be disadvantaged by the strict hierarchy of institutions headed by Tokyo Imperial University and the élite character of higher education, which injected competition of a desperate nature into the lower levels of the system. Private institutions catered to the needs of those unable or unwilling to use state higher education, but failed to shake its near monopoly of the establishment. The imperial universities continued to be a guaranteed path to success, especially for those without substantial wealth. Private education could mount only a limited challenge to the statist educational orthodoxy.

It is difficult to assess the degree to which the population subscribed to the orthodoxy the state sought to impose on it. Dissent was voiced by the government's political opponents, left-wing leaders claiming to represent popular dissatisfaction, isolated rebel intellectuals and the media, but coherently articulated alternatives rarely seemed compelling. Intellectuals often found themselves in an ambiguous relationship with the traditionalist bent of the state's orthodoxy. The long-standing respect for learning combined with the élitist nature of education since the 1880s produced in Japan a situation where to be an intellectual virtually conferred its own status. Those members of the immediate post-Tokugawa generation who did not become part of the establishment joined a free-wheeling social élite, whose major concern was the accommodation of individualist Western values to a state philosophy which tried to reinforce traditionalism and national identity. A sense of alienation felt by much of the intelligentsia was reflected in its writings. Literature and journalism tended throughout to play an *avant-garde* role and 'proletarian' writings remained conspicuous into the 1930s. As long as literature maintained a detachment from overt political pronouncement the state was relatively content to ignore its hostility towards tradition, satisfied that its appeal would be limited to the intellectual minority with the inclination and leisure for cultural activities. Most educational and religious leaders withdrew from open conflict with the state and limited their dissent to activities which the state did not care sufficiently about to suppress. The all-embracing nature of the ideology of the prewar Japanese state made it easier for it to assimilate a variety of dissenting views. This leaves a misleading image of compliance to the dictates of the state which conceals the true diversity of intellectual and religious life in pre-1930s Japan and takes no account of popular sentiment. The exercise of conscious control by the state was always open to question, at least until after World War I.

From the late 1920s the state did seek more actively to impose its philosophy throughout the cultural, intellectual and religious spheres, persuading within its fold some potentially hostile institutions and views and suppressing others. Conflicts between the 'traditional' and the modern, between the 'indigenous' and the Western, were increasingly resolved in favour of a real or simulated Japanese tradition which seemed the monopoly of the official orthodoxy. The 1930s–early 1940s were marked by a rejection of non-Japanese culture and of aspects of Japanese culture regarded as being tainted by Western and non-orthodox influences. The hedonistic lifestyle of the so-called 'modern' generation of the twenties,[6] with its Western-style entertainments and dress, gradually yielded to the conformity, hard work and dedication considered to be in the national interest. Heterodoxy became anathema and the arts, like education and religion, were more and more forced into the mould appointed by the state. The growing totalitarianism served to tighten existing control over most aspects of religion and education.

Stronger attempts to impose the emperor-centred State Shinto did not undermine the old rituals and folk customs of households and communities. Other newer religious groups had learnt to adopt a low profile, and were left in peace as long as their beliefs and activities did not appear to conflict with duty to the state. Some sects, however, now found their members subjected to persecution. Militant Buddhists were among those accused of allowing loyalty to their faith to take precedence over loyalty to the nation. The state had always seen Christian belief as a potential focus of opposition to nation-oriented traditionalism. Few Japanese Christians acknowledged any conflict between their patriotism and their Christianity, but in a period of anti-Westernism Christianity was distinctly vulnerable. Control was tightened by merging several denominations into a more easily controlled single body. Since the number of practising Christians was small it was Christianity's educational rather than religious role that was undermined. Japanese Christians were rarely persecuted by the authorities purely because of their religion; more common was the stigmatization of practising Christians as un-Japanese and, hence, disloyal. Any decline in open Christian religious practice was due as much to social disrepute as to positive oppression.

While open dissent from the religious community remained negligible, opposition from educational and intellectual circles was also stilled. Formal state education was already the tool of the official orthodoxy, and allowed little margin for non-conformity. The deprivations of the war years and the effects of conscription severely curtailed the extent of educational provision especially at the élite level, but left unchanged the broad system and values on which this provision had been based. Private education had modelled itself after the public sector in order better to compete with it, and higher education, in which it was of most importance, suffered particularly under the constraints of war. Rebels within the army were crushed and dissident intellectuals found themselves absorbed into the ranks of the national machine. A few resisters remained political prisoners – mostly socialists and communists – but the alienation and concern of many intellectuals at the trend of events seemed unable to withstand the growing momentum

197

of the consensus that Japan was beleaguered and all Japanese must demonstrate their patriotism at such a time of crisis. Prime Minister Konoe's 'think-tank' of the late 1930s (the Shōwa Research Association) is an example of the way in which dissenting intellectuals anxious for influence over policy could come to be identified with the authoritarian state and accommodate their views to its philosophy. As might be expected, a popular scepticism regarding the pronouncements of the state was common, but the contingencies of war reinforced the pressure to pull together. Only in the later stages of the conflict did doubts begin to surface with any confidence.

Defeat left much of the emperor system ideology discredited. Japan had lost despite her supposed spiritual advantages. The ideological vacuum was magnified by the efforts of the Occupation authorities to dismantle the old institutional structures. Both educational and religious reforms were regarded as priorities. The Occupation measures not only transformed the institutional framework, but fundamentally affected cultural and intellectual life as a whole. All religions were disestablished, including the State Shinto pivotal to the 'emperor system'. The emperor no longer claimed divinity. By ceasing to be an object of worship he would, it was felt, lose the powerful emotional hold over his people which had been so abused. The new constitution, when it appeared, confirmed a complete separation of religion and state in conjunction with the removal of the person of the emperor from any direct political power. Religious freedom was guaranteed. Leading politicians and members of the government were banned from visiting shrines in any official capacity. Restrictions were introduced on state funding of religious institutions, largely targeted at Shinto shrines.

The Occupation reforms, like those of the Meiji period, took little account of the rituals which made up popular religion, and were only partially successful in dismantling 'State Shinto'. Inherent contradictions remained in the position of the emperor, who was permitted as an individual to visit the shrines of his ancestors and carry out certain traditional ceremonies of symbolic importance to the nation. The relatives of some 2.5 million war dead enshrined at the Yasukuni shrine in Tokyo were deeply distressed by the prohibition of official respects, while Prime Minister Nakasone's visit there on the anniversary of Japan's surrender in August 1985 provoked criticism from other quarters.[7] The connection between grass-roots Shinto practice and loyalty to the emperor has remained tenuous, but the major elements in State Shinto are integral to Japan's historical development, and the devotion to nation and emperor pivotal to the old State Shinto has retained an emotional hold on many, including some of the post-disestablishment generation.

The rapid social and economic change since the Occupation has had a fundamental impact on established patterns of religion. Increasing urbanization has accelerated the breakdown of traditional communities. With religion so closely identified with the community, the reorganization of society around new forms of community has entailed Japanese religion adapting to this change if it is to survive. Large companies, for example, whose strong sense of community is often noted, often operate under the patronage of a specific *kami*. Japanese religion has also been more exposed to internationalist trends. Although even 'imported' doctrines have over the centuries acquired a distinctly Japanese flavour, organized Buddhism in particular has played an international role. The Western interest in Zen Buddhism from the late 1960s is one example of this.

The postwar years have also produced an upsurge in new or revived religious movements. A bewildering number of 'new religions' have grown and proliferated; some have prewar origins, and most are offshoots of the main religions. Some of these sects claim hundreds of thousands of followers, some count their followers in millions. The enthusiasm for these movements, especially from among the less advantaged members of society, has threatened the traditional strength of organized Buddhism. The swelling numbers of adherents of the new religions suggest they have provided a major outlet for spiritual frustrations which are not satisfied by the old rituals. Despite their immense following within Japan itself, most of the new religions have no universalist claims, and international conversion activities are thus limited. New religions springing out of existing beliefs have remained closely entwined with Japanese tradition and retain an element of ethnocentrism, which explains at least in part their popularity.

One sect has stood out by virtue of its sizeable membership both inside and outside Japan, and this is the Buddhist lay organization, Sōka Gakkai.[8] One of the manifestations of a limited Buddhist rejuvenation after 1945 was the growth of lay organizations. Sōka Gakkai claims a basis in the nationalist Nichiren Shōshū sect, whose prewar adherents were few but fanatical. The state regarded them as subversive, and persecuted the sect's leaders. By engaging in militant and aggressive methods of conversion after the war, registered Sōka Gakkai membership in Japan climbed to over eight million by the early 1980s. Far more claimed to be Nichiren Shōshū believers. Overseas activities have increased rapidly. Sōka Gakkai has been accused of acting as a state within a state. Its claims to universal validity are unrelenting and emphatic, and it has shown itself to be a highly authoritarian organization, with the top leadership possessing an alarming capacity to mobilize the mass of members. As such it is a real force both in domestic politics and on the international scene. In 1964 it founded its own political party, Kōmeitō, and although Kōmeitō is no longer officially the political wing of Sōka Gakkai it still draws much of its strength from Sōka Gakkai members.

Notwithstanding the influx of Western influences in the postwar years, organized Christianity has remained weak in Japan, except for a brief upsurge in the immediate postwar period. The hard core of strongly committed Christian believers has remained small in number and fragmented between different denominations. Christianity's role as a vehicle for education remains important. Christian schools and colleges founded in the prewar era still play a significant role, and new ones have been set up. Some incorporate a certain amount of religious teaching in their curricula, but at others religious practice comprises at most a daily assembly, which hardly counts as active proselytism. What interest students may have is rarely likely to meet with much encouragement and interest at home. While as the origin of modern Western civilization the Christian religion is considered worthy of respect, and perhaps study, for the majority the Christian religion in its entirety remains too alien, too un-Japanese to supplant the existing pattern of religious practice. Yet there are indications that Christianity has had some impact. Many of the new religious movements contain Christian elements. More importantly, the enthusiasm with which Japanese have embraced Christmas and white weddings suggest that specific Christian rituals are beginning to be absorbed into the totality of Japanese religion.

The Occupation's disestablishment of Shinto and guarantees of religious freedom were paralleled by a complete restructuring of the system and content of education. A new three-tier school education system was patterned after the American model. Under the so-called 6-3-3 system six years at elementary school and three at middle (junior high) school were compulsory for all. Three years attendance at high school was voluntary, and some high schools acted as vocational colleges, training students in specific skills. Higher education was to be provided by universities and various kinds of specialist colleges. This three-tier structure has remained substantially unaltered since its introduction.

The content of education after the reforms remained almost as standardized as in earlier years, but under the Occupation lasting modifications in that content were made, particularly in the field of ethical and moral instruction. The ideological slant of education was changed to minimize political indoctrination. Text books were rewritten and subject-matter ordered and presented in a way that would be ideologically neutral and conducive to democratic ideals. Nationalist practices such as military training and the recitation of the Imperial Rescript were dropped. The ideal of a politically neutral approach has remained largely unchallenged since the Occupation. Nevertheless, the neutrality of education was always likely to be hard to achieve, particularly in the light of attempts by the Ministry of Education progressively to tighten its control. It has in recent years been threatened by growing calls for the reintroduction of greater 'ethical' instruction to counter the supposed moral degeneration of the young and the worsening problem of bullying in schools. Official sanction of widely used text books[9] which seem to play down some of the worst excesses of Japan's twentieth-century history have provoked an outcry from China, Korea and other former victims of Japanese aggression. Among the most militant defenders of a freer education system have been the members of the powerful left-wing teachers' union. Relations between teachers (who are government employees) and the Ministry of Education have never been easy, and official attempts to encroach on the autonomy of teaching staff and centralize the system have been constant sources of tension.

Two of the most conspicuous postwar educational developments in Japan have been the expansion of private education and the increase in the numbers receiving higher education. High school and university education is no longer the prerogative of the few, which it was under the élitist old system. While compulsory education comes to an end after nine years, in practice more and more children have been continuing their education. By 1985 over 95 per cent of middle school graduates were progressing to high schools and around 30 per cent of high school graduates went on to some form of tertiary education, necessitating a drastic expansion of provision at these levels. Much of the demand was supplied by private institutions. Private higher education had expanded considerably in the interwar period, but the scale of the postwar expansion, especially in the university sector, has been quite unprecedented. State-run universities had hitherto been few and far between and the state was unwilling or unable to fill the gap. Now, while almost all children attend public elementary and middle schools, at higher levels, particularly post-high school, the proportion using the private sector rises rapidly. New universities and colleges of all kinds have proliferated, and reputations vary from the very good to the very mediocre. Specialist training colleges are numerous, as are the two-year course junior colleges, most of which cater to girls whose assumed aim in life is acquisition of marriageable skills. It is conspicuously the case, however, that the most respected private institutions are almost exclusively the prewar foundations.

The higher education sector thus comprises a mixture of private, national, prefectural and municipal institutions catering to varying needs and possessing differing reputations. The cost to the student varies greatly. At national universities fees are relatively low, while attendance at a private medical school may well be beyond the reach of most families, since grants and scholarships are not normally available. Entrance examinations are not standardized, and despite tentative moves towards a more uniform entrance procedure applicants still tend to take separate examinations (and pay the appropriate fees and other costs) for all the colleges to which they apply. Saving for education expenses has become a major element in the spending patterns of Japanese families, and even so most students engage in part-time work.

The huge variety of tertiary institutions has gone little way towards reducing the extreme competitiveness in the education system. The 'examination hell' of the prewar period has, if anything, become more acute. Not only do students compete for places for financial reasons. The varying quality and traditions of universities and colleges have caused them to be ranked in a strict hierarchy. Students achieving entry into the institutions at the top of the hierarchy are assured of the best employment opportunities. The hierarchy is based on the pre-1945 one. At the top are the national universities, led by Tokyo, and a few of the oldest private institutions. Competition to enter these universities is intense, and the effects of this have reverberated downwards through the whole system, producing a bitter fight to get into the best high schools, middle schools and even primary schools and nurseries. Since around two-thirds of all successful entrants to Tokyo University come from fifty élite high schools, and nearly one-third from only ten, it is to be expected that parents will do what they can to get their children into these schools. If they have a better chance of securing a high school place from a specific middle school, then entry to that, too, must be sought. The private sector operates additional favoured channels. Entry into Keiō elementary school, for example, tends to put children on the 'escalator' for Keiō University.

Competition is thus constantly reinforced at all levels of the educational sector. Both public and private institutions subject children to a strict regime of study and achievement, with success in the frequent tests and examinations the prime objective. A majority of children from middle school onwards receive extra-school coaching. One survey showed that in 1980 almost all of the successful applicants to Tokyo University had attended cramming school and averaged five hours homework per day for at least the previous three years. The imposition of severe strain on children through overstudy and parental pressure is common. There is increasing disillusionment with many aspects of the education system but it is the prestigious universities that are the key to removing the strains imposed by the 'examination hell', and a reluctance to do so has become built into the system.

This intensity of competition does not leave by the wayside the many that might be expected. Traditional teaching methods and schoolroom approach, an emphasis on instruction and rote learning rather than creativity and discussion, and a basic achievement orientation, have tended to keep all but a few within the fold. There is far less variation than in the UK, for example, both in assumed ability and in attitudes to educational attainment. There is a shared assumption that education is necessary, desirable and in the interest of all, that it is a means to social mobility, and that the acquisition of a substantial measure of education is within the capability of all individuals. The commitment to education means that Japan has a highly educated workforce. By the mid-1980s in Japan around 95 per cent of 16–18 year olds were receiving full-time education; in the UK the comparable figure was around 30 per cent. The disparity in higher education was also great, with figures of 30 per cent and 14 per cent respectively for 19–20 year olds. These numbers give no indication of the range of skills acquired. For example, Japan concentrates on applied science and social studies and is weak in pure science.

The state still views education as an agent for providing the skills required by the nation, and the measure of Japan's economic achievements suggests considerable success in this regard. However, while the high literacy and educational level of the workforce is of undoubted importance, just as significant for understanding postwar Japan is the inculcation of socio-political characteristics. So-called innate values of Japanese society – for example, orientation towards the group, a tendency towards hierarchical structures and a recognition of the importance of being Japanese – are to no small extent the product of careful social conditioning, in which the educational system has played a conspicuous part. It is likely that longer hours and years of schooling combined with the uniformity of the syllabus and teaching methods serve to reinforce elements of conformity and consensus within Japanese society. The content of education takes this further by discouraging individualism and teaching children to think of the benefit of the wider community. Rebellion against this regimentation for the most part follows certain ritualized lines. It is not focused in the private education sector.

Japanese cultural and intellectual life has not been monolithic in the postwar period. The arts have provided a platform for the maverick and *avant-garde*, although traditional art forms in theatre, literature and music are enthusiastically supported. Japanese cinema has a high reputation with both domestic and international audiences. Art forms have been exposed to strong foreign influences, but real devotees of Western and avant-garde art forms are few compared with the tens of millions of adherents of television soap operas and chat shows, which often demonstrate a didactic emphasis on social conformism. Early social conditioning and education have been the strongest influences upon intellectual, religious and cultural attitudes. The minority concerns of intellectuals have made little impact on the essential conservatism of popular religion and culture. In the prewar years orthodoxy possessed some ability to absorb and modify intellectual and religious influences which might in other cultures have served as a focus for heterodox belief. The ability to synthesize was made stronger by its very nebulousness. By a process of osmosis some potentially threatening elements were absorbed; the remainder were left alone to observe their traditionally self-imposed limits or to become the province of intellectuals and artists. While it is inappropriate to talk of a new conservative 'orthodoxy', there exist a loose collection of views which can be broadly categorized as 'traditional' or 'conservative', and which have something in common with the old orthodoxy.

Heterodox religious belief, culture and, to a lesser extent, education, do exist in Japan, but in the prewar period they failed to mount a convincing challenge to, let alone displace, the mainstream intellectual and social values. These values have remained dominant in the postwar years. Sōka Gakkai, for example, powerful enough in itself, seems to offer little threat to the most dearly held beliefs and values of traditionalist opinion. Japanese society has thus presented to outsiders an appearance of uniformity in intellectual and religious attitudes. Social conditioning and education have together been the major means of reconciling orthodoxy and heterodoxy, producing the large measure of conformity which does, in fact, exist. A basic consensus over the course of Japan's postwar development has rendered most intellectual currents outside the tradition alien and irrelevant to the majority of Japanese. How long this consensus will persist in the event of generational change or economic difficulties is impossible to predict.

NOTES

1 Shinto means literally 'way of the gods'.
2 The outstanding work in this respect is C. Gluck, *Japan's Modern Myths: Ideology in the Late Meiji Period* (Princeton, 1985).
3 Yoshida was a leader of the anti-Bakufu movement in the 1850s, executed in 1859 for plotting the assassination of a Tokugawa official. His influence on the pro-emperor movement was immense.
4 This was the statement issued in October 1890, of the ideological principles behind the education system, subject to regular ceremonial readings and worship in educational establishments.
5 J. M. Kitagawa, *Religion in Japanese History* (New York, 1966), p.185.
6 The words *mobo* and *moga* – short for 'modern boy' and 'modern girl' – symbolized this generation.
7 Nakasone was the first postwar prime minister to make such an official visit.
8 'Sōka Gakkai' means literally 'Value Creating Society'. The Japanese name is always used.
9 Text books used in state schools have to be approved by the Ministry of Education.

CHAPTER TEN
Oligarchy and Democracy

Japan has had constitutional government and parliamentary politics since the enactment of the Meiji Constitution in 1890. However, in the pre-1945 years control of the diet alone was not sufficient to govern the country. Challenges to parliamentary supremacy could be made through non-parliamentary institutions whose role in national politics was legally recognized. Party politics often became infighting within a small élite, which had little relevance to the broader issues of national power. Constitutional changes during the Occupation made the diet the highest government authority and reduced the number of élites with which it had to compete for power, but parliamentary politics has continued sometimes to appear peripheral to government decision-making.

From 1868 up to World War I political power in Japan was essentially wielded by an oligarchy. This oligarchy was composed largely of men from Satsuma, Chōshū, and, to a lesser extent, Tosa and Hizen, all domains that had been the main architects of the downfall of the Bakufu. The earliest leaders were those who had played a major part in the revolution, which provided a similar political cachet to that which members of the Chinese Communist Party gained from participation in the Long March of 1934–5. Their successors were protégés from the same *han*. It is among them that we find the great political names of the Meiji period – Saigō Takamori, Kido Kōin, Ōkubo Toshimichi, Ōkuma Shigenobu, Itō Hirobumi and Yamagata Aritomo.

Until the constitution of 1889 this ruling group was subject to few legal constraints. Its power rested on its ability to keep it. Its activity and decisions followed the dictates of national and international circumstances, and the result was an essentially pragmatic, step-by-step approach to policy. The greatest potential source of disagreement lay not in the practical response to day-by-day administration, but in personal ambition and the grand designs individuals harboured for the future. A serious constraint on the political decision-making of the Meiji oligarchy was the personalities and long-term aspirations of the leading members of the government and the need to resolve internal discord.

There was no unity of political views among the men who seized power in Japan following the 1868 revolution. They had been united only in their desire to replace the Tokugawa Bakufu by an alternative form of government. After the Restoration they remained for the most part held together by the desire to build up a strong Japan capable of resisting Western aggression and dealing with the West on equal terms. This shared goal, combined with the ruthlessness of the leading members of the oligarchy, served to maintain some appearance of political unity at least through the first three decades after the revolution. However, political rivalries and disagreements among the ruling élite were intense even throughout these years.

For the first year or two after the fall of the Bakufu the new regime had little time to spare for innovation. Such disagreements as did arise were minor and easily resolved. As the policies considered by the regime became rather more radical – for example, the abolition of samurai status and all that that implied – the potential for discord increased.

The first significant split in the ruling oligarchy after 1868 came over the issue of foreign policy. In 1871 the Iwakura Mission left Japan for a lengthy tour of Europe and the United States in pursuit of its overriding goal of revision of the so-called 'unequal' treaties. Led by Iwakura Tomomi, the delegation included Ōkubo Toshimichi, Itō Hirobumi and Kido Kōin, some of the most powerful figures in the government. Decision-making in Tokyo during their absence was dominated by Saigō Takamori and Itagaki Taisuke. One of the decisions Saigō and Itagaki came to was over the desirability of sending a Japanese military expedition to Korea in the wake of Korea's refusal to agree to diplomatic relations. This decision was overturned by the returning members of the Iwakura Mission. They believed that the gulf that existed between Japan and the Western powers was so great that Japan must concentrate on building up her own strength before engaging in external adventuring. This issue produced the first, and in many ways the most crucial, split in the Meiji oligarchy. No longer was it a question of one *han* against another; domains were divided within themselves. Ōkubo and Saigō, for example, both came from Satsuma. Ōkubo remained in government. Saigō Takamori returned to his Satsuma home, acting as a focus for conservative dissent until he found himself at the head of a major anti-government uprising in 1877. Itagaki Taisuke resigned, as did lesser figures such as Soejima Taneomi, Etō Shinpei and Gotō Shōjirō.[1]

The events of the next two decades were dictated by how far, and in what manner, these and other ex-members of the government attempted to demonstrate their opposition to their former colleagues. The potential of some of these former oligarchs for fomenting anti-government dissent was tremendous, should they care to exercise it. Anti-government activity at this time essentially took two forms; armed insurrection on the one hand, and peaceful agitation for constitutional and political reform on the other. The split over Korea spawned both kinds. Subsequent splits in the oligarchy added mostly to the ranks of the latter group, since the regime quickly achieved a monopoly of military power.

The path of armed opposition was followed by Etō Shinpei and Saigō Takamori. The pro-Bakufu forces had been defeated, but during the early 1870s the new government faced a series of uprisings led for the most part by disaffected former supporters, alienated by the pace and nature of reform. It was in part to provide an outlet for this samurai discontent that the government agreed to an armed expedition to Formosa in 1874, despite its earlier reservations over an invasion of Korea. These rebellions included those led by Etō Shinpei at Saga in 1874 and Maebara Issei at Hagi (Chōshū) in 1876.[2] The government had no difficulty in quickly putting down these disturbances, and those involved were severely punished. The Satsuma (Seinan) Rebellion of 1877 was an altogether different matter.

Saigō Takamori had viewed the Restoration as a vehicle for national regeneration, a return to all that was best in traditional Japanese values. In the trend of policy after 1868 he saw his aspirations as betrayed. Returning to Satsuma after his resignation, he opened a school aimed at promoting the samurai virtues and inculcating the conservative ideals in which he most fervently believed. He was a man of considerable personal charisma, and his presence attracted to the area many who shared his views and were equally disillusioned with the direction that government policy was taking. By 1877 his influence was immense and he had thousands of dedicated followers. Anti-government sentiment in

Satsuma became increasingly vocal, and the government began to fear a dangerous insurrection in the region. Plans were drawn up for administrative reform, and early in 1877 a precautionary attempt was made to remove arms and munitions from Kagoshima, at the southern tip of Kyushu. This move, in conjunction with the discovery of an alleged plot on Saigō's life, proved sufficient to spark off an armed rebellion among Saigō's followers. How far Saigō would have instigated such an uprising himself is debatable, but in the circumstances his hostility to government policy and his loyalty to his homeland and followers led him to put himself at the head of it. The rebels decided to march on Tokyo to present their demands, and began to move northwards. At Kumamoto, half way up the island, a resolute stand by the governor of the garrison and his men halted their progress, giving the government time to send reinforcements. Over the next six months the rebels were gradually driven back towards Kagoshima.

The central government responded to the crisis with alacrity. The cause of the Satsuma rebels had potentially nationwide appeal among conservatives and among samurai newly divested of their time-honoured status; it threatened the cause of reform and progress along Western lines. Every possible resource was brought into play to check the rebellion. Ten years after the Restoration, the government could now field its new conscript army, armed with modern weaponry, supported by an efficient marine supply line and a crucial new telegraph communication network. Saigō's followers embodied the old style. They fought with swords and rifles, giving their allegiance to traditional values and virtues; many were armed with little more than passion, dedication and samurai spirit. Even so the rebels proved resilient. The central government was forced to mobilize nearly 60,000 men before new technology and methods showed their superiority and the insurrection was finally ended in September. Saigō committed suicide following the final defeat at Kagoshima. His memory as an embodiment of nobility in defeat and all that was best in the samurai spirit has remained enshrined in the hearts of Japanese.

This major rebellion marked the end of organized military opposition to the new regime. The continuation of sporadic, isolated acts of violence, especially numerous in the 1930s, suggested that violence remained a legitimate outlet for political discontent, but for the most part the government's opponents after 1877 turned to political activity – even where it was illegal to do so.

By contrast, Itagaki Taisuke, who had also resigned from the government over the Korean crisis, began to mobilize support to press for a constitution and the formation of political parties in Japan. Returning to his native domain of Tosa, in southern Shikoku, Itagaki organized a welfare society for samurai, the Risshisha, which began to agitate for popular rights. In 1874–5 he cooperated with Gotō Shōjirō and Soejima Taneomi, who had resigned from the government at the same time, in organizing a nationwide campaign. A petition for an elected assembly was submitted to the government, and in 1875 the Aikokusha, Japan's first real national political party, was founded. This marked the beginning of what came to be known as the Freedom and People's Rights Movement (*jiyū minken undō*), a series of semi-popular campaigns, agitation and organizations which provided the main vehicle for the expression of anti-government opinions up to the establishment of the first diet in 1890.

Support for calls by dissatisfied ex-samurai for a parliament and a democratic constitution soon spread to better-off members of the farming community. Some historians have also maintained that the small but vocal agitation at national level was accompanied by a spontaneous upsurge of grass-roots sentiment and interest in Western-style democratic politics.[3] Harsh restrictive action by the government hindered the activities of popular rights campaigners, but towards the end of the decade a nationwide movement revived. Ideologies and genuinely held political ideals played an important role in the movement throughout these years, but of equal, if not greater, significance was the fact that the elemental parties and political organizations which spearheaded the popular rights movement were essentially born out of opposition, out of their leaders' exclusion, or withdrawal, from the locus of power. This characteristic influenced their tactics and attitudes, and also those of their political successors, the conservative parties of the twentieth century.

Concerned by the presence outside the government of the vocal Itagaki, and of the powerful Kido Kōin, who resigned over the Formosan Expedition of 1874, the government arranged a meeting with the two in Osaka early in 1875. At this meeting it succeeded in luring them back into office with a promise of constitutional proposals and appointments as senior councillors (*sangi*). The respite was short-lived. Kido was in effective retirement from 1876 due to ill-health. Itagaki had resigned again before 1875 was out, accusing his colleagues of betraying their promise of constitutional development. Even so, the initial momentum of the popular rights agitation was not for the present resumed. Government restrictions were one reason. Another was that during the later 1870s leading members of the Meiji oligarchy began to refine their own views on constitutional government. Constitutional rule, a legislature, and the whole political-legal apparatus that went with them, were regarded as necessary for the securing of foreign approval and respectability.

The dominant figures of the early Meiji years were Iwakura Tomomi, a court noble, Saigō Takamori and Ōkubo Toshimichi from Satsuma, and Kido Kōin from Chōshū. By the late 1870s the last three were all dead, and Iwakura now exercised power in conjunction with a younger triumvirate of Yamagata Aritomo and Itō Hirobumi from Chōshū, and Ōkuma Shigenobu from Hizen. All three had played a crucial part in the reforms of the early Meiji years. The difference in the constitutional proposals put forward by the members of this ruling group was to be a root cause of the second major split in the Meiji oligarchy.

By the late 1870s Iwakura and Itō envisaged the enactment of a constitution some ten or fifteen years hence; they believed in the need for imperial control over the constitution, non-party cabinets, and for strict limitations on the powers of the cabinet and elected diet. The response of other figures in the ruling group, for example Yamagata and Inoue Kaoru (also from Chōshū) suggested that a consensus along these lines was probable. Ōkuma, however, bided his time, keeping one eye on the resurgent popular rights movement. Early in 1881 he proposed the implementation of constitutional government within the next two or three years, with cabinets responsible to an elected legislature, which would in turn possess considerable powers. Ōkuma's statement appeared little short of revolutionary to his more conservative colleagues, and opened up a serious rift in the oligarchy.

Hostility between Itō and Ōkuma had been simmering for some time. Both were rising stars of the group in the mid-1880s, and competed for the mantle of Ōkubo Toshimichi, the most powerful individual in the government, after his assassination by a disgruntled samurai in 1878. Over the next year or so Itō gained the edge, and Ōkuma, believing himself to be at a substantial disadvantage due to his Hizen origins (i.e. the fact that he did not come from Satsuma or Chōshū [Satchō]), became increasingly dissatisfied with his own situation. His dissatisfaction was increased by the Satchō majority's conspiring to reduce his powers in 1880.

211

Ōkuma's disaffection explains in large part his growing support for a change in the ruling status quo; he saw himself as the main beneficiary of representational government. His openly radical proposals served to make public the existence of disagreements within the oligarchy. The quarrel was with difficulty patched up, but was reopened with even greater bitterness by a scandal over the sale of government assets in autumn 1881.

In the early 1870s the government had set up a special department, the Hokkaido Colonization Bureau, to be responsible for the development of the northern island of Hokkaido. The bureau had invested considerable sums in development projects, and its investments had increased substantially in value. During 1881 Kuroda Kiyotaka, head of the bureau, gained government approval to sell off these assets, to a group of influential businessmen closely associated with Satsuma and Chōshū. The estimated value of the assets was now ¥30 million, but the group was to pay less than ¥400,000, payable over thirty years without interest. News of the sale leaked out, provoking a public uproar against 'clan-faction' (*hanbatsu*) government and 'political merchants'. Ōkuma sided with the opponents of the sale and openly campaigned with them against his colleagues. The oligarchic consensus was now broken for good, and the Satchō majority decided that Ōkuma had to go. He left the government in October 1881, and was followed by nearly twenty other senior bureaucrats/politicians, who resigned for either ideological or personal reasons. Almost all were from regions other than Satsuma and Chōshū. While men from the court – Iwakura and Sanjō Sanetomi – remained influential, the government was now more conclusively than ever dominated by men from these two domains – Itō, Yamagata, Matsukata Masayoshi, Inoue Kaoru, Kuroda Kiyotaka. They and their protégés maintained a hold on power until well past the turn of the century. The political crisis of 1881 introduced the era of Satchō dominance, the era *par excellence* of *hanbatsu* government.

Ōkuma, like some of his ousted predecessors, turned to political agitation against his former colleagues, but within a changed framework of operation. A revival of the popular rights movement in the late 1870s had culminated in the formation of the League for Founding a National Assembly (*Kokkai Kisei Dōmei*) in March 1880. By the end of the year this body's campaign claimed to have the support of over 100,000. The growing agitation caused serious concern within the government, whose members were broadly agreed that such sentiments would be best kept in check by some form of representative assembly. This pressure, combined with the government's own previous deliberations, was the background to an announcement issued in immediate response to the crisis of autumn, 1881. This statement declared that the proposed sale of the Hokkaido assets would be cancelled. It also promised that a constitution providing for the operation of political parties in an elected legislature would take effect from 1890. The months after the crisis witnessed the founding of political parties that could look forward to constitutional politics and the possibility of real influence.

Two major parties were formed within a short time in the hope of influencing the content of the promised constitution. The first was the Jiyūtō[4] founded by Itagaki Taisuke in October 1881. Itagaki had remained the leading light of the popular rights movement throughout the 1870s. He had maintained pressure on the government through his Aikokusha, and then through the League for Founding a National Assembly, which formed the basis of the new party. The Jiyūtō's ideology was strongly influenced by the thought of Rousseau and other French thinkers. It called for the extension of liberty, equality and happiness, but beyond that remained distinctly vague. Itagaki hoped to pressurize the government into making the new constitution as liberal as possible, providing a legislature with wide powers and responsibilities, elected by a large majority of the people. Local groups affiliated to the Jiyūtō were set up throughout the country. Support came from many strata of the population, but increasingly from the poorer sector of the farming community. Support in Tosa remained particularly strong.

Ōkuma soon followed Itagaki. Early in 1882 he and his followers founded a second party, the Kaishintō. The core membership comprised discontented intellectuals, ex-bureaucrats and personal followers of Ōkuma. The party retained throughout an urban bias. The Kaishintō's ideals emphasized 'moderation' by comparison with the Jiyūtō; members acknowledged a debt to English liberalism and parliamentarianism. Like the Jiyūtō, the party hoped for a widely elected legislature, with considerable powers, and a cabinet responsible to the diet, rather than the 'transcendental' cabinets upon which the oligarchy appeared bent. Neither party questioned the position of the emperor at the apex of government.

For a short while these parties were highly active. They held rallies, produced papers, were active in local assemblies and conducted a sustained campaign to recruit members and put pressure on the government. The government responded first by sponsoring its own political party, the Teiseitō. Increasingly it also took harsh measures to control and restrict meetings, publications and political activity in general, and suppressed anything that could be interpreted as remotely treasonable. These measures seriously weakened the new parties.

Other factors contributed to the decline of the parties over the next few years. In the first place, the environment within which these parties were operating was relatively static. They had no chance of political power until 1890. Without knowing the provisions of the new constitution they could make little preparation for its arrival. Secondly, the strength and reputation of both parties was seriously impaired by the internecine rivalry between them. Thirdly, and of most immediate seriousness, in the years 1882–4 the whole popular rights movement was discredited by the involvement of local groups, many of them claiming to be linked to the Jiyūtō, in violent and subversive activities, some of which were openly aimed at the overthrow of the government. A root cause of these incidents was the increase in rural poverty intensified by the deflationary policy of the early 1880s, but the Jiyūtō leadership could exercise no control over the acts of local discontents. The incidents served to make even harsher government control over the more peaceful extra-government political activities. The influence exercised by Ōkuma and Itagaki themselves remained a constant source of concern to the government, but before 1882 was out Itagaki had been persuaded to avail himself of government funds for a lengthy trip abroad. Both he and Ōkuma became increasingly convinced that in such a hostile environment their groups could achieve little in the immediate future. The Jiyūtō was disbanded in October 1884. Shortly after, a significant part of the Kaishintō leadership, including Ōkuma, withdrew from the register of party members, leaving the official party no more than a rump.

The existence of a formal party has not been necessary for the maintenance of political ties in Japan. Kaishintō members who resigned from the party retained extensive informal contacts with it; many of them participated formally in the Kaishintō's successor parties of the 1890s. The same cohesiveness was to be found among ex-Jiyūtō members when they resumed formal political activity. The Itagaki group maintained an essential continuity from the 1870s through to the early years of the twentieth century. The Ōkuma group also held together for some thirty years. The two together dominated party politics. Contacts between members of the group were maintained not merely on the political level, but also in the spheres of business, education, journalism and welfare. Similar personal contacts operated among members of the ruling group.

The factor which united these early parties was their leader. They and their successors were held together by personal loyalty and tactical considerations borne out of exclusion from power. If small, a party was a personal faction; an increase in size tended to make a party a combination of several such personal factions. In the so-called 'proletarian' parties which emerged during the 1920s, and in their left-wing successors, ideological considerations played a far greater role, but for the centrist and conservative end of the political spectrum personal factions – formal or informal – have been a major element in party organization over the last century. This characteristic owes much to the nature of Japanese society (see Chapter Four). Its origins also lie in the birth of the early parties in a context of personal opposition to those in power, rather than their emergence from ideological aspirations or spontaneous mass movements.

During the latter 1880s extra-government political activity was relatively stilled. Stringent laws and harsh policing were used to suppress the more 'dangerous' elements of the anti-government movement. Itagaki and Ōkuma were offered membership of the new peerage established in 1884 or government posts in an attempt to remove their threatening opposition. Ōkuma served as Foreign Minister from 1888 to 1889, but hostility to his proposals for treaty revision resulted in the loss of a leg in a bomb attack. The most active anti-government campaigner between 1887 and 1889 was Gotō Shōjirō, out of government since 1873 and a close associate of Itagaki. The Daidō Danketsu movement, which he led, fell into disarray after Gotō, too, accepted the lure of a government post in March 1889.

With the promulgation of the constitution in February 1889, the framework for party activity at last became public knowledge. Neither the parties, nor even the drafters of the constitution, were able to predict accurately how the constitution would work in practice, but party politicians could now prepare for the first general election, scheduled for July 1890. The constitution placed severe limitations on the power of the legislature by vesting sovereignty in the emperor and giving power to competing élites that were not responsible or subordinate to the diet, such as the cabinet, the Privy Council, the military and the bureaucracy. The *genrō*,[5] or elder statesmen, comprised a further, extra-constitutional élite.

The existing ruling oligarchy was determined to keep a hold on power even after the promulgation of the constitution and their own withdrawal from important government office. Men such as Itō, Yamagata, Matsukata and their protégés, notably Saionji Kinmochi and Katsura Tarō, took the title of *genrō* and as a body were regularly consulted on the conduct of political affairs by emperor, cabinet and the other institutions of government. No major political move was made without first seeking their advice. The choice of a new prime minister was *de facto* decided by the *genrō* through to the 1920s. Even after that the sole remaining *genrō*, Saionji, wielded immense influence. By this informal institution the political importance of the Meiji leaders long outlived their formal tenure of office.

The powers of the legislature were further restricted by the regulations relating to the diet itself. It consisted of two chambers. The upper house, the House of Peers, consisted of members of the nobility and imperial house, imperial appointees from among leading political and economic figures and representatives of top taxpayers. The lower house was elected on the basis of a highly restricted franchise. In 1890 little more than 1 per cent of the population could vote. The powers possessed by the two chambers were identical, except that the lower house could vote down the budget. Even here there was a safeguard in the stipulation that if a budget was not approved that of the previous year automatically came into force. The emperor could dissolve the diet at will.

With cabinets not responsible to the diet, and their members not selected from among the parties represented in the diet, the legislature appeared on paper to be little more than a talking shop, an outlet for the venting of dissatisfaction (but not subversion). It was not intended to be a vehicle for participation in governmental decision-making. The diet was to prove far less passive than had been hoped. Growing conflict between the ruling oligarchy and politicians in the diet culminated in 1900 in Itō Hirobumi's decision to forge an alliance with party politicians and act as the head of a new political party with representation in the diet.

The two major groupings in the diet at this time were still headed by Itagaki and Ōkuma. Itagaki's followers had readopted the name of Jiyūtō for their party. Changing its name to Seiyūkai in 1900, it continued to operate under that title until 1940. Ōkuma had resumed the formal leadership of the Kaishintō, but shifts in the party's name and membership on several occasions after 1896 tend to obscure the fact that here, too, there was a substantial line of continuity from what was essentially Ōkuma's personal following. During the 1890s the antagonism between the followers of these two men was intense. It dated back to the fierce quarrels of a decade previously and the personal rivalry between the two leaders.

In the early years of the 1890s the diet sought to exercise what power it had. The result was a series of clashes revolving around lower house refusal to pass the budget and several dissolutions followed by elections. That of February 1892 was conspicuous for Home Minister Shinagawa Yajirō's attempt to interfere in the conduct of the election. The extensive and violent use of the police to sway electors benefited the oligarchy in no way whatsoever. The vigour of the conflict, and the fear that the constitution was just not operable, increasingly forced members of the oligarchy to canvass for the support of one or other of the largest political groupings. Party leaders became more receptive to these overtures as their hostility seemed to get them nowhere. Since some of them were also former government members they were aware of the openings a compromise might create.

The leading oligarchs disagreed over how far to compromise with the diet. Yamagata was strongly opposed to any concessions at all. Despite his objections both Ōkuma and Itagaki held cabinet posts during 1896–97. In 1898 the oligarchy, unable to find a prime minister with the degree of diet support required to make the system work, approached Ōkuma and Itagaki with a view to their establishing a joint administration. Ōkuma served as prime minister and Itagaki home minister, for a few months. Their political followings briefly merged to form a single group, the Kenseitō, but bitter conflict between the two ensued. Ōkuma resigned, backed neither by a diet majority nor by the oligarchy. The new 'party' reverted to its two constituent factions. Despite this fiasco, the diet made life difficult enough for the ruling group to compel a greater degree of accommodation with the party politicians. A change in tactics was accelerated by the nascent left-wing and labour activity of the years 1890–1900.

The new approach took two major directions. Even stricter legislaton was introduced to suppress and restrict political and labour activity outside the diet. Controls were consolidated in the Peace Police Law of 1900, which included a ban on political activity by women, minors and the military, and on labour organization and strike activity, as well as providing for extensive Home Ministry and police powers to control or prohibit political meetings and associations. Inside the diet the oligarchy attempted to establish

217

some sort of *modus vivendi* with the parties. After some negotiation Itō Hirobumi broke new ground in forming from among various groups in the diet a new party of his own, the Seiyūkai. The major element in the Seiyūkai was the remainder of Itagaki Taisuke's Jiyūtō. Itagaki himself retired from politics. By this stroke Itō attempted to secure for himself, and subsequently for his protégé Saionji Kinmochi, the guaranteed support of a large section of the diet membership, while yet retaining cabinet independence.

This form of accommodation was strongly resisted by Yamagata Aritomo. It was not until 1912–13 that his protégé, Katsura Tarō, moved to ally with other political groups, and former Ōkuma supporters became the major element in another new party, the Dōshikai, after Katsura's death in 1913. Such a marriage was achieved despite Yamagata's continuing hostility. The ambiguous position of Ōkuma himself as both party politician and oligarch – a focus of loyalty who was neither in the cabinet nor in the diet but who yet had the prestige of a senior statesman – created further difficulties. Despite this fundamental Itō–Yamagata difference their two protégés, Saionji and Katsura, alternated as premier for the years 1901–13 in an atmosphere of relative tranquillity, each group reluctant in the light of the wider interest to avail itself of its power to obstruct the other. While diet–cabinet conflict did not cease, it was relatively subdued for a while, as party leaders followed what one writer has called 'the politics of compromise'.[6] This period of accommodation between diet power and old-style oligarchic rule also enabled the political parties in the diet to consolidate their stature and respectability *vis-à-vis* the rest of Japan's ruling class.

During the first two decades of the twentieth century, party leaders worked particularly hard to consolidate their connections with the bureaucracy, the nobility, the *genrō*, the business world and the military. They were relatively successful in all these spheres. There was frequent movement between the upper echelons of the bureaucracy and the parties, a legacy dating back to the early Meiji years when bureaucracy and politics were less discrete. Members of the oligarchy and their followers became increasingly identified with particular political groupings, either through formal office or through unofficial affiliation. Leading military and naval figures, especially those closely identified with the old ruling group oligarchy, used these connections to assume leading positions in political parties. 'Reliable' party politicians might be elevated to the peerage, which often meant that they could be politically active within the framework of the House of Peers.

Businessmen became dietmen, and parties were highly dependent on business funding.

This anxiety to be part of the establishment is not surprising in the circumstances. The origins of the first parties, the limited franchise and the highly restrictive framework within which they were compelled to seek power, conditioned early diet politicians to make the most of the system rather than work to enhance their popular appeal. In the existing political environment mass support served little for the achievement of practical political power. Party politicians were aware that their best chances of influence lay in increased contacts and accommodation with the remainder of the oligarchy and with other élites, notably the military and the bureaucracy. The House of Peers and Privy Council were also forces to be cultivated. Both the political environment and their own inclinations led the parties to become increasingly élitist, identified with the ruling class, and divorced from the concerns of the mass of the populace. The parties rarely spoke out for 'popular' interests and did little to try to improve social and working conditions. They failed to support left-wing movements in the face of government suppression, which became especially marked from 1907 and culminated, in 1910–11, in the trial for treason of Kōtoku Shūsui and other radicals. They followed a chauvinist line in foreign policy. They never claimed to be popular, and worked hard to achieve what in the context of the times could be seen as political respectability. The lack of popular support, and the extensive practice of machinations, compromise and even corruption in the pursuit of naked political power, had serious implications for the 1920s and 1930s and left a legacy that endured into the post-1945 period.

The 'politics of compromise' did not always allow the cabinet an easy ride. There were occasions on which the parties attempted to demonstrate their independence. In 1912–13 anti-*hanbatsu* protests about the high-handed action of the Katsura cabinet and calls for proper constitutional government culminated in the fall of the administration. Unusually, the 'parties' on this occasion showed the ability to combine both with each other and with extra-party elements in the organization of a massive and highly effective popular protest movement. The following year the opposition parties in the diet nearly achieved the downfall of the succeeding cabinet, under Admiral Yamamoto Gonnohyōe, following revelations of ministerial corruption over naval contracts. The parties proved unable to repeat this degree of success, but these protests foreshadowed the end of the *hanbatsu* period. The virtual Satchō monopoly on power almost since the Restoration had been maintained in the face of growing criticism through the provisions of the Meiji Constitution, dominance in the army and navy and the institution of the *genrō*. After the resignation of Admiral Yamamoto (of Satsuma) in 1914, the *genrō* were again forced to look outside the Satchō élite for a premier.[7] They turned to the veteran Ōkuma Shigenobu, who for two years was prime minister, backed by his traditional locus of support now reborn as the Dōshikai.

These years saw the outbreak of war in Europe, and an attempt by the government in Japan to capitalize on the situation to enhance Japanese influence in East Asia, and particularly in China. Like so many of their predecessors, and many of their successors, the sights of Ōkuma and his cabinet were firmly fixed on foreign policy and not on domestic political change and the establishment of a firm political constituency for the party. The Ōkuma government resigned following conflict with the *genrō*, to be replaced by General Terauchi Masatake, formerly governor of Korea and protégé of Katsura and Yamagata. Terauchi, a non-party premier of Chōshū origins, lasted for two years with the support of the Seiyūkai, but the weakness of *hanbatsu* government was again exposed by popular protest.

The economic boom that Japan experienced during World War I resulted in considerable inflation in the country. With much of Japan's massive trade surplus frozen in foreign accounts, the shortfall was made up by the creation of money and credit. The price rise produced tremendous profits for some, but others were severely hit. Speculators and merchants were accused of rice-hoarding, and in mid-1918 a series of riots affected more than half the prefectures of the nation, lasting for several weeks. These Rice Riots were by far the most serious incidence of popular discontent since 1868; they posed a real threat to the maintenance of law and order and the existing status quo. Martial law was declared and the rioting was eventually stilled, but the Terauchi administration could not survive such an upheaval. Terauchi's resignation brought nearly fifty years of Satsuma–Chōshū domination to an end.

The new cabinet marked a new stage in the evolution of party politics in Japan. Hara Kei was neither an oligarch, nor an oligarchic protégé. Working first in the bureaucracy and in business, Hara had for sixteen years been one of the Seiyūkai leaders in the diet. In 1918 he became the first prime minister to hold a seat in the lower house and head a cabinet formed from the majority party in the diet. In recognition of this Hara was known as the 'commoner' prime minister. For many this change marked the real advent of 'Taishō democracy', the term given to the more liberal period of Taishō – early Shōwa when the influence of the political parties was greater than at any other time during the prewar years.

Expectations of radical institutional reform from Hara's government proved ill-founded. Hara had perhaps become too used to conciliation and his party too bent on being identified with the establishment. A major victim of this conservatism was the suffrage movement. Despite limited extensions of the franchise since 1890, the diet in 1918 was still elected by a small number of better-off Japanese. A campaign for universal manhood suffrage dated back to the days of the popular rights movement, and had enjoyed strong popular support in the 1890s, but even supposedly sympathetic premiers, such as Ōkuma, had done little to advance the cause. A male suffrage bill passed the lower house in 1911, only to be rejected by the House of Peers. The campaign had revived as part of the 1912–13 constitutional government movement. The Rice Riots gave it further impetus. However, parties such as the Seiyūkai had a vested interest in the continuing restriction of the vote to wealthier citizens. An extension of the franchise could endanger the existing parties' domination of the diet and the influence they had achieved by tailoring their policies and activities to the interests of the wealthy minority that elected them. The popular unrest manifested in the Rice Riots and the beginnings of an active trade union and socialist movement during these years suggested that if universal male suffrage were granted the existing parties might lose out to more progressive competitors. Hara extended the franchise only slightly in 1919, and the Seiyūkai was never reluctant to try and restrict the left-wing movement.

Hara's appointment to the premiership initiated a period of over a decade when, except for a reversion to non-party cabinets in 1922–4, party government was in operation, although Prime Minister Tanaka Giichi (1927–9) was a Chōshū ex-military man recently elevated to party presidency. During the early part of this period the 'established'[8] parties were subject to several splits and reorganizations; most were caused by personal ambitions and hostilities, or by disputes over tactics. Despite such rifts, and the name changes that accompanied them, there were considerable continuities in party membership. The Seiyūkai, despite losing some of its members, remained largely intact, and the consolidation of its opponents under the new name of Minseitō in 1927 meant these two major groupings dominated conservative party politics through to the end of the 1930s. The essential continuity of both the Seiyūkai and its competitors throughout the prewar years pointed in the direction of a two-party system. These two political groupings provided the governments of the twenties and the early thirties, but in many respects sharp policy swings were not evident. Both parties consistently opposed radical change. Both gave considerable attention to foreign policy, although differing on how aggressively the expansion of Japanese interests abroad should be pushed forward. They were less than vigorous in coping with economic problems at home. Indeed the deflationary policy pursued by governments during the twenties served to exacerbate domestic discontent and poverty.

The two parties realized that they had a common interest in defending their power in the face of any attempt to reimpose non-party cabinets. The appointment of two consecutive non-party premiers in 1922 and 1923 provoked a united stand from the members of various parties. Although proving that parties acting together could create a powerful pressure (the participating parties gained an absolute majority in the May 1924 election), a failure to arouse public interest ultimately rendered this movement far less effective. The parties seemed unable, or unwilling, to identify issues of immediate popular concern and could not automatically rely on a wide basis of support.

The all-party movement at this time also exerted considerable pressure for the enactment of universal manhood suffrage, and this was at last conceded in May 1925. This measure increased the electorate from 3 million to over 12.5 million. The government simultaneously provided itself with a major safeguard against the potential dangers of this move in the form of the notorious Peace Preservation Law. This law was aimed at suppressing activities, and even ideas hostile to the Japanese state as it was then constituted. Any desire to alter the *kokutai*, or national polity, was culpable, as was any wish to abolish the system of private property. The law's provisions were ill-defined, and it was able to cast its net as widely as the inclinations of the government of the day suggested. It was used to suppress not merely the communists and 'subversive' left-wingers who were its original target, but Japanese of a whole variety of views, both moderate and extreme. Women continued to be excluded from the vote and from party membership. Some engaged in political activities clandestinely, indirectly, or by subterfuge; others campaigned more openly in the vocal female suffrage movement.

One product of the period of Taishō democracy was the so-called 'proletarian' parties, espousing the left-wing views to which Hara had so feared that manhood suffrage would give a fillip. Socialist ideas had had their advocates in Japan since the 1890s, but active support was limited to a small number of intellectuals. Early attempts to build social democratic parties had encountered official suppression, and the prevailing official hostility to all ideas of socialism or labour organization had inhibited further attempts. After World War I a small but growing labour movement appeared. It was dominated in succession by moderate socialist, anarcho-syndicalist, and communist ideologies. An illegal communist party was also founded. The enactment of universal male suffrage in 1925 spawned a succession of parties whose aim was to wrench power away from the established parties and provide more genuine representation of the interests of the newly enfranchised masses. These parties are normally referred to as 'left-wing' parties.[9]

The role of organized labour and political representation of the working classes is dealt with in Chapter Eleven, but it is appropriate here to suggest how far the left-wing parties had a different pattern of behaviour from the existing conservative parties. Both were born out of opposition to those in power. Both appeared initially to have little chance of acquiring power. The same society influenced their modes of operation, yet they were qualitatively different in two major respects. In the first place, the leaders of the proletarian parties had, in most cases, existing power bases as leaders of the labour union and social movement. Organizations and trends within organized labour were reflected in political organizations; the same leadership was often common to both, and different factions of the movement produced different political parties. Secondly, while few of the proletarian parties would openly have subscribed to a fundamental change in the national polity, they had much clearer ideological views than their conservative counterparts.

In many respects, though, these parties were subject to the same constraints as their forerunners and inherited their weaknesses. They, too, had to cope with established oppression, which could easily result in the disbanding of a party and the imprisonment of individual members if either ideology or activity was considered to have become too subversive. To have any hope of continuing legality, criticism of certain aspects of the state had to be kept reasonably muted. They were no less subject to schism and factionalizing, although ideology became just as important a determinant as personalities and tactics. The new parties had a base in organized labour, but the labour movement itself was small, and not all union members were concerned with politics. They thus also lacked at their inception a broad popular or class base of support, and conspicuously failed to build one up during the interwar years, although economic and social circumstances would appear to have offered a favourable chance of doing so. Much of the energies of all parties was spent on internecine disputes, and on the left there was ideological bickering of a kind hardly calculated to enlist mass support. All displayed a reluctance to criticize the governments of the day, especially over foreign policy, for fear of seeming disloyal and unpatriotic.

Thus while political parties of all shades gained a certain ascendancy during the 1920s, they remained without any broad popular base, frequently divided against themselves and too apt to entertain short-term considerations of tactics, power and personality. The terms of the Meiji Constitution also meant that this ascendancy was always under threat from the existence of competing élites. To suggest a change in the constitution would have been treachery. Only the illegal communist movement dared to propose such an alteration. In the last resort the parties' lack of popular base and credibility in the eyes of the people, compounded with the constitutional constraints under which they operated, meant that they could not stand their ground in the face of a determined onslaught from other groups provided with competing powers under the constitution. Armed with popular appeal, the military and its supporters in the bureaucracy, the upper house, the court and the privy council acting together produced a situation in which the parties were repeatedly forced to compromise or go under.

The conservative parties of the prewar era attempted to become part of the establishment in order to achieve a hold on power. The proletarian parties' response to the same challenge was to polarize. The radical faction became more and more in danger of total annihilation by the state. By the early 1930s radical left-wing and communist-dominated organizations had all but disappeared in the face of effective government suppression, leaving the field of radical politics open to the extreme right. The more moderate left compromised with the establishment in an attempt to join it, but this was a difficult task. It had no basis upon which it could build up contacts with the military, the bureaucracy and the traditional political establishment, all of whom were innately hostile to any form of left-wing ideology. The only way in which these parties could gain any acceptability in the eyes of the establishment was by compromising their policies. They accordingly subscribed to the suppression of the radical left, the aggressive foreign policies of the twenties and thirties – albeit with sporadic token resistance – and sanctioned military-oriented trade and industrial policies, which were often to the detriment of workers and farmers. As the 1930s progressed, the leaders of the proletarian parties talked less and less of socialist policies and more and more of building a strong Japan with substantial influence in Asia. To this extent the policy gap between proletarian and conservative parties in the diet narrowed, as both followed the lead taken by non-party interests.

The growing strength of the military and the right wing in matters of national policy[10] served to undermine the credibility of the political parties, whose members were often viewed by these elements as dangerous liberals. Party politicians were subjected to sporadic physical attacks by extremists. In November 1930 Prime Minister Hamaguchi was shot in protest at the London Naval Treaty. He died the following year. The acute crisis brought about by the great depression and the necessity of coping with the consequences of the Manchurian Incident of 1931 exposed the weakness of party cabinets. In an attempted coup in May 1932, the assassination of Prime Minister Inukai Tsuyoshi of the Seiyūkai, for over forty years a diet member, marked the renewal of the practice of non-party cabinets. Admiral Saitō Makoto, Inukai's successor as premier, presided over a cabinet of 'national unity'. Saitō's successors in the 1930s – an admiral, a general, a diplomat, and two peers (one a court noble, the other president of the Privy Council) included party politicians in their cabinets, but they were rarely voices of dissent. Not until after the end of the war was a party politician again to serve as premier. Without cabinet dominance, and lacking a popular basis of support, the diet became little more than a rubber stamp for already determined policies. United attempts to block increasing military intervention in the making of policy were never made.

After the start of the China War in 1937 all the parties fell into line behind the armed forces, as might be expected in such a crisis. Even so, as military control over policy-making increased, and the war dragged on, many government leaders felt that the continuing existence of political parties undermined the necessary domestic commitment and national unity. The idea of a mass party along the lines of Hitler's National Socialists was increasingly canvassed. In October 1940 a body called the Imperial Rule Assistance Association

(IRAA) was founded as the nucleus of a new political structure. Unresisting to the end, the remaining major political parties – one proletarian, three conservative – spontaneously disbanded. Independent political parties ceased to exist until 1945 and the IRAA became the core of such legal political activity as existed for the next five years.

Although intended to be an exclusive political structure aimed at concentrating national political power, the role of the IRAA was vaguely defined as enabling the emperor's subjects to assist imperial rule. Headed by the prime minister and manned by local officials, it had numerous branches throughout the nation, but failed to take on the character of a mass party, having instead its own political association. The IRAA effectively ended up as an instrument of national bureaucratic control. Taking over some ministerial responsibilities, it also had nominal control over, and absorbed, many hitherto independent organisations of all kinds. These tended to constitute competing influences within the association, undermining the homogeneity of its control and the coherence of its direction. The IRAA was dissolved shortly before the end of the war in June 1945. Its functions were easily assumed by other departments and it was barely missed.

Party political activity effectively ceased to exist during the years 1940–5. The people were mobilized towards an unquestioning pursuit of victory, and increasingly the hardships of their existence left little time or inclination for politicking. Political discussion was in any case officially discouraged. Political infighting at the top levels – among individuals, ministers and sections of the military – was, however, rampant. The army was the most important arbiter of policy during these years, and political manoeuvring at the top centred on attempts to curb this military power. Military control was never absolute. Although party politics could not operate effectively, the forms of constitutional government were retained. The cabinet and diet continued to function, and there was even a general election in 1942, albeit one where most of the candidates were officially recommended.

In the early years of the China War the cabinet was for much of the time led by Prince Konoe Fumimaro (premier 1937–9, 1940–1), but despite Konoe's active prosecution of the war in China he was not the creature of the army. His promotion of a new political structure based on the IRAA was at least in part an attempt to create a body strong enough to resist army influence. His attempts to reach a negotiated settlement with the United States over Japan's actions in China and Southeast Asia led to disagreements with the army, and an inability to resist army pressure was a major factor in bringing about his resignation. Konoe's successors of the war period were all military men, but even so did not always see eye to eye with military ambitions. General Tōjō Hideki, prime minister 1940–4, attempted to coordinate cabinet, army and navy policy and strengthen central control by monopolizing many of the senior cabinet and army posts himself. He was at least in part successful in reducing disagreements, but his aggressive stance and unwavering belief in a Japanese victory at all costs, despite an increasingly disastrous situation, produced coordinated and effective opposition to his policies and influence. Under his successors, General Koiso Kuniaki and Admiral Suzuki Kantarō, cabinet/army disagreements worsened. The focal conflict was between the more diehard, who desired a fight to the finish on Japanese soil, and those who were willing to countenance the thought of surrender on the grounds of the need to avoid further loss and suffering.

With Japan's surrender, the constraints on party activity were removed. The Occupation decision not to have direct military rule, but to operate through the elected Japanese government, immediately made party politics again of considerable importance. Four sizeable parties were founded before 1945 was out, and the next decade produced a plethora of parties of various shades of the political spectrum. The first postwar general election was held as early as April 1946. The framework within which the new parties operated was very different from that of earlier years. Even before the 1946 election the Occupation authorities had suspended many provisions of the Meiji Constitution, lifted restrictions on the activity of all parties (including the Communist Party) and announced universal suffrage. These freedoms, and others intended to provide for democratic and responsible government and prevent the resurgence of Japanese militarism, such as wider diet powers and responsible majority party cabinets, were embodied in the new constitution of 1947.

Many of the members of the new political parties had belonged to parties in the pre-1940 years. This remained true despite the purges to which many, mostly conservative politicians were subject. Often the postwar leadership consisted of the rising young politicians of the 1930s. One exception was Yoshida Shigeru (1878–1967), who held the premiership for much of the Occupation period. A former diplomat, who had supported a strong policy in China, Yoshida had nevertheless been regarded by the army as dangerously liberal. This credential enabled him to avoid being purged and engage in party politics from late 1945. The continuities of personnel contributed to both left-wing and right-wing parties' suffering from some of the same defects as the prewar parties – for example, a tendency to division/factionalism for ideological, personal or tactical reasons, and a lack of committed popular support. Other constraints on party behaviour were the need to act under pressure from external decision-making authorities, and, for the left, a degree of official suppression.

The first election after the war was a victory for the conservative wing of politics (represented by the Liberal and Progressive Parties), but the May 1947 election made the new social democratic Japan Socialist Party (JSP) the largest party. During the next seventeen months the JSP cooperated with conservatives in two cabinets. The coalition nature of these cabinets, and the overall control of SCAP, prevented any introduction of radical socialist policies, but the apparent widespread support in the country for the socialist and labour movement alarmed the authorities, leading to prohibition of a general strike, and the legal prohibition of certain rights to strike. In the light of worsening US – Soviet relations there followed the 'red purge' of 1950, in which many suspected of left-wing sympathies suffered. The policies pursued by the Ashida coalition cabinet of 1948 led to divisions in the Socialist Party, and left-wing support never recovered. Since 1948 the conservative parties have maintained an unbroken hold on power, which the left wing has appeared powerless to challenge. Japanese politics since 1955 have been dominated by one conservative government party and four opposition parties.

Fragmentation of parties on both wings of the political spectrum was a feature of the years of the Occupation, but this was brought to an end in 1955 when the reunification of the two wings of the JSP, separate for some four years, stimulated a consolidation of conservative forces into the Liberal Democratic Party (LDP). Since then the Japan Communist Party (JCP), the LDP and the JSP have continued unbroken, although a 'moderate' faction of the JSP under Nishio Suehiro broke off in 1960 to form the Democratic Socialist Party (DSP), and a small group of LDP members formed the semi-independent New Liberal Club in 1976.

The LDP has become firmly established in postwar Japan as the party of capitalism and big business. It has promoted economic growth on the basis of free enterprise, but has attempted to direct capitalist development in accordance with what it sees as the national interest. The LDP has pursued this policy within a framework of close cooperation with the US and its allies. The party has always strongly supported the 1952 Security Treaty with the United States, and became an active promoter of the build-up in defence forces initiated during the Korean War, while trying to respect popular hostility to rearmament. Some elements of the LDP have desired a revision of the provisions of the constitution which restrict Japan's military strength, but this requires a two-thirds majority in both houses of the diet. The maintenance of this pro-US policy has brought with it barely cordial relations with the Soviet Union (a peace treaty has yet to be signed) and from the early 1970s an enthusiastic fostering of relations with the People's Republic of China. Economic and cultural relations with Southeast Asia have also been an LDP priority. To all intents and purposes, the LDP leadership's policy has been to keep Japan economically successful, capitalist and closely identified with the US camp, to enhance Japan's interests and standing in Asia and, increasingly, to achieve for Japan diplomatic and political influence in the world commensurate with her economic might.

The conservatives set out in the 1950s to make economic recovery and growth a priority, and the success of this policy was already becoming self-evident by the end of the decade. The most strident arguments of the 1950s, both between LDP and opposition parties, and within the LDP itself, were over not economic, but foreign policy. These culminated in the security treaty crisis of 1960, when the opposition parties resorted to extra-parliamentary tactics to try to prevent renewal of the treaty, and the public outcry compelled Prime Minister Kishi Nobusuke to resign after forcing its passage. The emphasis on a high rate of economic growth was renewed with Ikeda Hayato's famous 'Income Doubling Plan', and maintained under his successor as premier 1964–72, Satō Eisaku. In the early 1970s the LDP government was delivered a series of blows in the form of the 'Nixon shocks' of 1971 (Nixon's visit to Beijing and the devaluation of the dollar) and then the 1973 oil crisis, which caused inflation to accelerate and significantly slowed down growth. The ability of the Japanese economy to weather these crises has upheld the ability of the LDP to keep a hold on power without any marked policy change. Indeed, the frequency of changes of premier due to factional shuffling – Nakasone, who gained the premiership in 1982, was the fifth prime minister in eight years[11] – suggests that the LDP had energy to spare for internal machinations. This confidence was borne out by the sweeping election victory of July 1986.

The policies of the opposition parties, while often dogmatically stated, have appeared less clear cut, especially since they have had no chance to demonstrate the concrete efforts of implementing them. The most important opposition party, the JSP, has a strong Marxist heritage, although most of its policies can be categorized under the heading of moderate socialism; its platform since the 1950s has included extension of the welfare state and greater public ownership. In foreign policy a majority of the JSP has consistently opposed renewal of the US – Japan Security Treaty and favoured a more neutralist international position. The DSP, which broke away from the JSP over its support for the treaty in 1960, has remained more centre-left. It has advocated the advancement of socialism by democratic, legal means, including greater welfare provision, progressive taxation and the encouragement of cooperative forms of organisation. Its opposition to dictatorship by either left or right and its advocacy of a national, rather than class, basis for socialism, has put it at loggerheads with the JCP, the third major opposition party. Prewar JCP policies were dictated by Moscow, but from the early 1950s faced a dilemma in the division between Soviet and Chinese communist ideology. Party differences over this point have persisted, but it has managed to maintain some, albeit fluctuating, success with the electorate.

The only totally new political foundation of the postwar years has been the Kōmeitō, or Clean Government Party, founded in 1964 to further the political aims of the powerful Buddhist sect, Sōka Gakkai. This is the last major opposition party. Kōmeitō has continuously advocated the purification of politics, the spread of welfare and other policies geared to a renovation of society according to religious principles. The formal connection with Sōka Gakkai was wound down in the early 1970s, but the party has continued to draw on the movement for much of its support. The nature of its political emphasis makes it difficult to locate on the conventional left – right political spectrum. Despite its advocacy of 'humanitarian socialism', Kōmeitō has never been a socialist party and is vigorously anti-communist. On some policy issues, though, it has been in agreement with the more left-wing parties; for example, in the degree of opposition to nuclear power. Kōmeitō views itself as the possible focus of a coalition of moderate, non-conservative elements.

The LDP's monopoly on power since its formation in 1955 has had a fundamental impact on the way both it and other parties have behaved. The reasons for this continuing domination are complex and have been exhaustively researched by scholars. Certainly, they cannot be totally separated from the political practice of the prewar years, especially the assiduity with which the conservative parties cultivated contacts with the bureaucracy, big business and other leaders of society, and essentially became part of the establishment. The overlap of prewar and postwar political and bureaucratic personnel helped to re-establish this tradition. The bureaucracy remained conspicuously powerful after 1945, and the retirement of bureaucrats in their fifties in favour of political involvement (invariably as LDP members) has remained a common career pattern. Many others have gone into business, and since members of these groups have in addition frequently come from similar educational backgrounds they have constituted a relatively homogeneous élite. Socialist dietmen have usually come from a very different background, in particular from journalism or organized labour, which has started them off at a disadvantage *vis-à-vis* the establishment.

The LDP has also benefited from presiding over economic success and being in a position to dole out perks put at its disposal by its hold on power. At a local level politicians have stood a greatly increased chance of getting elected if they have been able to promise with a fair amount of certainty that their election will bring specific advantages to the constituency. In this way conservative politicians in particular have managed to build up over the years strong networks of support within their constituencies. Their chances of satisfying their electors have been further enhanced if they have been able to join one of the stronger personal factions within the LDP which is likely to provide candidates for ministerial office.

At a national level three decades of LDP rule have been marked by an unprecedented degree of economic prosperity especially appreciated by those who experienced the deprivations of the war and early postwar years. The years of high economic growth rates after the 1950s brought improvements in material living standards to the population as a whole and provided the LDP with a proven record of success. Many Japanese have thus had little reason to believe that a government of different political hue could do any better, or even as well. While voters may not always have approved of all of the LDP's policies, they have continued to give them their vote on the grounds that the evil they know is better than the one they don't. The continuing domination of the LDP has constantly reinforced this inertia, especially since a non-LDP government would be manned by relatively unknown politicians with no experience of government at national level.

The sweeping LDP victory at the polls of July 1986 underlined there was more to LDP success than inertia. Other, more calculated, means have assisted the LDP to hold on to power. Chief among these has been the inordinate predominance awarded to the rural vote in national elections by means of the distribution of the multi-member constituencies. Rural areas in most countries have traditionally been more conservative than their urban counterparts, and Japan has been no exception to this. The land reforms of the Occupation established a rural community of owner farmers which has enjoyed considerable prosperity in the postwar years, and the maintenance by the LDP government of assured prices for many agricultural goods, especially rice, has made sure that this prosperity has continued.

Money has also played a major role in LDP politics. While there are legal provisions covering election expenses, the limits on expenditure are high, and strong business and factional connections have meant that LDP members have had access to considerable sums. Furthermore – and this applies not merely to the LDP – gift-giving has long played an important role in contacts in Japanese society, thus the line between legitimate electioneering expenses, social convention and corruption has been extremely difficult to draw.

The success of the LDP has depended in part on the nature of its opponents. Lack of government experience is a disadvantage in any parliamentary democracy. The inadequacy of the opposition's bureaucratic and business contacts in the context of Japanese society casts doubts on its ability to operate as a viable government within the existing constitutional framework. In the eyes of many Japanese none of the opposition parties has really managed to establish itself as a credible alternative government, whether by itself or in coalition. The longer the LDP maintains its hold on power the more serious become these deficiences. Moreover, to many Japanese some of the policy statements of the socialist parties have sounded dangerously radical and disputatious, giving the impression of aiming at the fundamental destruction of a tried and tested status quo. Ideological disagreements within parties have been blown up to absurd proportions, obscuring any semblance of party unity.

Notwithstanding the importance assigned to the diet by the constitution, party politics has essentially remained of much less importance in national life than, for example, in Britain. Much of the major political decision-making in Japan has gone on outside the sphere of party politics, outside the diet, and with little in the way of popular consultation. The LDP, like the other parties, has shown a continuing disinclination to seek a broad basis of popular support. Its approach to the electorate has been one of mutual backscratching, and experience suggests it will continue to get elected as long as it is seen to be delivering the goods. Prewar and postwar parties have failed to cultivate a committed and active membership. In recent years the membership of all parties has increased. Prime Minister Ōhira used his position as chairman of the LDP 1976–8 to increase party membership very considerably, but this campaign was in part a stratagem to secure his own election to party leadership through a vote by party members. It was not a genuine campaign to recruit members on a basis of ideological conviction. LDP membership by the late 1970s stood at 1.5 million, but how much of this increased membership was committed and active is hard to say. The JSP, despite substantial union and electoral support, had a membership of no more than 50,000 at the same time. The JCP membership of nearly half a million was highly committed to active support, but the party has found it difficult to elicit support outside organized labour. Kōmeitō, relying on the Sōka Gakkai constituency for much of its 150,000 membership, and the smaller DSP, could muster little more than 200,000 members between them. Consequently all but a small minority of the Japanese population has not been actively involved in party politics at all, though a high proportion of those eligible have turned out dutifully to vote at elections.

A great deal of Japanese politicking and decision-making, especially at local level, has not been directed primarily by party loyalties but by long-standing social conventions and attitudes. Important influences include patronage; social, educational and bureaucratic hierarchy; local interests; and, perhaps more than anything else, personal loyalties and commitments. This characteristic has led to a persistence of political factionalism. Less pronounced in the opposition parties, it has been very marked in the LDP, which has appeared for much of the time to be little more than a coalition of personal factions. A faction built up by a leading politician through the use of influence, patronage, contact and even money, has frequently on retirement been passed on intact to that politician's leading protégé, providing him with a ready-made power base. The larger the faction the more influential it has tended to be, since the bigger the weight it can wield within the party. The party leadership (and hence the premiership) and the make-up of the cabinet have been determined by negotiation between the party's main factions. The nature of external contacts and their importance to the maintenance of factional influence have meant that individuals outside the diet and outside the party have often had a strong influence over these factions. In the early 1980s former Prime Minister Tanaka exercised a major political decision-making power as leader of the largest LDP faction despite almost total incapacitation through illness.

The way in which Japanese political parties have operated in the postwar period has served to perpetuate their reliance on older traditions of social and interpersonal interaction. This *modus operandi* has been reinforced by the existence of a similar pattern in bureaucratic circles. On paper the Japanese political system would appear to provide more than adequately for the operation of a democratic system in the Western sense, but the reality has been very different.

The Meiji Constitution was hailed as an advance along Western lines, and served to channel political protest into parliamentary politics, but the pre-1945 constitutional framework was not in any genuine sense democratic. The architects of the constitution aimed at the achievement of a constitutional, yet absolute, monarchy, and as such parties of every hue were perhaps destined to fight a losing battle. Moreover, only a small number of Japanese politicians aimed at democracy in the Western sense of the word, the majority believing that Japan was qualitatively different from the West, and needed to build up her own unique constitutional and political framework in accordance with existing beliefs and modes of conduct. What in due course resulted was not a unified nation under an absolute emperor, nor a parliamentary democracy, but a series of major groupings, each of which could utilize the imperial position to impose its own policies on the rest of the population.

The framework that shaped party political behaviour for half a century before 1945 has left an enduring legacy. The persistence of older patterns of behaviour have, in turn, affected national perceptions of the way in which the democratic system does, or is able to, operate. Politicians have rarely been highly esteemed and outsiders have often turned to bureaucrats rather than politicians to influence policy. The interaction between the constitutional framework and its Japanese environment has resulted in the emergence of a unique political system. It would be foolish to contend that Western-style democracy is the ideal for all nations, but while the LDP may keep Japan committed to the Western camp there must be no illusion that the existence of a Western-style democratic framework and political parties provides the whole story of political decision-making in Japan.

NOTES

1   Itagaki and Gotō were from Tosa, Soejima and Etō from Hizen.
2   Maebara, a Chōshū samurai, had resigned following disagreements with Ōkubo and Kido in 1870.
3   E.g. Irokawa Daikichi and the school of 'people's history' in Japan.
4   For the sake of clarity most Japanese political parties are here referred to by their Japanese titles, except where there is a widely-used, unambiguous translation.
5   It is more appropriate to retain the Japanese word *genrō*, since it implied a specific group of elder statesmen active at a particular period of Japanese history.
6   T. Najita, *Hara Kei in the Politics of Compromise* (Cambridge, Mass., 1967).
7   Saionji, though a member of the court nobility, was strongly identified with *hanbatsu* government as Itō's protégé.
8   The Japanese term *kisei* (established, existing) is used to refer to the conservative parties (e.g. Seiyūkai, Kenseikai, Minseitō) in contrast to the 'proletarian' parties of left-wing inclinations which emerged in the 1920s.
9   Doubts may attach as to how far it is appropriate to segment the Japanese political spectrum in the traditional left-right way, or indeed how far these parties and their successors really are socialist, but it is appropriate in this context to adhere to this terminology, not only because such terms will be widely found in literature relating to Japanese political parties, but also because they represent a division which genuinely existed in terms of ideology, class interests and approach to change.
10   See Chapters Eight and Thirteen.
11   LDP regulations stipulate that no member can serve as prime minister for more than two successive two-year terms. Nakasone had this regulation suspended to allow him a fifth year, but was succeeded by Takeshita Noboru late in 1987.

CHAPTER ELEVEN
Popular Protest and the Working Class

Communal protest in Japan was in evidence during the Tokugawa period, and has recurred throughout the years since 1868, despite vigorous suppression by the authorities. Popular protest was motivated by a variety of issues and took various forms. On more than one occasion it brought down the government and threatened the stability of the state. However, for the most part, the socialist and left-wing movement which claimed to represent the interests of the masses proved unable to tap this popular discontent.

In the Edo era Japan was a caste society in which the populace was divided into four main groups: warriors (*bushi*), farmers, artisans and merchants. Towards the end of the period the distinctions between these various castes became to a certain extent blurred, but the formal structure continued to operate until abolished after 1868. At the same time, though, the occupation, influence and wealth possessed by many members of these different groups bore less and less relationship to their ranking in the social hierarchy. Moreover, while the peasant status assigned to some 80 per cent of the population theoretically ensured their right to at least some of the fruits of their labour, the number of landless and tenant peasants increased markedly. In both town and country a growing proportion of the population had little from which to make a living but the sale of its labour. A division of labour well beyond that provided for by official decree was also becoming apparent. These developments signified a growing emergence of economic rather than military strength as the dominant factor in social and political power.

As in many other pre-industrial and industrial societies, the benefits of wealth, influence and culture accrued to relatively few.

236

The majority of the population continued to live in subservience, poverty and ignorance. Tokugawa Japan remained governed by a small élite. The stratum of society that could be termed a bourgeoisie was very narrow and the mass of the population comprised a lower class fated to drudgery and a low standard of living.

The Tokugawa period produced few intellectual currents which claimed to champion the causes of the lower strata of the population. The majority of ideologues gave no attention to improving the lot of the lower classes of society. Invariably samurai born and bred, they showed little inclination to question the basic tenets upon which society and their own privileged position within it rested, and devoted most of their time to criticizing their confreres at the top of the social ladder. There were exceptions; religious teachings in particular could produce thinkers of a highly radical cast of mind. One eighteenth-century religious figure, Ishida Baigan, for example, devised a rationale for commercial activity which had wide appeal. Members of the sect founded by the thirteenth-century Buddhist priest, Nichiren, were the inheritors of a long and radical popular tradition. In the confusion of the late Tokugawa period a wave of utopian and millenarian sentiment swept through segments of the peasant and artisan classes, as evidenced by the term 'world renewal' (*yonaoshi*) attached to some of their more extreme protests. For some these movements marked a sublimation of an inability to cope with the unsettled atmosphere of the time and bring about improvements in the people's material way of life.

More conspicuous in Tokugawa history are the violent manifestations of popular discontent which recurred throughout the period, though rarely on a scale to pose a serious challenge to the supremacy of the ruling élite or the basic assumptions of the system. The most feted of these was the revolt led by Ōshio Heihachirō in 1837 in famine-ridden Osaka. Ōshio remains a popular hero of Japan's past, but his position as a Confucian scholar heading an urban riot hardly makes the episode representative of popular protest in the Edo period. Less dramatic, but of more fundamental importance, were the localized peasant uprisings which broke out continually all over the country. Their incidence and severity varied according to the quality of the harvest and the demands of local authorities and commercial élites, but there was an overall tendency for them to increase as the economic basis of the status quo became ever weaker, and as peasants became more dependent on the market. These violent protests were a reaction against the increasing exactions of the ruling class and the depredations of their representatives and other wealthy élites in the countryside. Protest leaders often sought to turn the rhetoric of the ruling class against them by accusing them of failing to fulfil their obligations as rulers. Provincial authorities were caught between the Bakufu on the one hand and the peasants on the other, and feared open revolt sufficiently to try to temporize before using outright force.

The changing nature and scale of revolt has been widely construed as evidence of a growing class conflict in Japan. Certainly, society in the villages was becoming increasingly polarized through changes in the economy. With rare exceptions, though, protesters sought improvements within the system rather than any revolutionary change. Unlike in China, where unrest was endemic for much of the eighteenth and nineteenth centuries, the authorities never lost administrative control over large areas of the country for sustained periods; moreover, no element of the population inside or outside the ruling class could specifically mobilize this widespread peasant discontent and harness it for broader political purposes. The local scale and local concerns of almost all revolts further reduced any capacity for shaking the Bakufu or domains into modifying the status quo. Peasant uprisings remained a constant anxiety to the ruling class, but the Restoration of 1868 was never more than a 'palace coup', in which popular participation and popular sentiment were conspicuously unimportant.[1]

Among the first reforms of the post-1868 regime was the abolition of the prevailing caste system, although recorded family status continued to set *shizoku* (warrior) families apart from the remainder of the population. Nevertheless, the order of the day was now the achievement of success in the world on an individual's own merits, and the government's attempts to introduce education for all suggested a genuine commitment to national advancement through maximizing individual knowledge and ability. That despite this the previous élites retained the leadership of society by virtue of superior education, wealth, influence and contacts will come as no surprise. During the Meiji period at least a disproportionately large percentage of leading businessmen, politicians, bureaucrats and other professionals came from samurai families; merchants, rural entrepreneurs and quasi-samurai were also well represented. The chaos of the 1860s had certainly produced some rags-to-riches stories, and some members of the lower classes now capitalized on increased opportunities for success, but for most Japanese neither their way of life nor their standard of living underwent any immediate change.

The frequent incidence of peasant uprisings continued for more than a decade after the Restoration, but revolts were harshly suppressed. They remained localized events which caused far less concern to the new regime than the samurai-led rebellions during the same years. The old causes of peasant unrest, such as corrupt officials, high prices and excessive taxes, persisted despite the abolition of the old land tenure system and the land tax reform, which for the first time bestowed on the peasant the legal right of land ownership. Peasants soon found, however, that such rights could be a burden as well as a privilege. The government's deflationary policies of the early 1880s reinforced economic pressures which increasingly compelled peasants to forfeit their land-ownership rights to others. Tenancy and the number of landless peasants grew rapidly. Urban discontent was as yet not widely manifest, although changes in economic conditions had brought deprivation to certain artisan groups, for example silk weavers. The number of non-agricultural workers remained small.

During the 1880s it appeared that a link might be forged between discontent in the countryside and the growing popular rights movement. Most popular rights activity was restricted to an élite group of activists at national level and wealthy provincial farmers and businessmen, but there was also an intense interest in problems of national policy and constitutional reform among the more educated members of some village communities. Some local activists orchestrated or became involved in forceful anti-government protests, sometimes for ideological reasons, but more often as an expression of the discontent and economic difficulties widespread among the agricultural community in the early 1880s. In the wake of the popular rights movement local groups sprang up all over the country. Some of them affiliated to the national popular rights parties, and more incorporated the name of one of them, the Jiyūtō, into their titles. Some groups were involved in violent incidents which served to bring the national opposition leaders into disrepute and increase government suppression of its opponents. The beliefs claimed by the popular rights parties, in particular the Jiyūtō's advocacy of Rousseau's natural rights theories, would appear to have offered a platform from which to champion the causes of the lower classes, but despite the involvement of thousands of protesters at incidents in Fukushima (1882) and Chichibu (1884), the gulf between national and provincial leaders of the movement and the discontented peasantry remained tremendous. No coherent mass movement arose. Popular anti-government protest declined in the later 1880s, but less than a decade later the rapid changes in the Japanese economy provoked a renewed concern about the problems it brought in its wake. Now the desire to improve the: lot of the working classes was influenced less by French liberalism or Russian populism, hitherto popular, but by ideas of Christian socialism and social democracy, and by the ideology of class.

The introduction of Western political ideologies had been part. of the influx of Western ideas and practices since the late Tokugawa period. Such ideas guided not only the activities of the popular rights movement, but also those of the government in drawing up the constitution. Works relating to socialist and social democratic ideas were translated into Japanese from the early 1890s, and drew the attention of a small group of intellectuals. The initial appeal of socialist ideas was minimal; there was no substantial industrial proletariat to speak of, and little consensus could be reached on the nature of development attained by Japan herself. Marx's 'Asiatic mode of production' owed much to his European predecessors' image of Asia, and nothing to a knowledge of Japan. Nevertheless, sporadic interest culminated between 1898 and 1900 in the formation of various groups, which studied the applicability of socialist ideas to Japan. Best known of these groups was the Society for the Study of Socialism (*Shakaishugi Kenkyūkai*) of 1898, whose membership included leading figures of the early left-wing movement, such as Kōtoku Shūsui, Katayama Sen and Abe Isoo.

Some of these intellectuals were also behind the first attempts to organize labour in Japan. Socialist and social democratic ideas by now wielded considerable influence in the US and parts of Europe. Left-wing ideas brought with them to Japan an awareness of movements such as Chartism or trade unionism dedicated to improving the lives of workers outside the ruling élite and the bourgeoisie, namely the labouring classes in both rural and urban areas. In Europe the First and Second Internationals suggested the possibility of solidarity across national boundaries. Knowledge of these developments spread in Japan the notion that organized action by members of the working class to improve their living and working conditions, aided and abetted by intellectuals, was, in fact, possible.

Although in Japan most workers were still employed on the land, it was towards urban workers that the first attempts at organization were directed. In the rural community discontent had been reduced

from a high point in the 1880s, and the agricultural sector was relatively prosperous compared with earlier years. Moreover peasant
farmers tended to be scattered, conservative and subject to landlord
domination. They were potentially far more difficult to organize
than factory workers who had less control over their working lives.
Skilled workers in particular had considerable industrial muscle,
since they were crucial to the nation's industrial development and
could not easily be replaced. In addition, public concern at both
rural and urban poverty increased conspicuously at this time, as
the appalling living and working conditions in many parts of
the country were exposed by such works as journalist Yokoyama
Gennosuke's *The Lower Social Strata of Japan (Nihon no Kasō Shakai)*
(1898) and a Home Ministry report of 1903 entitled *Conditions of
Workers (Shokkō Jijō)*. Ideology, social concern and pragmatism thus
came together to stimulate intellectuals' initial attempts at industrial
organization in the late 1890s. The women workers who made up
a majority of the factory labour force suffered from conspicuously
bad employment conditions and had shown themselves capable of
sporadic labour protest. Predictably, though, intellectuals looked
first towards skilled male workers. Under the auspices of the League
for Founding Labour Unions (1897–1901), Takano Fusatarō and
Katayama Sen, two intellectuals who had spent extended periods in
the United States, led attempts to organise iron workers, printers
and railway workers. The League also campaigned for protective
labour legislation and published a journal *Labour World (Rōdō Sekai)*.
At the same time Ōi Kentarō, long associated with the more radical
wing of the popular rights movement, founded the Greater Japan
Labour Association to research into labour problems, promote
labour unions and improve welfare facilities for workers.

The instigators of these activities were very few in number, and
the worker response a strictly limited one. The ascription of caste in
the Tokugawa period had engendered certain shared sentiments,
but these could hardly be termed class consciousness. Even where
the interests of management and workers were clearly often at
variance with each other, the concept of a formal expresson of this
conflict in the formation of workers' organizations was alien to the
hierarchical, group-oriented slant of Japanese society. However,
the increasing influence of economic imperatives had, since the
mid-Tokugawa period, stimulated in elements of the peasantry in
particular a mass awareness of common interest. This enabled a
perceptible advance in the organization of labour and the promotion
if its awareness of its rights. Despite the minute numbers involved,

this advance proved sufficient to provoke a strong retaliatory action from a government alarmed at the thought of a heightening interest in socialist ideas implicitly or explicitly hostile to the status quo. The class orientation of socialist thought, the concepts of historical materialism and revolution for a new economic order were regarded by the authorities as an inherent threat to the unity of the Japanese state and the fundamental premises upon which its system of rule rested.

Under the Peace Regulations of 1887, drafted to combat the popular rights agitation, the police had powers to ban mass meetings and exclude specified individuals from within a certain radius of Tokyo city centre. In March 1900, the government passed stringent measures to restrict still further anti-government activity and protest, in the form of the Peace Police Law. Among the most important provisions of this law were a ban on political activity by women, minors, police and members of the armed forces; a ban on labour organization and strikes; extensive police and Home Ministry controls over associations, meetings and demonstrations, especially those with a political content. The law gave the Home Ministry the right to prohibit any association. The Peace Police Law effectively suspended attempts to organize labour and put a major damper on left-wing political activity. It overshadowed the activities of labour and the left wing in general for the next quarter of a century, until partially superseded by the equally restrictive Peace Preservation Law of 1925.

An indication of the government's willingness to use the Peace Police Law came in May 1901, when Japan's first left-wing political party, the Social Democratic Party (*Shakai Minshutō*), was immediately banned by the government when party leaders refused to water down the party's moderate social democratic platform, which included equality and universal suffrage. The restrictions on labour and political activity meant that would-be socialists expressed themselves in journalistic, welfare and research activities. A major centre of interest in socialist thought became the *Yorozu Chōhō*, a newspaper run by the journalist Kuroiwa Ruikō, whose writers included Kōtoku Shūsui, Uchimura Kanzō and Sakai Toshihiko. After 1903, when Kuroiwa broke with many of his team over the issue of a possible war against Russia, the focus for socialist activists for the next eighteen months was an organization known as the Heiminsha (Commoner Society), whose members discussed socialist theory and carried out welfare and propaganda activities. A weekly journal called for socialism, pacifism and 'commonerism'.

Official censorship was rigorous, and both this publication and its successor closed within a year.

Those who called themselves socialists at this time were a highly heterogeneous group.² They included Christian socialists and social democrats as well as supporters of direct action, anarchism and international revolution. For a time the common interests of the group held it together, but the combined tensions of government oppression and internal disagreements produced a growing rift between 'moderates' and 'radicals' after 1905. The split was exacerbated by the increasingly vocal commitment to direct action of Kōtoku Shūsui, who, during a spell in prison and an extended visit to the United States in 1905–6, had become an anarchist. The advent of a marginally more liberal government under Saionji Kinmochi in January 1906 encouraged a limited rapprochement between the various groups. The same month a legal socialist party, the Japan Socialist Party, was founded. Before long, however, there was again conflict between direct actionists and Christian socialists, and the government's view that the former constituted a public danger led it to ban the party little more than a year later. The rift in the left-wing movement was never to be healed. Right through the prewar period it consistently failed to achieve a united front to champion the interests of the working classes.

During the period following the demise of the Japan Socialist Party suppression of the left wing worsened. Many members were imprisoned for their activities and journalistic and propaganda activities subjected to the stringent censorship laws. While the proponents of direct action were the main target of official proscription, more moderate Christian and social democratic factions were frequently tarred with the same brush. The government campaign against the left wing culminated in the so-called High Treason Incident. In January 1911 a group of socialists and anarchists, including Kōtoku Shūsui, were found guilty of plotting to assassinate the emperor. Kōtoku maintained to the end that he had early on withdrawn from any conspiracy that might have existed, but both he and his mistress, Kanno Sugako, were among twelve defendants executed. Many regarded the plot as a fabrication by the authorities. Certainly it provided a convenient method of removing from circulation the more radical figures of the left wing and scaring the rest. It initiated what has been termed the 'winter period' of Japanese socialism. Until the end of World War I, overt left-wing political activity was virtually non-existent and advocates of socialist ideas who remained in Japan kept a very low profile.

The early socialist activists, despite their attempts at labour organization, had little more success than their predecessors in the popular rights movement in identifying with the wider complaints of the working class. It was essentially a movement of intellectuals for intellectuals. This was at least in part the result of a distinctly unfavourable environment. The ban on trade unionism and industrial action, and the far broader powers of suppression claimed by successive governments, made it extremely difficult to spread left-wing ideas and organizations. Few Japanese were prepared to jeopardize their livelihoods, their freedom and even their lives for an obscure creed which in the the short run at least offered little hope of change. The ideas themselves were complex, new to Japan and alien to much of the Japanese tradition. Marxist thought had been conceived within the framework of an industrialized European nation, and the question of its applicability to a non-Western European, non-industrialized nation provoked conflict and schism in Japan no less than in countries like China and the Soviet Union. The industrial proletariat was still very small. Even in 1915, of a total employed population of around 16 million, barely 900,000 were factory workers,[3] some 60 per cent of them women. The peasantry was conservative, would-be capitalist and difficult to organize.

Yet activists cannot be totally exonerated. The left wing faced an uphill task in steering essentially conservative, chauvinist popular sentiment towards working-class solidarity, but there was a strong current of popular protest throughout this period. Spontaneous outbreaks of discontent erupted from the peasant uprisings of the early 1870s, through the sporadic labour protests of the late 1880s and 1890s up to the famous Rice Riots of 1918, which amounted to the most serious challenge to the establishment in the whole prewar period. The working class was far from being totally passive, but the left wing failed to make contact with its protests, still less to organize them. Right-wing, nationalist sentiment, by contrast, achieved at least one conspicuous success during this period in orchestrating popular sentiment for political purposes; the Hibiya Riots of September 1905, which followed the announcement of the peace treaty with Russia, were serious enough to bring the capital under martial law.

The years of the 1914–18 War produced an unprecedented boom in the Japanese economy. Industry, trade and shipping expanded, the country accumulated substantial balances overseas and some Japanese became enormously wealthy. However, the boom was accompanied from 1916 by accelerating inflation, in which wage levels increasingly fell behind commodity prices. While the wholesale price index doubled between 1915 and 1918, rice prices rose even more. The price of rice in August 1918 was three times that of August 1915. Industrial unrest increased rapidly in 1917, but it was not only urban workers who suffered. The farming and fishing population were hit both by the rising prices of the consumer goods they needed to purchase and by the increase in the price of rice itself. Poorer members of the community were compelled to sell their own rice, buy back at inflated prices, and see the profit go into the pockets of middlemen, landlords or retailers. Speculation was rampant. In July 1918, fishermen's wives in Toyama Prefecture participated in a violent demonstration against rice hoarding. The protest initiated a series of spontaneous riots which spread over a large part of the country, lasting for several weeks and leading to the imposition of martial law. They were by far the most serious incidence of popular protest faced by any Japanese government since 1868 and were brought under control only by military force and mass arrests. Thousands were eventually charged, a large number of *burakumin* among them. The riots forced the government to place controls on the price of rice, and after the disturbances were stilled the cabinet resigned. Its successor sought to prevent a recurrence of such an outburst by promoting cheap imports of rice from the colonies along with greater domestic production.

The government and the ruling élites were severely shaken by the scale of the Rice Riots. They moved to forestall a successful attempt by the left wing to mobilize worker protest by adopting a more conciliatory attitude which appeared to acknowledge the existence of working-class problems. This softening of attitude was made more urgent by the worldwide upsurge in labour and socialist activity which followed on the heels of the successful Bolshevik seizure of power in Russia in 1917. The years of the war brought strains in many societies to a head, and in Russia and Germany at least had precipitated revolution. An international ferment of left-wing thought and activity spread to Japan, where the economic problems caused by the war years and the depression of 1920–1 made for greater receptivity to such ideas. The increasing proportion of male workers in factory industry occasioned by war expansion seemed to offer greater hope of labour militancy. The advent of the first real party prime minister, Hara Kei, in the wake of the anxieties raised by the Rice Riots, produced a government which appeared disinclined to use the full extent of the draconian laws at its disposal, especially in regard to labour union organization. The result was a brief flourishing of left-wing and trade union activity in Japan, which has contributed to this more liberal period's being known as the era of 'Taishō democracy'. These years saw left-wing ideas beginning to spread outside the middle class, the wholesale conversion of much of the intelligentsia to socialist thought and a short-lived but vigorous proletarian cultural movement.

The term 'democracy' is something of a misnomer. Left-wing groups were still highly restricted in their political activities. the provisions of the 1900 legislation could still be used, and frequently were, to place stifling controls on meetings, demonstrations and associations. The continuing property qualification for national elections restricted the electorate to around 10 per cent of males over twenty-five, excluding from the franchise that part of the population which left-wing parties claimed as their main constituency. Hara Kei disappointed many by rejecting the case for universal manhood suffrage, and it was not until 1925 that the combined efforts of opposition parties succeeded in achieving this goal. The apparent futility of much political action before 1925 encouraged would-be socialists to turn their attention to propaganda, welfare and labour organization. With the exception of the Japan Socialist League of 1920–1, which embraced individuals of a variety of left-wing views and foundered on their disunity, the main vehicles for left-wing activity at this time were not narrow political bodies but student or labour associations.

One brighter event during the years of 'winter' had been the initiation of a movement which foreshadowed renewed efforts to organize labour. In 1912 a Christian intellectual, Suzuki Bunji, had established in Tokyo a group dedicated to the mutual welfare of workers. He gave it the name Yūaikai (Friendly Society), and it had some similarities with the early English friendly societies. To avoid legal prohibition under the 1900 Peace Police Law, the Yūaikai emphasized Suzuki's strongly held belief in the desirability of harmony between capital and labour, and refrained from anything that could be regarded as union activity or industrial action. Despite the limitations on the scope of its activities, Yūaikai membership rapidly increased to over 20,000 by early 1917. Members came from a growing range of occupations, branches were set up outside Tokyo and a regular publication issued. A women's section was set up in 1916. The Yūaikai provided a forum for the exchange of views on labour issues, and members became increasingly involved in raising the consciousness of their fellow employees. Against a background of industrial expansion and growing working-class unrest Suzuki's desire to keep the Yūaikai approach cautious and conservative was increasingly undermined. Yūaikai involvement in labour organization increased and, from 1917, in strikes as well. It was a shift of which the establishment had to take notice, but which paled into insignificance besides the unorganized challenge to its authority which the government faced in 1918 from the Rice Riots.

During 1918 the government acknowledged the Yūaikai's role as the main focus of labour activity by making its leader, Suzuki Bunji, an official Japanese representative at the inaugural meeting of the International Labour Organization. Not all Yūaikai leaders were by now as cautious as Suzuki himself. Many openly advocated a more overt commitment to unionization and support for industrial action. During Suzuki's absence at the ILO meeting the radicals gained the upper hand in a Yūaikai which by mid-1919 had 30,000 members. On his return Suzuki was compelled to accept that the association was now a labour union federation, and declared his support for socialist ideas. Late in 1919 the Yūaikai refused to cooperate in the work of the Kyōchōkai, a government-sponsored organization, whose goal was the establishment of harmony between capital and labour. It took the more militant name of general Federation of Labour (Sōdōmei).[4] This shift marked a growing radicalism in the whole left-wing movement and a decline in the dominance of Suzuki himself. Sōdōmei became a major force in the spread of unionism and industrial action.

In the early years after 1918 there was a limited coming-together of intellectuals and workers, of theory and practice. The more radical members of Yūaikai/Sōdōmei who had promoted the change in the direction of its activities from 1917, and who were most active in organizing labour and industrial action and spreading socialist propaganda, were themselves intellectuals. Others came from a less élitist background. Labour leaders also had strong contacts with radical intellectual groups such as the Shinjinkai, whose members were mainly past or current students of Tokyo Imperial University. The Shinjinkai was in turn closely involved with slum settlements and welfare as well as discussions of ideology. Unable to free itself of the divisiveness which beset the whole left-wing movement, however, Sōdōmei was caught between, on the one hand, caution and a desire for government approval, indeed an anxiety to avoid being banned altogether, and on the other pressure from its more radical contingent for stronger action. This conflict weakened the influence of Sōdōmei, and, such was its prominence, the labour movement as a whole.

The 'winter period' had placed a curb on left-wing and labour activity, but it also served as a gestation period during which knowledge and understanding of left-wing thought among Japan's intellectuals had become more widespread and more sophisticated. Even the embryonic socialist movement had produced a major split between advocates of direct action, and more moderate, mostly christian-influenced, social democrats. The revival of socialist and labour activity after 1917 produced far greater diversity of views and tactics, which made it even more difficult for the left-wing movement to present any sort of united front. Despite its early militancy, after 1923 Sōdōmei leadership represented the moderate, cautious end of the left-wing spectrum. Activists who wanted a more radical line had their own competing organizations. Right through the 1920s labour organizations, and the political groupings which they spawned after manhood suffrage was introduced, suffered from repeated schism and conflict. Disagreements over policy, ideology, tactics and personalities split the ranks of the Japanese left-wing movement. No organization proved capable of playing the role of a 'broad church' that could contain the differences. Furthermore, increasingly severe government suppression of the more radical elements of the movement caused more moderate factions to go out of their way in being conciliatory towards government policy. The extent of this compliance totally compromised their proclaimed beliefs and aims.

Against the background of a diversity of left-wing views there were clear shifts over time in the balance of support within the movement. In the years 1920–2 the labour movement was dominated by anarcho-syndicalist views, which owed much to the direct action thought of Kōtoku Shūsui. Kōtoku's main disciple and leader of the anarchist faction was Ōsugi Sakae. Faced by the limited prospects of successful political action, the concept of achieving revolutionary change through labour unions was appealing and Ōsugi proved a dynamic leader, but by 1922 a struggle for control between anarcho-syndicalists and communists had split the movement. Support for Bolshevik ideas had been growing since their visible success in the 1917 revolution and the founding of the Soviet Union, the first proclaimed workers' state. By contrast, anarchists were encountering considerable difficulties both in the Soviet Union and elsewhere. The attempted revolutionary tactics and policies of the anarcho-syndicalists appeared ill-suited to a time of recession and provoked harsh government oppression. The restrictions placed on the activities of much of the leadership culminated in 1923 with the police murder of Ōsugi Sakae and his close associate and mistress, Itō Noe, in the upheaval following the great Kantō earthquake. In a bitter conflict between adherents of the two doctrines the more radical wing of the labour movement increasingly supported the tactics (advocated by Bolsheviks) of concentrating on political issues and campaigning for popular support, as well as strengthening labour organization.

These sentiments found their organized expression in the Japan Communist Party, founded in 1922 by a small group of intellectuals which included Sakai Toshihiko and another figure of the early socialist movement, Yamakawa Hitoshi. Since the party's existence was prohibited under the terms of the Peace Police Law, its activities had to be carried on underground. Many members were arrested. The constraints of illegality in conjunction with doctrinal pressures from Moscow – where Katayama Sen, originally a Christian socialist, was now an influential member of the Comintern – caused JCP tactics and ideology to steer a fluctuating course. Unity was lacking even among those who called themselves communists. In March 1924, a majority of the party agreed, against the wishes of Moscow, to disband the party until a more favourable time presented itself. It was re-established in 1926. During 1926-7 Japan's leading party theorist was one Fukumoto Kazuo, but before long Fukumoto's over-emphasis on the importance of theory was strongly criticized both by Moscow and by members of the JCP. The JCP returned to the Comintern fold after the pronouncement of a new set of theses in 1927, but the relationship between the illegal Japanese party and the Moscow-based Comintern was never an easy one.

Yet socialist thought, in particular the ideas of Marx, Engels and Lenin, had a lasting impact in Japan through their appeal to the intelligentsia. During the 1920s Marxist terminology and concepts were adopted by many intellectuals, including some who did not subscribe to Marxism, or even democratic socialism, as political creeds. For those seeking an alternative to the official state ideology and anxious about political and economic trends, the Marxist framework became a widely used pattern of conceptualization. Its influence survived the clamp down on left-wing political activity in the late 1920s. Doctrinal disputes among Marxist members of the intelligentsia continued into the 1930s and were reflected in academic controversy. The Marxist interpretation of Japanese history proved particularly contentious. The two leading factions in this debate over the nature of Japanese capitalism – the Moscow-identified Kōza group and the 'dissident' Rōnō group – disagreed over how far the Meiji Restoration was, or was not, a bourgeois revolution, and, as a result, over what kind of strategy Marxists should adopt for the future. While originating in disagreements over JCP strategy, the dispute fulminated between academics throughout the early 1930s and has lived on in the historiography of the postwar years. Yet these intellectuals failed to use socialist doctrines effectively to mobilize the energies of the working class. Socialism was not widely regarded as a remedy to the discontent that so many felt. Both labour organizations and left-wing political parties proved totally inadequate in building up a basis of mass support or addressing themselves to the immediate needs of their constituents. Instead they emphasized to the government their conciliatory attitude or engaged in damaging ideological disputes of a more or less recondite nature.

The period 1918–26 was a period of increasing labour protest, much of it organized; it was a time of growing awareness of social inequalities during which members of the ruling class became increasingly concerned to channel dissatisfaction away from themselves. Employer and government efforts to compromise with and conciliate employees and the mass of workers, highly limited though they may have been, testify to the existence of a growing realization that oppression was not necessarily the only way to respond to popular discontent and labour unrest. As early as 1919 government and private enterprise had sponsored an organization (the Kyōchōkai) to investigate social and labour problems and promote conciliation between employers and employees. The legal position of unions remained ambiguous, but the number of labour union members increased (Sōdōmei claimed a membership of 37,000 in 1925) and there were several successful campaigns of industrial action. Other left-wing groups attempted to organize the rural community and encourage poor owner farmers and tenants to stand up for their rights. Some large employers moved to combat labour problems by improving working conditions and wages, in the hope of creating a committed, skilled and stable workforce.

The interwar period has often been seen as the time when the contemporary Japanese system of industrial relations was established. Some writers have dated its genesis far earlier, seeing in it a carry-over of Tokugawa values into the modern period. In large companies at least, constant manoeuvring between employers and labour against a background of government intervention and economic problems produced a shift in employer policy during these years. Employers pressurized by rising labour activism and the need for skilled workers adopted seniority and bonus payments to reduce labour turnover and introduced company unions to keep out outside labour organizations. Some of the institutions associated with the postwar industrial relations pattern – in particular life-time employment, seniority pay and company unions – did begin to appear, in theory if not always in practice. Other features modern commentators assign to contemporary Japanese factories – for example, company loyalty – were little in evidence. Collective, bargaining hardly existed. Shifts in labour relations policy therefore set a precedent for developments after 1945, but they affected a minute percentage of workers and evidence suggests that employers in particular had no hesitation in abandoning their inducements to labour when they were strong enough to do so.

Labour unrest continued for much of the 1920s and 1930s, yet much of it went uncoordinated. The success rate in strikes, for example, was just as high when unions were not involved. Even as labour and social movements were becoming more vigorous, labour was being put in an increasingly weakened position by the postwar slump, the dislocations of the international economy and the deflationary policies of the Japanese government. All these factors encouraged, and even compelled employers to amalgamate firms and rationalize their workforces and labour management policies.

During the early 1920s' heyday of organized labour, popular protest was deprived of a formal outlet for political expression. The passing of the Universal Manhood Suffrage Act in May 1925, granting the franchise to all males over twenty-five, changed the prospects for left-wing political action and led to the founding of a series of 'proletarian' political parties of varying shades of opinion. Free expression of left-wing views remained restricted by law. The Peace Police Law of 1900 was still in operation, although some of its provisions had been amended or partially ignored in the more liberal early postwar years. In 1925 much of its previous function of controlling political thought and activity was taken over by the new Peace Preservation Law, passed almost simultaneously with the suffrage act. The Peace Preservation Law was less explicit in its restrictions than its forerunner, and for that very reason potentially far more draconian. It contained wide-ranging sanctions against any move to subvert the private property system and the national polity (i.e. the status quo); even the discussion of any such change was prohibited. The law made illegal any activity by the more radica! elements of the left, such as the JCP, whose pro-revolutionary stance made it an obvious target. More seriously, its blanket powers could be, and were used to restrict the activities and campaigns of any opponent of the government of the day. The legal 'proletarian' parties which were founded after 1925 were frequently forced to bend over backwards to avoid the restrictions of the Peace Preservation Law.

The left-wing parties of these years were weakened further by the same schisms and divisions that beset the labour movement. The years 1926–32 produced a series of proletarian parties sponsored by the leaders of Sōdōmei and other national labour organizations and for the most part the leadership of the political and labour movements was one and the same group of men. Conflict and lack of unity in the one was mirrored in division in the other. Disunity in left-wing politics appeared endemic, and not until 1932 did the less radical elements whose existence was still tolerated by the authorities form a single united party, the Social Masses' Party (*Shakai Taishūtō*). Under the leadership of Abe Isoo, the veteran Christian socialist, and Asō Hisashi, a younger intellectual and Sōdōmei leader, the Social Masses' Party supported a social democratic platform opposed to communism, capitalism and fascism. It seemed to offer at last a viable opposition to the established conservative parties. Conditions in 1932, however, were already such that this unity, such as it was, had come too late. The established parties themselves were bowing to right-wing and military pressure. The increasingly oppressive policies adopted by successive governments towards the left had effectively emasculated its ideology and forced it to toe the line on major issues. The Social Masses' Party did not, and could not, provide an effective opposition.

The strategy and tactics of social democrats were affected in other ways by the continuing prohibition of the radical left. Strategies of compromise proved divisive among moderates themselves. Supporters of more radical views responded to official restriction by founding 'moderate' political organizations as a front, under cover of which they could spread their ideas. They also infiltrated and took over legal social democratic organizations already in existence. The authorities frequently used 'dangerous' left-wing activity as an excuse to ban an organization, penalizing radical and moderate members alike. When it became apparent that an organization was dominated by radicals, the moderates would often split off to form a new organization, leaving the rump to be banned by the authorities. The response to oppression by both wings of the movement drove them further and further apart, widening the gulf between those who were prepared to risk official hostility by supporting more radical views and activities and their cautious counterparts, who contended that the only method of progress was to act and speak within the law and maintain some sort of legal existence that could offer support to the cause of the masses, however limited. These tactics exacerbated an existing tendency towards schism and realignment on ideological grounds. Nor were personal antagonisms and ambitions absent from these divisions.

Although Marxism retained a strong hold on the intelligentsia throughout this period, the JCP remained illegal. Communist attempts to increase popular support in the late 1920s meant increasingly intense government efforts to eradicate the still vocal communist leadership. Organizations associated with the movement were banned and massive waves of arrests in March 1928 and April 1929, followed by the imprisonment of many, decimated the active leadership of the communist movement. The more fervent communists were still in prison at the end of the war in 1945, but many weakened under the tremendous pressure exerted on them to recant their views and openly profess their adherence to the official ideology. The 'conversion'[5] in 1933 of two of the JCP's leaders, Sano Manabu and Nabeyama Sadachika, was followed by a wave of similar conversions among the many imprisoned communists. Communist influence and organization was insignificant until 1945.

The increasingly oppressive government attitude, and the wide-ranging provisions of the Peace Preservation Law, meant that many who had no formal connection with the communist movement, and whose views were far less radical, were branded as subversive elements. Radical right-wing nationalists (though not anti-capitalist national socialists) could be exonerated of any attempt fundamentally to alter the status quo, but social democrats and even liberals were likely to find their views culpable in the eyes of the law. It is not surprising, therefore, that those unwilling to be seen as opposing the government had to act with the utmost caution and were slowly driven towards the official (right wing) line. The approach of the legal proletarian parties is ample demonstration of this. If such organizations wished to preserve an existence at all, opposition to the official line had to be restricted to the most minor issues. The radical right was likely to regard opposition on major matters as treachery, even if the authorities themselves did not. As official pressure and the influence of the right wing increased during the early 1930s, the proletarian parties were to be found condoning the invasion of Manchuria. In 1937, when out of a total of 466 diet seats the Social Masses' Party achieved thirty-seven – the maximum number reached by the 'proletarian' opposition in the prewar years – it was already supporting the war with China and the mobilization of the economy and people which it necessitated.

That the prewar peak of proletarian party electoral representation should have been so low points to a general lack of popular support for and interest in parties of left-wing persuasions. No less than in the case of their conservative counterparts, the lack of any considered attempt by the proletarian parties to cultivate a broad popular base damaged their prospects and was a major factor in their inability to stand up against the tide of militarism and ultranationalist thought. This absence of popular support was due to inadequacies in the parties themselves, to government restrictions and to the relatively late stage at which they appeared on the scene.

The parties' approach to securing mass support was influenced by the fact that throughout the interwar years the left-wing political and labour movements were led mostly by intellectuals. The intellectual approach was not always best suited to securing mass support. These leaders saw their natural constituency as being organized industrial labour, and to that extent labour organization and political activity went hand in hand. However, industrial labour still accounted for a small proportion of the occupied population (20 per cent in 1930), many of whom were outside factories. The advance of labour organization even within the factory sector was very slow. At its prewar peak in 1931 less than 8 per cent of the industrial workforce belonged to a labour union. Some of this 8 per cent was accounted for by management-steered company unions. The unionization rate among male workers in heavy industry was disproportionately high, meaning that labour in some important sectors was totally unorganized. This so-called 'natural' constituency was therefore very small in size, and the efforts of party members to appeal to the broader, unorganized mass of the population, even the urban poor, were both limited and ineffectual. The rural sector received scant attention, and unity with left-wing sections of other disadvantaged groups, such as *burakumin* and Koreans, was not widely in evidence.

A failure to accommodate a rather rigid ideological approach to the realities of interwar Japan was only one factor in the parties' lack of support. That proletarian parties also looked to have little prospect of being able to implement policies which might improve the welfare of the mass of the population was part of a vicious circle of reduced electoral support. Government oppression deterred all but the boldest members of the population from supporting the more radical activists. Participation even in mild industrial action or campaigning on behalf of a social democratic political party could result in police action or the loss of a job. Since the poor in particular could ill afford to take such risks most workers concluded it more advisable to endure an inequitable status quo. Popular protest sparked off by agitators or by those who felt they had little to lose could have a bandwagon effect, as in the Rice Riots, but for the most part serious eruptions of discontent or violence were forestalled by rapid action or channelled into directions where they did the establishment little damage. In the mayhem that followed the 1923 earthquake, for example, Koreans were the main target of popular hostility.

By delaying the growth of the labour movement and postponing until 1926 the formation of proletarian parties, the authorities put them at a distinct disadvantage in the struggle for popular support. By the time the movement was permitted a degree of freedom of action after World War I the ideology of the *kokutai* had been the object of official propaganda and educational inculcation for nearly fifty years. A substantial proportion of the Japanese population had been born and educated since the promulgation of the constitution in 1889. In a nation that was still dominantly agrarian, the rural areas remained a bastion of support for conservative views. The urban-based socialist parties showed little evidence of interest in workers in the countryside. The Christian, Kagawa Toyohiko, led attempts to ameliorate widespread peasant discontent and poverty, and to incorporate the numerous tenant disputes into the framework of a national movement, but these never affected more than a minute percentage of the total farming population. The army, which achieved substantial political power in the 1930s, had long made strenuous and successful efforts to forge a close relationship with the rural community, and had established a strong basis of support for the conservative values it held so dear. In as far as any part of the political spectrum appeared to offer a positive solution to the problems of the working class in the interwar years, it was the army and the right wing with their 'nationalist' policies, and not those who called themselves socialists.

The rapidly expanding industrial community towards which organized labour and the proletarian parties directed their efforts also suffered from severe dislocation in the interwar years. The constraints of the international economy, extensive enterprise rationalization and stringent deflationary policy in the 1920s brought unemployment and wage reductions. The conditions of workers were worsened by the onset of world depression in 1929. The harsher social effects of prolonged industrial depression were partly mitigated by the reflationary policies adopted after 1932, and the rapid recovery and growth in both light and heavy industry during the 1930s brought a rapid increase in the number of industrial workers. By 1938 around six million workers were in manufacturing, some two-thirds of them in factories employing over five workers. As the urban proletariat grew, so, too, did the potential basis of support for left-wing organizations, but by the mid-1930s such policies were hardly on offer to the general public. Radical left-wing activity had been totally suppressed. Recalcitrants were imprisoned, forced underground or overseas. The ideology of their more moderate colleagues had been effectively emasculated, and the remaining legal organizations expressed little dissent at the increasingly aggressive and militaristic policies of successive governments. In the factories labour more and more came under the wing not only of company unions, but of the officially-promoted 'patriotic' labour union organization. This gradually replaced Sōdōmei and its affiliates. In 1940, with the reorganization of the political structure, these 'patriotic' unions were brought together under a national body known as the Greater Japan Industrial Patriotic Society. Independent labour organizations ceased to exist. The compulsory membership characteristic of the bodies of the new political structure meant that by 1941 the Society claimed over five million industrial workers. This figure is no more an indicator of an active labour movement than is the extension of the 'patriotic' unions to almost every factory.

In Japan, as elsewhere, the coexistence of industrial and agricultural problems in the interwar period facilitated a shift towards more radical policies. Discontent and an awareness of differing class interests certainly existed, but these were never mobilized by the left on a national scale or transformed into conscious, class-based action. The long years of indoctrination and oppression under the regime of the Meiji Constitution, plus the strength of traditional values as a focus of stability in a time of rapid change, produced in the mass of the population a common awareness of national interest which transcended the potentially divisive sense of class. The right wing was successful in monopolizing the hearts and minds of both rural and urban workers, enabling the labour and productive forces of the nation to be efficiently mobilized in the services of the war against China, and then in the Pacific War. The rapidly deteriorating situation after 1943 took its toll in a decline in individual commitment, but there was little inclination to engage in organized labour protest, which was, in any case, too dangerous to contemplate.

Once the constraints of the wartime situation were removed there was an explosion of activity on the labour and left-wing front. The Labour Union Law of December 1945 guaranteed workers' right to collective action, and labour unions covering a whole range of industries and occupations sprang up in unprecedented numbers. By the end of 1946 some 40 per cent of the industrial labour force belonged to labour organizations. Social democrats came together to form the Japan Socialist Party, which advocated pacifism and a peaceful transition to socialism. The revolutionary left was represented by the rebirth of the Japan Communist Party, now for the first time a legal organization. This activity was greeted with delight by the Occupation authorities as a sign of democratic potential.

Both socialist and communist parties at this time were dominated by prewar figures. The most prominent figures in the JSP were Katayama Tetsu and Nishio Suehiro, both socialist representatives in the diet in the 1930s. The communist leaders Tokuda Kyūichi and Shiga Yoshio had both been in prison since 1928, and early in 1946 the leading role in the JCP was taken over by Nosaka Sanzō, who returned from fifteen years' exile in the Soviet Union and China. Support for these two parties mushroomed in the early years of the Occupation. A wave of popular enthusiasm carried the JSP to the position of largest single party in the diet in the spring 1947 election. This permitted Katayama, supported by two smaller parties, to form a cabinet, the only time a socialist party has done so in Japan's parliamentary history. An inability to carry out avowedly socialist policies led to divisions within the party, and the cabinet resigned early in 1948. Although it was a partner in a short-lived coalition cabinet under Ashida Hitoshi later the same year, its popular support collapsed. In the 1949 election the number of JSP members in the diet fell by over 50 per cent, to only forty-eight. For a while the JCP too enjoyed tremendous prestige among a broad segment of the population and was a vigorous articulant of popular protest. It too enjoyed diet representation and was a powerful influence in the labour movement.

This upsurge in 'proletarian' political activity was closely tied to the labour movement and the increase in the number of workers in labour unions. Land reform in 1946, by creating an agricultural sector dominated by owner farmers, minimized rural discontent, and brought a qualitative change in the nature and motivation of collective action by farmers. No such radical reform affected the urban proletariat, which inherited many problems from the prewar period. Distress increased as the number of unemployed, destitute and displaced persons was swelled by millions of repatriated soldiers and civilian emigrants. The inability of the urban/industrial sector to support the vast numbers who relied on it not only increased the burden on the rural sector but stimulated the radicalism prevalent in labour activity in these years. By 1948 union membership had reached nearly seven million (almost 20 per cent of the workforce). The legal framework for labour organization established by the Occupation gave labour considerable advantages. At the same time a distinctive pattern of unions emerged. Most unions in private industry were enterprise unions, and where an enterprise had more than one plant each plant tended to have its own union; these then cooperated under the aegis of an overall enterprise union. This pattern had begun to emerge in large companies in the interwar years, and the tradition had been maintained in the 'patriotic' labour unions of the war period. At the same time, though, industry-wide or professional unions made their appearance among groups such as teachers, national railway employees and civil servants. Most of these unions were affiliated to national federations whose roles were largely of a political nature. It was these unions that spearheaded much of the militant union activity in the years 1946–9. Moreover, the incapacity of management to control and manage enterprises in the wake of collapse of the old system and economic anomie served to encourage labour demands far beyond the minimum wage rises needed to keep pace with rampant inflation. Union success in conflicts with employers further reinforced labour assertiveness. Strikes and disputes were recurrent and a general strike planned in 1947 was banned by the authorities.

The strength of organized labour and its domination by the radical left, coinciding as it did with deteriorating US–Soviet relations and the prospect of a communist victory in China, was distinctly alarming to the Occupation authorities and its conservative Japanese backers. As policy shifted towards reconstructing Japan as a bastion of the Western capitalist camp and a haven of bourgeois democracy, steps were taken to restrict labour and socialist activity. In May 1950, General MacArthur proposed unsuccessfully to ban the JCP. A 'red purge' in the second half of 1950 restricted communist leaders and drove thousands of party members and purported sympathizers from their jobs, creating an environment in which many communists took to underground activity. Restrictions on labour activity included the prohibition of collective bargaining and industrial action by civil servants, a hitherto militant group. Simultaneously there commenced the depurging and rehabilitation of individuals purged at the end of the war.

The blatant anti-communism of the authorities and their restrictive attitude towards all suspected of sympathy with left-wing views weakened the radical left among organized labour and led to a general decline in support for socialist alternatives. The effect on the socialist and labour movements themselves was, ironically, not dissimilar to the pattern of the prewar years, with government oppression producing disunity and disarray. Left infiltration and domination of hitherto centrist organizations combined with the moderates' desire for self-preservation provoked a series of splits and realignments. Increasingly divided within itself, in 1951 the JSP formally split into two parties over the issue of the Security Treaty with the United States. The two factions did not reunite until late in 1955. Extreme militancy promoted by the dominant faction in the JCP in the early 1950s weakened its internal unity, and discouraged supporters afraid of a renewal of official antipathy. In the labour movement an anti-communist alliance was formed at national level; but as this organization moved to the left further splits occurred. Purges and restrictions at all levels removed communist dominance and weakened the movement as a whole.

The labour movement never regained the militancy of the immediate postwar years. On the basis of the substantial powers they acquired in the early years of the Occupation, unions remained a force to be reckoned with, but management response of maximum accommodation and the overwhelming dominance of company unions in private enterprise meant that they increasingly tended to become part of the establishment. Most private enterprise unions were located in companies where conditions were already good and improved rapidly during the high-growth period. Members came to enjoy the famed lifetime employment and seniority wages of Japanese industrial relations after the early 1950s.[6] In an era of prosperity the financial benefits of a rise in productivity became self-evident, and this led workers to cooperate with management to boost the company as a whole. The annual wages round, known as the 'spring offensive', emerged as a highly ritualized process in which the general level of wage increases was set by a few 'market leaders' entrusted with the initial settlements. Strikes came to serve as a demonstration rather than an ultimatum.

The particularist nature of unions has had two major effects. Firstly, unions have not been a horizontal unifying force bringing together all workers as a class. Since managers, too, are union members, they have reinforced company solidarity and shifted the labour problems posed by, for example, recession, on to the backs of non-unionized labour, reinforcing the dual structure of the labour market. Secondly, organized labour as a whole has failed to achieve any substantial unity. There has been no single national body representing organized labour. By the mid-1980s there were two large focal organizations, Sōhyō and Dōmei, and two smaller ones of some importance. Each attracted a different element of the union movement and was associated with a different part of the political spectrum. Lacking a unified voice in a country dominated by conservative politics and big business, organized labour has never achieved a position where it is an acknowledged party in official discussions, and has little say in decision-making at the top levels.

After the two wings of the JSP were reunited in 1955, left-wing political groupings in Japanese politics were relatively stable. Only one split has produced a major new party. In 1959 a small group of the JSP, led by Nishio Suehiro, left the party over the Security Treaty issue, and in January 1960 formed the Democratic Socialist Party. Advocating the advancement of socialism by democratic means, such as welfare programmes and cooperative management, the DSP has played down the importance of a class basis for socialism, opposing dictatorship of left or right. It has drawn much of its support from small business and white-collar workers, but its organization, representation in the diet and political prestige have remained very weak. Unable to secure a firm niche between LDP and JSP, it has never become a political heavyweight.

The JSP has remained by far the largest opposition party; it has adhered to a platform of democratic socialism achieved through peaceful means, and unarmed neutrality. Although it has embraced a range of left of centre views, it has had little in common with the JCP, whose membership is large but whose diet representation is small. Antagonisms have been frequent and concerted action from the two, as in the Security Treaty crisis in 1960, has been rare. Socialist politicians have remained highly dependent on support from organized labour, but in recent years the national labour leadership has seemed to be more united than the opposition representatives in the diet.

Even in the unlikely event of cooperation between these left of centre opposition parties, and the still more unlikely one of their working with a non-socialist opposition party, Kōmeitō (which is daggers drawn with the JCP), a parliamentary majority over the ruling Liberal Democratic Party seems remote. At the time of the 1960s Security Treaty renewal, for example, desperation and frustration led the opposition parties to resort (in vain) to extra-parliamentary tactics. They have been little more successful since in increasing their influence over policy-making. The JCP's attempt to present a 'lovable' image appeared for a time in the early 1970s to be a successful tactic, but notwithstanding the fluctuations of election results, the left has achieved little fundamental improvement in its overall position, and shows signs of having come up against a ceiling in terms of representation.

Despite the conservatives' unbroken enjoyment of political power since 1949, the Japanese population have not always acted in a supine manner, unquestioning of the hierarchy imposed upon them and unwilling to protest against government decisions. There have been very active manifestations of popular discontent. The 1960 Security Treaty crisis produced an outbreak of popular unrest on a scale that shook the country to its foundations. The war years were still recent enough for political opposition and organized demonstrations to be able to tap a nationwide residue of pacifist, and, in particular, anti-nuclear sentiment. The defence issue is still capable of arousing strong feelings on both sides.

Since 1960 many dissatisfactions have been channelled into 'citizens' movements', which have concentrated on consumer and environmental issues. Of these the anti-pollution agitation has been the most vociferous. Protest over the notorious mercury poisoning of hundreds by a plant at Minamata, in Kyushu, was only the most conspicuous part of a movement that has had considerable success in restraining the unbridled activities of big business and spreading an awareness of the social costs of the high rates of economic growth. A consciousness of the potential political price of its economic policies compelled even the highest levels of the government to take stock.

These movements were not narrowly political, but highly practical. They tended, if anything, to deal directly with the decision-making bureaucracy, circumventing elected assemblies.

Purely political expressions of dissatisfaction have been far less common. The skilfully orchestrated protest against the building of Tokyo's new airport at Narita has provided a continuing focus for left-wing, anti-government activity, and the terrorist activities of the Japanese Red Army show a revolutionary streak, but for the most part the organizations charged with political and labour representation of the working class and poor have been lulled by the establishment and the widespread prosperity into distinctly muted dissent. The weakest and poorest members of the community have too much to lose by engaging in radical protest activity. The majority of the working class have been the beneficiaries of rapidly rising standards of living. Neither the media nor the intelligentsia, both of which have a strong anti-establishment strain, have had much success in mobilizing popular dissatisfaction. Nor, in fact, have they shown much inclination to work hard in this direction.

Overwhelmingly, the citizens' movements and other popular protests have concerned themselves with causes and deprivations that are common to the nation as a whole and are conspicuously lacking in any class sentiment. Some sociologists have argued that the segmentation at lower levels conferred by the Japanese social structure renders popular movements less able to rouse the majority and revolution unlikely. The unity conferred by being Japanese appears to be the most successful in overcoming the negative effects of this segmentation. The sense of belonging to a locality, group or organization, rather than to a class, has been bolstered up by labour and industrial relations policies. The existence of company unions has encouraged all members of the group to subscribe to the existence of a common cause rather than define their interest according to their level in the occupational hierarchy, i.e. whether they are workers or managers. Moreover, the relative job flexibility within companies precludes the existence of trade or craft identity; the absence of restrictive practices, and the real possibility of ascending the hierarchy up to management level, create an awareness of change and hope within the status quo which is inimical to the whole perception of class prevailing, for example, in Britain. The majority of workers whose existence depends on the lower level of the dual manufacturing and service structure do not enjoy such conditions, but there are huge barriers to the organization and coordination of worker protest in these sectors, and workers here, too, have benefited from economic growth.

The postwar years have brought about phenomenal improvements in the standard of living of virtually all Japanese, giving them a chance of comfort, if not wealth, and fostered the belief that social mobility is high. Although figures suggest that the rate of social mobility has declined, and is now little different from that in the UK, the fact remains that most Japanese would define themselves as middle class. The categorization has few overtones of opprobrium, nor is 'working class' necessarily a designation to be proclaimed with particular pride. Where an individual is defined by his role in working for the nation and the group and the chance of improvement is clearly laid down, to label any stratum as 'working class' appears somewhat fatuous. Disadvantaged groups there certainly are, notably the Korean minority and the *burakumin*, but the labour and left-wing movements have singularly failed to try to work for these elements of the population, either because they have been unable to identify with their problems or because they have taken the view that a broader improvement in the welfare of the putative working class will bring in its wake better conditions for these groups as well.

Yet left-wing thought, inadequate though it may have been in its appeal to the majority of the population and in generating political action, has remained influential in Japan. Numerous intellectuals have been, and still are, active subscribers to socialist theories. Far more have been affected by the way in which the language, perceptions and approaches of academic writing are influenced by a Marxist conceptual framework. Theorizing has, to say the least, been lively, and the political parties of the left have been closely tied in to this trend. However, it is the degree to which socialist theory accords to the practicalities of postwar Japan that will govern its real influence in motivating a broader element of society. There clearly exists in Japan a large stratum of society whose economic circumstances might lead it to be termed working class, even if its members do not so designate themselves. However, those political organizations that claim to represent the members of this stratum seem conspicuously to have failed to take account of the realities of working-class life. They have dealt in theories which appear to have little relevance to constituents who live in a successful capitalist economy which promises them every chance of material prosperity. They speak of an urban proletariat which has little awareness even of its own existence. Japanese asked about class divisions in their

263

society often categorize the populace into rich and poor; Japan is more than ever before a plutocracy. The divisions that exist in Japanese society are not widely perceived of as class divisions, and only when the traditional theoretical approach can come to terms with this reality – or change it – will socialism have any chance of increasing its influence.

NOTES

1 This is not to deny that peasant unrest was an important indicator of the decline of the Tokugawa system.
2 The term 'socialists' is used here in the broad sense found in much of the literature. J. Crump, *The Origins of Socialist Thought in Japan* (London, 1983) disputes the use of 'socialist' to describe these individuals' ideas.
3 A factory was defined at this time as an operation employing ten or more workers.
4 Short for Japan General Federation of Labour. Between 1919 and 1921 the word 'Yūaikai' was appended to this title as a gesture towards its origins.
5 The Japanese word *'tenkō'* (conversion, about-face) is used for those who retracted their communist ideals in the 1930s.
6 Union members were by definition 'core' workers in firms who enjoyed these benefits, in contrast to peripheral temporary or part-time workers.

CHAPTER TWELVE

The Role of the Military

The image of the samurai is one of the conventional images of Japan familiar to many foreigners. The importance attached to the samurai is not a mistaken one; the samurai were Japan's ruling class from the twelfth century and the concept of the samurai ideal, the warrior ethic, was fundamental to the development of Japanese culture in the years prior to the Meiji period. Samurai lost their formal status in the early 1870s, but the samurai ideal remained powerful, and the military forces built up during the Meiji period played a crucial role in national affairs up to 1945.

China was essentially a civil society throughout her history, but Japan, despite extensive cultural borrowing from China, experienced the emergence of a warrior ruling class. By the end of the eleventh century great warrior families were beginning to encroach on the power of the ruling court nobility, whose servants they in theory remained. Following an internecine struggle between the leading Minamoto and Taira families, during the 1180s the victorious Minamoto Yoritomo built up a national administration controlled from his home city of Kamakura, just south of present-day Tokyo. This military government, which exercised influence over much of the country, was called the Bakufu. The emperor later bestowed upon Yoritomo the title of *shogun* and he remained nominally the servant of the emperor, exercising secular power in his name. In fact, from Yoritomo onwards, the shogun exercised absolute secular power, and the emperor became little more than a sacred and religious functionary. Despite occasional attempts by members of the imperial family to regain power, the rulers of Japan from this time through to 1868 were all military men. Many took the title of shogun. Where military families established dynasties – Ashikaga, Tokugawa – the title became hereditary. The possessor of the title of shogun was not always the real holder of power. This role might pass to a close adviser or relative, again a member of a warrior family. For over 700 years Japan was dominated by a small group of families whose *raison d'être* as a ruling élite resided in its ability to fight and exercise military strength.

The military families always remained outsiders in court cultural circles. Over the years they evolved a separate culture, with its own distinct codes of conduct and behaviour. The warrior ethic, or the ideals of *bushidō*, the way of the warrior as it is often referred to, developed over centuries. *Bushidō* has been compared to the chivalry of mediaeval Europe. This analogy is valid in as far as *bushidō* emphasized the virtues of bravery, loyalty and honour. A warrior had a pre-eminent loyalty to his lord and had to preserve his own and his master's honour, by death if need be. Prior to the early seventeenth century, when Japan was plagued by frequent internal conflict, the emphasis of *bushidō* was on military capability and on the codes of conduct and practices that would reinforce fighting efficiency.

Policies and developments from the late sixteenth century had a fundamental impact on the nature of warrior rule and the military ethic. First of all, an attempt to impose a rigid caste system on Japanese society drew a sharp formal distinction between the samurai (*bushi*) families and the remainder of the population, setting the warriors apart as a ruling caste by right. This process was begun by the military ruler Toyotomi Hideyoshi with his famous 'sword hunt' edict of 1588. The edict banned farmers from carrying weapons, in an attempt to divest those with no claim to samurai ancestry of all arms and make arms-bearing the sole right of the samurai caste. The Tokugawa rulers reinforced this policy by seeking to remove samurai from the land, compelling most to reside in castle towns rather than in the countryside. Samurai retainers received stipends from their lord in lieu of land income. The stipend initially corresponded to the volume of production of the earlier land-grant. Some marginal samurai continued to farm land and live in rural areas. In some domains the distinction between farmer and samurai never became clearcut, and older patterns persisted. This was particularly true of Satsuma, in southern Kyushu, and Chōshū, in western Honshu, where the Tokugawa Bakufu had less influence. In most of Japan, though, the majority of samurai were taken out of the agricultural sector, making cultivation essentially the task of the peasantry. The role of the warrior class was to rule and defend the domain.

Secondly, the warrior ethos was modified in accordance with the type of government and society desired by Japan's rulers. The most important influence in this respect was Chinese Neo-Confucianism. Certain elements of Neo-Confucianism were used to bolster the position of the samurai as a ruling class. These included an emphasis on a rigidly hierarchical society; the primacy of the values of loyalty and filial piety; and the relegation of trade and commerce to the lowest position in an agrarian-based economy whose basic task was to support the ruling élite. A policy of national isolation after 1639 served further to keep 'barbarian' influences away from the country.

The rigid restrictions placed on the patterns of behaviour of the three other major castes of society stimulated them to a certain extent to evolve their own subcultures. Even at the end of the Tokugawa period the difference in social structures between peasant and samurai, for example, remained very great. This did not prevent the samurai ideal from permeating the value system of the rest of the population. During the course of the two and a half centuries of Tokugawa rule the Neo-Confucian influenced warrior ethic came to be regarded by much of the population as the ideal; some members of the other strata of society sought to incorporate it into their own views and attitudes. By the end of the Tokugawa period, the *bushidō* ethic was no longer exclusively the preserve of the 6 per cent or so of the population who had samurai status.

Tokugawa rule brought to Japan an unprecedented 250 years of peace. This peace pre-empted the need for substantial military activity on the part of the samurai class, the rationale of whose very existence was to fight. Warriors continued to undergo military training and carry swords to indicate their status, and the maintenance of large standing armies by the various lords was regarded as an important factor in keeping the peace, but few samurai ever fought except in training, as a recreation, or in the occasional dispute over impugned honour. Taken off the land and prohibited from engaging in most alternative occupations, the *bushi* were in danger of becoming an idle, potentially disruptive group. They were encouraged to take education, and the vast majority were employed by their lords as administrators. By the nineteenth century they had essentially been transformed from a military caste into a ruling class of civilian bureaucrats and politicians. They retained as their guiding values those which had originated on the battlefield – valour, loyalty, honour, dedication to duty. By the nineteenth century in particular some of the barriers separating the warrior rulers from the rest of the populace were breaking down. Economic change and financial straits brought influence to many wealthy non-samurai and forced some *bushi* to engage in prohibited occupations to keep themselves and their families alive. Wealth, influence and status became increasingly incommensurate with each other. For the most part, though, the formal distinctions between samurai and the remainder of the population were preserved.

The Meiji revolution of 1868 was essentially a *coup d'état* by one part of the ruling class against another. Those who seized power were samurai, the losers were other samurai. The civil war itself left much of the population untouched. Significantly, though, those domains which led the coup, notably Satsuma and Chōshū, were not only old enemies of the Tokugawa, but also those in which the separation between warrior and farmer had never become absolute. Given its traditional role as a ruling class, its superior education and experience of leadership, the warrior caste might be expected to continue to provide Japan's leaders. The samurai class retained power for several decades despite the abolition of formal social hierarchy and samurai status, and despite changes in the economic system which forced samurai to make their own livings.

The new *bushi*-led government moved quickly to dismantle the old political and economic system in the interests of uniting the country under a strong central government. By 1871 the rigid four-caste system was abolished. The population was recategorized as *shizoku* (warriors), *sotsuzoku* (lower or marginal samurai) and *heimin* (common people). The following year the category of *sotsuzoku* was abolished, its former members being divided between the other two categories. While these terms continued to be used to denote lineage and implied social status, they lost most of their formal weight. In 1876 sword-bearing was also prohibited. Two swords were the traditional insignia of a samurai, making him instantly recognizable as a member of the ruling class. A samurai in theory needed little justification to use his sword against a commoner.

The samurai also lost the formal financial bond with his lord, although emotional ties remained strong. The old domains were transformed into prefectures or other units of local government by 1871. Payment of samurai stipends, hitherto the responsibility of the daimyo, was taken over by central government, but the financial burden incurred by this was so great that from 1876 ex-samurai were compelled to have their stipends commuted for a lump sum, usually payable in government bonds, which could be invested. Within a decade of the revolution, therefore, the samurai as a class had been deprived of both formal status and income.

One of the most important tasks facing the new government, given its objective of making Japan strong and independent, was the building of a large, modern army and navy. One possible option was the wholesale transformation of the samurai class, or at least part of it, into new fighting forces armed with modern weaponry and techniques. However, traditional samurai combat was individualistic and ill-suited to the techniques of nineteenth-century European warfare, and the technological gap was huge. In the interests of both domestic unity and efficiency the new leadership decided to start afresh with the building of a conscript army. This policy was announced late in 1872. Officers were to be professionals, but a substantial part of the armed forces was to consist of men conscripted for a period of years from all sectors of the population. The idea of recruiting members of the armed forces from outside the warrior class incensed many samurai. It was less contentious for Satsuma, Chōshū and other domains where the distinction between samurai and farmer was relatively vague, and whose leaders had made conscious attempts to recruit commoners into their forces even before the 1868 civil war. Men from these domains, of course, were now the country's rulers.

The net effect of these reforms was that samurai voiced a growing discontent which threatened to destabilize the government itself. The regime was compelled to take action. The proposed military expedition to Korea in 1873, and that which actually took place to Formosa in 1874, were both partly motivated by the need to find an outlet for samurai discontent. It was not to be the first time that domestic unrest was diverted into foreign aggression. In addition, the government undertook a major programme of samurai rehabilitation. *Shizoku* were employed in a variety of capacities, where they might earn salaries. Many joined the bureaucracy or undertook other administration, and a large number joined the armed forces. They were encouraged to invest in business, manufacturing and agriculture, which would help them to be financially self-sufficient while at the same time promoting the economic development of the nation. This programme was not totally successful, but stilled much of the disquiet. A minority of samurai failed to cope with the new pattern of their lives, either through an inability to adapt, or because they believed that acceptance of the new norms would inevitably bring about the decline of the inherited traditions which had made them what they were. This latter group harboured resentment and dissatisfaction, which erupted in rebellions such as those at Hagi in 1876 and Satsuma in 1877, and became a powerful factor in the emergence of right-wing ultranationalist thought.

Not that the rest of the populace was initially pleased to find itself conscripted into the new military forces. Some of the peasantry, from whom most conscripts came, construed the word 'blood tax' in the official notification as implying a form of human sacrifice. It took a while to dispel this misconception. Conscription also depleted the manpower resources available to a peasant cultivator, by removing the strongest and most able part of the labour force whether or not it was harvest time. Many educated or wealthy families used any means at their disposal, legal or illegal, to avoid the conscription of their sons, worsening the burden on those less favourably positioned. By the late 1880s the law had been tightened to prevent the propertied classes from finding these loopholes, but military service still tended to be regarded as a burden, not as a privilege or an accolade. The mantle of the samurai did not instantly fall upon the shoulders of the new armed forces. The need for an army was accepted by the population, and its leaders enjoyed considerable prestige, but membership of the armed forces did not confer an automatic charisma.

The government's prime target was for its army and navy to be both modern and efficient. Size would come later. To this end experts were brought over from Europe to advise on the training and equipping of modern forces, first French, and then Prussians, in the case of the army. Naval advisers were largely British. The advisory role of these men was crucial to the efforts of Yamagata Aritomo and Ōyama Iwao, the main architects of Meiji Japan's modern army. Foreign advisers cooperated closely with Japanese officers, most of whom were former samurai.

At first almost all equipment, especially major items such as ships, had to be imported, but by expanding production in the arsenals it inherited from the Bakufu, the government was before long able to provide for many of its own military needs. Warship production was minimal until well after the turn of the century, but basic items such as firearms and uniforms were largely home-produced by 1900. Manpower was no problem, nor was finance. Military expenditure was a priority and accounted on average for over 30 per cent of annual government expenditure for the years 1880–1912.

The net result was impressive. By 1877 the new conscript army was sufficiently able and well-equipped to achieve victory over conservative rebels from Satsuma, fighting in the traditional manner. By 1893 Japan had a standing army of over 60,000 men, with the potential for far greater mobilization. She had a small but efficient navy, and confounded general predictions by achieving a sweeping victory over the inefficient and demoralized Chinese armed forces in 1894–5. Japan's success was attributed to greater use of technology, superior tactics, strategy, operation and leadership, as well as more highly motivated and dedicated manpower. Success in the war was a fillip to further military expansion, strengthened Japan's position in the international economy and made her for the first time a colonial power. The increasingly imminent prospect of war with Russia from the mid-1890s quickened the pace of the military build-up, and Japan's military and naval capacity effectively doubled in the decade 1895–1904. The war against Russia 1904–5 was an immense financial burden, but the armed forces again emerged with considerable credit, if not with the crushing victory for which the public hoped. Within little more than fifty years of the end of seclusion Japan had defeated both the largest nation in East Asia and one of the most powerful in Europe. She had 150,000 men under arms and the most powerful fleet in the Far East.

The latter part of the Meiji period brought the armed forces not only military success, but a privileged constitutional position. Under the 1889 Meiji Constitution the emperor was the supreme commander of the armed forces. Army and navy ministers as cabinet members did partake in a certain measure of joint cabinet responsibility, but the chiefs of staff, presiding over the strategic/tactical side, were free of popular, legislative and even cabinet control, being responsible to the emperor alone. An additional regulation operative until 1913 and again from 1936 stipulated that the army and navy ministers had to be serving officers. This effectively gave the armed forces a veto on the composition of the cabinet, since both army and navy could order their minister to resign and refuse to provide a replacement. In these provisions there existed legal and constitutional sanction for independent action by the military.

This power was not initially exercised. The armed forces, like the civilian government, were dominated by men from the *hanbatsu* domains of Satsuma and Chōshū, many of whom were also politically active. Army policy and planning was guided by men such as Yamagata Aritomo, Katsura Tarō and Terauchi Masatake – all of whom were at some time prime minister – and army leadership

271

remained the preserve of Chōshū through to the 1920s. The navy was equally identified with the Satsuma interest group, through men such as Saigō Tsugumichi, Yamamoto Gonnohyōe and Tōgō Heihachirō. The *hanbatsu* domination of both civilian and military authorities provided for a community of interest between the two while oligarchic power persisted, through to the late Taishō period. Not until later, with the decline of *hanbatsu* government and the divergence of military from civilian interests, were steps taken by members of the military to exploit their constitutional position.

The members of the new military did not at once become the samurai of the new age, although victory against China and Russia enhanced the prestige of the army in Japanese society, and the army came to be regarded as a guardian of nationalist and traditional values by the more conservative elements of the population. The conscription system provided the army with a strong connection with the inherently more conservative rural areas, since a majority of conscripts came from these areas. Returned men served in the reserve for a period of years and enjoyed a high status in their communities. They became a channel through which the values held dear in the army – discipline, order, service to the nation – could be disseminated to the rural population. The army later increased its control over village activities by the formation in 1910 of the Imperial Reservists' Association, which became a leading force in village life. Over the next two decades military-sponsored organizations impinged further on the life of the rural community. The introduction of compulsory military training into schools in 1925 extended military influence further over the population as a whole.

During the Meiji period strenuous efforts were made to detach the mass of the armed forces (though not their leaders) from the arena of day-to-day politics. An abortive army uprising in Tokyo in 1878 (the so-called Takebashi uprising), motivated by non-payment of rewards after the Satsuma campaign the previous year, distinctly alarmed the authorities. Their response was two declarations laying down the guidelines for a military ethic. The Admonition to Soldiers and Sailors (*Gunjin Kunkai*) of 1878 emphasized the need for bravery, loyalty and obedience, and warned against political activity. The 1882 Imperial Rescript to Soldiers and Sailors (*Gunjin Chokuyu*) stressed the same values, tying them in with the traditional samurai ethic, and again enjoined against political activity. The Peace Police Law of 1900 formally prohibited political activity by members of the armed forces. By detaching the military from politics the authorities reinforced their position as servants of the emperor. With official sanction the armed forces became the bastion of loyalty to the emperor and the 'impartial' guardian of the interests of the nation in a system in which the imperial mandate was the ultimate sanction. When armed also with the legal power to impose what their members considered to be in the national interest, they were in a truly formidable position.

Although for much of the Meiji period the army and navy as institutions had little political role, their leaders wielded significant political influence as members of the ruling oligarchy. Some military leaders served as prime ministers. Despite the discouragement of political activities by the broad mass of soldiers and sailors, retired generals and admirals often went on the reserve list to enter party politics, and in this capacity were politically important. Political involvement and the growing need to come to terms with the developing political parties of the diet after 1890, brought military leaders into close contact with parties, contacts eagerly cultivated by party men anxious to gain a stake in power. General Tanaka Giichi, for example, became leader of the Seiyūkai and served as prime minister 1927–9. The reputation of the forces as the guardians of imperial and national honour, however, still caused them to proclaim that they were 'above' party politics. Two admirals, Katō Tomosaburō and Yamamoto Gonnohyōe, served as successive prime ministers 1922–4 when 'politically neutral' premiers were considered desirable, and a return to non-party 'transcendental' cabinets was marked by a succession of forces premiers in the 1930s. By this time the cabinets of national unity they headed were deemed to be the only ones capable of having the national interest truly at heart.

Until shortly before World War 1 the armed forces had been the beneficiaries of a programme of almost unlimited expansion. By 1912 Japan had a standing army of almost a quarter of a million men. However, the financial burden incurred by lavish military spending, notably the heavy foreign borrowing engaged in during and after the Russo-Japanese War, was potentially devastating to the Japanese economy. The reluctance of the Saionji cabinet in 1912 to finance further expansion in the armed forces led to a political crisis and the resignation of the cabinet. Scandals over naval corruption[1] further undermined the reputation of the military. Pressure for retrenchment received an added impetus from the post-1919 depression, and from the beginning of the Taishō period military prestige suffered a reversal in the face of the growing influence of party politics, and then the worldwide disarmament movement. This produced an element of rancour and resentment among some members of both services.

The most significant impact of the international arms limitation movement after World War 1 was on the Japanese navy. The 1922 Washington Naval Limitation Treaty provided among other things for a 5:5:3 ratio on capital ships for the US, Britain and Japan. While the fact that the Japanese navy was sufficiently powerful to be the object of international negotiation was in some ways flattering, the actual ratio that was decided on was not. Japan had fought for a 10:10:7 ratio. The final outcome led to a split in the delegation, and its members faced a barrage of criticism at home for having given way. The agreed ratio, the ten-year halt on the building of capital ships, the stop on Pacific fortifications and other conditions of the treaty were considered by many in the navy to be fundamentally detrimental to Japan's security. Their apparent imposition bred resentment.

The strength of the army was never the subject of international negotiation, but successive Japanese governments in the early-mid-1920s sought for financial reasons to restrict its size. In 1925 it was reduced from twenty-one divisions to seventeen. In the long run these cutbacks if anything benefited the army. They enabled it to rationalize both manpower and equipment, adopting new technology and discarding old, and increasing its efficiency as a fighting force. Moreover, to alleviate the problems of redundancy among army officers affected by the retrenchment, a programme of compulsory military training in schools was initiated. This programme served to impress the values dear to the military onto the minds of the most receptive members of the population. The restraints on military expansion created much severer resentment within the armed forces.

Rising resentment helped to stimulate a revival of political interest among military personnel. Some members of the armed forces believed that it was not appropriate for them obediently to carry out the commands of their civilian political masters where the latter seemed to be acting against the national interest and abusing the imperial mandate. During the 1920s this process of politicization was most marked among Japanese troops in Manchuria and China; from the late 1920s it spread to the main body of Japanese forces at home. From the turn of the century Japanese troops were stationed on Chinese territory to protect foreign settlements and other concessions. Troops were also stationed in the colonies of

Formosa and Korea to enforce Japanese rule. The other nucleus of Japanese troops in mainland Asia was the so-called Guandong Army, which guarded the Manchurian Railway concession and the Japanese leased territory of Port Arthur and the Liaodong Peninsula (gained after the victory over Russia in 1905). Over the two decades after its establishment the Guandong Army expanded rapidly in both size and influence. It attracted the cream of the younger officers, as well as some whom the authorities preferred to keep at arm's length from mainland Japan, a potent combination which contributed to an increasing politicization of the officer class. Moreover, the relative autonomy enjoyed by the leaders of the Guandong Army – the head of the army had considerable influence over the affairs of Guandong Province – enhanced its political advantage in its dealings with the authorities in Japan. During the 1920s the Guandong Army became a stronghold of the military's political ambitions.

These political ambitions related initially to Japan's policy in East Asia.[2] Civilian governments in Japan proved less able to control armed forces stationed outside the home islands, and this produced a development in the field of foreign policy which came to be known as dual diplomacy. This was the phenomenon whereby Japanese forces abroad took independent action, leaving the government at home to pick up the pieces. The first suggestion of this was in China in 1927, when Japanese forces in the Shandong area clashed with Chinese nationalist troops. The incident escalated, requiring the despatch of further troops from Japan. Local incidents of this kind might, perhaps, be expected where troops from the two countries were in close proximity, but much of the independent action taken by Japanese forces in mainland Asia was of a more calculated nature, aimed at pressurizing the government at home into ex post facto acceptance and justification of certain policies. The most conspicuous examples of this dual diplomacy were the assassination of the Manchurian warlord, Zhang Zuolin, in 1928, and the Manchurian Incident of September 1931. The Zhang assassination did not lead to the hoped-for occupation of Manchuria, which ended up committed to the Chinese nationalist cause. By contrast, the Manchurian Incident was conspicuously successful in bringing about a Japanese takeover of Manchuria and the establishment of a puppet state of Manchukuo, policies for which many members of the army had long campaigned.

The political ambitions of a hard core of officers soon spread to domestic affairs. The army was no more united in the solutions it proposed to the problems facing Japan. The military as a whole was a bastion of conservative values, but influential minorities within the armed forces were committed to radical change. The result was a running conflict within the military which reached its peak in the years 1930–6.

A major split in the navy had started with the terms of the Washington Treaty in 1922; dispute over the degree of civilian control over naval matters and the relative international strength of the imperial navy simmered throughout the 1920s. It erupted again with full fury with the signing of the London Naval Treaty by the Hamaguchi cabinet in 1930. This treaty, reluctantly negotiated and signed by Navy Minister Takarabe, extended the existing 5:5:3 ratio to auxiliary ships and renewed the stop on the building of capital ships until 1935. Ratification of the treaty was forced through despite the objections of the naval chief of staff, who maintained that its provisions constituted a threat to Japan's freedom to act in East Asia and jeopardized her basic security. He argued that only the supreme command could make a final judgment on such matters of strategy, tactics and operation. The civilian authorities, the treaty's opponents claimed, had violated 'the independence of the supreme command'. This view gained strong support from within the army; it suggested that a whole range of decisions could be justified on the grounds of operational necessity. Even after this crisis had passed, factional disputes within the navy continued through much of the 1930s.

During the 1930s both army and navy were also subject to what was largely a gulf between senior officers and some of their junior counterparts, who were strongly influenced by ultranationalist thinking. These younger officers believed that Japan could only play her full role in Asia if a radical programme of reform were undertaken at home. At the risk of oversimplifying this distinction, historians have tended to formalize it in the case of the army in the rift between the *tōsei* (control) faction and the *kōdō* (imperial way) faction. Members of the *tōsei* faction believed in the need for modification of the existing status quo to achieve 'control' over the nation and make Japan a defence state geared to Japanese expansion on the mainland, and to the conduct of war in Asia and beyond. They advocated the entrustment of affairs of state to military leaders who were the true servants of the emperor and guardians of 'traditional' values. These leaders would cooperate with 'progressive' bureaucrats and others to mobilize Japan's economy and society in a way most likely to enable her to achieve her Asian destiny. The most famous figure in the group was General Tōjō Hideki, prime minister 1941–4.

The *kōdō* faction, though led by senior officers, consisted mainly of younger field officers, many of whom believed that forceful action was necessary to enable a takeover by the army and the implementation of radical reform to remove the barriers between the emperor and his people and fulfil the principles of the *kokutai* (national polity). The nationalist writer, Kita Ikki, was widely respected by them. The members of the *kōdō* faction were part of a larger assortment of nationalist would-be activists within the army. Both factions included those whose association stemmed from personal rather than ideological reasons. Both were reacting to the attempts to impose arms limitation.

Radicals in the armed forces perpetrated a series of assassinations and attempted coups during the period 1931–6, sometimes with the cooperation of civilian ultranationalists. Twice during 1931 members of the Sakurakai, an informal nationalist society within the army, were involved in abortive plans for a *coup d'état*. The failure to punish the conspirators encouraged other attempts. In May 1932 young naval officers managed to shoot dead Prime Minister Inukai Tsuyoshi. Recognized members of the *kōdō* faction assassinated General Nagata of the Military Affairs Bureau (a powerful *tōsei* faction figure) in 1935. Actions such as these found support among many junior officers. Some had served in Manchuria and believed that Japan could not wield her rightful influence in Asia without a radical change of government at home. Others, less interested in territorial aggrandizement as part of Japan's destiny, sought a regime at home that would deal more positively with the depression and the rural impoverishment that was devastating some of the villages from which many of them came. The reform policies they espoused were strongly anti-capitalist. Brought up to believe that the army was the only truly non-partisan, patriotic élite, they believed that the armed forces should be the major architects of what they termed 'national renovation', or a 'Shōwa Restoration'.[3]

The disruption caused by this radical assortment was out of all proportion to its numbers. In engaging in violence at home the radicals followed a tradition of opposition by violence which went back to the Meiji period and which was not without honour.[4] The perpetration of a series of political killings and attempted *coups d'état* in the early 1930s, which disposed of some notable national figures, revealed a considerable reluctance on the part of the military authorities to take strong disciplinary measures to curb insubordination by junior officers acting 'in the name of the emperor' or because of 'sincere motives'. This was strongly revealed even in the attempted coup of 26 February 1936, an incident on a far greater scale than any of the earlier ones.

Towards the end of 1935 *tōsei* leaders took measures to disperse *kōdō* supporters, as factional interest polarized further after the murder of Nagata in August. On 26 February 1936, before some transfers could be carried out, over 1,000 soldiers, led by junior *kōdō* officers, occupied key buildings in the centre of Tokyo. Leading political figures were attacked, and Finance Minister Takahashi Korekiyo and Lord Privy Seal Saitō Makoto were among those killed. Top *kōdō* officers failed to give overt support to the calls for a Shōwa Restoration and a new domestic order. Martial law was declared to cope with the crisis, but the military leadership waited to assess the degree of support for the rising before taking measures to suppress it. Two days later, when it had become apparent that the coup lacked widespread support outside the army, a show of military force persuaded most of the rebels to return to barracks. The ringleaders were arrested and prosecuted. Thirteen officers and four civilians were later sentenced to death. The purge was extended to the ultranationalist thinkers Kita Ikki and Nishida Mitsugu, whose ideas were claimed to have influenced the young officers. The measures taken to disperse the remaining core of *kōdō* officers weakened the faction irrevocably, and confirmed the *tōsei* faction as the leading force in the direction of military policy. Discipline, it was said, had been restored. Thereafter there were no more extremist army plots.

The 26 February rising marked the growing pre-eminence of the military in domestic politics. The prime minister at the time, Admiral Okada Keisuke, barely escaped with his life; his cabinet resigned less than a fortnight later. His successor, Hirota Kōki, a former diplomat, presided over a cabinet of national unity, which openly maintained strong connections with the *tōsei* faction. War with China further strengthened support for cabinets of national unity, which included a growing number of military men. The political influence of the military was also strengthened by the revival in 1936 of the stipulation that army and navy ministers must be generals or admirals on the active list. In the army, the army (war) minister, chief of the general staff and inspector-general of military education acted as a decision-making triumvirate, which deliberated on the appointment of a new army minister. Any refusal by the army to nominate an appropriate representative could bring down a cabinet. In as far as the armed forces controlled the making and breaking of cabinets in this way, their wishes could not be ignored by other political decision-makers.

The years after 1932 produced a rapid military build-up. The expiry of the Washington and London agreements initiated a huge programme of warship and other armaments production after 1935, and ended all attempts at international naval limitation. As the crisis in East Asia deepened with the advent of war with China in 1937, national unity inevitably took precedence over political bickering. As might be expected, the conflict favoured even greater military involvement in politics. From 1937 Japan was turned into the defence state which *tōsei* army leaders aimed for; politics, the economy and society were all geared to a successful prosecution of war, first with China, and then with the US, Britain and the Allies. Military influence was based firstly on constitutional prerogatives which enabled the military legitimately to exercise influence at the highest levels. There was never an attempt after 1936 to establish direct military rule. The forces had also, unlike the political parties, build up over the years a considerable stock of popular support, much of it through national organizations which became even more active during the 1930s. The military had been the main beneficiaries of the expansionary economic policies of the early 1930s, which had brought little substantial improvement in standards of living to the mass of the population, and its more radical elements were able to tap popular chauvinism and demands for a radical change in the way Japan's domestic affairs were organized. The pursuit of Japanese advancement in Asia as a vindication of Japan's national honour and a solution to problems at home seemed, to many, a positive and coherent response to domestic ills. The military became the voice of national aims and ambitions, as well as the means of carrying them out.

The navy played a lesser role than the army in national policy-making during the war years 1937–45, but the army was unable to impose its will, and there was rarely unanimity on strategy and the conduct of the war. Prosecution of the fighting was bedevilled by conflict between the two armed forces, which was never satisfactorily resolved. The hostility was partly the result of the army's political dominance, which was resented by some members of the navy. It was also the result of different strategic priorities and needs. For the navy, charged with the task of defending Japan's seaborne approaches, colonies and mandated territories, the main enemy was one that could approach from the sea and endanger Japan's supplies of raw materials from Southeast Asia, notably the oil on which the fleet depended. The navy regarded the United States and Britain as posing the major threat to Japanese interests, and to that extent was reluctant to antagonize them. The army's priorities were different; less directly affected by any possible embargo on oil supplies, and geared to land operation, the army's preoccupation lay with mainland Asia. Japanese-controlled territory in Northeast Asia enjoyed a common border with Russia, the long-standing threat to Japan's interests in the area. The desire by some members of the army to strike northward against the Soviet Union was not unassociated with its struggle in China, in which the navy played a relatively minor part. Army strategy had for years been geared to a struggle with the Soviet Union. However, in clashes with the Soviet Union in 1938 and 1939 Japan had come off worse and many feared full-scale conflict with the USSR. Hitler's initiation of war against the Soviet Union in 1941 made some members of the army and their civilian supporters more anxious to strike against the Soviet Union while she was tied up on her Western borders. Bitter experience, as much as naval pressure, led Japan to adhere to the non-aggression pact with the Soviet Union, which was eventually broken by the Soviet Union in August 1945. The revelation of this decision to Moscow by the Sorge spy ring which operated in Tokyo enabled the Soviet Union to concentrate on resistance to the Germans. When the decision to advance 'southward' was made, the army was as yet unprepared to play a major part.

The inter-forces dispute was exacerbated by the way in which each force was administered. Each had its own airforce and independent organization, which meant that they frequently failed to cooperate to best advantage. They had long competed ferociously for budget advantage and continued to fight fiercely for dwindling supplies during the later stages of the war. Major military decisions remained throughout subject to inter-force rivalry up to the very highest levels.

At the level of political decision-making, where the army predominated, a major part was played by the authoritarian General Tōjō Hideki, sometimes misleadingly viewed as a Japanese Hitler. Tōjō became premier in October 1941, and held the post until July 1944. His was the strongest individual voice in the conduct of the war, and he increasingly centralized all political and strategic decisions, accruing considerable power to himself in the process. By 1943 Tōjō held simultaneously the war and munitions portfolios, and in early 1944 he became chief of the general staff as well. He hoped by this move to rid himself of the traditional intra-army conflict between the political (army minister) and strategic (chief of staff) sides, but it was not totally successful. Despite the great power he enjoyed Tōjō was in the end brought down by his failure to bring the war to a successful conclusion. He resigned in the face of political manoeuvring by military and civilian colleagues and intense pressure from the country's senior statesmen.

Army control over the population as a whole became much tighter after 1937. Operational necessity became the overriding factor in making decisions at all levels, and military needs took precedence over all else. As such military considerations affected every aspect of the lives of all Japanese, often in a distinctly arbitrary fashion, and petty tyranny by local army officers and men was common. Extensive control over the material aspects of the life of the community was reinforced by the use of the military police *(kenpeitai)* to control matters of law and order, potentially subversive ideologies and public unrest. In Korea and Manchukuo the military police were the main agents of suppression of nationalist sentiment.

At the time of the Boxer Rebellion of 1900, and the Russo-Japanese War, Japanese forces had been praised for the honourable and gentlemanly way in which they conducted themselves. In the campaign against China, and in the Pacific War, such standards of conduct ceased to operate. In the name of a 'holy' war against inferior peoples brutality became widespread. The fall of Nanjing in December 1937 initiated a particularly appalling spate of murder, rape, torture and looting. Prisoners of war reported the most appalling atrocities. Such behaviour made the Japanese army an object of abhorrence outside the country. Even within Japan the high-handed attitude adopted by some members of the army towards civilians and subordinates made it the object of hatred.

As the war dragged on the prestige of the military declined further in the face of desperation among the people and the growing realization that Japan could not possibly win. Yet so great was the army's stake in victory that this was never publicly admitted. There was a growing divergence between the interests of military and people. The army authorities continued to proclaim a belief in victory, and, when that became impossible, called for a battle to the death on Japanese soil. Surrender was agreed in August 1945 despite army opposition. An attempt by a small number of army officers to prevent the emperor from broadcasting Japan's decision to surrender – considered crucial to military acceptance of the decision – narrowly failed. Several top army officers committed suicide rather than face the reality of defeat. The mass of conscripts was too exhausted to object and, indeed, positively welcomed an end to the fighting.

The Occupation authorities were convinced that military leaders were largely to blame for Japan's excursion into war. The conduct of the war had further labelled the army as a malign influence. The demobilization of Japan's armed forces, the demilitarization of Japan and the introduction of 'democratization' policies intended to prevent any future resurgence of Japanese militarism, became the major objectives of Occupation policy. With the repatriation of Japanese soldiers and sailors, some five million members of the armed forces were demobilized and returned to their native towns and villages. Thousands were prosecuted for offences in the conduct of the war in minor war crimes trials throughout the former occupied areas. Civilian and military leaders considered responsible for leading Japan into aggressive war were indicted in front of the International Military Tribunal for the Far East in Tokyo. Of the seven defendants eventually given the death penalty only one, ex-prime minister Hirota Kōki, was a civilian. The number included Tōjō Hideki. Factories geared to military requirements – by now a substantial part of Japan's manufacturing industry – were dismantled, many of them designated to be sent abroad as reparations. By the end of 1947 the Japanese army and navy no longer existed.

Demobilization and the destruction of Japan's capacity for waging war was a more easily defined task than the wider demilitarization of Japanese society and the prevention of a resurgence of popular support for aggressive militaristic policies. Occupation experts defined two major areas of Japanese society as bastions of militarist support: the *zaibatsu* (huge financial and industrial combines dominating the Japanese economy) and the rural community. The industrial-military complex was subjected to an extensive deconcentration and anti-monopoly programme. The rural community was transformed by a major land reform, whose aim was to remove widespread tenancy and build a nation of prosperous owner-farmers with no interest in the pursuit of aggressive policies. Efforts were made to remove the channels for military influence over political affairs. Many leading politicians and bureaucrats of the war period not charged as war criminals were purged from office; the purge was extended to the economic sphere. The Meiji Constitution was immediately suspended to invalidate any constitutional hold by the military on political decision-making.

The single most important tool for preventing a revival of militaristic policies was the new constitution of 1947, which provided for a new political system in which the military had no role. The ninth clause aimed to prevent the reappearance of any Japanese military capability.

The official English translation of this clause reads:

> Aspiring sincerely to an international peace based on justice and order, the Japanese people forever renounce war as a sovereign right of the nation and the threat or use of force as a means of settling international disputes.

> In order to accomplish the aim of the preceding paragraph, land, sea and air forces, as well as other war potential, will never be maintained. The right of belligerency of the state will not be recognized.

This clause of the Occupation-drafted constitution conveys the very strong feeling at the time that Japan should be permanently demilitarized. Its apparent finality took many Japanese by surprise, but it found widespread popular support.

The Japanese were not in a strong position to object to Occupation policies, but even so, this onslaught did not cause an outcry. The level of support for the military which the allies believed existed might have led the authorities to expect greater protest. However, the armed forces were discredited by having failed in their ultimate *raison d'être*, the successful prosecution of war on behalf of the nation. Japan's surrender also marked a defeat and discrediting of the whole prewar system and its policies, of which the military had been vocal advocates. On a practical level as well as an ideological level the military had failed to live up to popular expectations; defeat discredited the military and much of what it stood for. The Japanese people seemed to be unconcerned with the fate of their military leaders; they took little interest in the war crimes trials, offered few objections to total and ostensibly permanent demilitarization, and in general took the view that failure was in itself proof of the inadequacy of the military, its policies and its conduct. Subsequent pressure for a change in the demilitarization policy came in the first instance not from the Japanese people or government but from the United States, in the context of a changed world situation which produced the 'reverse course' in Occupation policy.

The 'reverse course' was stimulated by the rise to power of the Chinese Communist Party in 1949, worsening relations between the US and the Soviet Union, and the onset of the cold war. The United

States and its allies increasingly felt the need to create in Japan a capitalist, pro-US camp in East Asia, rather than the economically limited, neutral state originally envisaged. With the outbreak of the Korean War in 1950 Japan provided the UN (US) forces with a crucial base from which to conduct the war and secure supplies. Ostensibly to maintain domestic security in this difficult period, the Occupation authorities promoted in July 1950 the formation of a National Police Reserve of 75,000 men. By July 1952, this body had been expanded and combined with the Maritime Safety Board to provide a Self Defence Force (SDF) numbering nearly 150,000 men. The SDF's tasks were the maintenance of law and order and the prevention of direct and indirect foreign aggression. Unlike its predecessor it consisted of volunteers. Before the end of the Occupation, therefore, Japan was already provided with the core of its postwar military capability.

By the mid-1980s the SDF comprised nearly a quarter of a million men in its land, sea and air forces and was armed with a wealth of a highly sophisticated equipment. Rapid development and growth were to some extent impeded by constitutional and other restraints aimed at preventing any resurgence of Japanese militarism, as well as by public hostility. Much equipment had to be imported since the redevelopment of the armaments industries has been a sensitive issue, with aircraft production, for example, closely restricted. Some Japanese entrepreneurs have come to see both civilian and military aircraft production as a rich potential source of profits, but nothing approaching a military-industrial complex along prewar lines has emerged. Budget constraints on defence spending have never been imposed by law, but since the end of the Occupation the convention has operated that annual expenditure on the SDF should not exceed 1 per cent of GNP. Although the size of Japan's GNP means that even this 1 per cent is now substantial, Japan has remained largely dependent for its external defence on US protection. The issue of Japanese defence capability is closely tied to US policy, and to that extent the authorities are subject to fluctuating pressure to either increase or decrease spending both from abroad and at home.

Many observers have argued that the existence of the SDF is clearly anomalous given the terms of the constitution. The ninth clause of the 1947 constitution would appear specifically to prohibit the existence in Japan of any sort of standing armed force, even if it is intended purely for defence. Objections from opposition parties, for example the JSP, who have supported unarmed neutrality, have been particularly vocal. On numerous occasions cases have been brought in the courts disputing the constitutionality of the SDF, but lower court decisions in favour of such contentions have always been overruled on reaching the Supreme Court. This constant defence by members of the Supreme Court of the constitutionality of the SDF has given rise to accusations of political bias on the part of top members of the judiciary, and many have called into question its genuine independence at the highest level.

Even those who have supported a certain measure of Japanese rearmament have been aware of the anomalies posed by the ninth clause of the constitution. These, they have argued, should be removed by revision of the constitution. Such views have had substantial support in the ruling Liberal Democratic Party. However, constitutional reform requires a two-thirds majority in the House of Representatives, and despite its landslide victory in the July 1986 elections the LDP has never been able to attain this majority, since members of the opposition parties have, almost without exception, been committed to keeping the constitution as it stands.

Nor has a large majority of the Japanese people been pressing for revision of the constitution. Polls in the early 1980s suggested that while only a minority were in favour of complete disarmament and disbanding the SDF, the majority regarded the existence of some sort of military capability as no more than a necessary evil. The level of general esteem for the SDF has not been high. SDF bases and personnel have frequently encountered non-cooperation and even antagonism and hostility from local groups and communities, especially where environmental issues have been concerned. The SDF has also been a target for bodies opposing the existence of US troops in Japan and the whole US – Japan mutual defence strategy. People have rarely welcomed the idea of US bases in their locality.

Moreover, memories of the war have died hard and have been passed on to the next generation. So fervent has been the anti-nuclear sentiment since the Hiroshima and Nagasaki bombs of August 1945 that not only have all nuclear weapons been banned from Japanese soil and territorial waters,[5] but attempts to promote even the more peaceful uses of nuclear power, such as energy generation, have met with enormous opposition. The economic prosperity of the 1960s and 1970s pointed to the apparent benefits of a low level of military expenditure, and the population has since then become increasingly consumer-oriented. In the face of lack of popular support the ruling LDP has been reluctant to court disaster with the electorate by raising the profile of defence matters, and has been keen, for example, to make a public show of excluding all SDF personnel from direct participation in political decision-making.

This lack of widespread enthusiasm for the SDF shows that it has not secured the control over public opinion achieved at one time by the pre-1945 armed forces. The military claimed in the 1930s and 1940s to be latterday samurai, but despite these claims they have never been fully accepted as the true bearers of the samurai tradition. Much of this tradition died with the Restoration. For the rest, from the Meiji period other groups – bureaucrats, businessmen – claimed to embody the old ideals. In as far as any Japanese in the postwar years has been seen as a modern samurai, it is the company man, with his dedication to duty, loyalty to organization and nation, hard work and spirit of self-sacrifice. The prestige of the SDF has grown slowly, both *vis-à-vis* the authorities and among the people as a whole. SDF leaders have close contacts with government; they are controlled by a minister of state with a seat in the cabinet and their advice on strategic matters is listened to carefully. A career as an SDF officer has not been shameful, but it has been a second-rank career. While most of the early SDF leaders had experience of participation in the war, this was decreasingly the case during the 1970s. By the early 1980s the top ranks were almost exclusively manned by graduates of the post-1956 Defence Academy. It is hard to say what difference the coming to power of a postwar generation will make, although the choice of an SDF career indicates a certain commitment to the concept of armed forces in Japan.

What influence the SDF has achieved since its formation has been based on an assessment of the international situation, the desirability of, and Japan's need for, armed forces, and the competence of the SDF as a fighting body. Japan's increasing worldwide economic interests, the proximity of the Soviet Union, and US pressure, have all proved conducive to the growth of armed forces capable of protecting Japan's extended interests and playing a part in world affairs more commensurate with Japan's growing economic strength. The SDF has not succeeded in filling the post-1945 vacuum in military (or other) values or establishing itself as the spiritual guardian of the interests of the state. However, despite the lack of political power and public charisma on the part of the SDF, fears of a resurgence of Japanese militarism have been expressed both inside and outside Japan. Some observers have argued that some of the characteristics of Japanese society and politics which made it easier for the military to lead the people along the road to war are still very much in evidence. As such, many have construed all statements in support of the past as inherently promoting militarism. Certainly members of the older generation, like their counterparts elsewhere, look back with nostalgia and abhor the changed circumstances and morality of the younger generation. This nostalgia is shared by some of that younger generation, but this cannot necessarily be construed as a desire for rearmament. Discussions of the defence issue are based on practical politics, and not merely on nostalgia.

Over the last century the interests of the armed forces have both conflicted and coincided with the interests and desires of the nation as a whole, but before 1945 the military successfully proclaimed itself as the guardian of Japan's national polity and traditional values. As the main agent of the disaster of the China and Pacific Wars, the army lost not only its political influence, but also its charisma. It has had to rebuild itself a new status within the context of dependence on its political masters and a detachment from overt political activity. Like the armed forces in the Meiji period, it has had to establish its 'impartiality' in serving the national interest, but the changed domestic political framework and international environment have deprived the military of the channels through which it exercised power and the issues on which others could be charged with abusing the imperial mandate. Moreover, while present prosperity continues, few Japanese can be expected to perceive military adventures as being in their best interest.

NOTES

1   The revelation in 1914 that the German firm, Siemens, had employed bribery to secure contracts in Japan led to further exposures of corrupt dealings by the navy and its suppliers.
2   It should be noted that politically conscious officers did not share a common coherent view of Japan's needs in Asia. There was a tremendous divergence of opinions, and bitter disagreement was frequent.
3   Implying a national transformation as profound as that following the Meiji Restoration of 1868.
4   The Meiji government had first been resisted by force, e.g. in the 1877 Satsuma Rebellion, and assassination attempts, successful or otherwise, had been made upon a number of leaders, including

Ōkubo Toshimichi, Ōkuma Shigenobu, Mori Arinori and, later, Hara Kei.

5   Something of a fiction since US ships have been assumed not to be carrying such weapons since exemption requests have never been made and the Japanese authorities have never asked outright.

CHAPTER THIRTEEN

Administration and Public Service

Since the late nineteenth century Japan has had a modern, Western-style bureaucracy for both national and local administration. Entrance to this bureaucracy has been secured on the basis of merit and competitive examinations. The Japanese bureaucracy introduced in the Meiji period aspired, like its British counterpart, to be the impartial servant of the political rulers of the country. However, a distinctive pattern of bureaucratic operation has evolved in Japan; its relations with other élites and its political role have in some respects been quite unlike those of the British civil service. Factors which have contributed to this include the heritage of Chinese influence, the unity of administration and politics in the early Meiji period, the Japanese social background and the constitutional framework within which the bureaucracy operated up to 1945.

China had a Confucian bureaucratic tradition dating back over many centuries. Entry into the national bureaucracy was secured by success in competitive examinations and conferred an élite status. The existence of this élite group enabled vast areas of Chinese territory to be controlled and taxed in the name of the ruling dynasty. Many of the countries of Southeast Asia, by contrast, had no such territorial administration for local control and the collection of tax by the state. Instead, these countries operated on the basis of patron – client relationships, in which the potentate was the most important patron, who exercised power indirectly through client rulers of lesser areas. Japan, as a country within the Chinese culture area, sought early in its history to introduce a Chinese-style bureaucracy, but the rise of the great military families and the emergence of a socio-economic system very different from that of China led to the appearance of a ruling military caste rather than a purely civilian bureaucracy. Relations between Japanese feudal lords of the mediaeval period and their followers were more reminiscent of the patron – client system than of the examination-based meritocracy of China.

The segmented nature of Japan during the Tokugawa period precluded the need for a national administration. Even so, the territory controlled by individual lords was often considerable, and the removal of the warrior caste from the land necessitated an efficient means of collecting the tribute needed to support it. Some of this task was delegated to local headmen, but intermediate levels of administration were still required. As the peace of the Tokugawa period brought an increasing complexity to agricultural and commercial affairs, and the ruling class became more and more involved in the economy, the need for an efficient administrative machine, for both Bakufu and daimyo, became even greater. This need was fulfilled by members of the ruling samurai caste, which was gradually transformed into a large, if somewhat unwieldy bureaucracy .

The establishment of a lasting peace under the Tokugawa effectively deprived the warrior caste of its *raison d'être*, which was to fight. The military pretence was kept up; all samurai practised the military arts, were coached in military discipline, bore swords as a mark of rank and were educated in the values appropriate to a warrior, but only for a very few was fighting much more than a pastime. The majority of retainers, while trained to defend and serve their lord, had no chance to manifest their loyalty in actions on the battlefield. Instead, they undertook the running of his domain. Daimyo in return were only too happy to find occupation for their idle retainers. As the Tokugawa period progressed, the number involved in these administrative tasks increased rapidly.

The biggest body of samurai administrators was that of the Tokugawa shogunate itself. The Tokugawa family needed retainers to administer its huge landholdings, and in its capacity of Bakufu required administrators to carry on the work of national government, supervising the various *han* and deciding the policy, which affected them all. The largest section of this administration was that which dealt with day-to-day economic matters, in particular the collection of the rice tax which served as the foundation stone for the whole political and economic structure, its conversion into cash via the medium of merchants, and its distribution as stipends to those retainers directly dependent on the shogun. The administration of other taxes, and income from such sources as ports and mines, was also important. Other retainers dealt with educational, personnel and secretarial matters, as well as political affairs. Each individual domain had a parallel bureaucracy to attend to the affairs of the area. Here, too, many specialized in matters related to the economy. Despite the traditional view that commercial involvement did not accord with samurai status, by the end of the era very considerable numbers of *bushi* were highly trained in specialized economic functions. Furthermore, greater contacts between *bushi* from different areas, encouraged by such mechanisms as the alternate attendance system, helped administrative practices to become more uniform by the later years of the Tokugawa period.

The officials of the *han* were primarily concerned with the interests of the ruling class of the area. The daimyo required peace and stability to prevail in the villages under his jurisdiction, and for the requisite agricultural and other taxes to be paid. Providing these requirements were met officials rarely showed much tendency to intervene in more parochial affairs. In the more densely populated urban areas and castle towns samurai officials were more likely to be involved in local administration, but for the most part the system relied on the operation of the village as an informal unit of government at the local level. Within the village the administrative tasks that existed were organized on the basis of a traditional hierarchy of families. A considerable degree of what might be called self-government operated in the countryside, but there was no concept of a right to self-government. Assertion of local interests might be vociferous in the face of any challenge from another area, but rarely stood its ground against a higher authority. Even in the towns, the persistence of peace and seclusion hindered major interest groups, such as merchants, in asserting any sort of independent influence. As the Tokugawa period advanced, domain officials were increasingly compelled to take notice of the concerns of those outside the ruling class, but official intervention usually remained peremptory and *ad hoc*. Tokugawa administration represented sectional interest, not national unity.

The social gulf that existed between the *bushi* and the rest of society emphasized a division between administrators and populace also found in the Chinese bureaucracy. In China, examination success was the sole criterion for entry into the bureaucracy, whose members became over the years a race apart. In Japan, the dominant position of the *bushi* caste and the contempt in which most of their number held the remainder of the populace reinforced an assumption that the country's administrators were entitled to immense respect. An excessive awe of officialdom, and a particularly exaggerated self-importance on the part of officials themselves, were firmly established by the closing years of the Tokugawa period. This tendency, often summed up in the phrase 'respect for officialdom, contempt for the people' (*kanson minpi*), was given greater strength during the Edo years by the fact that administration was synonymous with rule.

The sweeping reforms aimed at centralizing the nation, which followed the political changes of 1868, rendered superfluous much of the work previously carried out by *han* and Bakufu bureaucracies. The abolition of samurai stipends and the reforms of agricultural taxation dismantled the whole economic basis of the Tokugawa system. At the same time fresh administrative requirements emerged from the needs of the new national government. Personnel were required to collect revenue, to see to financial outlay, to cope with the new demands of foreign policy, and to keep the peace. Large numbers of administrators were needed to implement the radical social, economic and political reforms which the government increasingly realized it had to make if it was to maintain Japan's strength and independence. The new system's need for an efficient bureaucracy more than matched the demands of the old.

The structure of the central administrative machinery went through a series of changes in the years 1868–74, before settling down into a fixed pattern of ministries with different, specified responsibilities along contemporary European lines. The most important ministries in the early years were those of Finance, Foreign Affairs, Home Affairs, Industry and Justice. The disposition of ministries and responsibilities varied slightly from time to time, but the basic arrangement remained the same. Until 1885 there was nothing equivalent to a cabinet; power was wielded by a small oligarchy consisting of the main architects of the Restoration and their protégés. Such men might, or might not, hold ministerial responsibility. Often they were merely entitled 'state councillor' (*sangi*) or 'imperial adviser'. Those who held power, however, were dependent on the bureaucracy for policy implementation; many of them had neither the expertise nor the experience required to administer. The make-up of this bureaucracy became a crucial factor in the success of the reform programme.

The earliest recruits into the new administration were those who came in on the coat-tails of the revolution – members of the four leading clans of Satsuma, Chōshū, Tosa and Hizen, and men from other domains that had provided support in the struggle against the Bakufu. These men were united by their shared role in bringing about the downfall of the Tokugawa. Most had some experience of *han* government, and a few had knowledge of Western learning or contacts with Westerners, but they were there, above all, because they had the right political credentials.

The new government rapidly came to realize that the scale of operation it had in mind required more and better trained administrators. They had not yet tapped the biggest single source of administrative expertise – those who had worked for the Bakufu. These men had experience of national administration and national issues, they had had far more extensive contacts with foreigners and Western culture. Their participation in the new administration had initially been ruled out by their identification with the Bakufu, and suspicions as to their loyalty to the new regime; but as the administration needed them, the doubts were soon overcome. Before 1869 was out the new government had started to recruit into its ranks considerable numbers of former Bakufu retainers, and others identified with pro-Bakufu domains. The members of this new intake largely worked where any technical or administrative expertise could be given full play, but where political responsibility was limited. Absorption into the new administration marked a high degree of rehabilitation into the good offices of the ruling group and stilled a potentially dangerous source of opposition. It also served to tide the new government over a critical period until it could begin to call upon the services of newly trained professional administrators. Some of these ex-Tokugawa retainers eventually rose to achieve a considerable measure of political power. The Bakufu naval leaders, Katsu Kaishū and Enomoto Takeaki, for example, rose to high office in subsequent years.[1] The majority, however, did not attain the highest levels, and their Bakufu background may well have ultimately played a major role in preventing their reaching the top political positions.

Despite this political gulf, the victors and losers of the 1868 civil war had a great deal in common. They were members of a single status group, and all considered themselves alike members of a ruling élite. Many Bakufu retainers had in any case been becoming increasingly unhappy about the direction of Japan's domestic political affairs, and welcomed the resolution of the situation and the formation of a powerful central government. By virtue of participation in national government and experience of international affairs, most former Bakufu retainers also realized that the overcoming of potentially divisive domain loyalties was crucial to national security. They therefore supported the move to establish a national administration. The two formerly combative wings of the administration had more which united them than divided them, and this cohesion meant that the bulk of the national administration was solidly behind the more progressive elements of the new government, strongly enhancing its effectiveness. After the end of the 1868 civil war the new government was to face by far the bitterest opposition not from ex-Tokugawa men, but from former supporters who felt that their traditions and regions were being betrayed by reforms at national level.

During the first decade and more after the Restoration there was no hard and fast line between the real power holders and the higher administrators who served them. While a system of ranks had been introduced there existed a very fluid, informal structure, and lower officials often wielded influence far beyond that implied by their nominal rank. For the most part, senior officials and top power holders willingly went along with proposals by their subordinates, especially if the matter required technical or administrative expertise beyond their own experience. In this period, more than in any other in Japan's recent history, the bureaucracy's power to administer was one with its power to engage in politics and make political decisions. Until after the establishment of the cabinet system in 1885 higher bureaucrats were also politicians and the executive was one with the administration. Building on the Tokugawa synonymity of rule and administration, this tendency towards political influence was reinforced by the fact that the issues involved were highly complex and the degree of relative ignorance substantial. In these early days almost all legislation was government sponsored, which made bureaucrats *de facto* policy-makers. This later led to attempts by outside bodies and individuals to influence the bureaucracy in its policy-making function, often by means which, in other cultures, might be regarded as corruption.

In the face of growing attempts to formalize the bureaucratic system this political character became less overt. The bureaucracy's political power was also reduced by the growth of competing élites and the increasing diversity of views concerning the national interest. Nevertheless this pattern of operation, once established, became crucial to the position and function of the bureaucracy in the governmental process, and was not easily discarded.

From the early years after the Restoration many Japanese regarded the introduction of a professional bureaucracy as crucial to the achievement of stable government, but it was not until 1893 that a system of examinations for entry into the higher civil service was fully established. With the introduction of examinations, the ranking, seniority and career patterns within the service became highly formalized. By the turn of the century the informality of decision-making which had marked the early Meiji years was virtually gone. Not all appointments to the higher bureaucracy were made on the basis of the examination system, but the non-exam appointments were rarely influential, and essentially remained peripheral to the working of the administration. From the start the examinations attracted the cream of Japan's youth, lured by the existing powerful influence of the national bureaucracy and the thought of working for the state in a period when an individual gained considerable credit from fulfilling an overtly patriotic rôle. The prestigious imperial universities rapidly became the main breeding ground for high-flying bureaucrats. In the years up to the outbreak of the Pacific War over 90 per cent of the bureaucratic élite came from the Law Department of Tokyo Imperial University.

Parallel with the institution of a national administration in the years after 1868, came a comprehensive system of local government. A local government bureaucracy to operate at prefectural, city, town and village level was regarded as crucial to the existence of a centralized nation state. This local bureaucracy was in the years up to 1945 closely integrated into a single system with the national bureaucracy. While many local officials spent their whole working lives serving in a single area, higher officials often moved between the provinces and the centre as part of a unified career pattern. Prefectural governors were often appointed from among the national bureaucracy and moved back to important posts there.

In the early years after the Restoration the development of local government was an immediate response to the difficulties posed by the abolition of the domains and the need for efficient control at local levels. The units of local government, for example the village, were designed for convenience, to serve the administrative needs of the state. They were seldom based on traditional communities, and rarely engendered much loyalty as entities from the populace. These units of local government built upon existing hierarchical tendencies, and were not in any sense democratic. The powers of elected officers were weak, and the introduction of local assemblies, under the stimulus of the popular rights' movement of the late 1870s – early 1880s, was rapidly compensated for by a strengthening of the already considerable powers of the appointed prefectural governor.

The final form of the pre-1945 local government system was established during the late 1880s under the guidance of Yamagata Aritomo. Yamagata conceived of local government as essentially bureaucratic rather than political in character. Local officials enjoyed strictly limited and closely defined powers. The system was such that there were many opportunities for the higher levels of government to intervene in the affairs of the lower. The prefectural governor, who was in effect a political agent of the central government, had inordinate powers in this respect. Local initiatives and inclinations were further dampened by a high degree of financial dependence of lower entities on higher ones. A slight loosening of the constraints on local bodies during the 1920s was a shift in emphasis reflecting the upsurge of liberal ideas rather than any alteration in the basic structure. The bureaucracy at all levels remained part of a tightly connected pyramid at whose nominal apex stood the emperor.

The institution of a professional bureaucracy failed to undermine its position as an instrument of rule, or introduce a concept of public service, except in as far as 'public' meant the requirements of the state. The changes did serve to introduce a *de jure* division between administration and political power, but the nature of the Meiji Constitution, added to the bureaucratic tradition, left the bureaucracy with tremendous influence. Despite its increasing professionalization, the postion of the bureaucracy overall remained something far removed from that of a servant of the people. The 1889 constitution formalized the structure of government at national level, with the emperor at its apex. The bureaucracy became officially the servant of the emperor, not of the government or the people. As an 'imperial bureaucracy', it was responsible only to the emperor. Each ministry was headed by a politician, a formal holder of political power, but bureaucrats could flout the orders of their minister on the grounds of the 'imperial' will. The bureaucracy's degree of public accountability, or indeed accountability to anyone other than the emperor himself, was thus minimal. The minister himself was responsible to neither diet nor people.

The constitutional position, in conjunction with the tradition of respect for officialdom and the bureaucracy's earlier involvement in national policy-making, meant that the administration maintained considerable political power. The weakness of the legislature reinforced this influence. However, the members of the civil service were not always united in their interests; the rendering of each individual minister responsible to the emperor led to a strong particularist tendency within ministries. This had in turn a divisive effect on the cabinet itself, weakening the whole institution of cabinet government. The constitutional position and characteristics common to the bureaucracy as a whole have often caused it to be viewed as a monolithic interest group, but inter-ministerial conflict rapidly became a feature of the bureaucratic institution in Japan.

The identification of the bureaucracy with politics also appeared more overtly in movements of individuals between the political and administrative spheres. In the early Meiji years, higher bureaucrats were also often politicians. Later on politicians from the conservative parties often served a bureaucratic apprenticeship before entering politics. Some of the most prestigious reached the highest bureaucratic level and then transferred to the leadership or top echelons of one of the parties. Takahashi Korekiyo and Wakatsuki Reijirō, both of whom served terms as finance minister and prime minister in the Taishō and early Shōwa periods, are examples of this career pattern.[2] Cabinets contained a high proportion of former bureaucrats. Other bureaucrats gravitated into the highest business circles.

The formidable influence of the bureaucracy at national level was reinforced by the integration of local and national government administration. The way in which provincial governors were appointed served to make them both administrators of national policy and political agents of the central government. The frequent transfers of personnel from one area to another, and the lure of the political influence of the national bureaucracy, tended to make prefectural governors and other senior officials much more concerned to adhere to the wishes of their national political overlords than to improve the lot of the area under their jurisdiction. Units of local government, from the prefecture downwards, became the agents of a monolithic authority centred largely on the powerful Home Ministry. Where necessary, local interest became submerged in national interest. Local interest groups, which became especially prominent in the 1920s, often found themselves in conflict with the local bureaucracy, and were rarely supported by it in any fight against national government. Where purely local issues were concerned, the local bureaucracy was highly sensitive to pressure from local élites, which reinforced ruling group solidarity and widened the gulf between bureaucracy and people. To this extent the bureaucratic centralization was highly effective in overcoming divisive regional issues and giving emphasis to a common national purpose.

Despite the continuing political influence of the bureaucracy, there was a shift in the emphasis of government activity after the early 1880s. At this time the government itself withdrew from much direct involvement in economic and other developments, concentrating on encouragement of the private sector. Many more entrepreneurial bureaucrats – especially those who felt that they might never achieve substantial political influence – felt that their talents could be put to better use outside the government and drifted away from it. By the late 1880s, with the perfection of the bureaucratic system, the government shifted its attention away from the establishment of the administrative machine itself, and from the definition of the powers and activities with which it was to be provided. The task of the bureaucracy was now to implement and administer policy in accordance with its stipulated responsibilities. At local level in particular, this change of emphasis pointed to local officials becoming less overtly political.

In fact, the all pervasive character of prefectural government administration right from the start served as a hindrance to the development of other potentially competing foci of influence, and the political role did not naturally fall to any other local entity. So many functions of different kinds were assumed by local officials in the early years of the Meiji period that not much was left for new organizations such as the political parties. This broad spectrum of activity stemmed from, and was reinforced by, existing social values. Local government rested on a strongly hierarchical social structure in a country where social diversity was relatively absent and opposition to established authority not undertaken lightly. The government machine continued to operate on a basis of coordination and conciliation, since open coercion was often socially unacceptable and there was no precedent for popular representation. The end result was a strongly hierarchical administrative authority which served both as a mechanism of political control from the centre and as a prime agent of social and economic development.

The administration could not rely purely on persuasion and custom to impose its authority. A police force was instituted during the first two decades of the Meiji period to ensure that the government's will was carried out, and to maintain law and order. The police system which emerged at this time was, like the administrative machine, under the jurisdiction of the Home

Ministry. It was highly centralized and authoritarian, and enjoyed considerable powers under the law. From the early twentieth century the regular force was supplemented by specialized units. These included the Special Higher Police, often referred to as the 'thought police', as its major task was to control protest movements and ideologies considered subversive by the state. Throughout the pre-1945 years the police force was closely identified with the bureaucratic machine. To that extent it did not merely ensure the maintenance of law and order, but was widely used for political purposes.

The key figures of this administrative system at the centre were the professional examination-entry administrators. These new bureaucrats were taught that they were essentially the servants of the state (as personified by the emperor), whose function was not to innovate, but to administer the status quo. Up to the late 1920s national officials continued to be relatively less concerned with policy formulation than administration, but the old tradition was to be revived in the 1930s with the rise of a new group of bureaucrats equally bent on innovation.

The bureaucracy was just one of the élites given competing powers under the Meiji Constitution. During the 1890s and early 1900s it did not exert its power openly, but wielded considerable influence through its associations with the *de facto* holders of power, elected or otherwise. During the more liberal period of 'Taishō democracy' its influence declined relative to that of the political parties, but contacts between bureaucrats and politicians remained extensive, and together they formed a reasonably homogeneous ruling group. A unity of interest between conservative party politicians and the upper echelons of the bureaucracy persisted into the 1930s. Even before this, however, the predominance of the party-bureaucratic nexus was coming under challenge from other élites, notably the army. A series of violent incidents perpetrated by military and civilian nationalists in the years 1931–6 added to the pressure, and the problems posed by the depression highlighted issues of national survival. In the circumstances some officials began to try to form an alternative view of what constituted their service to the state. More overtly political activities by bureaucrats increased, and the Meiji Constitution provided them with a legitimate channel to political power. Only a small number of officials identified with the motives of younger army officers and members of the civilian right wing who were prepared to engage in direct action to overthrow the system. A larger, far more significant, group believed strongly that considerable reforms were required to revitalize the state and carry out the emperor's 'true' wishes. This group became known as the 'renovationist' or 'reformist' bureaucrats (*kakushin kanryō*). Its members were prepared to work closely with army leaders in the creation of a defence state, and were a major force in determining the direction of Japan's policies in the late 1930s.

The 1930s produced considerable modifications in the structure and functions of government to cope with the prospect of war, especially at the more local level. When war became a reality this process accelerated. War in all countries has tended to produce a tightening of national control over all spheres of political, economic and social life. Japan was no exception to this pattern. On the bureaucratic level local entities and organizations of all kinds were more and more incorporated into the structure of government and executive power correspondingly increased. The demise of independent political parties – or rather their absorption in 1940 into the Imperial Rule Assistance Association intended as the nuclear body of the new, strengthened political structure – increased bureaucratic power further. As the war progressed the functions of the IRAA, whose remit was already somewhat vague, tended increasingly to overlap with those of the bureaucracy, and the two together served as a single instrument of national control and administration. All formerly independent groups, whether political parties, consumer associations, youth organizations, women's groups or any other, were absorbed into a single administrative machine geared exclusively to the needs of state policy. Its task was efficiently to mobilize the efforts of the people and all other national resources. A case in point is that of the neighbourhood associations (*tonarigumi*), whose establishment throughout Japan by the spring of 1941 enabled the authorities to exercise rigid control over the members of the population at the lowest level, while yet serving as a channel for participation by every family member in the greater affairs of the nation.

The breadth of function and operation possessed by the bureaucracy/IRAA meant that apart from the army, with which it did not always see eye to eye, it was the only instrument of government. Once again politics and administration were at one. Over the years 1941–5 bureaucratic control under military supervision extended further and further into the lives of the people. Significantly the major agent of control at this time was the military police (*kenpeitai*), which took over most of the functions of the regular police force. The military police were widely feared and their pervasive influence over the life of Japanese people was a powerful factor in army dominance.

The bureaucratic role in the formulation and implementation of national policy in the 1930s and 1940s had a basis in legal provision and customary practice. The Occupation's keenness to pin down the major participants in Japan's conspiracy to wage aggressive war changed the legal framework, but left much of the administrative machine intact, and failed to bring about a transformation in the nature of the bureaucracy in Japan. This failure has been widely interpreted as a failure by the Occupation authorities to appreciate the powerful political role of officialdom.

Yet the administrative machine was substantially affected by the political and constitutional changes brought about under the Occupation. Some officials were purged. The new National Public Service Law of 1947 to control the whole government service framework enshrined new codes of conduct and activity which ran counter to previous modes of bureaucratic operation. A new emphasis on local autonomy severed many of the connections between central and local bureaucracies, and officials increasingly tended to spend their careers in one or the other. Officials became in law subordinate to the wishes of a minister, who was in turn a member of a cabinet responsible to the Diet. The all-powerful Home Ministry was abolished and administration of the civil service became the responsibility of a new Administrative Management Agency established in November 1946 (later the National Personnel Authority). This body was responsible to the prime minister, and was headed by a minister of state who was also a member of the cabinet. Political involvement by officials was discouraged, and since the early years of the Occupation they were deprived of the right to strike.

Reforms on a similar scale affected the local bureaucracy. As at the national level, there was a partial purge of local government officials. A greater measure of local self-government was regarded by the Occupation authorities as crucial to the spread of democracy. The powers of local assemblies were increased, the franchise was extended to women and local executive positions became elective. Local elected bodies experienced a considerable strengthening of their rights *vis-à-vis* the executive. The new laws followed the Meiji precedent of establishing units on the basis of the needs of the state, and attempted to impose a uniform system of local government throughout the country. The new local government units were freed from central control through the Home Ministry, and many government functions were decentralized. Jurisdiction over many aspects of policing and education, for example, was delegated to units of local government. At all levels the open avenues to political power seemed to have been closed off.

At no stage, however, were the Occupation authorities able to inflict on the bureaucracy so drastic a reorganization that it would have rendered it incapable of carrying out its administrative function. The Allies had opted for indirect rule, and the incapacitation of the administrative machine in the years after 1945 would not only have rendered the Occupation reforms ineffectual but would have jeopardized the survival and recovery of the country as a whole. The country's need for administration from the start set the parameters for reform of the national and local government machine. Furthermore, the influence of the position and role of the prewar bureaucracy could hardly be expected to be dispelled overnight. The political power of the bureaucracy in the pre-1945 period rested on a number of factors. The weakness of the political parties, the lack of constitutional responsibility to the Diet and the limitations on cabinet power all played a part. The precedent of the early Meiji period, when government and bureaucracy were effectively interchangeable, was always influential. After 1945 party politics became a factor to be reckoned with, but politicians' status was still relatively low compared with that of bureaucrats. Moreover, the powers of the legislature were not always able to restrain the executive. Throughout the postwar years ministers' own control over their officials and responsibilities have been seriously weakened by the inordinately frequent reshuffles to which Japanese cabinets have been subjected. As with the British civil service, there are few political appointments, so the national bureaucracy has operated at a very high level of government. Most controversial political matters have been virtually sewn up before they even reach the Diet, and some commentators take the view that the bureaucracy has effectively run both the legislative and the executive.

The potential channels for bureaucratic influence have been reinforced by close relations between the bureaucracy and the conservative parties which have held power without a break since 1948 (since 1955 merged in the Liberal Democratic Party). There has been a persistent progression of many higher echelon bureaucrats into politics after retirement,[3] and the vast majority of them have entered the LDP. These ex-bureaucrats have continued to make up a substantial portion of the personnel of Japanese cabinets. The phenomenon has been so common that the recruitment of high-flying bureaucrats into politics (and industry) has its own term, *amakudari*. Significantly the literal meaning of this word is 'descent from heaven'. This close involvement has fostered cooperation and contact on policy matters between the ruling party and the bureaucracy. The mutual interdependence of the bureaucracy and conservative politicians has helped not only to sustain the latter in power, but to produce over the years a high degree of consistency and coherence in the formulation and implementation of national policies. The business community has acted as the third element in a triangular relationship which has been at the core of policy-making in Japan.

The traditional authority pertaining to the bureaucracy could not be instantly dissipated in 1945. The hierarchical nature of Japanese society and a long-standing view of the influence of officialdom have combined to make the bureaucracy still the lords rather than the servants of the people. The concept of public service has remained weak, if not non-existent, and the whole structure has rested on the assumption that the people at large will submit to bureaucratic authority. In as far as the bureaucrat sees himself as a servant at all, he is not the servant of the people, but of the state and his superiors.

The size of the bureaucracy has expanded considerably to cope with the developments of the postwar years, but its efficient functioning is still strongly dependent on a small élite of high fliers. This group has considerably widened its intake by comparison with prewar years, and the origins of its recruits has been very diverse, but the élite group has retained an intense homogeneity which is often viewed as the key to the independent power of the civil service. In a society where contacts between members of the same educational institution are pervasive and influential, the most important single source of entrants to the higher civil service has remained Tokyo University, and in particular the Law Faculty of that university. The strength of the educational faction explains at least in part the identity of interest between conservative politics, big business and the bureaucracy, which has been so important in postwar Japan. The high-flying entrants to the national civil service tend to constitute a single interest group whose members have more in common with their fellow alumni in big business or politics than with their bureaucratic colleagues from different educational backgrounds.

The intense competition to get into the Japanese bureaucracy at the higher levels is an indicator of the prestige attached to the institution. Repeated surveys suggest that a civil service career has been regarded by a majority of parents as the most desirable career for their male children,[4] and their preference is shared by most graduates of the top universities. Only careers with the leading corporations challenge this preference. The Japanese bureaucracy has been regarded both as a highly prestigious career in itself and also as a path to political influence. Competition to enter the two most influential ministries, the Ministry of Finance and the Ministry of International Trade and Industry, has been particularly fierce, and the pre-eminence of these two ministries looks set to continue despite substantial changes in the economic and political environment. This desire to enter the national administration has been reinforced since the Occupation by a certain backtracking on local autonomy. The difficulties attendant on financing and organizing large-scale undertakings at the purely local level contributed to this trend. The police and education systems have gradually been removed from local government jurisdiction and organized on the basis of a highly centralized system firmly directed from the centre. This centralization has not gone unopposed but little of the real or potential influence of the national bureaucracy has been siphoned off by the increase in local autonomy.

By contrast local government has come to be regarded as something of a backwater, and ambitious students have rarely considered it as a possible career. Despite the provisions of the law, local government has hardly proved independent. Local officials have tended to rely on guidance from a higher level of government, and this trend has been reinforced by two factors. The first is the continuing dependence of local entities on financial support from national government, which means local government has been unable to be self-supporting and financial allocations have fluctuated in accordance with the dictates of national policy. The second is an absence of functional demarcation between levels of government which has made it easier for the higher levels to interfere in the affairs of the lower. The legislative powers of the purportedly independent elected local bodies are in any case limited, and the powerful prefectural governor, albeit elected, has found his role determined by the relative strength of the pressure on him by central government from above and by local interests from below.

Characteristics of the methods of operation of the bureaucracy show that here, too, the reforms brought no absolute break with the past. The use of the circular letter system (*ringisei*) – whereby policy documents are drafted at relatively low levels and passed up through the hierarchy until they have received approval from all concerned up to the highest levels – has often been cited as an example of the continuation of prewar practice. Critics say that the practice encourages a lack of leadership and dispersal of responsibility, and the requirement of extensive circulation, often to twenty or thirty individuals, means that an inordinate amount of time is wasted. Attempts to remove or modify *ringisei* in the 1950s – 1960s were largely ineffectual.

The old particularism of ministries has been reinforced by this practice, and by the factional apportionment of cabinet posts. The perpetuation of a sense of rank and precedence among ministries has attached not just to ministers but right down through their staff. Despite its homogeneity the bureaucracy has been subject to severe ministerial conflict, and individual ministerial priorities have often received excessive consideration. An emphasis on the importance of seniority and the practice of using the generalist rather than the specialist has been maintained, and officials of the national government have enjoyed a broad functional remit. Since the 1970s calls for administrative reform have been common, but the gestures in this direction have been half-hearted and have in any case aimed primarily at removing the mounting budget deficit rather than revolutionizing the practices of the civil service. Many of these practices are not dissimilar to those pursued in the British civil service, but the full analogy does not extend to the political prestige and influence of the bureaucracy and the public perception of its position.

The key role of the bureaucracy throughout the modern period in Japan has been in the formation and execution of a cohesive set of policies on the part of the state. In the postwar years it has continued to play this role, not because of its constitutional position but because of the nature of Japanese society; the position enjoyed by officialdom in Japan since long before the Meiji era; and the lasting effect of the modifications in that position produced by the circumstances of the late nineteenth – early twentieth centuries. The change in constitutional position after 1945 appears to have impaired little the efficiency of national and local bureaucracies in the formulation and execution of cohesive national policies. The Ministry of Trade and Industry, for example, has the reputation of being particularly effective as an arbiter of Japan's postwar economic policies through the medium of 'administrative guidance'. This very success has helped to reinforce the substantial political influence of the bureaucracy. The experience of the postwar years has produced little evidence that a shift in attitude in the direction of a concept of 'public service' in the Japanese bureaucracy can be anything but slow. Acceptance of bureaucratic rule has remained widespread, and a clear-cut division between administration and politics has yet to emerge.

NOTES

1 Katsu Kaishū was Navy Minister 1873–5 and Privy Councillor 1888–99. Enomoto served in various ministerial capacities, including as Minister of Foreign Affairs, over the years 1880–97.

2 Takahashi was president of the Yokohama Specie Bank and the Bank of Japan before becoming Seiyūkai finance minister in 1913. Wakatsuki had become the most senior official of the Finance Ministry before entering politics in 1912.

3 Many bureaucrats retire in their early to mid-fifties.

4 More women are now beginning to enter the bureaucracy at administrative levels, but it is yet too early to say whether most will enjoy similar career patterns to men.

CHAPTER FOURTEEN

Conclusion – 1950s to 1980s

The enormity of the transformation which Japan has undergone since the desperate months of summer 1945 is not easy to comprehend. In 1949 Japan's trading deficit with the US was in excess of ¥146 billion, and Japan was a net importer of capital. In the financial year 1986 Japan had a trade balance surplus of ¥16,200 billion with the rest of the world, over half of it with the US, and was the world's largest supplier of capital. Direct foreign investment by Japan, traditionally at a low level, increased rapidly in the wake of the rising yen, and reached $22.3 billion in 1986; much went to East and Southeast Asia, but the US was the largest single host economy. At the end of the Occupation years Prime Minister Yoshida's first trip abroad was to the US to sign the San Francisco Peace Treaty in September 1951. Southeast Asian nations made agreement to the treaty conditional on a promise of Japanese reparations payments. The last of these payments was made in the early 1970s. Significantly, Takeshita Noboru's first foreign visit as prime minister was to Manila, for a meeting with the heads of government of the Association of South East Asian Nations, (ASEAN) in December 1987. Japan has become an economic giant, a substantial overseas investor whose export success is legendary and whose stock market dealings surpass in volume even those of Wall Street. From an occupied country, compelled to make considerable sacrifices to regain independence and autonomy, Japan became a US satellite and ally. A framework of dependence on the US was established, the influence of which has endured to this day, but at the same time Japan has gradually moved towards a point where she realizes that she can no longer refuse to exercise the part in international relations which naturally accrues to her from her immense economic strength. Her preoccupations with the US relationship, though remaining pivotal, are increasingly measured against the necessity of establishing amicable relations with other areas of the world, in particular the nations of Southeast Asia, the East Asian NICs (newly industrialized countries) and the People's Republic of China.

The Occupation authorities were idealists who sought to create a new Japan whose basic attributes were democracy and peace. They sought to establish a new constitutional framework with an independent judiciary, responsible cabinets, sovereignty resting with the people and equality for all. They strove for total and permanent disarmament. They tried to create a free-market, capitalist economic framework in which capital, labour and the consumer would all be partners. However, society could not be remade overnight. The new forms had to rest on historical legacy, and the opting by the Occupation authorities for a system of indirect rule meant that Japanese leaders were far more influential than the American presence might suggest. Moreover, the idealism was undermined well before the Occupation was ended by the strategic and political considerations of the US and her allies. The major parameters for Japan's history during the decades 1950s – 1980s – economic growth and the US connection – were established by defeat, Occupation and the terms of the San Francisco Peace Treaty, but Japan in 1952 was insecure, tentative and unsure of the future. The subsequent transformation of Japan has been the result of interaction between new structures and old attitudes in a constantly changing international environment.

A political chronology has traditionally served historians as a useful framework for an overview of a given period of a country's history. Such a framework has not been deemed appropriate in the major part of this book, and although a chronological approach is adopted in this final appraisal of the postwar years, it is a chronology determined less by political leaders and parties than by economic forces and international events. In Japan the standing of politicians has remained in general low, and this lack of prestige has been confirmed since 1945 by a succession of corruption and financial scandals which brought leading politicians into disrepute.[1] The 1976 Lockheed scandal, in which even former prime minister Tanaka was implicated, has continued to cast a shadow over Japanese politics for over a decade. Politicians in Japan, as elsewhere, are often forced to bow to the strength of extraneous pressure groups – public opinion, powerful citizens' movements, moderately anti-establishment journalism. At the same time, lack of public participation in political activity, the degree to which precedent and framework weakens the power of politicians *vis-à-vis* other élites, and the intense factionalism within the ruling LDP, have made it particularly difficult to judge how influential politicians have actually been during these years. Moreover, given the significance of group activity, consensus and compromise within Japanese society, it is never easy to determine the political influence accruing to any individual. Prime ministers have invariably come to the fore as a result of compromise and factional infighting rather than personal charisma. Postwar Japan has produced few prime ministers who have clearly led from the front. Few cabinet leaders have sought to achieve the high profiles of Yoshida Shigeru (1946–7, 1948–54), Tanaka Kakuei (1972–4) or Nakasone Yasuhiro (1982–7).

The early Occupation years produced a brief heyday of left-wing influence in Japanese politics, but this gave way in 1948 to an era of continuous conservative rule. So overwhelming has been the dominance of the conservatives since the late 1940s that, by the end of the 1960s, Western scholars were devoting considerable attention to analysing the conservative monopoly of power.[2] In the 1950s, however, the conservative hold on power appeared in many ways nothing like as strong as it does today. Yoshida Shigeru, prime minister for much of the Occupation period, was an abrasive figure who had cooperated with the US while yet managing to extract some concessions from the occupying power. However, his strategies and manner increasingly eroded his support both among conservatives and among the public at large, and Yoshida was forced to resign in 1954. His successors in the 1950s, all of whom had been active in politics or administration in the prewar years, presided over several years of instability and confrontation. Reorganized into a single united party (the Liberal Democratic Party) in 1955, the conservative elements in the diet used every opportunity to railroad through their desired policies and, in the opinion of many opponents, to abuse their strong parliamentary majority. While a major thrust of government policy was the recovery of the economy and the need for economic strength as a path to genuine independence, the ruling conservatives were also anxious to reappraise Occupation reforms in the light of their practicability and Japan's newly independent status. Over issues of domestic reform, in particular efforts to recentralize the police and education systems, there was bitter conflict with the minority parties of the centre and left, who were at every turn made only too aware

309

of their political impotence. Even more damaging confrontations occurred over defence policy. Hostile to the thought of anything other than a strictly neutralist foreign policy, and particularly to the idea of prolonging the mutual security arrangements with the US, the opposition found itself unlistened to and overruled at every step. High-handedness on the one hand combined with utter political frustration and a strong residue of pacifist sentiment on the other, to produce a national crisis in 1960, when the US – Japan Mutual Security Treaty (*Anpo*). came up for renewal. The revised treaty signed in January of that year removed the clause permitting US troops to intervene in the maintenance of internal law and order in Japan, but this concession failed to satisfy the treaty's opponents. For a period of months there were constant large-scale demonstrations as opposition party members attempted to obstruct a diet vote on ratification. Physical means, such as sit-ins, were adopted in an abortive attempt to prevent an extension of the diet session which would result in automatic ratification. Massive strikes and violent demonstrations continued through May and June, and a planned visit by General Eisenhower in June had to be cancelled for fear of the president's personal safety in the Japanese capital. At midnight on 19 June ratification occurred automatically. The opposition parties could do no more.

The *Anpo* crisis marked a culmination of several years of confrontation, but it also initiated a more conciliatory period in Japanese politics. No prime minister could continue in office in the face of such overt parliamentary and public hostility. Kishi Nobusuke, the ex-bureaucrat who had taken over LDP leadership in 1957 and presided over this unprecedented storm of unrest, resigned immediately ratification had been achieved. His departure opened the way for a less confrontational, more expansionist decade, during which economic growth and growing prosperity compelled politicians of all parties and the public at large to come to terms with a very different domestic and international environment.

The pursuit of economic recovery had been a goal throughout the 1950s. The Korean War, following hard on the economic stabilization programme enforced by the Occupation authorities after 1948, proved an unanticipated bonanza in Japan. Japan's use as a base for US forces provided a substantial injection of foreign exchange, a provision of purchasing power which had spin-offs for the economy as a whole, raised expectations and enhanced Japan's ability to purchase much-needed capital goods for reconstruction. Under the San Francisco Peace Treaty Japan had regained her sovereignty in 1952 but was burdened neither by international responsibilities nor by defence spending. Assisted by US support, Japan was enabled to rejoin organizations, membership of which bestowed international economic respectability. Japan joined the International Monetary Fund and the International Bank for Reconstruction and Development in 1952, and in 1955 became a full member of GATT (General Agreement on Tariffs and Trade). Postwar recovery initiated a world investment boom in the early 1950s. Technology was cheap and available and Japan had the advantage of maximum support from the world's technological leader, the US. By the mid-1950s prewar levels of production had again been reached. Reconstruction was over. The most substantial expansion during this decade was in the heavy industries, e.g. shipbuilding, iron and steel; the formerly dominant light industries lost their pre-eminence, which had already been eroded during the 1930s and the war years. Sponsorship of industrial structure – which industries to promote and which to phase down – was intentionally carried out by government bodies utilizing the basis of official direction of the economy built up since the 1930s. The relationship between bureaucracy and business – always strong – was reinforced.

With the opening of a new decade a new phase of economic growth was initiated, one which sought not merely economic strength as a foundation of national independence – a familiar theme from the Meiji period – but an increased emphasis on the material prosperity of the Japanese people. While Japan's lack of natural resources necessitated a continuing emphasis on export success, domestic consumer purchasing power became more and more of a major factor in the development of the economy. Government economic policy underlined this emphasis. Prime Minister Ikeda Hayato's famous 'Income Doubling Plan' of 1960 targeted a rapid rate of growth, with the ultimate aim of higher living standards and full employment. Its psychological impact in terms of rising expectations was immense. It helped to generate even more rapid economic expansion. Through the 1960s the annual growth rate of the economy, in terms of GNP, reached 10 per cent or more. Successive economic plans were superseded as goals were reached well before the target date. The apogee of popular ambition was the acquisition of consumer durables, in the first instance items such as televisions and washing machines, and latterly cars and air-conditioning. By the late 1960s most Japanese enjoyed a standard of living far beyond what they might have expected ten years earlier. The international exposition – Expo 70 – held in Osaka in 1970, with its slogan of 'progress and harmony', did more than demonstrate to the world that Japan was attempting to be international; it showed that many Japanese had money to spend. Visitors from all over Japan flocked to it in unprecedented numbers, not merely to look at foreign curiosities but to admire their own technological, material and organizational achievements.

Economic influence brought an increased need for a considered set of relationships with the outside world. Japan had joined the United Nations in 1956, but what the government's opponents considered a slavish adherence to the US-dependent relationship had proved contentious throughout the 1950s, slowly pushing all parties towards agreement on the need to attempt less divisive strategies. Domestic economic success had additional international implications. Expanding trade brought in its wake the need for enhanced foreign contacts at a time when Japan still faced the uphill task of rehabilitating herself in international eyes and throwing off the legacy of ill-feeling left by her conduct in earlier years. Japan's nearest neighbours, where close economic ties might be most naturally sought, were also those which had suffered most directly from her aggression – Southeast Asia, China, Korea. Throughout the 1960s Japan was paying out reparations; material payment had been made a condition for international recognition. Only vigorous US support and recognition of a mutual communist threat prevented disputes between Japan and Korea over fishing rights from becoming even more bitter. US pressure in 1952 to recognize Taiwan rather than the People's Republic as the locus of the government of China meant that trade and other contacts with the PRC were closely confined, although the economic relationship with Taiwan proved fruitful. Other countries further removed from Japan were mistrustful of Japan's role in international relations. Sensitive to the influence of the past, in the process of bridge-building embarked upon by Japan every effort was made to distinguish between trading and political contacts. The desire to eschew economic strength as a means of asserting diplomatic superiority was never concealed, and the 'economic animal' of Western imagination was born. This divorce of economic from political strength has died hard, producing to this day a substantial reluctance on the part of Japan to exercise a role in the international community commensurate with her position as one of the world's dominant economies.

The *Anpo* crisis not only marked a change in the profile of LDP activity, but also initiated a period of adaptation on the part of its opponents. Opposition parties were increasingly forced to acknowledge that the growing prosperity enhanced the LDP's popularity among the people as a whole, and particularly in the rural areas which were the bastions of LDP support. 'Pork-barrel' politics had a long tradition in Japan, and economic growth enabled the party in power not merely to fund large-scale construction and development projects in different localities to ensure provincial LDP dietmen retained office, but to maintain the system of support prices for agricultural goods, particularly rice, which sustained the party's popularity in the heavily over-represented rural areas. Agriculture declined in terms of population and contribution to GNP, but farmers became increasingly prosperous. Not only did opportunities for diversification into non-agricultural sources of income expand; mechanization and other advances in working capital increased land and labour productivity and the volume of production. Self-sufficiency in many agricultural products was prolonged by these improvements in conjunction with a rampant protectionism aimed at defying comparative advantage. Restrictions on imports were also used to shelter growing manufacturing industries long after they had passed the 'infant' stage. A yen pegged against the dollar became more and more undervalued, making Japanese exports relatively cheap in international terms.

The LDP's opponents did not find it easy to come to terms with the prosperity of the people and the fillip it gave to the ruling party. Support for the major opposition party, the Japan Socialist Party, stagnated in the face of party leaders' reluctance to accept change and a lingering heritage of doctrinaire Marxist beliefs. By contrast the standing of the Japan Communist Party improved after a difficult period in the 1950s. Determined not be identified too closely with the doctrines of either Beijing or Moscow, the JCP enjoyed moderate electoral success as it showed itself willing to compromise to cope with changing conditions. Any unified anti-LDP stand by the opposition parties was precluded by the DSP's support for the mutual security treaty with the US and the vigorous anti-communism of the religious-backed Kōmeitō (Clean Government Party). The LDP remained secure in its hold on power. Political-bureaucratic ties were strengthened by more ex-bureaucrat prime ministers in the 1950s and early 1960s – Kishi Nobusuke, Ikeda Hayato, Satō Eisaku – and the existence of a ruling triangle of bureaucracy-big business-conservative politicians was constantly reinforced. It seemed that ties of this kind, so familiar in the 1920s, had been no more than temporarily eclipsed by the military dominance of the intervening years.

The high rates of growth brought in their wake a substantial improvement in standards of living particularly welcome in the light of the deprivation of the war and immediate postwar years. There nevertheless began to emerge in the later 1960s a growing sense that material prosperity should not be the sole objective of human activity. Economic expansion had not been achieved without cost. There was substantial evidence that the impact of such rapid industrial growth was highly detrimental to many aspects of living. Scarce natural resources – for example, forest land – were fast being depleted. Industrial pollution was widespread, contaminating vegetation, rivers and coastal areas. In Minamata, Kyushu, hundreds of villagers succumbed, sometimes fatally, to mercury poisoning received through eating fish contaminated by effluent from a local chemical factory. Similar incidents occurred at several other locations. Many workers worked long hours in difficult conditions, often with little security and inadequate wages. Industrial-related diseases were not uncommmon. In the densely populated strip of land between Tokyo and Kobe which by 1970 housed around 50 per cent of the total population of over 100 million, housing space was desperately short, recreation facilities inadequate and commuting times unbearably long. British newspapers told of workaholic Japanese living in 'rabbit hutches'. Welfare provision was not substantial. Most individuals did not enjoy the benefits given to a minority of favoured groups, for example government employees or permanent workers in large businesses. Sickness and old age had to be provided for on an individual or family basis, and life expectancy was increasing. As the birth rate declined a rapid ageing of the population would take place from the last decade of the twentieth century. Savings for old age, education and other contingencies contributed to making the personal savings rate in Japan the highest in the world. Significantly, the efficient channelling of these savings into investment contributed substantially to economic growth. Ironically, though, this high rate could also be used as an excuse for not developing a welfare state. A further factor in change was the appearance of a postwar generation, whose attitudes were not conditioned by the experience of war and occupation. Japanese students did not remain isolated from the unrest of the late 1960s in Europe and the US. Around 1970 a wave of student unrest hit some Japanese universities. To many Japanese by the early 1970s it appeared that the basic aims of prosperity and affluence were being achieved, but at considerable cost. It was the start of a period of questioning, a greater degree of uncertainty about which direction to go.

This sense of uncertainty was confirmed by a series of events which shattered certain facets of the whole politico-economic framework that had operated since the Occupation and necessitated fundamental change. During the course of 1971 US policy inflicted on Japan two major blows. The first one was economic. The success of Japanese exports to the US had already begun to generate some friction, and in 1971 the US government announced restrictions on imports from Japan to the US and allowed the value of the dollar in the international exchange markets to fall from ¥360 to ¥300. In 1973 the yen was permitted to float, and despite government efforts to hold its level down it progressively gained in value against other currencies. While Japan compensated for declining US exports by turning to European markets, and exports continued to expand despite the rising yen, these moves suggested an end to the relatively free movement of goods and undervaluation of the yen, which had been major ingredients in Japanese export success.

The second of the 'Nixon shocks' was the announcement from Washington in 1971 that President Nixon was to visit Beijing. Nixon's visit heralded an end to the policy whereby the US had studiously avoided recognition of the People's Republic of China. For Japan, with its proximity to the PRC, the decision marked a dramatic change in the whole East Asian environment. If anything, more serious for the Japanese was the absence of prior consultation with Japan before the announcement of the Nixon visit. The US had cultivated Japan as its trusted ally and a bastion of capitalism in East Asia, but that ally could no longer rely on the US's making it a party to decisions of mutual importance. Japan had to be able to act unilaterally as well, and not be totally confined by the US relationship. The following year Japan's prime minister, Tanaka, responded by a visit of his own to Beijing, and diplomatic relations with the PRC were initiated. Within four years the two countries had signed a peace and friendship treaty.

A further politico-economic shock in 1973 hit a nation already unsettled by changes which called into question two major parameters of postwar development – export success and alliance with the US. The repercussions of the rise in oil prices of that year reverberated throughout Japan's economy and society. For a country dependent on imported raw materials and energy,[3] a country whose growth had been assisted by the relative cheapness and availability of these items in the 1950s and 1960s, the implications of the oil shock were particularly substantial. Japan imported $6 billion worth of oil in 1973, but $20 billion worth in 1974. The rapid rise in oil prices meant two things in particular to Japan: a substantial increase in the costs of production, which threatened to raise the prices of Japanese exports to non-competitive levels; and a dramatic object lesson, if one were needed, of how the country's industry was dependent on imported raw materials, and therefore how vulnerable Japan was – as she always had been – to pressure from those who controlled this raw materials supply. In 1974 for the first year since the war a negative growth rate was recorded. Inflation soared. The balance of payments plunged into deficit.

The first half of the 1970s saw the country trying to make adjustments to take account of this changed situation. Presiding over this new scenario in 1972–4 was Prime Minister Tanaka Kakuei, a self-made man from Niigata Prefecture, who had made his political career with the aid of his fortune. Tanaka was a product of the postwar boom very different from the university-educated, bureaucratic-oriented élite that had preceded him. Although equally brought to power on the back of factional politics, Tanaka adopted a higher profile than most other postwar prime ministers. He even enjoyed a certain measure of personal popularity – a relatively rare attribute among Japanese premiers. Tanaka's 1972 visit to Beijing betokened a dynamic response to the uncertainties of the day, but he failed to attack the fundamental problems of the politico-economic system from which he himself had benefited. In 1972 he published a *Plan for Remodelling the Japanese Archipelago*,[4] a grandiose scheme to relocate Japanese industry away to the peripheries to release congestion in the central foci of activity, and to translate economic growth into increased welfare for the Japanese people. Attitudes to such relocation and devolution were not overenthusiastic, and the oil shock halted the flow of funds essential to any such programme. Tanaka's popularity waned, and he left office in the face of heavy criticism of his financial dealings in 1974. Two years later he was under suspicion of corruption in the Lockheed scandal, but remained a powerful political influence.

Ministerial policy had little to do with the ability of the Japanese economy to weather the oil shock far beyond the expectations of many. Japanese industry had already moved far in the direction of energy-saving production, and Japan soon became the most cost-effective user of energy in the world. Within two years a positive growth rate was resumed, and the steady 3–4 per cent per annum level has been maintained ever since. Concern that a lower growth rate would prove damaging to an economy whose mode of operation had become geared to high growth rates has proved largely unfounded. Adaptation has been highly successful, and although during the 1970s and into the 1980s Japan's success in international markets has been attended by a damaging amount of friction, domestic prosperity and international economic importance have continued to grow at a rapid rate. Japan's response to the insecurity of raw materials and energy supplies has been to engage in strategic disposition of purchasing, avoiding as far as possible dependence on a single supplier. Diversification of sources of oil supply has proved more difficult, and Japan has remained highly dependent on the Middle East in this respect.

Notwithstanding the resilience of the economy, the shocks of the early 1970s combined with the longer term side-effects of economic expansion served to promote in Japan a more questioning attitude towards the pursuit of growth. Emphasis on the pursuit of welfare and the quality of life increased. The shift into high-technology, capital-intensive, labour-saving industries since the 1970s has produced a process of deindustrialization; the proportion of the population working in manufacturing has been decreasing, with more and more people being employed in the service sector. With reproduction now below population replacement level, pressure for labour-saving technology has increased still further, and this has been strengthened by calls for increased leisure time, more emphasis on family life and less commitment to the workplace, particularly from among the younger generation. Material prosperity remains important. Japan is a consumer-oriented society whose members expect to spend money and enjoy doing so, but sentiments have grown that material gain should not be the only fruit of past and present efforts.

More questioning attitudes at home combined with an increasingly dominant position in the world economy have meant that LDP governments have been compelled to tailor their policies accordingly. After the Nixon shocks Japan moved towards becoming a more independent agent in international affairs, but the parameters of the US relationship were maintained, and a reluctance on the part of Japan to assert herself in foreign-policy matters was apparent. In economic matters, however, Japan became increasingly exposed to international pressure on her policy decisions. This was also true of political matters, such as defence. A strong residue of anti-war sentiment in Japan, a feeling that the absence of high military spending has contributed to economic growth, and the controversial ninth clause of the constitution with its restrictions on Japanese defence capability, are enduring factors in Japan's international relations, particularly those with the US; and although into the 1980s conservative calls for an increased military role for Japan and a higher defence profile have become more audible, there is still strong resistance to an expansion of military spending or to changing the constitution. The US, despite facing considerable economic problems, has continued to bear much of the burden of Japanese defence, and this reluctance on the part of Japan to adopt a higher defence profile has been a bone of contention between the two countries. Japan has thus been increasingly brought within the framework of an international political economy, and so prominent has become her part in it that decisions made by Japan and concerning Japan have widespread international ramifications. Japan has had no choice but to show a greater sensitivity towards other countries' feelings.

In social terms, too, Japan became more exposed to external influences. More Japanese began to use their prosperity to travel overseas, more businesses operated abroad. The number of foreign visitors and residents in Japan also increased. Growing contacts with other countries and the rapidity and quality of communications and media coverage from the 1970s served to make some Japanese even less satisfied with the prosperity they had achieved. While growth-related issues, like pollution and the concentration of industry, continued to occupy many, others began to look for institutional reform of their society. Women influenced by personal frustrations and the women's movement inside and outside Japan called for true equality of opportunity, which would enable women to advance into spheres conventionally reserved for men. Equal employment opportunities legislation was enacted in 1986. Awareness that the education systems of other countries allowed for greater creativity and did not necessarily produce the 'examination hell' of Japan led to a growing agitation for educational reform and the government's setting up of a commission in 1984 to investigate the whole system. Tax reform became a pillar of Prime Minister Nakasone's domestic economic policy, and governments in the 1980s also campaigned for administrative reform as a means of curbing accelerating government expenditure, exacerbated by the maturing of pension and other welfare schemes. Both at home and from abroad, Japanese policy-makers and citizens were exposed to sustained pressures for fundamental change in the way their society operated. 'Internationalization' became a buzz-word.

Yet both in international eyes and in terms of domestic perceptions Japan remained strongly insular. The attitudes of both sides even in the 1980s reinforced the wall of impenetrability and incomprehensibility built up by a century of mutual suspicion against a background of differing cultural heritages. Foreigners in the late nineteenth century decided that the Japanese were a singular people, of a different ilk from Westerners. Japanese over decades found it in their interest to reinforce this perception, and perceptions, once rooted, die very hard. Moreover, Japan has changed dramatically in material terms since the Occupation, and material changes have in turn modified fundamental aspects of society, but the speed of change has been so rapid that it has been impossible for perceptions either inside or outside the country to keep pace with the transformation. Popular writing in the 1980s has continued to harp on the economic animal, the excessive work ethic, and the low standard of living in many aspects we consider crucial, such as leisure, housing, individualism, freedom from hierarchical relationships. Criticism of the way in which Japanese exports have by unfair means flooded the European market, while trying by every means possible to exclude imports from the EEC, is widespread, and redolent of the sour grapes view of the 1930s, with its notion of cheap labour and dumping. Japanese still work hard, and for the most part enjoy less living space than we do, but many aspects of Japan have been transformed even since the 1960s, and the image has become out of date.

In the 1960s Japanese industry was unduly protected, and Japanese labour cheap by international standards. Competitors experiencing the 1960s boom were only just beginning to complain of this. By the second half of the 1980s substantial pressure from outside Japan has brought the removal of many legal protectionist barriers, although informal ones cannot be abolished so easily. Even financial markets are being opened up to foreign firms. Hostility towards Japanese exports is based on a vision of Japan flooding the world's markets, when in fact Japan's export : GNP ratio is less than that of many other countries, never more than 12 per cent over the last few decades, compared with 20 per cent prewar and a similar figure in the UK now. Much of the stimulus for Japan's rapid growth has come from the existence of a substantial domestic market where there has been a strong

319

tendency to buy Japanese and where manufacturers and retailers have a continuing vested interest in making the consumer aware of how much his custom is valued. One authority[5] has suggested that ill feeling abroad over Japanese exports is probably caused more by the accurate targeting of Japanese exports and an acute sense of the inability of the US or EEC countries to overcome their own economic problems.

Internationally and domestically, Japan's economy has altered in other ways. Labour, still widely available in the 1960s, has since the early 1970s moved into a state of shortage. Japanese firms have responded by bringing in guest workers from overseas or moving production abroad. Labour has become very expensive, and the high value of the yen (*endaka*) on international markets has made Japanese goods far less competitive in monetary terms. The downturn caused by the increasing value of the yen has pared the profits of many enterprises to the bone. Government concern over budget deficits has promoted privatization of telecommunications and railways, retrenchment through administrative reform and cutbacks on welfare expenditure at a time when pension systems are coming to maturity. The economic dominance of Western Europe and the US has been challenged by countries other than Japan. Japan is no longer the only dynamic economy of East Asia, but is herself deeply concerned by the growing competition of the Asian NICs – Korea, Taiwan, Hong Kong, Singapore – which threaten her pre-eminence in the Asian Pacific area and beyond. The balancing of the country's relations with Asia and the Pacific area with dependence on OPEC supplies and the long-standing involvement with the United States has become one of Japan's major economic and political considerations.

Japanese perceptions have also become outdated. Japan's distinct reluctance to exercise influence in international relations commensurate with her economic might is partly due to an understandable wariness which is the legacy of recent history, but has also come about in part because an element of 'underdog' feeling still exists. From the Meiji period the nation's aim has been to catch up with, and surpass the West. Despite the prevalence of high-tec and consumer spending power, unequalled in Europe, except perhaps in the Federal Republic of Germany, there is a residue of sentiment that Japan is still in some ways a third world country. On a visual level it is only too obvious that Japan has more than achieved the goal of catching-up, but it takes time for the reality to sink in. Both Japanese and non-Japanese have to come to terms with Japan's position in the 1980s.

From the perspective of the second half of the 1980s Japan appears a success story. The disastrous events earlier in the century detract little from this image. Japan's dominance in the international economy has provoked a particular desire to learn from Japan's experience. Many observers believe that the development of the Japanese economy over the last century and more holds useful lessons for the third world. The 'learn from Japan' movement argues, at times obsessively, that the advanced industrialized nations of the West, too, have much to learn from the way in which Japanese industry operates. The enthusiasm to learn from the Japanese industrialization process has sometimes led to aspects of the Japanese experience being detached from the very domestic and external factors that gave rise to them. Moreover, Japan's industrial growth has had a distinctly negative side. The disasters of the 1930s and the Pacific War cannot be separated from Japan's integration into the international economy, and in the postwar years rapid industrial growth has exacerbated physical problems such as cramped housing and pollution. Japanese industrial development has also been inherently dependent on a mode of social and institutional operation, many aspects of which would be totally unacceptable to some Western societies.

Japan's recent history suggests that perceptions are often of greater importance than realities in determining historical events. The attitudes that Japanese have towards themselves as members of the Japanese nation have been particularly significant in this respect. Considerable emphasis has throughout the modern period been placed on the uniqueness of the Japanese cultural tradition, the position of the Japanese nation in international affairs, and the patriotic sentiments of the people. A desire to analyse what it means to be Japanese remains widespread, and Japanese people's perceptions of the world in which they live are conditioned by this sense of 'difference'. Outside Japan, references to the Japanese as 'different' are just as frequent. That the Japanese experience cannot be duplicated is in itself no hindrance to learning something constructive from Japan's history, but exclusivity and uniqueness are not the best terms in which to interpret the history of modern Japan. Japan has learnt from, and been transformed by, exposure to the outside world, and the reverse is equally true.

The twenty-first century is predicted to be the century of the Pacific. Japan's phenomenal development is already being followed by economic success in other Asian countries – Hong Kong, Singapore, Taiwan, Korea. It is impossible to say how accurate this prediction will prove to be, or whether Japan will continue to enjoy the benefits of an expanding economy, but recent experience suggests that there is one precondition for continuing Japanese progress in the future, which may also be of relevance to other nations. Much of Japan's success before and since the war has been due to the existence of a basic degree of consensus within Japanese society. From 1945 disaster and then success reinforced a common sense of identity and prolonged a shared willingness to work together. This consensus has led to a certain inertia in the way the Japanese view their society and the way in which its institutions operate. The impetus for radical change has advanced little beyond the structural reforms imposed by the Occupation authorities, and old habits have adapted to a changed environment. The disappearance of such a degree of unity and consensus would mark a major turning point in the evolution of modern Japan, and two factors in particular may pose a threat to its continuing existence. One is that it could well be called into question if economic growth and rising standards of living encounter serious setbacks. Secondly, the accession of the new Heisei emperor in January 1989 symbolizes the advent of a new generation, which has known little of the hardship and adversity of earlier years. Should this new generation feel unable to go along with the established consensus, the consequences for Japan, and the rest of the world, could be even more fundamental.

NOTES

1 These did not merely involve members of conservative parties. After 1948 the Socialist Party was discredited following collusion by some of its leading members with the Shōwa Electrical Fertilizer Company.
2 For example, see N.B.Thayer, *How the Conservatives Rule Japan* (Princeton, 1969); H.Fukui, *Party in Power* (Canberra, 1970).
3 A conscious decision had been made to run down the expensive domestic coal industry and depend on cheap imported oil.
4 English translation, K.Tanaka, *Building a New Japan* (Tokyo, 1973).
5 Ali M.El-Agraa, *Japan's Trade Frictions: Realities or Misconceptions?* (Basingstoke, Hants., 1988).

Chronology of Major Political and Economic Events in Japan Since 1853

1853　Arrival in Japan of US naval squadron under Commodore Perry charged with initiating relations with Japan; Perry issues an ultimatum and promises to return the following year
Death of shogun Tokugawa Ieyoshi; Tokugawa Iesada succeeds to position of shogun

1854　Return of Perry and conclusion of US–Japan Treaty of Friendship (Kanagawa Treaty)
Japan concludes treaties with Britain and Russia
Opening of first two ports for foreign ships to purchase necessities

1856　Arrival in Shimoda of Townsend Harris, first US consul to Japan

1858　Ii Naosuke appointed senior councillor (*tairō*) to deal with political crisis caused by disputes over foreign relations and shogunal succession
Conclusion of US–Japan Treaty of Amity and Commerce, followed by similar treaties with Holland, Russia, Britain, France (together known as the Ansei or 'unequal' treaties), providing for further ports to be opened to foreigners, foreign trade and extraterritorial rights for foreigners
Death of shogun Iesada; succession of Tokugawa Iemochi

1859　Execution of Yoshida Shōin for anti-Bakufu activities

1860　Assasination of Ii Naosuke

1862　Shogun Iemochi marries Kazunomiya, the emperor's sisters, as part of the strategy to establish a court-Bakufu alliance (*kōbu-gattai*)

1863　British ships bombard Kagoshima following murder of a British merchant by Satsuma samurai

1864　Ships from Britain, France, US and Holland bombard Shimonoseki forts following attacks on foreign ships by Chōshū

1866   Satsuma and Chōshū conclude an anti-Bakufu alliance and agree to work to restore the emperor to power
Failure of Bakufu military expedition against Chōshū
Death of shogun Iemochi; succession of Tokugawa Yoshinobu (Hitotsubashi Keiki)

1867   Death of emperor Kōmei; accession of Meiji emperor
Tokugawa abdication of political authority in favour of an imperial council of daimyo

1868   Satsuma–Chōshū–Tosa led palace coup; formal return of power to the emperor, abolition of shogunate and confiscation of its lands (Meiji Restoration)
Battle of Toba-Fushimi initiates 1868 civil war (Boshin War); Keiki declared an imperial rebel, but resistance to the new regime is rapidly overcome
Promulgation of the Charter Oath declaring aims of new 'imperial' government
Edo renamed Tokyo, and designated new imperial capital

1869   Return of domain registers to emperor (*hanseki hōkan*); daimyo become imperial governors of their domains

1871   Abolition of domains and establishment of prefectures as units of local administration (*haihan chiken*)
Japan concludes first commercial treaty with China
Departure of Iwakura Mission to negotiate treaty revision and study the West
Ryūkyūan fishermen massacred on Formosa by natives

1872   Abolition of formal status system; population categorized as *shizoku* (former samurai) and common people (*heimin*)
Promulgation of Educational Ordinance (*Gakusei*), aiming at establishment of universal education system
Opening of first railway between Tokyo and Yokohama
Opening of government's model silk mill at Tomioka
Announcement of system of conscription to establish a modern, regular army

1873   Commencement of land tax reform to establish ownership of land and tax liability, aimed at providing central government with a stable income
Dispute over invasion of Korea because of Korea's insistence on seclusion and refusal to recognize Meiji government; Saigō Takamori, Itagaki Taisuke, Gotō Shōjirō and others resign following return of members of the Iwakura Mission, who decide internal development must precede foreign aggression.

1874   First agitation for representative government
Suppression of Saga Rebellion, followed by execution of its leader Etō Shinpei
Itagaki Taisuke founds a political organization, the Risshisha, in Tosa

324

Kido Kōin resigns over decision to send troops to Formosa

Departure of Formosan Expedition as part of Sino-Japanese conflict over possession of Ryūkyū Islands

1875　Osaka Conference aimed at bringing back Kido and Itagaki into government

Itagaki founds Aikokusha to press for constitutional parliamentary government

Conclusion of treaty with Russia giving Russia Sakhalin in exchange for Japanese possession of the Kurile Islands

1876　Conclusion of Kanghwa Treaty between Japan and Korea; opening of Korea to trade, and Japanese possession of extraterritorial rights

Prohibition of sword-bearing by former samurai

Compulsory commutation of samurai stipends for government bonds, ending economic support for samurai as a class

Hagi Rebellion, followed by execution of its leader, Maebara Issei

1877　Satsuma Rebellion (February–September) led by Saigō Takamori, who commits suicide after the uprising is put down

Founding of Tokyo University, the government's first Western-style institution of higher education

1878　Assassination of Ōkubo Toshimichi, a major government figure, by discontented samurai

Takebashi uprising by disgruntled members of the Imperial Guard, rapidly suppressed

1879　Ryūkyū Islands incorporated into Japan as Okinawa Prefecture

1880　League for Founding a National Assembly established to succeed Aikokusha as main organization of popular rights movement

1881　Disagreement within government over constitutional proposals, especially those of Ōkuma Shigenobu

Protests over proposed sale of assets of Hokkaido Colonization Board

Government promises constitutional government after ten years, suspends the Hokkaido sale and expels Okuma from government

Founding of Jiyūtō under Itagaki Taisuke to campaign for democratic government

1882　Founding of Ōkuma Shigenobu's political party, the Kaishintō

Establishment of Bank of Japan as central bank along British lines

Anti-government protesters clash with police in resistance to attempts to impose a labour tax in Aizu (Fukushima Incident)

1884　Establishment of peerage system

Disbanding of Jiyūtō in face of government suppression and involvement of local members in anti-government incidents

Uprising in Saitama provoked by economic crisis put down by force (Chichibu Incident)

Ōkuma and other leaders leave Kaishintō

1885   Formation of NYK (Japan Shipping Company) following merger of Mitsubushi with its major rival
Arrest of Ōi Kentarō and others for plotting a coup in Korea (Osaka Incident)
Introduction of cabinet system

1887   Inoue Kaoru resigns as foreign minister over treaty revision proposals
Enactment of Peace Regulations aimed at excluding named opponents of the government from Tokyo

1888   Establishment of Privy Council

1889   Promulgation of Imperial Japanese Constitution (Meiji Constitution), providing framework of government to 1945
Attempted assassination of Foreign Minister Ōkuma Shigenobu over treaty revision proposals, and his subsequent resignation

1890   First general election, followed by convening of first diet
Imperial Rescript on Education promulgated, affirming 'traditionalist' principles that governed education up to 1945

1892   Second general election; clashes over government interference in voting leave many killed or wounded

1893   Institution of full examination system for entry into bureaucracy

1894   Foreign Minister Mutsu Munemitsu concludes Anglo-Japanese Treaty of Commerce and Navigation (implemented 1899), heralding an end to the unequal treaty system and the return of tariff autonomy
Outbreak of Sino-Japanese War over competing interests of the two countries in Korea

1895   Treaty of Shimonoseki ends Sino-Japanese War; Japan secures colonies, an indemnity, the opening of more treaty ports, economic privileges and most-favoured-nation treatment
Triple Intervention, in which Russia, Germany and France demand changes in peace terms; Japan compelled to give way
Japanese complicity in murder of Queen Min of Korea undermines Japanese influence there

1897   Formation of League for Founding Labour Unions marks emergence of early labour movement
Japan goes on the gold standard

1898   Promulgation of civil code along German lines, which remained intact until 1945
Society for the Study of Socialism marks growing interest in socialist thought

1900   Promulgation of Peace Police Law imposing severe restrictions on labour and political activity

Japan sends troops as part of international force to cope with effects of Boxer Rebellion in China

Formation of Seiyūkai under Itō Hirobumi, marking compromise between diet and oligarchy

1901 Formation of state-sponsored Patriotic Women's Association to help soldiers and their families

Government's Yawata Iron Works commences production

1902 Conclusion of Anglo-Japanese Alliance

1903 Publication by Agriculture and Commerce Ministry of *Conditions of Workers (Shokkō Jijō)*, exposing conditions of workers in a variety of industries

Kōtoku Shūsui, Sakai Toshihiko and other socialists form the Heiminsha, for a short time the mainstream of the Japanese socialist movement

1904 Outbreak of Russo-Japanese War over conflicting ambitions in Northeast Asia

1905 Portsmouth Peace Treaty ends Russo-Japanese War; protest rally in Hibiya Park, Tokyo, against the peace terms leads to widespread rioting

Korea becomes a Japanese protectorate; Itō Hirobumi first resident-general

1906 Formation of first Japan Socialist Party

Nationalization of railways to coordinate transport development

1907 Banning of Japan Socialist Party because of activity of direct actionists

Korean protests over protectorate agreement with Japan at international conference at the Hague find no international support

1909 Assassination of Itō Hirobumi by a Korean in Harbin

1910 Arrest of Kōtoku Shūsui and other left-wing activists for alleged plot on life of the emperor

Japanese annexation of Korea

Formation of Imperial Reservists' Association to strengthen army–village ties

1911 Execution of Kōtoku Shūsui, Kanno Sugako and ten others in the so-called 'High Treason Incident'

Recovery of full tariff autonomy

Founding of literary group Seitōsha (Bluestocking Society) by Hiratsuka Raichō and other women writers; emphasis of society gradually shifting towards female emancipation

Fall of Qing dynasty in China

1912 Death of Meiji emperor; accession of crown prince as Taishō emperor

Suzuki Bunji founds Yūaikai, a mutual aid society for workers later developing into a labour organization

1913   Founding of Dōshikai as focus of diet opposition to Seiyūkai

1914   Outbreak of World War I; Japan declares war on Germany under terms of Anglo-Japanese Alliance, and seizes German interests in East Asia and the Pacific

1915   Presentation of Twenty-One Demands to China, aimed at enhancing Japan's position there; China compelled to accept these in large part

1917   Japan makes substantial loans to China for political purposes (Nishihara Loans)

1918   Rice Riots; rioting over high rice prices affects much of Japan for several weeks July–August
Decision to send Japanese troops to intervene in Siberia to contain the Soviet advance
Armistice ends World War I
Radicals from Tokyo Imperial University found Shinjinkai, later dominating student movement

1919   Convening of Paris Peace Conference
March First demonstration against Japanese rule in Korea, brutally suppressed by Japan
Anti-Japanese demonstrations in China over Japanese occupation of Shandong Peninsula (May Fourth Movement)
Signing of Treaty of Versailles
Founding of government-sponsored Kyōchōkai (Harmonization Society) to promote harmony in the industrial world; labour refuses to participate
Founding of New Women's Association by Ichikawa Fusae, Hiratsuka Raichō and others to campaign for greater rights for women

1920   Japanese soldiers and civilians killed at Nikolaevsk in Siberia (so-called Nikolaevsk Incident); Japan occupies N.Sakhalin to demand compensation

1921   Convening of Washington Conference to discuss East Asian affairs and naval arms limitation; Anglo-Japanese Alliance to be superseded by Four Power Pact of Britain, France, Japan and the US; Nine Power Pact subscribes to China's integrity and an 'open door' policy

1922   Conclusion of Washington Naval Limitation Treaty; 5:5:3 ratio on capital ships for Britain, US and Japan accepted by Japan in face of domestic opposition
Founding of national Suiheisha (Levelling Society) as part of *buraku* emancipation movement
Withdrawal of Japanese troops from Siberia
Founding of illegal Japan Communist Party

1923   Great Kantō earthquake kills nearly 150,000 and destroys much of the Tokyo–Yokohama area; in ensuing confusion many Koreans attacked by mobs. Left-wing and labour activists killed by troops or police include Ōsugi Sakae and Itō Noe

1924 Dissolution of Japan Communist Party in face of official hostility
Effective US prohibition on immigration from Japan

1925 Japanese recognition of USSR; Japan withdraws from N.Sakhalin
Passing of Peace Preservation Law in attempt to restrict liberal and left-wing ideas and activities
Passing of Universal Manhood Suffrage Act
Founding of Women's Suffrage League to campaign for votes for women
Introduction of compulsory military training in schools and colleges following cutbacks in the army

1926 Japan Communist Party re-established illegally
Death of Taishō emperor; accession of Crown Prince Hirohito, taking name of Shōwa emperor

1927 Major financial crisis following closure of Bank of Taiwan due to unsecured debts; government forced to take short-term relief measures and prohibit smaller, less stable banks
Despatch of Japanese troops to Shandong (China) to support Manchurian warlord Zhang Zuolin and hinder possible unification of China
Formation of Minseitō as main opponent of Seiyūkai
Publication of 'Tanaka Memorial', supposed blueprint for Japanese policy in China submitted to emperor by Premier Tanaka Giichi

1928 First wave of arrests of JCP members
Japanese and Chinese troops clash at Jinan (China); Japanese troops eventually withdraw 1929
Members of Japanese Guandong army assassinate Manchurian warlord Zhang Zuolin

1929 Second wave of arrests of JCP members
Wall Street crash marks onset of world economic depression

1930 Japan returns to gold standard, suspended during World War I
Conclusion of London Naval Treaty; ratification in Japan forced through against intense navy opposition
Assassination attempt on Prime Minister Hamaguchi by member of the civilian right wing

1931 Abortive *coup d'état* attempted by members of nationalist Sakurakai (March Incident); plot kept secret and conspirators unpunished
Guandong army engineers occupation of Manchuria (Manchurian Incident)
Embargo on gold exports replaced (leaving of gold standard)

1932 Members of terrorist Blood League murder former finance minister Inoue Junnosuke, and Dan Takuma, managing director of the Mitsui group

Puppet state of Manchukuo established in Manchuria

Prime Minister Inukai Tsuyoshi assassinated by radical naval officers seeking 'national renovation' through direct action

Formation of Social Masses' Party (*Shakai Taishūtō*), largest prewar 'proletarian' party

Army sponsors founding of National Defence Women's Association to mobilize women

1933   Japan withdraws from League of Nations over criticism of Japan's involvement in Manchuria

1935   Intra-army factionalism causes murder of General Nagata Tetsuzan, Chief of Military Affairs Bureau

1936   Young army officers attempting a coup occupy central Tokyo for several days and kill senior political figures, including Lord Privy Seal Saitō Makoto and Finance Minister Takahashi Korekiyo (February 26 Incident); eventual suppression marks conclusive dominance of army's *tōsei* faction as arbiter of national policy

Japan moves towards a quasi-war economy

Conclusion of Anti-Comintern Pact with Germany

Kidnapping of Chinese leader Chiang Kai-shek (Zhiang Jishe) in Xian increases unity of Chinese response to Japan

1937   Issue of *Cardinal Principles of National Polity (Kokutai no Hongi)*, aimed at laying down orthodox ideology for Japanese people

Fighting at Marco Polo Bridge near Beijing leads to war with China; Japanese troops make rapid advances but Japanese occupation of Nanjing is attended by appalling atrocities

1938   Japanese and Russian troops clash at Zhanggufeng on the Soviet–Korean–Manchukuo border

Prime Minister Konoe Fumimaro calls for a 'new order in East Asia' to resist communist and Western imperialist interference

1939   Japanese and Russian troops clash at Nomonhan on the Manchukuo–Outer Mongolian border

1940   Japan establishes Chinese puppet regime under Wang Jingwei in Nanjing and officially recognizes it; the regime gains credibility neither inside nor outside China

Introduction of new political structure within Japan; dissolution of all political parties and establishment of Imperial Rule Assistance Association to concentrate political power and exercise national control

Japanese troops advance into Southeast Asia following agreement with the Vichy regime as part of anti-China strategy

Japan concludes Tripartite Pact with Germany and Italy

1941   Soviet–Japanese Neutrality Pact signed in Moscow

Japan resolves on southward advance and moves further into French Indochina on grounds of defending Japan and her essential supplies

US freezes Japanese assets and places embargo on oil exports to Japan

Negotiations over Japanese withdrawal from China and Indochina are unsuccessful; Japan initiates Pacific War with attacks on Pearl Harbor and the Malayan Peninsula. By spring 1942 most of Southeast Asia is under Japanese occupation

1942 Japanese losses at the naval battle at Midway mark a turn in the tide of war against Japan

1943 Establishment of the Ministry of Munitions in an attempt to improve coordination for the war effort

Greater East Asia Conference held in Tokyo in attempt to increase support for Japan within territories under Japanese control

1944 Resignation of General Tōjō Hideki (prime minister since 1941)

Allied bombing of Japanese mainland commences

1945 Soviet Union breaks Neutrality Pact and declares war on Japan

Atomic bombs dropped on Hiroshima and Nagasaki

Unconditional surrender of Japan

Allied Occupation of Japan commences; suspension of much of the old legislation and reappearance of political parties and labour unions; steps towards demobilization and demilitarization

1946 Renunciation of divinity by the emperor

Commencement of land reform and other major reforms relating to the economy, society and political structure

International Military Tribunal for the Far East opens in Tokyo to try government leaders accused of major war crimes

1947 Implementation of new Constitution of Japan to replace Meiji Constitution

1948 Introduction of new criminal and civil codes

Execution of seven IMTFE defendants, including Tōjō, for conspiracy to wage aggressive war

Introduction of economic stabilization programme and start of 'reverse course' in Occupation policy aimed at rebuilding Japan as a capitalist ally in East Asia in the face of worsening US–Soviet relations and the Chinese Communist rise to power

1949 Ministry of International Trade and Industry (MITI) established

Chinese Communist victory in civil war and establishment of People's Republic of China (PRC)

1950 Outbreak of Korean War

Institution of National Police Reserve to maintain internal Japanese security; developing later into Self Defence Force

Occupation purge of those suspected of communist sympathies

(Red Purge); depurging of many individuals purged after 1945

1951 Signing of San Francisco Peace Treaty and Japan–US Mutual Security Treaty; Soviet Union and PRC do not participate

1952 Allied Occupation of Japan ends

1954 Japanese fishermen affected by radiation from US hydrogen bomb explosion at Bikini Atoll; US compensation granted, and incident serves to stimulate anti-nuclear movement
Establishment of Defence Agency to control Self Defence Force aimed at prevention of direct and indirect aggression

1955 Reunification of Japan Socialist Party (split since 1951)
Conservative elements join to form Liberal Democratic Party

1956 Normalization of Soviet-Japanese relations (no peace treaty)
Japan becomes a member of the United Nations

1960 Democratic Socialist party under Nishio Suehiro splits from Japan Socialist Party over defence issue
Widespread disturbances over renewal of the security treaty with US (*Anpo*)
Ikeda cabinet resolves on 'Income Doubling Plan' to increase and spread benefits of economic growth

1964 Tokyo Olympics
Formation of Kōmeitō, political party sponsored by lay Buddhist movement Sōka Gakkai

1965 Normalization of relations with South Korea

1969 Widespread student unrest and popular agitation for return of Okinawa, held by US since the Occupation

1970 International exhibition Expo 70 held in Osaka

1971 Start of protests against construction of Tokyo's Narita Airport
Emperor visits Europe
Washington announces that President Nixon will visit Beijing, also changes in the exchange value of the dollar (Nixon shocks)

1972 US restores Okinawa to Japanese rule
Prime Minister Tanaka Kakuei visits the People's Republic of China; diplomatic relations established with the PRC

1973 Chisso Company found legally responsible for mercury poisoning of Minamata pollution victims (first case 1953)
Oil shock; Japanese and other economies hit by substantial rise in oil prices

1975 Emperor visits US

1976 Lockheed scandal breaks; top politicians and businessmen accused of corrupt dealings include former prime minister Tanaka Kakuei

1978   Conclusion of Sino-Japanese Peace and Friendship Treaty

1982   China protests over content of officially-approved Japanese history textbooks, which appear to play down Japanese aggression in Asia

1983   Japan begins to take measures to ease frictions caused by her export success and boost domestic demand
Shooting down of Korean airliner in Soviet airspace

1986   Equal Employment Opportunity legislation passed in attempt to improve women's employment opportunities

1989   Death of Shōwa emperor; accession of Crown Prince Akihito, taking name of Heisei emperor

Bibliographical Notes

The Western language literature on Japan has expanded dramatically in recent years, and a bibliographical section of this kind must by its very nature be highly selective. Texts mentioned here are but a small sample of the available literature; prime attention is given to books rather than papers in journals, and to the 1853–1952 period. The rate at which new works are appearing threaten to make bibliographical information rapidly out of date. Readers seeking more detailed information on Western language writings on Japan are advised to consult the *Annual Bibliography of Asian Studies* produced by the *Journal of Asian Studies*, and other bibliographical works, such as J.W.Dower, *Japanese History from Ancient to Modern Times: Seven Basic Bibliographies* (Manchester 1986).

GENERAL WORKS

The most expansive reference work on Japan and its history is *Kōdansha Encyclopaedia of Japan* (9 vols, Tokyo, 1983). On a much smaller scale is J.E.Hunter, *Concise Dictionary of Modern Japanese History* (Berkeley and Los Angeles, 1984). A multi-volume dictionary of Japanese history in French is in the course of production, and as of 1988 is as far as the letter 'K' (Maison Franco-Japonaise, *Dictionnaire Historique du Japon* (Tokyo)). For economic history there is M.Sumiya and K.Taira (eds), *An Outline of Japanese Economic History 1603–1940* (Tokyo, 1979).

General texts on the history of modern Japan are comparatively numerous, but the rapidity of change both in research on Japan and in the country itself mean that they can soon become out of date. G.R.Storry, *History of Modern Japan* (Harmondsworth, 1960) is still widely available. W.G.Beasley, *The Modern History of Japan* (London, 1976) is a clear and reliable account concentrating on diplomatic and political occurrences. E.O.Reischauer and A.M.Craig, *East Asia: Tradition and Transformation* (Boston, 1978) is a version of an earlier work which deals with East Asia as a whole, but which offers a compendium of information on Japan. For a briefer account of the evolution of modern Japan, P.Duus, *The Rise of Modern Japan* (Boston, 1976) is penetrating and well written. Of more recent works C.Totman, *Japan Before Perry* (Berkeley and Los Angeles, 1983) outlines the Tokugawa years and before, while J.-P.Lehmann, *The Roots of Modern Japan* (London, 1982) provides a stimulating account of the Meiji period. R.Buckley, *Japan Today* (Cambridge, 1985) is a trenchant look at Japan since 1945. H.Wray and H.Conroy (eds), *Perspectives on Modern Japanese History* (Honolulu, 1983) is a collection of brief essays highlighting some of the major points of debate among historians of modern Japan. Other useful compilations of essays are M.Jansen and G.Rozman (eds), *Japan in Transition: From Tokugawa to Meiji* (Princeton, 1986); J.Morley (ed.), *Dilemmas of Growth in Prewar Japan* (Princeton,1971); B.Silberman and H.Harootunian (eds), *Japan in Crisis: Essays in Taishō Democracy* (Princeton, 1974).

RELATIONS WITH OTHER COUNTRIES

Japan's relations with other countries are perhaps the aspect of Japanese history most widely written about by Western historians. Most of the texts concentrate more on the history of international relations – the traditional areas of war and diplomacy, but there have appeared works relating to more nebulous areas, such as cultural interaction. A good guide is J.Morley (ed.), *Japan's Foreign Policy 1868–1941, a Research Guide* (New York, 1976). The initiation of Japan's relations with the West after 1853 is covered in most of the general histories in some detail; W.G.Beasley, *Great Britain and the Opening of Japan 1834–1856* (London, 1951) is a detailed account of Japanese – British dealings at this time. I.H.Nish, *Japanese Foreign Policy 1869–1942* (London, 1977) gives a comprehensive picture of how foreign policy was debated and the issues involved; there is an appendix of translations of some significant foreign policy documents. A brief summary of Japanese – Western involvement in Asia is in G.R.Storry, *Japan and the Decline of the West in Asia 1894–1943* (London, 1979). Further volumes of use in understanding the history of Japan's relations with Britain are G.Fox, *Great Britain and Japan 1858 – 1883* (Oxford, 1969); I.H.Nish, *The Anglo-Japanese Alliance* (London, 1966); I.H.Nish, *Alliance in Decline* (London, 1972); P.C.Lowe, *Great Britain and Japan 1911–1915* (London, 1969). For Russo-Japanese relations see I.H.Nish, *The Origins of the Russo-Japanese War* (London and New York, 1985); S.Okamoto, *The Japanese Oligarchy and the Russo-Japanese War* (New York, 1970). Relations with the US are covered in many texts, for example, C.E.Neu, *The Troubled Encounter: The US and Japan* (New York, 1975); D.Borg and S.Okamoto (eds), *Pearl Harbor as History* (New York, 1973); A.Iriye (ed.), *Mutual Images: Essays in American – Japanese Relations* (Cambridge, Mass., 1975). Western images of Japan are discussed in J.-P.Lehmann, *The Image of Japan 1850–1905: From Feudal Isolation to World Power* (London, 1978), and A.W.Burks, (ed.), *The Modernizers: Overseas Students, Foreign Employees and Meiji Japan* (Boulder, Col., and London, 1985) looks at personnel exchanges in the early years of modernization.

There is a substantial literature on Japan's relations with Asia. A.Iriye (ed.), *The Chinese and the Japanese* (Princeton, 1980) takes an overview of relations between the two countries, and M.B.Jansen, *Japan and China: from War to Peace 1894–1972* (Chicago, 1975) looks at the two countries' dealings from the Sino-Japanese War up until the re-establishment of formal relations. For Japan's early relations with Korea, H.Conroy, *The Japanese Seizure of Korea* (Philadelphia, 1960) has yet to be superseded, although M.Deuchler, *Confucian Gentlemen and Barbarian Envoys* (Seattle, 1977) supplements our knowledge of the opening of Korea in the 1870s – 1880s. W.G.Beasley, *Japanese Imperialism* (Oxford, 1987) provides a picture of Japan's overall strategy and intentions in East and Southeast Asia, and M.Barnhart, *Japan Prepares for War: The Search for Economic Security 1919–1941* (Ithaca, N.Y., 1987) investigates the role of economic arguments in Japan's blueprint for Asia. More detailed information on Japan's colonial rule is to be found in A.C.Nahm (ed.), *Korea under Japanese Colonial Rule* (Kalamazoo, Mich., 1973) and R.H.Myers and M.R.Peattie (eds), *The Japanese Colonial Empire 1895–1945* (Princeton, 1985). There is no single good account of Japanese activity in Manchuria, but it is touched upon in G.McCormack, *Chang Tso-lin in Northeast China 1911–1928*

(Stanford, 1977) and W.F.Morton, *Tanaka Giichi and Japan's China Policy* (Folkestone, Kent, 1980). For the Sino-Japanese and Pacific Wars of the 1930s and 1940s there are J.H.Boyle, *China and Japan at War 1937–1945* (Stanford, 1972); C.Thorne, *Allies of a Kind* (Oxford, 1978). J.Morley (ed.), *Japan's Road to the Pacific War* (New York, from 1976) consists of several volumes of translations of a major Japanese series, and comprises a fundamental text for any reader with a strong interest in this period.

SOCIETY AND BELIEF

The best-known English language account of Japanese society is C.Nakane, *Japanese Society* (Hardmondsworth, 1979). The works of another leading Japanese scholar are also available in T.Fukutake, *Rural Society in Japan* (Tokyo, 1978); T.Fukutake, *The Japanese Social Structure* (Tokyo,1982). More recent volumes of particular value for the non-specialist are R.J.Smith, *Japanese Society* (Cambridge, 1983) and R.J.Hendry, *Understanding Japanese Society* (Beckenham, Kent, 1987). Portraits of Japanese village life are to be found, among others, in T.C.Smith, *Nakahara: Family Farming and Population in a Japanese Village 1717–1830* (Stanford, 1977); J.F.Embree, *Suye Mura – A Japanese Village* (Chicago, 1939); R.P.Dore, *Shinohata – Portrait of a Japanese Village* (London, 1978). A portrait of postwar urban life is found in R.P.Dore, *City Life in Japan* (London, 1958). There is relatively little on the historical development of the urban community, although T.R.H.Havens, *Valley of Darkness: The Japanese People and World War II* (New York, 1978) concentrates on daily life during this period, and the more recent rise of urban studies has helped to produce works such as E.Seidensticker, *High City, Low City: Tokyo from Edo to the Earthquake* (New York. 1983) and G.Allinson, *Japanese Urbanism: Industry and Politics in Kariya 1872–1972* (Berkeley and Los Angeles, 1972).

Education has been a growth area as well, and readers are no longer almost wholly dependent on R.P.Dore, *Education in Tokugawa Japan* (London, 1965) and H.Passin, *Society and Education in Japan* (New York, 1965), although the former in particular is still of great value. Recent works include D.Roden, *Schooldays in Imperial Japan* (Berkeley and Los Angeles, 1980); J.Bartholomew, 'Japanese Modernization and the Imperial Universities 1876–1920', *Journal of Asian Studies*, Feb. 1978. Religion and ideology have proved particularly difficult – and contentious – subjects with which to come to grips. J.M.Kitagawa, *Religion in Japanese History* (New York, 1965) is still something of a standby. More recent works are S.Murakami, *Japanese Religion in the Modern Century* (Tokyo, 1980) and K.Morioka, *Religion in Changing Japanese Society* (Tokyo, 1975). C.Gluck, *Japan's Modern Myths: Ideology in the Late Meiji Period* (Princeton, 1985) has helped to transform views of ideology in the Meiji period and subsequently. There is also S.H.Nolte, *Liberalism in Modern Japan: Ishibashi Tanzan and his Teachers 1905–1960* (Berkeley and Los Angeles, 1986), while T.R.H.Havens, *Farm and Nation in Modern Japan: Agrarian Nationalism 1870–1940* (Princeton, 1974) concentrates on the association between nationalist ideology and the rural sector. Several classic studies of ultranationalism are dated but still useful; they include G.R.Storry, *The Double Patriots* (London, 1957); I.Morris, *Nationalism and the Right Wing in Japan* (London, 1960). There are also many studies of individual thinkers and writers, for example C.Blacker, *The Japanese Enlightenment: A Study of the Writings of Fukuzawa Yukichi* (Cambridge, 1964); G.M.Wilson, *Radical Nationalist in Japan: Kita Ikki 1883–1937* (Cambridge, Mass., 1969); J.D.Pierson, *Tokutomi Sohō 1863–1957: A Journalist for Modern Japan* (Princeton, 1980). Studies of particular religious beliefs include J.W.White, *The Sōka Gakkai and Mass Society* (Stanford, 1970); H.Hardacre, *Kurozumikyō and the New Religions of Japan* (Princeton, 1986).

ECONOMIC DEVELOPMENTS

The economic growth of Japan has obviously attracted considerable attention, but, surprisingly, a good overview of Japan's economic development in the modern period accessible to non-specialists has not appeared since W.W.Lockwood, *The Economic Development of Japan* (Princeton, 1954) and G.C.Allen, *A Short Economic History of Modern Japan* (London, 1972). A more technical approach is to be found in R.Minami, *The Economic Development of Japan – A Quantitative Study* (Basingstoke, Hants., 1986). A long-standing interest in the economic development of Tokugawa Japan among Japanese historians has spread to Western scholars; many Western specialists on this period have concentrated on social and political factors, rather than exclusively economic ones. C.D.Sheldon, *The Rise of the Merchant Class in Tokugawa Japan* (repr. New York, 1973) and T.C.Smith, *The Agrarian Origins of Modern Japan* (Stanford, 1959) are both older examples of outstanding scholarship. There is also the controversial S.B.Hanley and K.Yamamura, *Economic and Demographic Change in Preindustrial Japan 1600–1868* (Princeton, 1977). For the Meiji period W.W.Lockwood (ed.), *The State and Economic Enterprise in Japan* (Princeton, 1965) introduces some major debates, and T.C.Smith, *Political Change and Industrial Development: Government Enterprise 1868–1880* (Stanford, 1955) is still without a competitor. W.J.Macpherson, *The Economic Development of Japan 1868–1941* (Basingstoke, 1987) has an extensive bibliography, and T.Nakamura, *Economic Growth in Prewar Japan* (New Haven, 1983) is an economist's picture of the overall pattern of prewar development. Postwar developments are covered in T.Nakamura, *The Postwar Japanese Economy* (Tokyo, 1981) and H.Patrick and H.Rosovsky (eds), *Asia's New Giant: How the Japanese Economy Works* (Washington, 1976). The ability to put the contemporary Japanese economy in a historical context makes G.C.Allen, *The Japanese Economy* (London, 1981) a particularly good introduction. C.Johnson, *MITI and the Japanese Miracle* (Stanford, 1982) concentrates on government involvement in the operation of the economy.

For the agricultural sector Y.Hayami, *A Century of Agricultural Growth in Japan* (Tokyo, 1975) is useful for reference. Specific areas of agriculture are covered in A.Waswo, *Japanese Landlords: Decline of a Rural Elite* (Berkeley and Los Angeles, 1977) and P.Francks, *Technology and Agricultural Development in Prewar Japan* (New Haven, 1984). R.J.Smethurst, *Agricultural Development and Tenancy Disputes in Japan 1870–1940* (Princeton, 1986) looks in particular at the state of the agrarian sector in the interwar years. For business and the industrial sector there is J.Hirschmeier and T.Yui, *The Development of Japanese Business 1600–1973* (London, 1975), while the *Proceedings of the International Conference on Business History* (Fuji Conference) have been published annually in Tokyo since 1976, and cover many aspects of Japanese and comparative business history. Studies of individual companies include W.M.Fruin, *Kikkoman: Company, Clan and Community* (Cambridge, Mass., 1983) and W.D.Wray, *Mitsubishi and the NYK 1870–1914* (Cambridge, Mass., 1986)

WOMEN

The history of Japanese women is a growth area, but productions have been of mixed quality. J.Lebra, J.Paulson and E.Powers, *Women in Changing Japan* (Boulder, Col., 1976) comprises a collection of papers on various aspects of women's activity in Japan, both historical and contemporary. Women in politics are studied in S.J.Pharr, *Political Women in Japan* (Berkeley and Los Angeles, 1981). The growth of the early women's movement is covered in S.L.Sievers, *Flowers in Salt: The Beginnings of Feminist Consciousness in Modern Japan* (Stanford, 1983). An account of the emergence of women's movements and activities, particularly in the Occupation and postwar years, is D.Robins-Mowry, *The Hidden Sun – Women of Modern Japan* (Boulder, Col., 1983), disappointing on an analytical level, but a useful source of information. The most valuable contributions in this area are perhaps R.J.Smith and E.L.Wiswell, *The Women of Suye Mura* (Chicago, 1983), an account of the lives of rural women in the 1930s, and G.L.Bernstein, *Haruko's World: A Japanese Farm Woman and her Community* (Stanford, 1983), which looks at women in the rural sector in more recent years. L.Crihfield Dalby, *Geisha* (Berkeley and Los Angeles, 1983) is a serious study of a legendary profession for Japanese women.

POLITICS AND THE STATE

The most comprehensive accounts of the political events leading up to the Meiji Restoration, and its immediate results, are probably W.G.Beasley, *The Meiji Restoration* (Stanford and London, 1973) and C.Totman, *The Collapse of the Tokugawa Bakufu* (Honolulu, 1980). For the Meiji period, J.W.Dower (ed.), *Origins of the Modern Japanese State: Selected Writings of E.H.Norman* (New York, 1975) includes Norman's classic *Japan's Emergence as a Modern State* (New York, 1940), in conjunction with a penetrating essay by Dower on the controversy provoked by the work, highly critical of more recent interpretations of Japan's history. The emergence of the prewar state is dealt with in G.M.Beckmann, *The Making of the Meiji Constitution* (Lawrence, Kans., 1957) and G.Akita, *The Foundations of Constitutional Government in Japan 1868–1900* (Cambridge, Mass., 1969). More recent works have tended to be narrower in scope than these earlier works. Y.Oka, *Five Political Leaders of Modern Japan* (Tokyo, 1986) analyses some leading political figures on most of whom there is surprisingly little in English, and offers a rare opportunity to read the work of a leading Japanese political scientist. The evolution of various political parties is covered in R.A.Scalapino, *Democracy and the Party Movement in Prewar Japan* (New Haven, 1953); G.O.Totten, *The Social Democratic Movement in Prewar Japan* (New Haven, 1966); G.M.Beckmann and G.Okubo, *The Japanese Communist Party 1922–1945* (Stanford, 1969). Studies of political activity after the founding of the Diet are to be found in P.Duus, *Party Rivalry and Political Change in Taishō Japan* (Cambridge, Mass., 1968); D.A.Titus, *Palace and Politics in Prewar Japan* (New York, 1974); G.M.Berger, *Parties out of Power in Japan 1931–1941* (Princeton, 1977); S.S.Large, *Organized Workers and Socialist Politics in Interwar Japan* (Cambridge, 1981); S.Minichiello, *Retreat from Reform: Patterns of Political Behaviour in Interwar Japan* (Honolulu, 1984); L.A.Connors, *The Emperor's Advisor – Saionji Kinmochi and Prewar Japanese Politics* (London, 1987). The best general account of postwar Japanese politics is probably J.A.A.Stockwin, *Japan: Divided Politics in a Growth Economy* (London, 1982). Local government is looked at in K.Steiner, *Local Government in Japan* (Stanford, 1965).

LABOUR AND POPULAR PROTEST

The Japanese historiography of this aspect of Japan's history is particularly dominated by the Marxist framework of debate, an approach rarely shared by Western historians. Moreover Japanese 'people's history' is very different from what might in Britain be called 'history from below' (see C.Gluck, 'The People in History: Recent Trends in Japanese Historiography', *Journal of Asian Studies*, Nov. 1978). Until relatively recently, most Japanese historians of labour and popular protest have tended to concentrate on the political dimension, and this interest is not strongly reflected in English language works. Recent years have produced several major works on popular protest in the Tokugawa period, of which S.Vlastos, *Peasant Protests and Uprisings in Tokugawa Japan* (Berkeley and Los Angeles, 1986) is the most accessible and rewarding. R.W.Bowen, *Rebellion and Democracy in Meiji Japan* (Berkeley and Los Angeles, 1980) considers popular unrest in the 1870s – 1880s, and D.Irokawa (ed. Jansen), *The Culture of the Meiji Period* (Princeton, 1985) analyses popular political awareness during the Meiji years from the viewpoint of 'people's history'. There is also J.V.Koschmann (ed.), *Authority and the Individual in Japan: Citizen Protest in Historical Perspective* (Tokyo, 1978). M.Hane, *Peasants,*

Rebels and Outcastes (New York, 1982) looks at the living conditions of the have-nots of the prewar period.

The question of Marxism and Japanese history is covered in several works, of which the most detailed, though not the most readable, is G.A.Hoston, *Marxism and the Crisis of Development in Prewar Japan* (Princeton, 1986). Left-wing activism is covered in many works, including F.G.Notehelfer, *Kōtoku Shūsui, Portrait of a Japanese Radical* (Cambridge, 1971); G.L.Bernstein, *Japanese Marxist: A Portrait of Kawakami Hajime 1879–1946* (Cambridge, Mass., 1976); J.Crump, *The Origins of Socialist Thought in Japan* (London, 1983).

Many Western analysts have looked at labour relations in Japan, but most lack a historical dimension. An outstanding exception is A.Gordon, *The Evolution of Labour Relations in Japan: Heavy Industry 1853–1955* (Cambridge, Mass., 1985). J.Moore, *Japanese Workers and the Struggle for Power* (Madison, Wis., 1983) concentrates on the postwar years. A contemporary study which raises issues of significance for the historical development of labour relations is R.P.Dore, *British Factory – Japanese Factory* (London, 1973).

THE MILITARY

There are numerous books on the Japanese samurai, for example G.R.Storry, *The Way of the Samurai* (London, 1978), but contributions on the military in modern Japan, despite their political influence, are less prolific. E.L.Presseisen, *Before Aggression: Europeans Prepare the Japanese Army* (Tucson, Ariz., 1976) looks at the building of modern armed forces in Meiji Japan. R.J.Smethurst, *A Social Basis for Prewar Japanese Militarism: the Army and the Rural Community* (Berkeley and Los Angeles, 1974) analyses army links with the countryside, particularly through the Reservists' Association. Political activity by young officers in the 1930s is covered in B.A.Shillony, *Revolt in Japan: The Young Officers and the February 26, 1936, Incident* (Princeton, 1973) and also in J.B.Crowley *Japan's Quest for Autonomy* (Princeton, 1966). Postwar developments can be followed in J.H.Buck (ed.), *The Modern Japanese Military System* (Beverley Hills and London, 1975) and M. and S.Harries, *Sheathing the Sword: The Demilitarization of Japan* (London, 1987).

Maps

Map 1 Modern Japan

HOKKAIDO

Aomori

Akita

Iwate

SEA OF JAPAN

Yamagata

Miyagi

Ishikawa

•Niigata

Sendai

anazawa•

Toyama

Niigata

Fukushima

Fukui

Nagano

Gunma

Tochigi

Gifu

Saitama

Ibaraki Mito•

•Nagoya

Yamanashi

Tokyo
Tokyo

Aichi

Shizuoka

Kanagawa
Kamakura• •Yokohama

Chiba

Shimoda

PACIFIC OCEAN

NSHU

Okinawa Islands

Okinawa

RYŪKYŪ ISLANDS

Map 2 East Asia in the 1930s

Index